Collateralized Debt Obligations and Structured Finance

Collateralized Debt Obligations and Structured Finance

New Developments in Cash and Synthetic Securitization

JANET M. TAVAKOLI

WILEY

John Wiley & Sons, Inc.

Published by John Wiley & Sons, Inc., Hoboken, New Jersey.
Published simultaneously in Canada.

For general information on our other products and services, or technical support, please
contact our Customer Care Department within the United States at 800-762-2974, outside
the United States at 317-572-3993 or fax 317-572-4002.

Wiley also publishes its books in a variety of electronic formats. Some content that appears
in print may not be available in electronic books.

For more information about Wiley products, visit our web site at www.wiley.com.

Library of Congress Cataloging-in-Publication Data:
Tavakoli, Janet M.
   Collateralized debt obligations and structured finance : new developments
in cash and synthetic securitization / Janet M. Tavakoli.
      p. cm. — (Wiley finance series)
Includes bibliographical references and index.
    ISBN 0-471-46220-9 (Cloth)
   1. Asset-backed financing—United States.   2. Mortgage-backed
securities—United States. I. Title. II. Series.
   HG4028.A84T38   2003
   332.63′2044—dc21

                          2003002598

Printed in the United States of America.

10 9 8 7 6 5 4 3

Acknowledgments

I would like to thank John B. Caouette, Vice Chairman of MBIA Insurance Corporation; James J. Croke of Cadwalader, Wickersham & Taft; John Cross, Director Portfolio Management & Risk Distribution at Standard Chartered Bank; Lang Gibson, Head of Structured Credit Products Research at Bank of America; Paulo Gribaudi, Global Head of Credit Derivatives in the Investment Banking Division of IntesaBci; Mark Hale, Group Strategist at Ansbacher & Co Limited; Robert R. Bliss, Ph.D., Senior Financial Economist and Economic Advisor at the Federal Reserve Bank of Chicago; and Philippe E. Zoetelief Tromp, Managing Director of Financial Security Assurance (U.K.) Limited for their help and advice. Thanks also needs to go to Katherine Evans and Linda Merizalde at Standard & Poor's New York. They provided updated data prior to publication. Michael B. Gordy, at the Monetary and Financial Studies Division of Research and Statistics at the Federal Reserve Board in Washington, DC, stimulated thought on capital treatment of securitizations.

Many of the ideas expressed in this book depart from mainstream thinking and current ethics in structured finance. Opinions on what is ethical or unethical are divided. I am responsible for any statements or conclusions, and no opinions or theories presented in this book necessarily represent those of the people I've thanked.

Special thanks to the excellent publishing and editing staff at John Wiley & Sons, especially Bill Falloon.

I welcome your comments on *Collateralized Debt Obligations and Structured Finance*. Please visit www.tavakolistructuredfinance.com.

J.M.T

Contents

CHAPTER 4
Credit Derivatives and Total Rate of Return Swaps   85

Collateralized Debt Obligations and Structured Finance

Introduction

What's new in structured finance? This book delves into the new rapid growth areas in structured finance, particularly the collateralized debt obligation (CDO) market, and some of the problems created by this rapid growth. The sea change in the CDO market from 1999 to the present is due to synthetic securitizations, which use credit derivatives to transfer risk. Recent new products require a fresh look at credit default swaps (CDSs) and total rate of return swaps in the context of synthetic securitizations. Synthetics introduce unique structural risks to CDOs and structured finance products. We'll look at recent changes in the CDS market with respect to language and settlement issues precipitated by their use in CDOs.

Another sea change is due to the way many securitization groups use their financial institution's balance sheets. Securitization technology originally moved mortgage-backed securities, consumer loans, and other loans off the bank's balance sheet so that banks could reduce balance sheet risk and do more business. Today, securitization groups are adding risk to the bank's balance sheet, adding risk to bank trading books, or placing risk in stagnant conduits in order to earn fee income. As a result, banks, investment banks, and conduit investors are more exposed to concentration risk and losses due to fraud.

The Sarbanes–Oxley Act of 2002 is meant to combat this on a corporate level for firms regulated by the Securities and Exchange Commission (SEC). We'll discuss its implications in some detail, because the global financial community tends to adopt financial standards initiated in the United States.

What do we mean by fraud? As we are all aware, fraud can be internal to a bank securitizing a deal, fraud can be external as when a corporation fudges its accounting, and fraud can take the form of a conspiracy when both external parties and internal deal makers agree to hide relevant facts.

Banks and investment banks are happy to air the dirty laundry of corporate malfeasance, but are more reluctant to admit it can happen to them. It does. Yet we shouldn't be surprised by it; we should actually expect to deal with it, and can take steps to guard against it.

For instance, we know that in the United States one-third of small businesses lose money and fail—not because of utility cost increases, not because of rent increases, not because big companies take their business—but *because of employee fraud*. Employees who commit fraud are sixteen times as likely to be managers or executives, four times as likely to be men, and five times as likely to have postgraduate degrees. We also know that many employees will commit fraud given the right circumstances. The right circumstances are known as the fraud triangle: need, opportunity, and the ability to rationalize one's behavior.

Knowing human nature, we can't expect it to change in big business, in big commercial banks, or in big investment banks. We can expect the individual to feel his needs are greater. The need for a Rolex, the need for an estate in Florida, the need for a castle in the south of France, the need for an enormous annual bonus: All of these needs seem to be greater in the finance business. Given the keen intelligence of the players and the complexity of structured financial products, the ability to rationalize behavior and opportunity may be greater as well. Decreasing opportunity increases sound business.

While we'll look at some instances of fraud, we'll also look at instances of gray area "opportunities" presented by structured products. We'll also look at opportunity costs due to both ignorance and intent.

We'll look at structural features of the well-established markets applied to the new growth areas. New products create new challenges for both structurers and investors. We'll compare the structural similarities and differences of the cash and synthetic market to better assess value of new products. We'll compare cash and synthetic CDOs, since synthetic securitizations use cash structuring technology.

The growth in the CDO market in the past five years has been accompanied by an unprecedented shift in the dynamics of the markets. In 1990, the CDO market consisted of roughly $2.2 billion in rated securitizations. In 1997, the $64 billion rated CDO market consisted chiefly of securitizations of cash assets. At the time, this appeared to be phenomenal growth, but the most amazing growth surge was yet to come. In 2001, global CDO issuance was around $200 billion, and for 2002, it is estimated that CDO issuance exceeded $250 billion. Synthetic CDOs—namely, securitizations incorporating credit derivatives technology to transfer asset risks and cash flows, made up more than 75 percent of this market. This is no accident. There is a seeming arbitrage advantage of synthetic versus cash assets caused by creation of a super senior tranche, the feasibility of increased leverage of the equity tranche, and model-based capital treatment for credit derivatives. The ability to make the synthetic arbitrage work with investment-grade collateral is another huge advantage over cash CDOs in the current credit environment.

CDOs are an evolving product, especially in Europe where special venue considerations introduce technological challenges relative to the more mature U.S. market. This market has enthusiastically embraced credit derivatives, since synthetic structures solve certain venue issues for risk transfer. Credit derivatives also often allow special gimmicks to be employed, which can produce certain regulatory advantages.

The CDO market experienced explosive growth during the past three years due to the introduction of the Euro, the market domination of very liquid European banks, and the introduction of synthetic CDO technology that allows banks to exploit their low cost funding while managing risk.

I've avoided giving away trade secrets, but have pointed out the keys to valuing new products. Models are complex and are considered proprietary information, and I believe there should be some barriers to entry to the market. Nonetheless, I review the basics of the market so that any reader with some knowledge of the capital markets will understand the components required to evaluate structured products. Where applicable, I provide illustrations of cash flow–based analysis to emphasize what is key and common to any sound model-based approach to value. While the rage is model building, the industry has produced many "model monkeys." They produce encyclopedias of code, but even if the code is correct, it is often of little practical value.

Richard Feynman once pointed out that students in Brazil memorized the definition and formulas for triboluminescence, but they had no idea what the formulas meant. Feynman wanted to send the students into a closet with a sugar cube and a pair of pliers to observe the faint blue flash of light produced by crushing the crystals. While the students could spout the theory of the production of light in the destruction of a crystalline lattice, they had no idea which crystals produce light when crushed or why they produce light. Complicated equations can usually be described with simple mathematics and physical examples, and that is the approach I use here. I'm not saying models have no value; I am a heavy user of models. I'm simply pointing out that if you don't know where you are going, writing a model isn't going to get you there.

Quality control in CDOs and structured credit products is uneven. A small number of firms have built sound business models with strong professional teams, but they are the exceptions. Many structurers and credit derivatives professionals are inadequately trained in the capital markets to be competent in their jobs, and the investor community is suffering the results. A major problem in today's markets is lack of cross training. The result is poor understanding of the basic mechanics of global financial market products. The problem is exacerbated by the fact that securitizations have recently become a lot more global.

Credit derivatives professionals often have never traded cash products or traded an interest rate swap. Some have no exposure to the bond markets, or even the currency or swap markets. Many cannot explain how to construct a par asset swap, one of the benchmark relative value instruments for their market. Some have no exposure to repurchase agreements. This lack of general knowledge has caused dangerous misunderstandings. For example, one credit derivatives professional at a top-five U.S. bank didn't know how to decompound the London InterBank Offered Rate (LIBOR) and further, didn't know the conventions for converting the rate to bond rates. He had just finished programming a total rate of return model; he had to reprogram it after learning more about interest rate and day count conventions.

I believe the reason this problem falls below the radar screen is that banks and investment banks rapidly grow these departments and need to dub ad hoc "experts" to satisfy a need. Qualifications and training take a back seat to fast formation of departments. Upper management is often confused by the complexity of these products and as a result, many institutions are going through growing pains. Some may not make it to full maturity.

Another reason this problem hasn't been solved is that upper management often has difficulty assessing true performance. If a group has lost money, there seems to be a ready and reasonable excuse. Many groups have no clear idea why they lose or make money. They make a bet and it either wins or it loses. There is no business model in place to support consistent revenue growth. If they make a little money, they persuade management that a hockey stick profit projection profile depicts the future of their fledgling department. The philosophy is to tell management what they want to hear, even if it isn't even close to the truth. Don't tell management the department is nothing more than just a few guys taking bets. Opportunity cost is invisible.

In Europe in particular, where synthetic securitizations often seem to pose a solution to sticky venue issues, there is a dearth of capital markets experience in the structuring community. Virtually any asset can be securitized and virtually anyone thinks he or she can do it.

One new entrant to securitized products told me he'd been an unsuccessful emerging markets trader, but now he felt he'd found his niche. Lack of experience was not an impediment. As a native Italian, he was able to speak both Italian and English fluently, and he felt that his bilingualism was significantly more valuable. He cloned mandate letters of his more experienced colleagues and sent them to banks to ask them to allow him to do their balance sheet securitizations. When that strategy wasn't successful, he simply lowered his costs. In his mind, that was all it took. The ability to offer creative structural solutions, or value-added, wasn't a chief concern for him. This attitude has the potential to hurt this growing market.

Cash flows can be manipulated to solve almost any problem; they can also be manipulated to hide almost any problem. Much of what we consider unethical practice is a matter of custom, legislation, and the time in which we live. That applies as much to financial practices as it does to social customs. Giving kickbacks in Europe was almost standard operating procedure until the Lockheed scandal caused vilification in the United States of its participants. Many Europeans were initially confused by the uproar, but in the end, the negative publicity caused the European business community to rethink this practice. Determining what is unethical is sometimes a difficult call, and opinions are divided. Nonetheless, I attempt to address this issue where applicable.

I do not delve deeply into tax products, because it would require an additional book to do them justice. Structured finance tax products have long hangovers. Investors may need product documentation for tax-related transactions years after the product matures. One Cayman Islands–based investor, in a tax structure that matured in the early 1990s, still gets phone calls from the U.S. Department of Treasury. Tax laws are constantly changing. Single venue tax code interpretation is complex, and cross-border tax code interpretation adds another layer of complexity.

Despite the caveats, I'm an enthusiastic proponent of structured financial products and welcome the growth of new products in the market. Wherever possible, I've tried to point out how existing structuring technology has benefited new markets and has the potential to create even better products. It is my intent to facilitate a clearer understanding of these products that will encourage investors to confidently participate in this fascinating market.

The CDO Paradigm Shift

In the past five years, synthetics have been the most powerful driving force for change in the way collateralized debt obligations (CDOs) are structured. Synthetics have gained increasing attention because of the rapid growth in the credit default swap (CDS) market. In 1996, the global CDS market was only $100 billion to $200 billion in size. Morgan Stanley estimates the CDS market grew to $2.4 trillion in 2002. The size of this over-the-counter (OTC) market is difficult to estimate, because transactions are private and off-balance sheet. It isn't surprising that different sources have different estimates of market size. The British Banker's Association (BBA) estimates that the CDS volume was close to $1.2 trillion in 2001, grew to $1.9 trillion in 2002, and will approach $4.8 trillion in 2004. These figures do not include asset swaps or total return swaps. Furthermore, the BBA estimates that about 50 percent of CDS trading takes place in London.

ESTIMATED MARKET SIZE

The collateralized bond obligation (CBO) market, not including collateralized mortgage obligations (CMOs), the precurser to the current new CDO products, began in the late 1980s when high yield or "junk bonds" had yields of about 13 to 20 percent.

In the United States, the Resolution Trust Corporation (RTC) was charged with liquidating positions held by savings and loan associations (S&Ls). Prior to this, savings and loans essentially enjoyed a put option to the U.S. government. They realized they could buy highly leveraged residuals from CMO transactions and could buy high yield bonds for yield. If there were no losses, they were heroes. If their positions didn't do well, they could put the S&L to the government and walk away. There was more to the crisis than that, such as fraudulent real estate loans, but this was a contributing factor to the S&L crisis in the United States. The fall of Drexel added further cheap high yield supply to the market, and changes in U.S. insurance capital regulations squelched demand for high yield product.

The beneficiaries were investors interested in diversified pools of cheap high yield bonds. Arbitrage CBOs were the answer. These deals were actively managed cash arbitrage CDOs. The early ones were exclusively leveraged market value deals. The supply glut of high yield bonds declined drastically in the 1990s, and the prices of high yield bonds rose with a corresponding decline in yield. Deal volume declined in the early 1990s. The emergence of the simpler cash flow CDO structure rekindled investor demand after 1995. This was the old paradigm.

By the late 1990s, there was a paradigm shift in the CDO market. A look at the reasons for almost nonexistent growth in the European market versus the U.S. market illustrates the sea change in CDOs and the causes for the paradigm shift.

As we can see from Figures 1.1 and 1.2, the European high yield bond market is minuscule compared to the U.S. high yield bond market. By 1999, the U.S. bond market was approaching $600 billion in size. In contrast, the European bond market was only about $35 billion in size. For more than a decade, the capital markets believed that this anemic issuance, combined with the multicurrency nature of the European issuance and investor market, would guarantee that Europe was never a significant factor in CDOs. The lack of supply of high yield bonds in Asia and Australia also inhibited their participation in CDO issuance.

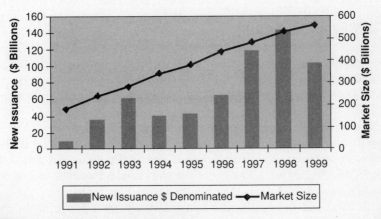

FIGURE 1.1 U.S. High Yield Bond Market
Sources: Moody's, S&P, and Westdeutsche Landesbank.

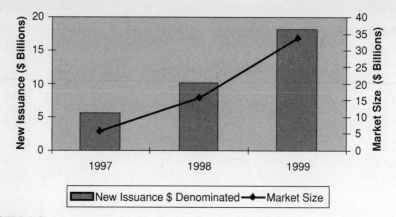

FIGURE 1.2   European High Yield Bond Market
Sources: Moody's, S&P, and Westdeutsche Landesbank.

Before 1995, virtually all CDOs were cash deals. A look at Figure 1.3 shows a change in the growth pattern beginning after 1995. The way the numbers are presented very much depends on who's reporting them. The numbers in Figure 1.3 are primarily CBOs and collateralized loan obligations (CLOs), but do not include the broad range of assets that can be securitized. Figure 1.4 lumps in other asset securitizations to report a much higher deal volume, but one can still see that the trend after 1995 indicates a change in the market.

Going back to the CBO/CLO market, we discover a pattern shift was mainly due to the introduction of *synthetics*. Structurers use CDSs and total return swaps (TRSs) to transfer the risk of assets, instead of selling cash (or physical) assets. As we will see later, the creation of a new tranche—the super senior tranche—gave an enormous boost to the deal arbitrage. It also created greater flexibility, and allowed for easier transfer of risk. In 1995, the CBO/CLO market was about $2.5 billion in size. By 1999, the CBO/CLO market was around $120 billion in size.

The growth spurt was chiefly due to the introduction of synthetic CDOs. Synthetics facilitate more efficient portfolio ramp-up, synthetics facilitate getting a higher average credit rating, and synthetics facilitate more efficient portfolio diversification. The synthetic arbitrage is facilitated by the feasibility of a smaller equity tranche, which creates more leverage. The synthetic arbitrage gets a further huge boost from the large, inexpensive super senior tranche that makes up the bulk of the synthetic deal.

Synthetic CDOs contributed to the explosive growth of CDOs in the European market, especially balance sheet deals. Many European banks

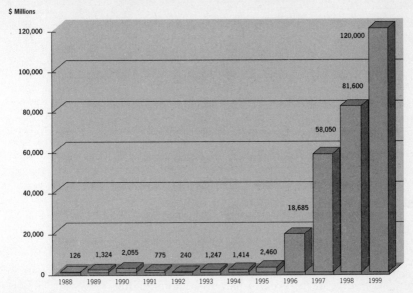

FIGURE 1.3 CDO Market Size—The Old Paradigm
Note: Above figures represent explicitly rated tranches of CBO/CLO transactions only.
Sources: Bank of America and Moody's Investors Service.

attract double the percentage share of discretionary savings relative to U.S. banks, making them very liquid. These European banks have a cheap source of funds. While the structure of the European market allows them a greater share of available savings, they haven't done well at generating high returns. They are under pressure to increase returns, lower costs, and

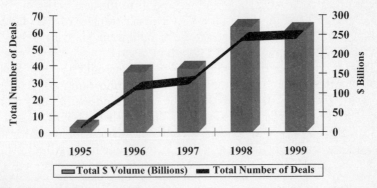

FIGURE 1.4 CDO Issuance 1995–1999
Source: Westdeutsche Landesbank.

manage risks better. Synthetic CDOs allow them to manage risk while employing their inexpensive traditional funding. The European bank funding advantage may disappear in a few years, but for now, synthetics are a welcome product for this market.

Another key shift in the market is the unprecedented number of credit downgrades and defaults in the past two years. Standard & Poor's reported an alarming recent increase in global corporate defaults. From the period from 1981 to 1998, global corporate defaults ranged from annual figures of $0.1 billion to as high as $23.6 billion in 1991. This period of low default rates has ended, at least temporarily. Defaults escalated from $40.4 billion in 1999 to $44.0 billion in 2000. Defaults then soared to $118.8 billion in 2001 with a further jump to $177.8 billion in 2002. The high yield market has been particularly hard hit, but investment grade credits have not been immune. Defaults in investment grade bonds over the past two years exceeded the cumulative total of the past twenty years.

Standard & Poor's reported that global investment grade corporate defaults ranged from 0–5 from 1981 to 2000. Investment grade corporate defaults climbed to 8 in 2001 and jumped to 17 in 2002. Speculative grade defaults ranged from 2–64 from 1981 to 1998, then climbed to 94 in 1999 and to 110 in 2000. In 2001, speculative grade corporate defaults jumped to 176 and remained high at 177 in 2002.

The increase in defaults and credit downgrades contributed to a growth rate of CDO downgrades of 318 percent in 2002. Most of the downgrades, about 74 percent, were in the high yield sector. The fact that the synthetic CDO arbitrage is viable using exclusively investment grade credits is a clear advantage for the synthetic CDO market.

The introduction of the Euro created a wider base of single currency reference assets in Europe. In addition, a wider investor base could participate in the deal when it was brought to market, because they were all purchasers of Euro assets. This helped boost issuance to about $200 billion in 2001, and issuance in 2002 is expected to be more than $250 billion when all the figures are in. Lang Gibson, Head of CDO Research at Bank of America, estimates issuance may top $269 billion. Figure 1.5 charts the explosive growth of the CDO market over the past 10 years, most of which has occurred in the past few years. The year-over-year growth from 2001 to 2002 of $50 billion exceeds total CDO issuance in 1996 plus all prior years. It equals the volume in 1997 when synthetic CDO issuance began to appear in the market. The explosive growth is due to the use of credit derivatives in the CDO market.

Figure 1.6 shows the breakdown of cash and synthetic deals as components of the total CDO market in 2002. *Whereas all of a deal's assets*

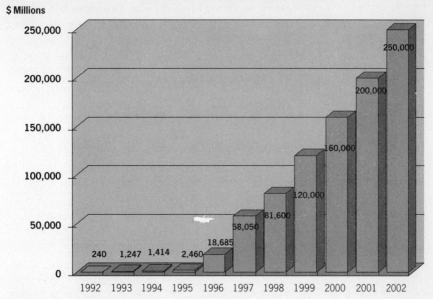

FIGURE 1.5   CDO Market Size 2002—The New Paradigm
Note: Above figures represent explicitly rated tranches of CBO/CLO transactions only.
Sources: Bank of America and Moody's Investors Service.

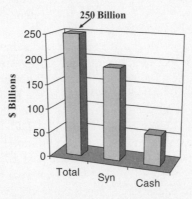

Synthetic Market is about 3 times the size of the cash market,
and more than 75% of the total CBO/CLO market.

FIGURE 1.6   CDO Market—Synthetic and Cash Breakdown for 2002
Note: Estimates as of January 20, 2003.
Sources: Moody's Investor Services and Bank of America.

were cash assets in 1995, by 2002, synthetics made up more than 75 percent of the CDO market. The percentage of the overall CDO market made up of synthetics varies by venue. The U.S. market is made up of only about 25 percent synthetic CDOs. Due to the greater volume of high yield bond and loan issuance, the U.S. brings more cash deals to market. In Europe and Asia, about 80 to 90 percent of the CDO market is made up of synthetics.

Synthetic CDOs usually fall into one of three categories:

1. Balance sheet CDOs,
2. Static synthetic arbitrage CDOs, and
3. Managed synthetic arbitrage CDOs.

Most balance sheet CDOs are regulatory capital-driven. Recently, several arbitrage-driven multisector balance sheet CDOs have come to market when banks used portfolios of mezzanine (BBB average-rated) tranches of multisector CDOs from their investment portfolios as the reference collateral.

The figures above understate the size of the synthetic market, because CDO statistics capture only a portion of CDO-related synthetic activity. Many cash deals employ synthetics to make up a portion of the total portfolio. Many synthetic arbitrage CDOs brought to market in 2001 and 2002 were *unrated*. We rely on rating agencies to compile most of the statistics. If a deal isn't rated, and if a deal is privately placed, we rely on word-of-mouth to compile deal data. Some portfolio swaps are privately placed, and some are untranched. Intermediations of synthetic product are not reported in CDO statistics. Neither are basket swaps, a separate but related category of synthetic activity.

In rough figures, balance sheet CDOs are about 45 percent of the synthetic CDO market. Static synthetic arbitrage CDOs are also about 45 percent of the synthetic CDO market. Managed synthetic arbitrage CDOs make up about 10 percent, or the remainder synthetic CDOs.

How did banks and investment banks manage to sell such a huge volume of new issuance to traditional (mutual funds, bank portfolios, pension funds, insurance company portfolios, hedge funds) CDO investors in such a short period of time? The answer is that most of the synthetic volume is not going to traditional CDO investors. While $250 billion total volume appears to be high, the sales of synthetic tranches and repackaged synthetic tranches are lower than the supply suggests. The super senior tranche makes up 85 to 95 percent of synthetic CDOs. This tranche is usually retained by the banks structuring the deals or is protected by monoline insurance companies.

Of the estimated $250 billion in CDO issuance in 2002, more than $187.5 billion is synthetic. Assuming the super senior tranche makes up 90 percent on average of the synthetic CDO, only about $18.75 billion of synthetic CDO product is available to traditional investors. Often, financial institutions that structure CDOs will retain the equity tranche in addition to the super senior tranche. They may feel like Wild Bill Hickok when he played poker with a man named Doc. Wild Bill was holding a winning hand of aces and eights. But he was shot in the back and killed. As we'll discover, investors in super senior and equity tranches may want to watch their backs.

CHAPTER 2

The Origins of Securitization

What is a securitization? What is a collateralized debt obligation (CDO)? Is this the same as structured finance? What is a synthetic credit structure? What is an asset-backed security? Market professionals agree all are structured products, but total agreement usually ends there. Market professionals often disagree on the definitions, so I will attempt to be clear regarding how I am using terminology in specific examples throughout this book. Some market definitions are confusing and redundant. We deal in a global market with people from a wide variety of professional backgrounds and ethnic origins. It is always best to agree on definitions of terms before engaging in any new transaction.

Structured finance benefits participants in various ways:

- Securitization may provide funding and liquidity by converting illiquid assets into cash.
- Structured finance can reduce borrowing costs. Often captive finance companies and independent companies can obtain capital at rates better than those obtainable for the originator of the securitized assets.
- Securitization may transfer the risk of assets or liabilities to allow a bank originator to do additional business without ballooning its balance sheet. Corporations use structured finance vehicles to finance assets used in the course of their business.
- Securitization can enable a financial institution to exploit regulatory capital arbitrage. At times, both banks and insurance companies engage in regulatory capital arbitrage as a prime motivation for securitization of assets that offer a low return on regulatory capital.
- Structured finance vehicles can be used to shelter corporations from potential operating liabilities.
- Securitizations and structured finance vehicles can be used for tax management.

To do all of the above, structures must address issues of bankruptcy, accounting issues, tax issues, and credit enhancement.

Structured finance and securitization can be vehicles for manipulating accounting statements and committing fraud, but these applications tend ultimately to work to the detriment of the deal sponsor. In this chapter we'll focus on the origins of securitization of pools of assets. In the following chapters we'll examine structured finance transactions that are designed for other purposes, such as special purpose corporations, or vehicles set up to finance the purchase of a single asset. These are all technically CDOs; however, in this book we'll use the term CDO to refer to securitization of pools of assets. This is the convention adopted by most market practitioners. In the next chapter, we'll examine shell companies, which may or may not be used for CDOs.

A securitization is a subset of structured finance, simply the creation and issuance of securities backed by a pool of loans, bonds, receivables, or future flows. The securities may be asset-backed bonds or notes issued by a special purchase entity that purchases the underlying assets, which are used as collateral to back the notes. In either case, the securities are backed by a pool of assets, and there are multiple obligors. The pool offers the possibility of portfolio diversification, even when it doesn't always deliver on this possibility. In many asset securitizations, the pool of assets is called the portfolio.

Virtually any type of asset or right to cash flows can be securitized. In the early 1990s, Prudential brought "death" bonds to the market. These were securitizations of the life insurance premiums owed to Prudential. The firm provided actuarial information showing drop-out rates and potential death rates of the premium payers so investors could get an idea of the future cash flows. Investors learned a new meaning for the term "deadbeat." This structure was one of the early "future flows" deals. The risk was whether or not the projected future cash flows would be realized due to the ultimate lack of future of the premium payers.

Traditionally, securitization has been a means for banks to reduce the size of their balance sheets and to reduce the risk on their balance sheets. This allowed banks to do more business and allowed investors access to diversified pools of assets to which they otherwise would not have had access. Securitization was a good deal for almost everyone.

THE CDO "ARBITRAGE"

There is no such thing as a CDO arbitrage. An arbitrage is a money pump. A true arbitrage guarantees a positive payoff in some scenario, with no possibility of a negative payoff and with no net investment. The opportunity to borrow and lend—at no cost—at two different fixed rates of interest, is an arbitrage. Another example is the ability to *simultaneously* buy and sell the *same* security in different marketplaces and earn a profit at no cost and with no risk. The efficient market hypothesis asserts that the market will take into account all relevant information and price risk accordingly. Therefore, arbitrageurs will force the rates to converge and drive the arbitrage out of the market. In other words, it shouldn't be possible to make a guaranteed risk-free profit.

Note that the process of buying bonds on the bid side of the market for later resale to customers at the offer side of the market is called trading. Often both sides of the trade do not occur simultaneously. Traders must assume market risk, thus trading isn't considered an arbitrage. Profits are not guaranteed. We often loosely—and incorrectly—use the word arbitrage to describe a hedged position that made money. For instance, we might say that a long bond position was "arbitraged" by a short sale.

Structurers of CDOs buy collateral and resell the collateral risk in another form at a lower all-in cost. As we shall see later, sometimes the risk is not completely sold and is held in a trading book due to distribution challenges. Sometimes the risk represented in the CDO tranches (the notes or liabilities issued by the CDO), are not exactly the same as the risk represented by the collateral of the CDO. Sometimes the residual risk is deliberately held in a trading book and "dynamically hedged." Sometimes an entire tranche, usually the super senior tranche, is held in the trading book with no hedge whatsoever, and is "marked to market" in theory, but not in actual practice.

Structuring groups that have separate profit and loss statements (P&Ls) from trading desks have some truth to the claim that they benefit from a CDO arbitrage, but their financial institution does not. The structuring group means that they put together a deal, pay themselves a structuring fee, pass the risk of distribution and management of the tranches to the trading desk, and declare victory for the structuring group. They have acted as the middleman, taken out a fee, and washed their hands of the risk management and distribution challenges. Many banks are set up this way. Smart banks recognize this moral hazard, link structuring and trading P&L, and track CDO profitability throughout the deal life—but many banks do not.

Financial institutions that structure CDOs come closest to approaching an arbitrage when they buy the collateral, tranche the exact risk represented by the collateral, and sell every tranche of the collateral through their distribution network. Time elapses between the accumulation of collateral and the closing of the transaction, especially in a cash asset–based deal. There is further delay before the deal is entirely "sold." Financial institutions make a secondary market in the CDO tranches, and occasionally have portions of CDOs in inventory that must be hedged. Still, most of the risk of the transaction has been distributed, and reserves are held as a cushion for the residual risk of ongoing trading and risk management. The financial institutions that use this business model have the cleanest type of transaction management from the arbitrage point of view, but it is still not strictly an arbitrage.

It is more correct to call the cash calculation of the CDO the "economics" rather than the "arbitrage." The economics of a typical CDO are calculated as follows:

> *Cash thrown off by the collateral plus interest on collateral, if any;* minus *structuring fees* minus *underwriting fees or sales fees (of the tranches or liabilities)* minus *legal fees* minus *trustee fees* minus *management fees, if any;* minus *administration fees* minus *special purpose vehicle fees* minus *rating agency fees* minus *listing fees* minus *the payments due on the CDO notes (the tranches, which are the liabilities, of the CDO) equals profit.*

Later we'll look at the CDO economics in more detail. We'll examine the failure of "arbitrage" terminology to describe the fluctuating profitability, and sometimes the loss, in these transactions, especially for financial institutions that do not distribute all of the liabilities of the CDO.

PORTFOLIO DIVERSIFICATION AND CREDIT EVENTS

Diversification is not a guarantee against loss, only against losing everything at once. Of the CDOs that have performed poorly, the cause has been chiefly due to the poor performance of the underlying corporate collateral. In 2001 and 2002, major defaults included Adelphia Communications; American Tissue; Argentina; Armstrong; Crown Cork & Seal; Enron; Global Crossing Ltd.; Kmart; Marconi; National Century Financial Enterprise, Inc.; Railtrack; Swiss Air; RBG Resources et al.; UAL Corp. (the parent of United Airlines); US Airways Group, Inc.; WorldCom; and others. These defaults, combined with a rash of downgrades in sectors like telecoms, have caused downgrades of CDO tranches in unprecedented large numbers. Even McDonald's Corporation wasn't immune from bad news. It announced its first quarterly loss ever in December 2002.

While investors need to consider the degree of portfolio diversification, it is arguably even more important to look at the type of risk in the portfolio, and the individual names in a portfolio. It is possible to diversify into uncharted territory and actually introduce imprudent risk in the name of diversification. The cash flow structure of the CDO is also important for tranche buyers evaluating risk. We'll revisit these caveats in Chapters 5 and 6 when we compare CDO structures.

Diversification is a necessary condition to a successful CDO, but it is not a sufficient condition to a successful CDO. I don't usually introduce a concept by saying people shouldn't rely too much on it, but in this case, a little caution is a good thing. Recent gaming of diversity scores has led some CDO investors to be complacent about risk. Diversification is merely one of several important structural features. Now, let's step back and look at this key concept in investment theory in the context of securitization.

For the moment, assume portfolio returns are normally distributed. Now that we've assumed a distribution of returns, we can use historical data to calculate the mean, variance, and correlation of the assets. A standard approach is to weight portfolio assets with fractions that add up to one and then calculate the portfolio standard deviation (volatility) and expected return. The standard deviation of the portfolio, $\sigma_{(Pn)}$, is simply the square root of the variance of the portfolio, $\sigma^2_{(Pn)}$. The standard deviation is also known as the volatility of the portfolio and is calculated as follows:

$$\text{Risk} = \sigma_{(Pn)} = \sqrt{\sum_{i=1}^{n} (\omega_i^2 \cdot \sigma_i^2) + (n \cdot \omega_1 \cdot \omega_2 \cdot \ldots \omega_i \cdot \rho_n)}$$

where ω = the weighting of the asset
n = the number of assets in the portfolio
σ_i = the standard deviation of the ith asset
Cov_n = the covariance of a portfolio of n assets

A simple example for a two-asset portfolio is as follows. If ω is the weight of the first asset, the weight of the second asset will be $(1 - \omega)$. The portfolio expected return is:

$$\omega r_1 + (1 - \omega)r_2$$

where r = return on the assets

$$\text{Variance} = \omega^2 \sigma_1^2 + (1 - \omega)^2 \sigma_2^2 + 2 \omega (1 - \omega) \text{Cov}_{12}$$

where σ_1^2 = variance of asset 1
             σ_2^2 = variance of asset 2
       Cov_{12} = covariance of assets 1 and 2
    Variance = volatility of the portfolio

For a portfolio of two assets of equal weights, let's assume asset 1 has an expected return of 20 percent with a variance of 0.04, and asset 2 has an expected return of 12 percent and a variance of 0.03. I'll further give you data that the covariance of the assets is 0.02.

The expected return of the portfolio is:

$$0.5 \cdot 0.20 + 0.5 \cdot 0.12 = 0.16 \text{ or } 16\%$$

The portfolio variance is:

$$0.5^2 \cdot 0.04 + 0.5^2 \cdot 0.03 + 2(0.5)(0.5)0.02 = 0.0275$$

The standard deviation of the portfolio return is:

$$(0.0275)^{1/2} = 0.1658$$

The volatility of the portfolio is 16.58%.

If I want to calculate my value-at-risk (VAR) at the 99 percent confidence level, there is a 1 percent chance the portfolio will lose more than 22.63 percent.*

What happens when we add an asset? Let's assume we now have a three-asset portfolio of equal weighting. Asset 3 has a return of 16 percent and its variance is the same as that of asset 2 or 0.03. The covariance of the assets is 0.1. The covariance is lower than for the two-asset portfolio, because the portfolio is now more diversified (more on this later).

The expected return of the portfolio is:

$$0.33 \cdot 0.20 + 0.33 \cdot 0.12 + 0.33 \cdot 0.16 = 0.16 \text{ or } 16\%$$

$$\text{Variance} = \omega_1^2 \cdot \sigma_1^2 + \omega_2^2 \cdot \sigma_2^2 + \omega_3^2 \cdot \sigma_3^2 + 3 \cdot \omega_1 \cdot \omega_2 \cdot \omega_3 \cdot Cov_{123}$$

The portfolio volatility is:

$$(0.33)^2 \cdot 0.04 + (0.33)^2 \cdot 0.03 + (0.33)^2 \cdot 0.03$$
$$+ 3 \cdot (0.33) \cdot (0.33) \cdot (0.33) \cdot 0.01 = 0.011968$$

The volatility of the portfolio is 0.1094 or 10.94%.

---

*Note: The 1 percent tail is $2.33 \cdot 0.1658 = 0.3863$ away from the mean. The level of VAR is $0.16 - 0.3863 = -0.2263$

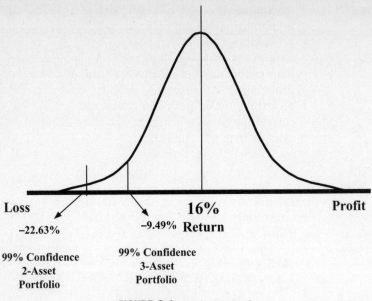

Loss

16%

Profit

−22.63%

−9.49% **Return**

99% Confidence
2-Asset
Portfolio

99% Confidence
3-Asset
Portfolio

FIGURE 2.1   Value-at-Risk

At the 99 percent confidence level, there is a 1 percent chance the port-folio will lose more than 9.49 percent.*

Although the expected return of both the two-asset and three-asset portfolios is the same, the volatility of the portfolio is lower, and the prob-ability of sustaining the same magnitude of loss as the two-asset portfolio is also lower. We want to minimize the volatility of the losses to minimize the volatility of the expected return. Figure 2.1 shows the benefit of reduc-ing the VAR in the portfolio.

Another way of looking at this is to say that if I take into account my expected losses, I get my expected return. If I don't get my expected return, it is due to the fact that I experienced *unexpected losses*. Unexpected loss is a measure of the volatility of the expected loss. Most market professionals are familiar with the following formula for calculating unexpected losses due to credit events:

$$UL_{(u,c)} = \sqrt{\Sigma \rho_{ij} n_i n_j \sqrt{\frac{(P_{(ui\,|\,c)})(1 - P_{(ui,c)})(P_{(uj\,|\,c)})(1 - P_{(uj,c)})}{(1 - P_{(c)})}}}$$

---

*Note: The 1 percent tail is 2.33 · 0.1094 = 0.2549 away from the mean. The level of VAR is 0.16 − 0.2549 = −0.0949.

where $UL_{(u,c)}$ = unexpected loss or credit event risk (default)

$\quad\quad P_{(ui|c)}$ = probability of default of asset i

$\quad\quad P_{(uj|c)}$ = probability of default of asset j

$\quad\quad P_{(ui,c)}$ = joint probability default of asset i and counterparty

$\quad\quad P_{(uj,c)}$ = joint probability default of asset j and counterparty

$\quad\quad P_{(uj,c)}$ = probability of counterparty default

$\quad\quad P_{(c)}$ = probability of default of counterparty

$\quad\quad \rho_{i,j}$ = correlation of default between asset i and asset j

$\quad\quad n_i$ = asset i's weight in the portfolio

$\quad\quad n_j$ = asset j's weight in the portfolio

Portfolios with only market risk tend to have normal returns because losses due to market risk are often normally distributed (also known as a Gaussian distribution) and have the familiar bell-curve shape. The distribution of credit losses, and therefore expected returns in a portfolio that has credit risk, is *not* normally distributed. As one risk manager said after looking at the lopsided shape of the returns, "I've been skewed." Credit returns are skewed, or lopsided, with a long fat tail as shown in Figure 2.2.

Mean and standard deviation, calculated assuming a normal distribution, do not adequately describe credit risk. Most portfolio managers use a horizon analysis. They assume a future time period and measure VAR due to upgrades, downgrades, and defaults; then they estimate a distribution of

Credit Return Distribution

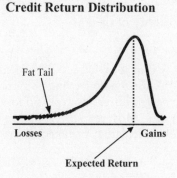

Market Return Distribution

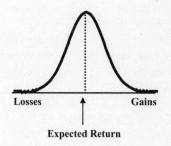

Credit returns tend to have
skewed distributions.

Market returns tend to
have normal distributions.

FIGURE 2.2   Credit Return versus Market Return Distributions

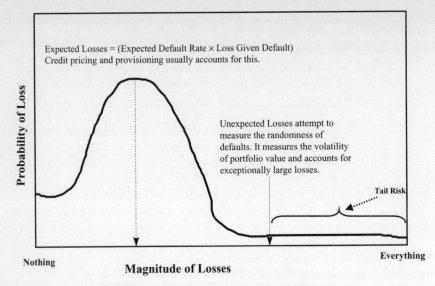

Expected Losses = (Expected Default Rate × Loss Given Default)
Credit pricing and provisioning usually accounts for this.

Unexpected Losses attempt to measure the randomness of defaults. It measures the volatility of portfolio value and accounts for exceptionally large losses.

Tail Risk

Probability of Loss

Nothing

Magnitude of Losses

Everything

FIGURE 2.3   Expected and Unexpected Losses

portfolio value. Figure 2.3 shows how a portfolio manager might view expected and unexpected losses on a portfolio. The portfolio manager might use these estimates of expected and unexpected losses to determine how much capital or reserves to set aside to account for these credit risks.

So is that it? If we estimate *expected losses* and *unexpected losses*, what else could there be? One would think the term unexpected losses would cover everything we didn't cover when we estimated expected losses. Unfortunately, there is more. Unexpected losses are only an estimate of how bad it can get most of the time. Anything not captured up to the point we measure unexpected loss is called "tail risk." That's just another way of saying it's the variance of risk (or the variance of return) due to everything else we didn't think about. We might experience an extraordinary loss due to fraud, for instance.

If we use the model for a normal distribution, a five-standard deviation credit event should only happen once in every 7,000 years. But in the marketplace, we see this happen once or twice in a decade. Banks that held large concentrations of Enron, RBG metals, Global Crossing, or WorldCom credit risk might argue that it happens even more frequently than that.

We want to maximize expected return. We want to minimize variance of return. Diversification is the Kevlar vest we wear to avoid taking a fatal shot from variance of return. At least, that's the theory. We're still exposed in areas not protected by the vest, but the best protection is to avoid getting shot at in the first place.

TERMINOLOGY

A CDO is backed by portfolios of assets that may include a combination of bonds, loans, securitized receivables, asset-backed securities, tranches of other CDOs, or credit derivatives referencing any of the former. Some market practitioners define a CDO as being backed by a portfolio including only bonds and/or loans, but most market practitioners use the former definition. I'll use CDO as an umbrella term for asset securitizations and drill down from there.

Up to the end of the 1990s, CDOs all used special purpose entities (SPEs), also known as special purpose vehicles (SPVs), that purchased the portfolio of assets and issued tranches of debt and equity. The SPE purchased the assets from a bank's balance sheet and/or trading books. These are known as *true sale* structures.

SPEs are usually bankruptcy-remote, meaning they are *delinked* from the credit risk of the bank arranger (also known as the originator). The bank arranger can earn servicing fees, administration fees, and hedging fees from the SPV, but otherwise has no claim on the cash flows of the assets in the SPV.

Formerly, banks and investment banks underwrote the CDO tranches to provide the funds—often along with bridge financing—for the purchase of the portfolio assets, which backed the tranches. This is no longer always the case. Synthetic securitizations eliminate the need for a special purpose entity, albeit they may also use an SPE to issue limited recourse notes linked to a CDO's tranched credit risk. We'll examine these structures later.

TRUE SALE, HYBRID, AND SYNTHETIC STRUCTURES

Figures 2.4 and 2.5 show simplified versions of the true sale structure and a purely synthetic structure. Notice that the true sale structure doesn't have one of the tranches found in the synthetic structure. That is a super senior tranche, and we'll talk about the advantages of this tranche in detail later. We'll also discuss the applications of true sale and synthetic structures with respect to arbitrage and balance sheet deals.

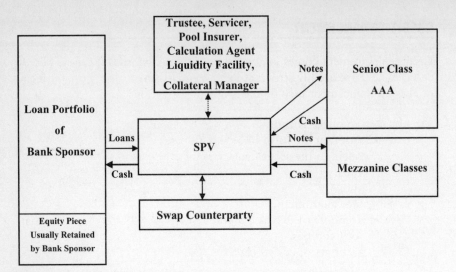

FIGURE 2.4   Simplified True Sale Balance Sheet Collateralized Loan Obligation (CLO)

The choice of structure type will take into account tax, accounting, and regulatory constraints. It will take into account the types of assets the vehicle can issue. It will take into account investor preferences for the type of product the vehicle can issue. We'll examine these issues in the section on SPEs later in this book, when I also cover the terminology of SPEs.

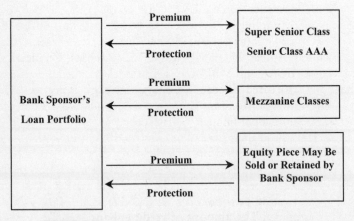

FIGURE 2.5   Simplified Synthetic Balance Sheet CLO

CREDIT ENHANCEMENT

Credit enhancement comes in a variety of forms, and several types of credit enhancement are usually structured into a single transaction. Popular forms of credit enhancement include the following:

- Initial overcollateralization.
- Subordination in the form of an equity piece.
- Junior lenders to the securitization vehicle.
- Credit wraps.
- Surety bonds.
- Government guarantees.
- Reserve accounts of excess coupon spread not required for immediate payment of liabilities.
- Reserve accounts of excess cash.
- Credit derivatives.
- Cash flow diversion once prespecified conditions or *triggers* are met.

Conduits may employ letters of credit (LOCs) and liquidity lines to ensure cash flow requirements, and may also add a *clawback* LOC to protect against payments being reclassified as preferential in the event of bankruptcy.

Several years ago, LOCs were a common form of credit enhancement for credit card securitizations. Recently, a structurer asked me what happened to all the LOCs, were they too expensive? It isn't that the cost is prohibitive—although it may become prohibitive under BIS II—but rather that an LOC has less value as credit enhancement because so many banks had been downgraded.

Monoline insurance companies provide *credit wraps*, which are *financial guarantees*. Monoline insurance companies are the only entities allowed to provide financial guarantees under New York law, where most securitizations are closed. Ambac Financial Group, Inc. (Ambac), Financial Security Assurance, Inc. (FSA), and MBIA Inc. are all AAA rated, and dominate market share for structured finance wrapping, although other monolines are active in this business. Monoline insurance companies started out providing wraps for U.S. municipal finance, but branched out into structured finance to diversify the risk in their portfolios. Ambac, FSA, and MBIA, in particular, have made a concerted effort to judiciously diversify into global risks. Non-U.S. risk is less than 10 percent of each of their portfolios, so they will probably continue to be major factors in the global market in the future.

The highest rating possible on a wrapped tranche is the rating of the credit wrap provider. The amount of credit enhancement depends on the deal structure. The amount of enhancement is expressed as a multiple of the expected loss level. For instance, to get an AAA rating, a general rule is that the credit enhancement must equal five times the expected loss level. The amount of enhancement required declines for lower rating requirements.

Investor satisfaction with the performance of wraps under duress is very high. The view of investors and rating agencies is that the wrap providers guarantee uninterrupted cash flows. The credit wrap also serves to preserve the rating of tranches in jeopardy of downgrade. Some Aaa tranches of CDO would have been downgraded by the rating agencies in recent past, but they maintained their Aaa ratings only by virtue of the credit wraps supplied by Aaa-rated monolines.

Multiline insurance companies, or *sureties*, may provide surety bonds or performance bonds. The surety bond guarantees the principal or obligor will perform its obligations under a contract. This is different than a financial guarantee. For instance, a commercial surety bond can be an advance payment bond that indemnifies against default on prepaid supply transactions involving the delivery of physical commodities.

The difference between a *financial guarantee* and a *credit derivative* is that the buyer of protection in a credit derivative contract does not have to own the underlying security or actually suffer a loss, as we'll see in the section on credit derivatives. In the recent past, protection bought in the form of credit derivatives has outperformed protection bought as surety bonds in non-CDO structured finance products. We'll look at one example involving Enron and J.P. Morgan in the chapter on credit risk dumping. This has important implications for future use of surety bonds.

Overcollateralization is achieved through investment in more collateral than is required to meet the CDO's static cash flow requirements. The SPE may invest in more physical assets, or equity investors may inject additional cash into the deal. Cash injections are usually invested in virtually risk-free assets such as short-term government assets.

Tranching creates more than one class of debt within a given structure. Junior investors provide credit enhancement for senior investors. Investors in subordinated classes earn a higher coupon, but have higher risk to their initial principal investment. The subordinated debt holders agree to absorb losses before the senior debt holders. Several tranches may exist in one deal, and the payments due to each tranche holder are defined in the prospectus according to the tranche payment priority. The more certain the payment, the higher the credit rating and the lower the nominal return. The less certain the payment, the lower the credit rating and the higher the nominal return.

Issuers may deposit cash in a reserve account or a trust account and these funds can be used to meet principal and interest payments as needed. Excess spread may also be trapped in a reserve account. Excess spread is the current cash flow remaining after payment of investor coupons and fees.

The excess spread account may be used for the benefit of all of the tranche investors to offset loss in value from nonperforming assets. Remaining funds would revert to the deal manager or the first loss investor at maturity, but this is not necessarily the case. In many structures, the reserve account is for the benefit of the first loss investor only.

CDO CLASSIFICATIONS

Any potential future stream of payments or future value can be securitized. The following summary shows broad classifications one should be on the alert for in evaluating reported CDO data. Statistics on CDO issuance are often reported according to type of collateral classification. Many CDOs securitize assets from more than one asset class, making it difficult to generalize. Different reports may use different definitions and benchmarks, so it is important to read the classification criteria to understand reported data.

One important class is consumer receivables, which include auto loans, auto leases, home equity loans, and credit card receivables. Student loans have unique characteristics and are grouped into their own category.

Mortgage-backed securities (MBSs) are usually categorized as residential mortgage loans (single family, multifamily, condominium, cooperatives) or commercial mortgage loans. Manufactured housing loans are often grouped into a separate category due to unique homeowner profiles.

Commercial and industrial loans include investment grade corporate loans and high yield corporate loans. Small business loans in the United States have their own category due to the government guarantee and unique structural features. In Europe, small- to medium-size enterprise loans are grouped into a multicountry category. These loans are smaller in size than usual commercial and industrial loans, and the obligors are often not publicly rated. Investment grade corporate bonds and high yield corporate bonds are often viewed as separate categories.

Receivables such as computer leases, aircraft leases, marine leases, and equipment leases are usually grouped separately. Utility stranded costs have been securitized for years and are their own category. Equipment loans and equipment leases are considered a separate small- to medium-size loan category. Expectations of payments, such as delinquent tax liens, are a separate category. Future flows deals are another separate category, but are sometimes included in the emerging markets statistics category.

Bonds backed by receivables such as the right to televise Formula One sporting events, or cable subscriptions, are also sometimes classified as CDOs, although they are usually lumped into the broader category of structured finance.

Private equity and hedge fund of fund securitizations are in separate categories. Nonperforming loans also have a separate category. Investment grade sovereign debt may be included in bond obligations, but emerging market debt is usually considered separately (although this debt is often found in high yield bond obligations).

I just mentioned assest that can be used in the CDO portfolio, but even the asset definitions are subject to debate. For instance, asset-backed securities (ABSs) are structured securities in which the underlying collateral is itself a pool of loans or receivables.

A CLO is a type of CDO. CLOs are backed by a portfolio of loans. The term CLO is reserved for a securitization that is exclusively backed by loans. The first rated CLO backed by U.S. bank loans was brought to market in 1990.

A collateralized bond obligation (CBO) is another type of CDO. The first rated CBO backed by high yield bonds was brought to market in 1988. CBOs are backed by a portfolio of secured or unsecured senior or junior bonds issued by a variety of corporate or sovereign obligors. Often a CBO will include loans in the portfolio, but the majority of the collateral usually consists of bonds. CBO transactions realize the positive spread between a portfolio of higher-return, higher-risk assets, often rated below BBB; and lower-cost, highly rated CBO securities issued to purchase the portfolio of bonds backing the CBO.

A collateralized mortgage obligation (CMO) is backed by MBSs also called mortgage pass-through securities. CMOs and the individual tranches of CMOs are also called MBSs. This terminology is usually reserved for the U.S. market, and we'll briefly look at this later. Ironically, CMOs, the CDO precursors, are usually excluded from CDO reports and are not considered in the definition of CDOs by many market professionals.

Structural differences in the European market did not lend themselves to the same type of cash flow tranching as the U.S. market. Often European mortgages do not enjoy government support. A look at the German market illustrates just some of the differences between the U.S. and European MBS market. The German Pfandbriefe market has been in existence for more than 200 years. The underlying mortgage loans must have a loan-to-value ratio of less than 60 percent, so the overall credit quality is deemed to be AAA. In the U.S. market, MBSs are a balance sheet management tool. In the German market, however, Pfandbriefe cannot be prepaid and are kept on the bank's balance sheet, although they may be pledged as collateral. Securitization of other types of MBSs as a balance sheet management tool has gained momentum only in the past three years after a very slow start.

CDOs are further classified as synthetic (credit derivatives) or cash. Some CDOs are backed by combinations of cash and synthetic securities.

CDOs are either arbitrage deals, balance sheet deals, or both. Both can be any combination of cash and synthetic underlyings. Arbitrage CDOs take advantage of greater market prices for the underlying obligations versus the price at which the combined liabilities can be sold. Balance sheet CDOs are normally used for regulatory capital relief, although funding may be another motive for a balance sheet deal.

Arbitrage CDOs are either market value CDOs or cash flow CDOs. They can be backed by either cash assets, synthetic assets, or a combination of both. Cash flow CDOs make up 85 to 90 percent of the arbitrage market, and are growing at a much faster rate than market value CDOs.

MARKET VALUE CDOs

Market value CDOs make up approximately 10 to 15 percent of the arbitrage CDO market. Market value deals, like most CDOs, will either (1) pledge assets to a trustee to back debt for the benefit of the investors, or (2) have a bankruptcy remote SPV buy the assets and pledge the collateral to back debt or equity (or preferred stock) for the benefit of the investors. Market value deals may also use a third, less common, structure. Investors have a claim on all of the assets in the fund and the seniority of their claim depends on the class of debt or equity (preference shares or preferred stock) they own.

Market value structures meet principal (if applicable) and interest liabilities by generating cash from trading assets and from interest on invested assets. If a collateral pool consists of defaulted bonds or loans, the market value structure is usually used, because these assets do not generate predictable cash flow streams, but have significant market value upside potential. Managers who have good track records trading investment grade debt and high yield debt often prefer market value deals.

Market value deal managers trade actively and aggressively and usually employ leverage. Of course, not every trade results in a gain. Both credit and market considerations are important to market value deal managers. Investors who must mark-to-market their assets might prefer market value structures, since market value CDO managers must mark-to-market the CDO's portfolio.

The ratio of the market value of assets to the face value of liabilities is the focus of a market value CLO. Market value deals require overcollateralization or a "haircut." The overcollateralization protects investors from asset price volatility due to changes in general interest rate movements, general credit spread movements, or other general market movements. Market value CDOs require maintenance of a minimum overcollateralization level. If this level is breached, the assets must be sold to pay down liabilities or the assets must be sold and exchanged for highly rated liquid instruments. This is known as a *trigger event*. The rating agencies monitor the debt coverage ratios. The performance of a market value CDO depends upon the manager's trading ability.

CASH FLOW CDOs

Nonsynthetic *cash flow* CDOs invest in cash assets as collateral. The structure passes principal and interest payments generated by cash flows of the underlying collateral through to the investors. For a deal to be successful, the cash flow from the collateral pool must meet all deal liabilities including the interest and principal obligations from the notes issued by the CDO. The cash flows are hedged, reinvested, and tranched by time and seniority. The rating of a note depends on the probability of cash flow sufficiency to service that particular note. If the cash flow deal is properly structured, investors only experience a loss if there are defaults in the collateral pool.

Cash flow CDOs backed by a pool of cash obligations require a manager, whereas synthetic cash flow deals may or may not have a manager. For the cash asset–backed CDO, the manager's role is more limited than that of a market value CDO manager. The manager is carefully chosen for credit expertise rather than trading expertise. The cash flow CDO manager of a cash instrument–backed deal chooses the initial diversified portfolio of cash instruments and chooses credits to purchase during the reinvestment period. The manager may also participate in a workout in the event of default to maximize recovery. We'll examine these structural details when we compare cash and synthetic CDOs.

Deals can be managed or unmanaged. Only deals, which reference a static pool of assets, can dispense with a manager. This is most common with arbitrage synthetic CDOs, or cash CDOs, where a fixed pool of assets is used in a pass-through-type structure.

Cash CDOs are usually broken into broad categories that represent the bulk of the issuance:

- High yield loans.
- Multisector.
- Investment grade corporate (which normally includes one quarter to one third high yield collateral).
- High yield bonds.

Synthetic CDOs are backed by credit default swaps (CDSs) on a diversified pool of reference obligors. The CDSs can reference any type of cash obligation. They can be either balance sheet deals or arbitrage deals and are often classified into three categories:

1. Managed CDOs,
2. CDOs with right of substitution, and
3. Static CDOs.

Managed CDOs will have an actively involved manager and may look similar to a market value CDO in that the underlying pool of assets is actively traded in an attempt to add value. Some managers are more passive and trade only to avoid losses. CDOs with the right of substitution have managers that may not be "arms-length" managers. The bank arranger's structuring group may handle management activities that allow them to trade out of credits according to pre-set rules. The object is to trade out of deteriorating credit before default and trade into a higher credit quality obligation.

Static pools of CDSs back a static CDO. No trading is allowed. By definition, this is a cash flow CDO. Synthetic static arbitrage CDOs differ from cash CDOs that are also cash flow CDOs because the synthetic deal normally has no preplanned reinvestment period. Since the CDS market allows cash flow maturities to be defined at the deal inception, there is no need for reinvestment, other than possibly to reinvest recovered amounts after a default, if any.

We'll examine the advantages and disadvantages of managed versus static CDOs when we compare cash and synthetic CDOs.

This menu of different products may seem confusing at first. The structural details are indeed important, and we'll review various structural features later. As we've already seen, the key is to avoid getting shot in the first place. The place to start evaluating the fundamental value of any securitization is with the pool or portfolio. If an investor doesn't like the names in the portfolio in the first place, no structure can make up for it. If the investor likes the names in the initial portfolio, then the negotiation begins for the best possible structural protections.

THE ORIGINS OF U.S. SECURITIZATION

Most of today's securitization technology originated in the U.S. financial markets. The origins teach us about structural features that can be applied to today's markets. Also, the origins teach us about how resistant we are to learning the hard lessons experience has to offer. A quick look at the U.S. MBS and CMO markets allows us, for the moment, to isolate the cash flow risk without worrying about credit risk.

In the U.S. market, MBSs are not included in the definition of ABSs, but the European market includes MBSs in this definition. In the U.S., the term *asset-backed security* is reserved for securitizations backed by credit card receivables, auto loans, auto leases, student loans, home equity loans, and manufactured housing loans. This list doesn't include other more obscure receivables that are securitized in the U.S. market. The fact that MBS is not included in the definition of ABS in the United States is an artifact. MBS securitization so completely dominated the U.S.-structured market at its inception that it required a name of its own.

The Government National Mortgage Association (Ginnie Mae or GNMA), the Federal Home Loan Mortgage Corporation (Freddie Mac or FHLMC), and the Federal National Mortgage Association (Fannie Mae or FNMA) are the three entities that caused a major leap forward in U.S. securitization. These three entities set guidelines and created pools of residential mortgages. FHLMC and FNMA are **respectively a *public company and a private company* sometimes called** *government-sponsored entities*. Each of these pass-throughs pay both a coupon and pass-through principal prepayments. Interest payments have a delay to account for collections.

The U.S. market views the issuance from these entities as risk-free, or as good as an obligation of the U.S. government, but that isn't strictly true. GNMA is a government agency, and *GNMA pass-throughs*, also known as *agency pass-throughs*, are backed by the full faith and credit of the U.S. government. FHLMC and FNMA are respectively a *public company and a private company* sometimes called *government-sponsored entities*, and FHLMC and FNMA pass-throughs are known as *conventional* pass-throughs. The U.S. market perception is that the government would never allow FHMLC or FNMA to default because it would shake the investment community to the core. The credit risk is viewed as negligible. As we say in the United States, it is close enough for government work.

This perception of safety for FHLMC and FNMA is not shared in the European market, and this initially made marketing of these securities in Europe more problematic. When U.S. deal arrangers tried to sell floating rate mortgage-backed securities in the European market, they met with initial resistance. Investors were initially suspicious of the creditworthiness of GNMA. As investors learned more about the entities, the resistance to investment abated. In much of Europe, GNMA is usually assigned a 0 percent Bank for International Settlements (BIS) risk weight, whereas FHLMC and FNMA are assigned a 50 percent BIS risk weight, as they are in the United States.

It was this perception of lack of credit risk in the United States that made reward for the cash flow risk of these securities all the more appealing. Many institutions that could not invest in options or take high degrees of interest rate risk could purchase these securities because of the sterling creditworthiness of the issuers. Life just got a lot more interesting for wide classes of investors in the United States! This is because when an investor bought these securities, they were short an embedded call option—the right of the U.S. homeowner to prepay his mortgage.

How did this work? Suppose a mortgage pass-through traded at a discount. Securities of an issuer without credit risk trade at a discount if the coupon is lower than the issuer's coupon of a new issuance at par. One can see this in the U.S. treasury market as interest rates fluctuate. Since interest rates had been volatile, by 1986 there were a variety of outstanding issues with a variety of coupons. For a discounted issue trading at a price of 99, one received a lower coupon than a current issue would offer, but if interest rates declined, it was likely that mortgage prepayments would speed up. Then one would get repayments of principal at 100. If one bought a premium security, one could enjoy a high coupon, but the investor hoped that prepayments declined. Then the high coupon could be earned for a longer period of time. Since there was "no credit risk" investors could place bets that weren't obvious to their constituencies.

Travelers, for instance, bought GNMAs with double-digit coupons at high premiums in the mid-80s. This allowed them to report extremely high current income—at least for a while. Unfortunately for them, interest rates were both volatile and dropping. Prepayments sped up—a lot! Their high premium securities began prepaying at par or 100. Travelers took a mark-to-market loss, while simultaneously losing a large portion of the cash flow stream of those high coupons.

The lower interest rates rubbed even more salt in the wound. The prepayments and remaining coupons had to be reinvested at lower rates. Suddenly GNMAs were no fun anymore. It was a debacle. Too late to stanch hundreds of millions in losses, but early enough to avoid further major losses, Travelers bought long-dated U.S. Treasury (UST) zeros as a hedge. Zeros have the property of popping up in price for large declines in interest rates. Travelers chose 20-year UST zeros since these were trading cheap relative to the UST interest rate curve. This partially offset the loss on the GNMAs. The hedge provided no current income, however.

This example may seem unrelated to current events, but it actually exemplifies pivotal concepts. It is a theme that gets replayed with variations many times over the course of the coming years. Let's take a moment to dissect some of the components. We'll see these ideas again in various forms in other structures. Today we still combine high cash flow equity with zero coupon bonds in principal-protected structures.

Suppose for a moment that Travelers had owned high coupon premium bonds that had no prepayment risk and no credit risk. The duration of those bonds would initially be shorter than current coupon bonds in the market due to their high coupons. These coupons have to be reinvested at lower interest rates. These bond prices would move inversely with interest rates, so as rates dropped, the price of the bonds would rise, but not as much as a bond with a lower coupon.

Which of the bonds below will have the greatest effective yield to a 6-month horizon if rates decline 100 basis points (bps)?

| Bond A | 7% coupon | 30-year maturity | 10% yield |
| Bond B | 12% coupon | 30-year maturity | 10% yield |

Bond A has the longer duration and will therefore have a larger increase in price if rates decline 100 bp. Bond A's effective yield, and its total rate of return to the 6-month time horizon will therefore be greater than Bond B.

Travelers was already behind the eight ball when interest rates dropped. Being short, the embedded call option only made a bad situation worse. It was as if they bought a bond and then sold a structured call option, which is only partially exercised when prepayments speed up. The selling of the call option gave them more income initially, but it resulted in even more pain than they otherwise would have experienced.

During which of the following scenarios will the implied option premium of the embedded call option be highest?

- Low volatility with rates falling.
- Low volatility with rates rising.
- High volatility with rates falling.
- High volatility with rates rising.

The premium will be highest when volatility is high and rates are falling. This is the scenario Travelers experienced. Since they are short the option, the higher implied option premium means that the price of the bond will decline rapidly. These bonds were highly negatively convex, which means the duration of the bonds fell rapidly. In fact, instead of rising, the price of these bonds started falling when interest rates fell.

Travelers searched for a hedge. Initially, they couldn't find anything at a price they were willing to pay. Treasury zeros seemed to be the answer, although they would have been happier to have stumbled on the solution earlier. Since Travelers owned securities that are negatively convex due to a short call option, they wanted something that had a high degree of positive convexity and would have characteristics similar to a call option. At the time, 20-year maturity treasury zeros seemed to provide an answer to part of their problem.

I once heard a professor tell his class that zero coupon bonds have zero convexity, but it isn't true. Formulas and academic definitions can obscure the utility of a financial instrument, its value as a tool. Forget the labels. Cash flows are what matter. Duration and convexity, as defined in the bond markets, are definitions linked to price performance. Modified duration is conventionally defined as the percentage price change in the full price of a bond for a 100 bp movement in rates. Convexity is a second order term helpful in describing how far off duration's predictive power can be in a nonstatic world. Table 2.1 shows the price behavior of a 20-year zero coupon bond with a bond equivalent yield (BEY) of 6 percent for increments of 25 bps as rates move in a range from 5 percent to 7 percent.

You'll recall that you price a 20-year zero with a semiannual BEY of 6 percent as follows:

$$100 \times (1 / (1 + .06/2)^{40}) = 30.6556.$$ I rounded to 30.66 for the table.

As interest rates move and the bond is repriced, the drop in price when rates rise is less than the increase in price when rates decline. This is due to the fact that the zero coupon bond has positive convexity. As one can see from the pricing formula, longer-dated zeros have the most convexity. The long-dated zeros have about three times the convexity of a similar maturity current coupon bullet bond. The highly positively convex

TABLE 2.1 The Price Behavior of a 20-Year Zero Coupon Bond with a BEY of 6%

BEY	Price	DP
7.00	$25.26	($1.25)
6.75	$26.51	($1.31)
6.50	$27.82	($1.38)
6.25	$29.20	($1.45)
6.00	$30.66	0
5.75	$32.18	$1.53
5.50	$33.79	$1.60
5.25	$35.47	$1.69
5.00	$37.24	$1.77

zeros can be combined with negatively convex securities to create a price performance hedge.

How did Travelers determine a hedge ratio? They guesstimated. This was a time when no one had a good handle on how to value the embedded prepayment option. Prepayment data was just in the process of being loaded into large databases. The models seemed to have more code than the Cray computer—at the time—in the Pentagon. Even after better data and better pricing models existed, a hedge ratio for a security like this is still a guesstimate. The uncertainty of prepayments makes the option, and therefore the price behavior of the security, an educated guess. Even if the price behavior could be exactly determined, the hedge is imperfect because the price behavior of treasury zeros differs from that of MBSs. Duration and convexity are known as *first* and *second* order terms, respectively, in a differential equation that attempts to model the performance of these bonds. We require even more terms than that to model the performance of MBSs.

A popular method at the time was to use a minimum variance hedge ratio. Suppose you had a series of prices of a security, X, and a series of prices for a security, Y, for a range of parallel shifts in interest rates. Security X behaves like a GNMA pass-through, similar to the security purchased by Travelers. Security Y behaves like a long maturity UST zero. Let Scenario 5 be today's base case rate. Scenario 1 is the lowest rate scenario and Scenario 10 is the highest interest rate scenario. The other numbers denote equal gradations in between. The prices under a series of rate scenarios might look like those in Table 2.2.

Denote the mean of each of the series of prices using the letters in italic and calculate differences from the mean and the square of the differences from the mean (see Table 2.3).

$$\text{Mean of } X = 104.27$$
$$\text{Mean of } Y = 30.407$$
$$n = 10$$

TABLE 2.2 Prices Under a Series of Rate Scenarios

Rate Scenario	1	2	3	4	5	6	7	8	9	10
X	102.00	102.50	103.00	105.50	105.30	105.20	105.10	104.80	104.70	104.60
Y	39.11	35.47	33.79	32.18	30.66	29.20	27.82	26.51	25.26	24.07

TABLE 2.3 The Differences from the Mean

Rate Scenario	1	2	3	4	5	6	7	8	9	10
$Xi - X = a$	−2.27	−1.77	−1.27	1.23	1.03	0.93	0.83	0.53	0.43	0.33
$Yi - Y = b$	8.70	5.06	3.38	1.77	0.25	−1.21	−2.59	−3.90	−5.15	−6.34
$(Xi - X)^2$	5.15	3.13	1.61	1.51	1.06	0.86	0.69	0.28	0.18	0.11
$(Yi - Y)^2$	75.74	25.63	11.44	3.14	0.06	1.46	6.69	15.19	26.49	40.16
$a \cdot b$		−19.76	−8.96	−4.30	2.18	0.26	−1.12	−2.15	−2.07	−2.21	−2.09

We can easily calculate the variances and standard deviations of the price series as follows:

$$\text{Variance of } X = (X - Xi)^2/n = 1.4601$$
$$\text{Std Dev of } X = (\text{Variance } X)^{1/2} = 1.21$$
$$\text{Variance of } Y = (Y - Yi)^2/n = 20.60136$$
$$\text{Std Dev of } Y = (\text{Variance } Y)^{1/2} = 4.54$$

The covariance is calculated as follows:

$$\text{Covariance} = \text{Sum } \{(X - Xi) \cdot (Y - Yi)\} / n = -4.02119$$

The covariance is also known as the *moment of the joint distribution* and is a measure of the direction of the relationship between these two series of data. If the relationship of the price changes as interest rates shifted were independent, the covariance would be zero. A positive number would indicate that the prices were positively related, so a higher price of the GNMA would tend to correspond to a higher price of the UST zero. That doesn't seem to be the case, because the number is negative. This suggests that a *higher* price of the GNMA tends to correspond to a *lower* price of the UST zero. The direction of the relationship tends to be negative.

How would I compare the strength of this relationship with the strength of other relationships? In order to do that, we've developed yet another term. This was necessary because sometimes we might want to look at other types of relationships and compare strengths. For instance, we might want to look at bonus compensation compared with the number of years of service of an investment banker. The problem is that the units are not the same. The units of the covariance are dollars–years. We create a unitless measure of the strength of the relationship by dividing the covariance by the product of the standard deviations of the two series.

The Greek letter ρ is often used to denote the correlation coefficient. In the case of our two price series:

$$\rho = -4.02119/(1.21 \cdot 4.54) = -0.73.$$

In this case, the prices are negatively correlated. If the correlation coefficient were zero, the two price series would be uncorrelated. If it were a $+1$, the prices would have a perfect positive correlation, and the volatility of the portfolio would be the sum of the individual asset volatilities. If it were a -1, the prices would be perfectly negatively correlated. The volatility of the portfolio would be the difference of the individual asset volatilities, and the risk would be minimized. The correlation coefficient is always between $+1$ and -1, but not 0.

Correlation has the drawback of being the measurement of a linear relationship. As we shall see when we are looking at credit risk, we can't just assume the relationship is linear. We could do more statistical work and try to determine the amount of the variance accounted for by this linear regression, but we can put this aside and employ other techniques as well. Continuing with this example, I'll suggest an approach, which will serve us through a variety of correlation problems.

The minimum variance hedge ratio is calculated as follows:

$$\rho_{xy}(\sigma_y/\sigma_x) = -2.75$$

This means I can own 2.75 of the GNMAs for one of the treasury zeros. Or put another way, I buy 0.36 zeros for every GNMA I own.

I might want to buy fewer of the zeros, however, and just hedge for extreme price moves. A profile of the two securities might then look as shown in Figure 2.6.

Notice the price behavior of the two securities. They are nonlinear. We saw this effect already for the zero. We can see why it must also be so for the GNMA. An intuitive way to think of this is that although these premium priced high-coupon MBSs are now dropping towards par in price as interest rates fall, this cannot continue forever. As the price approaches par, the price drop will slow down. Convexity is a second order effect. Duration can still be negative, yet convexity can *become* positive. When duration is negative, convexity can be either positive or negative. For instance, if I'm driving and I'm accelerating, my velocity is positive and my acceleration is positive (positive duration, positive convexity). If I take my foot off the gas pedal, I decelerate, albeit my velocity is still positive and dropping (positive duration, negative convexity).

Pattern of Price Behavior

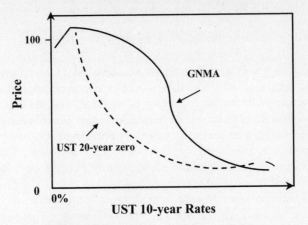

FIGURE 2.6   GNMA vs. UST Zero Hedge

Consider that the formula for duration is defined as follows:

$$D = -100/P \cdot dP/dY$$

Then, convexity is simply:

$$100/P \cdot d^2P/dY^2$$

where C = convexity
    D = duration
    P = the price of the bond
    Y = the yield of the bond

Convexity can be written as the following expression:

$$C = -dD/dY + D^2/100$$

How did I get that? I did it as follows:

$$C = 100/P \cdot d^2P/dY^2 = 100/P \cdot d/dY(dP/dY)$$

We know that $D = -100/P \cdot dP/dY$ and therefore $dP/dY = (-D) \cdot P/100$. Substituting, we get

$$C = 100/P \cdot d/dY(-D \cdot P/100)$$
$$= -100/P \cdot dD/dY \cdot P/100 + 100/P \cdot (-D) \cdot dP/100 \cdot dY$$

Substituting and canceling terms, we get

$$C = -dD/dY + D^2/100$$

One could calculate a hedge and try to keep rebalancing it as conditions change. This is known as *dynamic hedging*. I define dynamic hedging as dynamically recognizing one's losses.

The challenge is that most of the assets we'll examine will exhibit non-linear behavior for the variables we wish to examine. For this reason, I prefer to do scenario analysis. This allows you to create a hedge that performs well in the scenarios you find most unpalatable. The hedge may let you down in scenarios in which you can afford to take a loss. It may also let you down in scenarios in which you have an offset somewhere else in your holdings. But the hedge will perform in the scenarios in which you can't take a loss and in which you don't have an offset somewhere else in your portfolio. This approach has an added advantage of making one clearly think through the performance of one's holdings as well as the objective of keeping those holdings.

Scenario analysis has the added plus of forcing an investor to think about appropriate stress tests for a portfolio. Historical knowledge, coupled with imagination of future possible scenarios, helps in the management of any portfolio. Imagination is important because it helps us create scenarios that may not be reflected in historical data. For instance, in evaluating corporate exposure, it may be useful to imagine a worst-case scenario of fraud.

When it comes to hedging, there is more than one answer to the problem, and all of them are imperfect, which is the definition of a hedge. If a hedge were perfect, and if one could still make money after paying for perfection, it wouldn't be called a hedge; it would be called an arbitrage.

COLLATERALIZED MORTGAGE OBLIGATIONS

Investor demand for more perceived safety, combined with investor demand for even more structural choices, spurred investment banks to create CMOs. The CMOs were mainly backed by GNMA, FHLMC, and FNMA pass-throughs. Some CMOs used nonagency collateral, and these traded at wider spreads due to additional perceived credit risk. These securitizations took cash flow technology to unprecedented heights. The imagination is the only limit to the number of ways one can carve up these cash flows. CMOs were issued by special purpose corporations (SPCs), real estate mortgage investment conduits (REMICs), trusts, finance subsidiaries, and real estate investment trusts (REITs). Today the REMIC structure dominates the market due to tax considerations.

The first CMOs had only four sequential pay slices, or tranches. The first three tranches received interest or coupon payments and the fourth

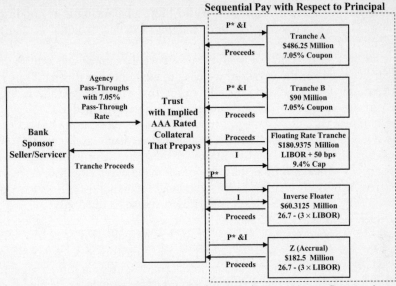

Sequential Pay with Respect to Principal

*Principal payments are allocated to each tranche in sequence. The floater and inverse floater receive a
pro-rata share of principal from the original tranche, which was third in the sequence.*

FIGURE 2.7   Simplified CMO Structure

tranche accrued coupon payments. Sequential pay meant the first tranche
paid down principal with a portion of the remaining cash flows. Once this
was fully amortized, the second tranche received principal payments until it
too was retired; then the third tranche began receiving principal payments;
then the fourth tranche received payments. The goal was to have enough
cash flow from the pool to retire all tranches by the stated maturity even
when one assumed low reinvestment rates and zero prepayment rates.
Figure 2.7 is a simplified sequential pay CMO with fixed-rate tranches; a
floating rate tranche; an inverse floating rate tranche; and an accrual bond,
also called a Z tranche.

The collateral has a 7.05 percent pass-through rate and a weighted
average coupon (WAC) of 7.675 percent. The weighted average maturity
(WAM) is 357 months. I took one of the tranches and created a capped
floating rate note and an inverse floater. Every floater must have an inverse
floater when the collateral consists of pass-throughs that pay fixed coupons.
The floater and inverse floater can have an infinite number of combinations,
but the sum of the interest paid on the pair must equal the interest available
on the original fixed coupon tranche.

In this example, I created the floater and inverse floater out of a tranche
that was originally $241,250,000 in size with a 7.05 percent coupon. It was

the third tranche in the sequential pay sequence. Seventy-five percent of the tranche is a floater and 25 percent is an inverse floater. The floater pays London InterBank Offered Rate (LIBOR) + 50 bps and has a 9.4 percent cap. The inverse floater has three times leverage with respect to LIBOR. This means that as LIBOR decreases, the inverse floater coupon increases threefold. The generic formula for an inverse floater of this type is given as follows:

$$C - (\text{Leverage Factor} \times \text{LIBOR})$$

where C = a constant and is the cap on the inverse floater coupon

Leverage Factor = the amount of leverage with respect to the last LIBOR fixing

LIBOR = the last LIBOR fixing for the CMO

The inverse floater for my CMO has a cap of 26.7 percent. This inverse floater does not have a floor coupon, albeit some CMOs have inverse floaters with a minimum coupon in addition to a cap. The leverage factor is three. The inverse floater coupon is calculated at any given time as follows: $26.7\% - (3 \times \text{LIBOR})$, where LIBOR is the fixing at the last coupon reset period.

The Z, or accrual tranche, is the only tranche that does not receive interest each month. The interest accrues and is added to the principal balance. The foregone interest is used to pay down the tranches ahead of it in the sequential pay structure, each in their turn. Investors who are concerned with reinvestment risk can reduce that risk, since this tranche has no reinvestment risk until all of the other tranches are paid off.

The interest payments on the deal are disbursed to the A, B, floater, and inverse floater each month, based on the amount of principal outstanding (the amount not prepaid, if any) at the beginning of the period. The Z tranche accrues interest based on the principal plus accrued interest in the previous period, and the Z tranche current interest is used to pay down the outstanding previous tranches in sequence.

Tranche A receives principal payments until it is completely paid off. Next, tranche B receives principal payments until it is paid off. Next, the floater and inverse floater receive pro-rata principal payments until they are paid off. After all of the other tranches are paid off, the Z tranche receives principal payments until the original principal balance plus accrued interest is paid off.

The servicer, the entity that collects cash flows and pays monthly principal and interest to the CMO's trustee, receives a fee. The right to service the CMO is traded in an active secondary market. The price of servicing behaves like that of an interest-only (IO) tranche. The longer the CBO tranches are outstanding, the longer the servicer earns fees. As the CMO prepays, the amount of servicing fees decline.

Residual cash flows are what is left over after all obligations are met. These cash flows come from a number of sources. One source is the difference between the WAC on the pass-throughs and the lower WAC on the combined CMO tranches. Deals are sometimes overcollateralized (especially nonagency issues), and another source of residual cash flow is from the higher principal amount of the underlying collateral and the lower combined principal amount of the CMO tranches. When excess reserve funds are reduced, due to lower maintenance requirements as the deal prepays, this is an added source of residual cash flows. If market rates are higher than the low cash flow reinvestment rate assumption used in structuring the deal, the excess cash may be paid out as residual income.

Investors asked for even more complicated structures. For instance, bonds with planned amortization classes (PACs) allow investors to enjoy a predetermined amortization as long as prepayments stayed within a predefined range. Traditional corporate bond investors were encouraged by the perceived lack of credit risk, greater certainty of cash flows compared to a MBS pass-through, shorter maturity, and competitive coupon compared with lower-rated corporate bonds. If prepayments strayed outside the range, it could be a problem, so investors learned more about prepayment data and trends.

Floating rate tranches satisfy demand of banks and other entities that fund versus LIBOR, and the floaters have caps. For every floater, there is an inverse floater. These can be offered in a separate tranche, or embedded in residual cash flows. We'll talk more about residuals later in this book. In early deals, the buyer had to look closely at the way the floating rate coupon was calculated. Some initial floating rate tranches paid on a 30/360 day-count (bond basis), and some on an actual/360 basis (money market basis). As we'll see later, this is a material economic difference, and unwary investors were sometimes exploited. Some CMOs paid monthly, some quarterly, and some semiannually. All had delay days, which sometimes varied by deal—added choices came with added complications.

Some deals had tranches that could receive only interest, called *interest-only* tranches (IOs). Other tranches received only principal and were called *principal only* tranches (POs). These and even more volatile combinations were created. One's view on prepayments became very important.

Wall Street invested millions of dollars and man-hours developing prepayment models. A slavish religious-like belief in the model outputs developed.

Models are wonderful tools, but they are just that. They have their limitations and chief among them is the data and the assumptions we make about the continued reliability of the data. The problem with data is that it is an observation of something that has already happened. By definition, it is history. It's a good idea to leave a margin around the edges of model dogma to make room for new ideas and observations. If you put too much at stake in a model's ability to predict future prepayment rates, or anything else for that matter, you are asking for trouble.

Still, we celebrate the model *du jour*, the genius *du jour*, and the trader *du jour*. If a trader says he can predict the market, stay away from him. Most traders aren't clear on why they make or lose money in a wild market swing.

If you have sixty-four people in a room each tossing a coin, the chances are fifty–fifty that each person will toss heads on the first flip. Thirty-two people will toss heads on the first try. Thirty-two people begin thinking they control the outcome. The next toss, sixteen people will toss heads two times in a row. Sixteen people become very cocky.

One person will flip heads *six* times in a row. This person will be dubbed a genius. What genius?! What cockamamie twaddle!

The next thing you know, another firm has signed the lucky person to a two-year contract at a minimum of $1 million per year. Who knows? Maybe that lucky person will toss heads seven times in a row! When the coin comes up tails, and the formerly lucky person loses a pile of money, he can't figure out what went wrong. His ability to predict the market seems to have deserted him.

In 1993, I had the opportunity to talk at length with a Morgan Stanley trader of very volatile tranches after she'd had a profitable week.

I said I was nervous about the size and hedges of one of the positions she traded, because no one could predict homeowner prepayments. One could get a fair idea of the boundaries with a model, but one couldn't predict an exact number. Prepayment behavior sometimes gave one a nasty surprise. It was unknowable. Perhaps finding more investors and lightening up the holdings would be prudent.

I knew the trouble with this recommendation was that there weren't enough buyers, so a trader's willingness to position these tranches allowed Morgan Stanley to bring more deals, which led to more fee income, which led to higher bonuses . . . you get the idea.

She eyed me aggressively. I persisted, and she began squirming. She started to look uncomfortable. I recognized the feeling. It's the feeling I get right before I face an unpalatable truth that I've worked hard to avoid. She suddenly got up and strutted to the trading floor. She barked an order to a trading assistant. She returned relaxed, having asserted some control. I recognized that, too. Push that unpalatable truth right back in the closet where it belongs.

She asserted *she* knew how to predict homeowner prepayments, and thus she knew how to predict the behavior of *her* market. She used Morgan Stanley's prepayment model! It was the best in the business. *She knew the unknowable.*

She made only one error. She forgot to share her insight with American homeowners. Interest rates went down and homeowners rushed to refinance at unprecedented rates. The price of those volatile securities plummeted like an eagle shot from the sky. Before the year was out, Morgan Stanley lost a lot of money in that trading book. It was enough to get her fired, along with her boss, who also knew how to predict homeowner prepayments.

Many yield-hungry investors also lost a lot of money. I'll digress with an example. One of my colleagues at PaineWebber dubbed one of my customers "The Hammer." The Hammer worked for the New York subsidiary of a Japanese trading company. The trading company leveraged its investment portfolios. In fact, these weren't investment portfolios; they were *hedge funds*. The Hammer was on the Tokyo board of directors and had a secure lifetime job. He also had a high stakes gambler's appetite for risk. His firm was famous in Japan for making hundreds of millions of dollars in the currency exchange market, angering Japanese banks by making money in yen–dollar arbitrage at their expense. Although he could not speculate in currencies as head of the New York office, he found other ways to indulge this passion. He was lucky. So far, this strategy had paid off, but if one relies only on luck, there is nothing to fall back on when it runs out.

I showed The Hammer two deals. Each deal was a combination of two securities, an inverse floater and an interest-only piece. One of the combinations had a yield of 14 percent; the other had a yield of 15.25 percent. Not bad in 1991, when 30-year treasury bonds were yielding less than 8 percent.

There was just one catch.

The effect of the prepayment rate was highly leveraged for the combination with the 15.25 percent yield. (The cash flows were path-dependent and highly sensitive to the path.) If interest rates declined and prepayments sped up, future cash flow from these securities disappeared faster than the bullet train.

Forever.

I explained: "The combination with 15.25 percent yield is much riskier than the other deal. If interest rates go down, the security *vaporizes*, along with the money you paid for it. I recommend the other deal, which isn't nearly as sensitive."

The Hammer glared at me.

"Thank you for your advice, Tavakoli-san," he said dismissively. "Our Tokyo office thinks that interest rates are going *up*, not down, so your warning is not needed."

"While that may be true," I continued, "for just a *little* less return, you can eliminate a *lot* of the risk. The deal with the 15.25 percent base case yield requires a big bet that interest rates will stay constant or only rise slightly. Even if you are right in the short term, if interest rates later drop below today's levels, you will rapidly lose value."

"The guy from Kidder Peabody never talks to me like that!" The Hammer looked angry enough to reject *both* proposals.

He looked down at the proposals and made me wait. Finally, he sat back with a slow but fluid movement.

"Tavakoli-san, is there a special *discount* on price?"

"No, I'm afraid that isn't possible," I said evenly. Then I went for the close. "May I have your order on the deal with 15.25 percent in the base case?" (I believe in an informed adult's freedom to choose.)

The Hammer actually smiled! I had learned my lesson. No more depressing talk of risk.

"Yes," The Hammer chuckled, still smiling. "*I'll take it.*"

And that was that.

But what happened to the trade, you ask?

Oh, yes, the trade. Interest rates kept declining, and prepayments kept speeding up. A few years later, The Hammer called me. His mortgage-backed holdings sustained several years of losses. For fiscal year end March 1995, the losses were $200 million. He lost his lifetime job.

I offer these examples to show there is a way to carve up cash flows to meet any investor desire. Many Japanese banks benefited from the purchase of floating rate tranches with high caps. Many global investors earned income unavailable to them with other investment alternatives. Some investors crave certainty and predictable income; others crave risky income. Human nature hasn't changed. We'll see the same pattern of risk profiles recreated with different instruments as this book describes the evolution of structured products.

CHAPTER 3

Structured Finance and Special Purpose Entities

Special purpose entity (SPE) is a global term, and is used interchangeably with the term special purpose vehicle (SPV). An SPE is either a trust or a company. Special purpose corporations (SPCs) are used for a variety of purposes, including structured risk management solutions. In securitizations, the SPE houses the asset risk either through the purchase of the assets or in synthetic form. The assets are then used as collateral for notes issued by the SPE.

SPEs are powerful structured finance tools. SPEs can be either onshore or offshore. Because of their normally off-balance sheet, bankruptcy remote, and private nature, SPEs can be used for both legitimate and illegitimate uses. Most of the structures discussed in this book are legitimate uses of SPEs. I point out several structures along the way that lend themselves to money laundering, disguising loans as revenue to misstate earnings through wash trades, concealment of losses, embezzlement, and accounting improprieties. Even when used legitimately, the way the issuance of SPEs is represented is sometimes ethically marginal.

All of the following are examples of SPEs: SPCs that may or may not be special purpose subsidiaries or *captives*, master trusts, owners trusts, grantor trusts, real estate mortgage investment conduits (REMICs), financial asset securitization investment trust (FASIT), multiseller conduits, single seller conduits, and certain domestically domiciled corporations.

SPEs are often classified as either *pass-through* or *pay-through* structures. Pass-through structures pass through all of the principal and interest payments of assets to the investors. Pass-through structures are therefore generally passive tax vehicles and do not attract tax at the entity level. Pay-through structures allow for reinvestment of cash flows, restructuring of cash flows, and purchase of additional assets. For example, credit card receivable transactions use pay-through structures to allow reinvestment in new receivables so bonds of a longer average life can be issued.

For securitization of cash assets, the key focus is on nonrecourse (to the originator/seller) financing. The structures are bankruptcy-remote so that the possible bankruptcy or insolvency of an originator does not affect the investors' right to the cash flows of the vehicle's assets. The originator is concerned about accounting issues, especially that the structure meets requirements for off-balance sheet treatment of the assets, and that the assets will not be consolidated on the originator/seller's balance sheet for accounting purposes. For bankruptcy and accounting purposes, the structure should be considered a sale. This is represented in the documentation as a *true sale at law* opinion. The sale is also known as a *conveyance*.

The structure should be a debt financing for tax purposes also known as a *debt-for-tax* structure. Tax treatment is independent of the accounting treatment and bankruptcy treatment. An originator selling assets to an SPE will want to ensure that the sale of assets does not constitute a taxable event for the originator. The securitization should be treated as a financing for tax purposes, that is, treated as debt of the originator for tax purposes. This is represented in the documentation in the form of a tax opinion.

The structured solution to the bankruptcy, true sale, and debt-for-tax issues varies by venue. For example, if a U.S. bank wants to securitize receivables, the structure requires two SPEs to avoid a federally taxable asset sale and to achieve off-balance-sheet financing and a bankruptcy remote structure. In the United States SPEs are usually organized as trusts (for tax reasons) under the laws of the state of Delaware or New York. The first SPE is a wholly-owned, bankruptcy-remote subsidiary of the originator/seller, and the SPE buys the assets in a true sale. The assets are now beyond the reach of both the creditors of the originator/seller and the originator/seller. Wholly-owned subsidiaries are consolidated with the originator/seller for U.S. federal tax purposes, so this achieves the debt-for-tax objective. The second SPE is the issuer of the debt [or asset-backed security (ABS)] and is entirely independent of the originator/seller. It is a bankruptcy-remote entity. The second SPE buys the assets of the first SPE as a true sale for accounting purposes, and a financing for tax purposes. A schematic of this structure appears in Figure 3.1.

Other venues are more problematic, and the regulations with respect to the local equivalent of the U.S. bankruptcy court's automatic stay procedures, accounting rules, and tax laws must be verified with specialists who have local expertise.

For example, two entities are required for Italian securitizations. The first entity can be onshore and purchases the assets. The onshore entity cannot issue bonds, or it will attract heavy Italian taxes. The second entity is offshore and issues the bonds.

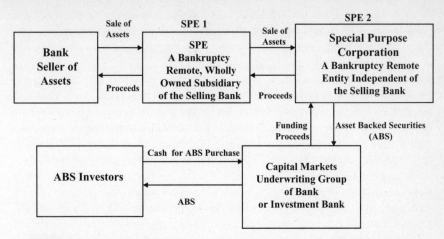

FIGURE 3.1 Double SPE Structure for U.S. Accounting and Tax Regulations

Synthetic securitizations do not get true sale treatment for accounting purposes, since no asset has been sold. This is true whether the vehicle is an SPE or a credit linked note (CLN). The motive behind these structures is to reduce regulatory capital according to regulatory accounting principles. These are usually balance sheet deals for bank regulatory capital relief. Partial funding is feasible with a hybrid structure. A corollary motive is to get credit risk relief. We'll compare and contrast synthetic and true sale structures for balance sheet management in Chapter 7.

SPCs AND HISTORICAL ABUSE

SPCs, also known as *shell corporations*, have been around in various forms for decades. They've been used and abused throughout their history. I've mentioned some legitimate uses of SPEs, but recent U.S. corporate scandals threaten to give them a bad name, so it is worthwhile to spend some time discussing abuses.

SPEs are a convenient tool for criminals. They are often offshore, usually bankruptcy remote, and the ownership structure is undisclosed. The board makes investment "decisions," but these are virtually dictated by the entity that structured the SPE in the first place. The entity that paid for the original setup costs is the "puppet-master," or the actual driver of the vehicle.

There is nothing wrong with SPEs in and of themselves, just as there is nothing wrong with any other tool. A hammer can be used to build a house or used like "Maxwell's silver hammer," to kill someone. A car can be a vehicle for driving children to school, or can be the vehicle used as a getaway car in a bank robbery.

Enron used SPEs to indulge in creative accounting. Enron's prolific SPEs may have inspired other chicanery. For instance, the U.S. Department of Justice charged three British bankers working for Greenwich NatWest (now part of Royal Bank of Scotland) with wire fraud. Allegedly they invested in an Enron SPE, neglected to inform their employer, and diverted more than $7 million that belonged to NatWest. The allegation isn't clear whether they acted independently or with the knowledge of Enron officials. We'll discuss Enron in more detail in various sections later, but my point is, they weren't the first and they weren't even the boldest. Recent events are a surprise only to those who have forgotten their financial history. While the Enron crowd is colorful, they pale compared to others.

In the mid-1970s through the early 1980s, the august hierarchy of the Catholic Church participated in a financial game of "shells and shills." In 1974, the crash of Franklin National Bank was the largest bank crash in the history of the United States up to that time. Michela Sindona was sentenced to 25 years in federal prison for his role in the collapse. He ran a money laundering operation for the Sicilian and U.S. Mafiosi. A United States Comptroller of the Currency's report showed Big Paul Costellano, among others, had a secret account at Franklin National Bank. Few people in the securitization business remember Sindona's name, but at the time he was internationally famous for his bold financial crimes.

Sindona didn't care for prison and sought revenge when his longtime friend Roberto Calvi, the chairman of Banco Ambrosiano (also known as "the priests' bank"), turned his back on him. Sindona told Italian banking authorities to start investigating Calvi, Calvi's foreign SPCs, and Calvi's links to the Vatican Bank. The Vatican Bank lost $55 million when Franklin collapsed. Archbishop Paul Marcinkus was also a suspect when it was revealed Sindona paid a total $6.5 million to him and to Roberto Calvi. The payment was allegedly for a stock price-inflating scheme involving three banks: Franklin, Ambrosiano, and the Vatican.

Paul Marcinkus got his big break in the early 1970s when a knife-wielding assassin lunged at Pope Paul VI during a papal tour in the Philippines. Marcinkus is a huge, charming American of Lithuanian heritage. He tackled the assassin, saved the Pope's life, and instantly became a star in the Vatican. Pope Paul VI gratefully made Marcinkus head of Vatican Intelligence and Security. Then, with Cardinal Spellman's backing, Marcinkus became chairman of the Istituto per le Opere di Religione (the Institute of Religious Work, known in Europe as the IOR), better known in the United States as the Vatican Bank.

Among other functions, the Vatican Bank administered some of the tithe, also called "Peter's pence," that the global congregation of the faithful contributed to the collection basket during the ceremony of the Mass. The faithful give their hard-earned, after-tax money with the trust it is being used to spread the word of the gospel and to do good works.

Paul Casimir Marcinkus was born in 1922 in Cicero, Illinois—Al Capone's neighborhood. He was bishop of Orta, chairman of the Vatican Bank, Chief of Vatican Intelligence, and Mayor of Vatican City (makes CEO sound drab, doesn't it?). The Vatican is a sovereign state, surrounded by Italy. Archbishop Marcinkus headed both the bank and the intelligence service. That seems a bit like allowing the CIA to run the Federal Reserve Bank. Who watches the watchers? I would have loved to have sat in on one of their risk management meetings. Oddly, guys like this never seem to invite people like me. All those pesky questions can really slow down a meeting, and the charming archbishop liked his spare time; he was an avid golfer.

When Pope Paul VI died in 1978, the College of Cardinals elected Albino Luciani, the cardinal of Venice. He ascended to the papal throne as Pope John Paul I. The new pope was furious with Marcinkus. Marcinkus had sold the profitable Venetian Bank, Banco Cattolica del Veneto, to Roberto Calvi over the then Cardinal Luciani's vehement objections. He vowed if he became pope, he would put an end to Archbishop Marcinkus's power and influence over Vatican affairs.

Pope John Paul I didn't have a chance to implement his plan. He reigned only 33 days. Vatican intelligence said Pope John Paul I died of natural causes, although he was reputed to be in good health. Speculation over the cause of his death inspired a scene in the movie *The Godfather, Part III.*

Pope John Paul II's election was a stroke of luck for Marcinkus. The Polish pope was initially an outsider in the Vatican power structure. He was the first non-Italian pope since Hadrian VI in 1522, almost five hundred years earlier. Marcinkus and the pope became fast friends; both were hulking Slavic men, and they instantly hit it off. The traditional Italian Vatican power structure gradually lost its control. Marcinkus helped the pope find his power base and Marcinkus reported directly to the pope.

The Vatican Bank (IOR) controlled several offshore shell companies involved in embezzlement of funds from Banco Ambrosiano. For example, the IOR accepted time deposits from Banco Ambrosiano's Lima Peru operation. The IOR lent the money to a Panama shell company. At maturity, the IOR refused to pay claiming the Panama company owed the money, but the Vatican Bank held the share certificates for the company as controlling fiduciary for Banco Ambrosiano.

In 1982, Banco Ambrosiano collapsed. Roberto Calvi, with the assistance of the Vatican Bank, looted $1.3 billion from Banco Ambrosiano. The

Vatican Bank paid a $250 million settlement to the defrauded depositors of Banco Ambrosiano, but the Vatican Bank admitted nothing. Calvi had turned to the Catholic Church in his hour of greed, and the worldwide Catholic community unknowingly gave a large donation to help cover his malfeasance. Catholic priests take a vow of poverty. Members of the congregation sometimes wonder just whom it is the priests have vowed to impoverish.

Marcinkus used the Alzheimer's defense, although today it may be known as the Ken Lay defense. "I'm not a crook, I just can't help it if I don't have all my wits." He claimed he didn't know what the bank was signing. He studied law in Rome and was chairman of the Vatican bank for 10 years, yet he claimed he'd never read or didn't understand the documents the bank signed. He said he trusted Calvi and claimed Calvi took advantage of his naiveté.

Calvi fled to London carrying a briefcase stuffed with incriminating documents. Flavio Carboni, another bank officer, joined him. That evening, Roberto Calvi's corpse was found hanging under Blackfriar's bridge. His pockets were stuffed with rocks, and it was rumored his wrists looked as if they had been bound with rope that was later removed. In 2003, it was deemed murder. Carboni and the documents were missing.

Carboni eventually resurfaced. Italian officials arrested him as he was attempting to extort $900,000 from Vatican officials in exchange for Calvi's stolen documents. Bishop Pavel Hnilica, a key member of Marcinkus's inner circle, was arrested trying to buy back the incriminating documents.

Marcinkus was never arrested. He lived in the Vatican for years, never stepping foot in Italy where he would have faced an indictment. Eventually, the Vatican came to an agreement with Italy to drop the charges. Marcinkus now lives in the United States.

If you can't trust the Vatican Bank to safeguard your money, whom can you trust? The answer is no one. At least, one can't just accept things at face value without doing independent verification.

That's why the financial markets are pushing for greater transparency. Banks insist that one know one's customer. Suspicious transactions must be reported. The trouble is that many of these transactions appear legitimate on the surface. At the time of Calvi's creative workmanship, it would have been extremely difficult to untangle the ownership structure of the shell corporations, especially with bank officers involved in the deception.

As an example of how a web of shell corporations obscures ownership, let's suppose I'm a drug lord with lots of cash. My circle of friends seems to have the same problem I do. We want to spend our money to buy nice things, but people don't want to do business with us if they can trace the money back to our enterprises. We might begin by using couriers to carry currency out of our home countries. We might even buy gems and jewelry and smuggle them out. I might make a very generous donation to my church in my home country, which later shows up as a bank balance in my name in another country. The money is transferred directly from the church account to the account of several shell companies to disguise its true ownership.

I'd use some corporate-friendly venues to set up the phony corporations. Now suppose you are investigating me and find an account set up in the name of RANA Corporation, and you suspect this account has links to my drug money. The only reason you suspect this is because you got a tip-off. Apollo Corporation owns 60 percent of RANA, and Delphi Corporation owns 40 percent of RANA. Tech Corporation owns 30 percent of Apollo, and Mark Corporation owns 70 percent of Apollo. Lana Corporation owns 50 percent of Delphi, and Capa Corporation owns 50 percent of Delphi. Are you still with me? Or have you fallen asleep after wading through a stack of documents that could sink a ship?

I own Tech Corporation. RANA Corporation's only assets are a $1.2 billion cash account in a Basel bank. That means that of the $1.2 billion, my share is 30 percent of 60 percent of $1.2 billion, or $216 million. And that's just in the RANA account. Tech Corporation also has part ownership in a few other corporations.

These are private corporations. They don't have to disclose anything. It is extremely difficult—if not impossible—for you to discover that I'm the true owner of Tech. It's also difficult for you to discover the true owners and ownership interests in the other corporations.

This is what all the fuss is about. Legitimate means can always be twisted to serve illegitimate purposes. The legitimate international banking community is doing its best to crack down on money laundering and suspicious movement of money across borders.

This may be one of the reasons you are getting e-mails from Nigerians asking for your letterhead and bank account numbers. Is it because these generous people want to make you $55 million richer? Actually in their case, I don't believe their intent is to create a complicated web of money laundering. They're probably just after your bank account number so they can impersonate you and loot your account. Come to think of it, they might be on to something. It seems much more direct than Calvi's machinations, and it has an added personal touch.

Although all the facts of Enron's SPC saga haven't yet been revealed or unraveled, the few that have been made public resonate with familiarity. Corporations were set up with complex ownership structures. Loans were made, interests were conflicted, pockets were lined, and officers faced indictment.

RBG Resources plc, Allied Deals Inc., Hampton Lane Inc., and SAI Commodity Inc. allegedly used shell corporations to falsify transactions and fraudulently secured cashable letters-of-credit.

American Tissue was the fourth largest tissue company in the United States before its bankruptcy in 2001. Several lawsuits include the following allegations. The owners allegedly borrowed hundreds of millions of dollars and diverted the money through a network of affiliated corporations. American Tissue was owned by Middle American Tissue as its sole asset, which was owned by Super American Tissue. It's estimated that American Tissue had more than 25 subsidiaries. One of the owners set up around 45 companies, which were affiliates of American Tissue. American Tissue lent money to the affiliates, and the loans required no interest payments and had no maturity. American Tissue bought machinery for several million dollars, and sold it to one of the owners for one dollar just two months later. Arthur Andersen, American Tissue's auditor, is being investigated by the U.S. Department of Justice for allegedly taking a role in shredding American Tissue documents.

Some applications of SPEs are not currently illegal, but may come under the scrutiny of public policy in future. In an example of art imitating life, the U.S. television show, *The West Wing,* about the internal workings of the White House, offers a typical example. One of the president's staff formerly worked for a law company that created SPCs for each oil tanker an oil company proposed to purchase. To keep costs low, the oil company chose old clunkers that probably should have been junked. The SPCs financed the tankers 100 percent. If there was an event such as an oil tanker leak, the law firm created a liability shield. But if litigation penetrated the liability shield, the SPCs would have no real assets, only debt. The oil company was judgment-proof. It's not illegal, merely sleazy. Of course that's television, but perilously close to reality.

Abuse won't disappear. People with a mind-set to pull a fast one assume that those who don't just don't know how to pull it off; or if they do know how, they don't have the guts to do it. Some of Enron's officers appeared to share this view. Shareholders seemed to like others to do their thinking and were willing to aggressively overvalue stocks. Bankers were willing to accept overvalued shares as collateral, and debt holders were willing to overvalue the right to convert into overvalued shares. Enron knew how to talk to Wall Street. They knew that saying it louder makes it right. They knew that acting self-assured translates to assurance. Given it is so easy to pull off a shell game, what is surprising is that it doesn't happen more often. What makes the capital markets work—and for the most part they do work—is that at its core are people whose word is their bond. Nice guys may not always finish first, but they last, and they finish.

SPEs AND SPVs

As we've discovered, both special purpose companies and special purpose trusts are called special purpose vehicles (SPVs) or special purpose entities (SPEs). The terms SPE and SPV can be used interchangeably, but it is important to distinguish between the corporate and trust structures. SPEs support various customer- and investment-oriented activities for banks, investment banks, insurance companies, and corporations. SPEs have been used for years as a tool to support securitization assets. SPEs can be onshore, domiciled in the home country of the deal arranger, or offshore.

There are multiple considerations and choices in setting up an SPE. Set-up time can vary from four weeks to three months. To illustrate key points, I offer the following observations about some of today's issues in setting up an SPE. Tax issues, accounting issues, bank regulatory issues, and other structural issues are always in flux. At any given time, there is no substitute for deal service providers who are well versed in the current state of the issues.

There is no easy answer to the question: "Where is the best place to set up an SPE?" It depends on the structured finance application, among other considerations. SPEs are currently set up in a variety of tax-friendly venues including Delaware and New York (in the United States), Luxembourg, the Netherlands, the Caymans, Ireland, Jersey, Guernsey, and Gibraltar.

While SPEs in the United States are often, but not always, set up as trusts for tax reasons, in non-U.S. venues, the SPC is a common structure. Venues can be chosen wherever an SPE structure is allowed, but as a rule only tax-friendly venues for the specific structured finance application are chosen.

While choice of venue usually revolves around tax issues, other considerations can be important. For example, many investors in Germany will buy notes issued by SPEs, but often require an Organization for Economic Cooperation and Development (OECD) issuer. Therefore, the SPE must be set up in an OECD country. Among the OECD countries, the Netherlands, Luxembourg, and Ireland are currently the most commonly used tax-friendly venues.

In tax terms, we want the SPE to pay zero tax on payments flowing in and out. We want to avoid corporate income tax at the venue of the SPE and the bank sponsor. There are two withholding tax issues: (1) withholding tax at the source, the venue of the incorporation of the SPE, on Euro Medium Term Notes (EMTNs) issued by the SPEs; and (2) withholding tax imposed on the underlying assets purchased by the SPEs by the country in which the assets were originated. The goal is that neither interest nor dividends paid by the SPEs is subject to withholding tax, so an ideal venue does not impose this tax.

If we choose a venue such as the Cayman Islands that does not have tax treaties in place with most jurisdictions, there is no mechanism for reclaiming tax withheld (if any) on the underlying asset income from the country of origin. The SPE will purchase assets that are not subject to withholding at the country of the assets' origination so that investors will not suffer a reduced return.

If instead we choose a venue with tax treaties in place, assets that suffer withholding tax may specifically be chosen so the withholding tax can be reclaimed. Several years ago it was popular to purchase Italian government bonds and repackage them in a Luxembourg domiciled SPE. Luxembourg had a double tax treaty with Italy, the withholding tax was reclaimed, and repackaged notes backed by the Italian government bonds were sold to investors in venues without Italian tax treaties. The investors enjoyed the gross coupon effect of the Italian government bonds that was otherwise unavailable to them. Figure 3.2 shows a simplified example.

This is a legitimate use of an SPE. Tax evasion is illegal; tax avoidance is legal. In this instance, German investors realized the full benefit of the gross income from the Italian government bonds.

We do not want to suffer tax on the SPE's income. In Europe, we also want to avoid value-added tax (VAT) and stamp duties. The goal is to have zero tax leakage, if possible. Venues such as the Caymans, Jersey, and Guernsey offer this advantage, but may not enjoy ready investor acceptability.

Other venues such as the Netherlands, Luxembourg, and Ireland also offer several tax advantages. There is no withholding tax on note interest.

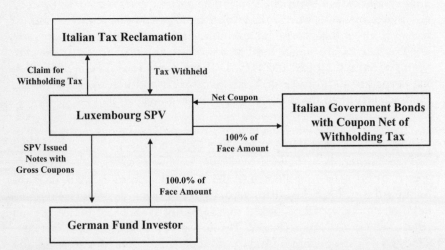

FIGURE 3.2 Luxembourg Domiciled SPV with Italian Government Bond Collateral

There is no stamp duty. There may be a very small VAT on servicing and administration for the SPE. There is no withholding tax on deposits. Among these three venues, there are other considerations that may affect the final choice. The Netherlands seems to take several weeks longer to provide tax rulings for SPEs compared to Ireland and Luxembourg. In the Netherlands, there seems to be a turf war between Amsterdam and Rotterdam. Most SPEs are set up in Amsterdam. For speed, one might choose Ireland or Luxembourg. In Ireland, the SPE must fit within the Irish tax securitization code. This may drive up the cost slightly relative to Luxembourg. United Kingdom-based deal arrangers might find it more convenient to deal with Ireland, because Ireland uses an English law–based system. Lately, Ireland has been the fastest of the three venues in actual set-up time, usually two to three weeks once the paperwork is in order.

Once the venue is agreed, there are still more considerations.

DOCUMENTATION

The documentation varies somewhat by venue. Program documents may include an offering circular, a master trust deed (a structure not usually recognized in the Netherlands), a program agreement, an agency agreement, a master swap agreement or International Swap and Derivatives Association (ISDA) agreement, various legal opinions, tax rulings, a trustee agreement, custody agreement, letter of appointment for the process agent, and board resolutions. SPE documents include a memorandum and articles of association, a declaration of trust of shares in the SPE, and a management or administration agreement. Each EMTN has a pricing supplement and may have a supplemental trust deed, a local legal opinion for the investor, swap documentation, SPE venue legal opinion, board resolution, or other additional documents. Rated EMTNs may have even more documents including corporate authority, a declaration stating that the notes are legal and binding, a true sale opinion, or wrap documentation.

EXAMPLE OF A MULTIPLE ISSUANCE ENTITY (MIE)

The following example illustrates typical issues one might address in the establishment of SPEs used for repackaging. Earlier, we saw repackaging SPEs used to create CLNs linked to tranches of synthetic transactions and prespecified underlying collateral. That is a popular use of an SPE. One possibility is to issue the notes from an SPE that uses a pool of underlying collateral. Another possibility is a structure used for synthetic collateralized debt obligations (CDOs) that requires the notes be issued as limited recourse notes from an MIE, which we'll review in Chapter 5.

In this example, a U.S.-based bank sets up two independent Cayman Islands–incorporated SPEs that are SPCs to support various customer oriented activities for its London branch. English law governs the EMTN programs of the SPEs. These non-U.S. vehicles target non-U.S. investors, but they allow for the possibility of occasional sales to U.S. investors. The SPEs' legal structure ensures the cash flow integrity of the SPEs. It ensures the transaction is treated in a tax efficient manner. It ensures specific types of investors will not be precluded from investing in the EMTNs of the SPEs bylaws, adverse tax consequences, or regulations applicable to them. It ensures offerings and sales of securities comply with applicable securities laws of the relevant jurisdictions. Finally, it ensures any issues sold to U.S. investors are private placements exempt from Securities and Exchange Commission (SEC) registration. For U.S. sales, the exemption is provided by Rule 144A of the Securities Act for sales to qualified institutional buyers (QIBs).

The Cayman Islands are a tax haven. The SPCs are exempt from all corporate tax, both United States and foreign. The choice of the Cayman Islands may limit the bank's ability to distribute repackaged product to European investors who prefer an OECD issuer. Sales to the SPE from the bank arranger's trading book, or other source's trading book, are treated as any other trading asset.

If assets are sold to the SPE from the bank arranger's balance sheet, however, the dual SPE structure outlined earlier might have to be utilized for tax purposes. That is not the primary purpose of this SPE, so that circumstance should be a rare event, and applicable only to that specific transaction.

The vehicles are qualifying special purpose entities (QSPEs) for Financial Accounting Standards Board (FASB) purposes. By definition, they are off-balance sheet, bankruptcy-remote entities. The assets are put presumptively beyond the reach of the bank transferor's creditors through a true sale. Furthermore, the bank is not obligated to repurchase the transferred assets. Setting up the SPE in this way insulates the customers from the bank's credit risk, and ensures the assets don't re-emerge on the bank's balance sheet, even though the SPE may often purchase assets from the bank sponsor's books.

Accounting rules are always subject to change. FASB continually reviews the conditions to be imposed on active SPE assets through equity ownership, management agreements, or other means. They have regular meetings on SPEs, sale criteria, transfers of financial instruments, and modification of the definition of a QSPE.

The SPEs are multiple issuance entities. The MIEs issue notes that reference only the underlying collateral specific to each note (unlike the structure in which the collateral for all the EMTNs is a reference pool of assets). The noteholders do not have a claim to any other asset owned by the SPE. Each set of assets is funded separately with its own EMTN tranche combining the risk characteristics of the underlying assets and/or derivatives. The derivatives may be hedges or may actually be an underlying asset, such as a credit derivative.

Banks often have other vehicles that are rated and funded, customarily with U.S. commercial paper (CP), and the vehicles issue indivisible obligations with identical risks for each investor. They cannot be used for the purpose under discussion. They are unsuitable for issuing discrete risk, ring-fenced notes linked to a specific asset.

With the MIE structure, each EMTN tranche has its own unique risks, which are passed directly to the investor. Each tranche remains unaffected by credit or market events that may affect other tranches. Each tranche will have its own swap transaction and unwind trigger events, if applicable. This is known as *ring fencing* and is a critical feature of MIEs. Ring fencing ensures that assets are secured for the benefit of the swap counterparty and noteholders of a particular tranche. The underlying assets are available only for the benefit of the swap counterparty and noteholders, and are unavailable to any other creditors. No other assets of the SPE are available to a noteholder and/or the swap counterparty except those relevant to their specific note.

Ring fencing is achieved in the following manner: The documentation specifies appropriate ranking security interests for the relevant noteholders and the counterparties. The noteholders' and swap counterparty's claims are limited recourse. This means the claims are satisfied by the note's underlying collateral only, not any other collateral in the SPE dedicated to other notes. The documentation ensures that default under one issue will not trigger a default in another issue of the SPE. This is known as *no cross-default*. The SPE signs a new swap confirmation, if any is required, for each issue. The "single agreement" contractual netting provisions of the ISDA Master Agreement are not applicable for other tranches issued by the SPEs.

It is the legal counsel's responsibility to ensure the creation, perfection, and priority of all security interests. This is especially important in nontraditional asset classes such as CDOs, high yield obligations, and emerging markets obligations. The obligations are held by a foreign depository (from the U.S. perspective), and the foreign depository laws must not conflict with the interests of the noteholders and derivative contract counterparties of the SPE.

The SPE gives the security trustee a security interest over the underlying asset/s for the benefit of the swap counterparty and the investor. The relative ranking of the noteholder and swap counterparty varies. Often banks will provide a swap to the SPE and attempt to hold a senior position to the noteholders. Many investors are unaware this occurs. Other investors are aware of the distinction and often will not tolerate this. They insist the bank provider of the swap hold a *pari passu* position to the noteholder, and sometimes request a subordinate position to the noteholder, although this may not be acceptable to the bank derivative provider.

In the case of credit derivatives, the underlying collateral must be reserved first for the settlement of the credit derivative contract, and must be senior to the interests of the investor. This isn't in conflict with appropriate seniority, however, since this credit risk is the risk the investor set out to take.

Limited recourse means that payments are owed by the SPE only to the extent that equivalent amounts are received on the underlying assets. To the extent that there is a shortfall, claims are extinguished. After enforcement of the security, no further action may be taken against the SPEs, and no winding-up proceedings may be taken. Limited recourse provisions exist with respect to the noteholders, swap counterparty, security trustee, charitable trust directors, paying agents, administrator, and any other parties involved in the transaction.

CAYMAN DOMICILED SPEs

A Cayman-domiciled charitable (not for profit) trust owns the shares of the SPE. Share capital, also called equity capital, for each SPE is nominal, usually around $1,000. The Cayman counsel will recommend the board of directors, who are independent of the bank setting up the SPE. The board must be comprised of Cayman residents. The board's purpose is to make decisions on whether to enter into transactions brought to it by the bank. If the initial proposal allows the board to consider deal proposals from outside banks and companies, they may do that, too. The SPEs will purchase assets and will have the power to execute derivative transactions. The SPE receives a small fee for each transaction accepted by the board. In practice, the board ratifies every deal brought to it by the bank provided it meets the criteria specified in the SPE's documentation. That is usually all of the deals.

The SPE purchases separately funded dedicated assets for each note. Each set of assets (or single asset) has its own EMTN tranche combining the risk characteristics of the underlying assets and derivatives. The structure of each issuance is driven by each investor's risk appetite. There is no restriction on the final maturity of the EMTNs other than the initial 20-year corporate tax hiatus in the Cayman Islands, which shortens in direct proportion as the SPEs age. The structurer may specify the volume of issuance for internal bank approvals, but the SPEs will each have the ability to issue up to $10 billion of EMTNs per the articles of incorporation.

The structurer anticipates and specifies eligible assets at the inception of the SPE. The SPE may only purchase these prespecified assets. Eligible assets usually include investment grade debt, noninvestment grade debt, unrated debt securities, assignable loans, equities, leases, receivables, and loan participations of nonbank sponsor-affiliated entities. The proposed SPEs will not engage in participations of loans on the U.S. bank sponsor's balance sheet due to FASB considerations. In this example, the SPEs can purchase receivables and leases. These will probably be rare securitizations, and the SPEs pass through the cash flows and risks of these underlying assets directly to the EMTN investors. The SPEs may also hold credit derivatives and other derivative instruments as assets.

Notice that eligible assets include assets on which withholding tax has been levied by the country of origination, even though withholding tax cannot be reclaimed by the Cayman Islands. On a net revenue basis, these assets are normally noncompetitive with structures that are able to capture gross revenues on assets. There is usually no specific prohibition of the purchase of these assets, however.

Figure 3.3 shows a typical generic repackaging. The SPE purchases assets. The assets are prefunded from proceeds of an EMTN issued by the SPE and underwritten or sold by the bank arrangers (bank sponsor's) capital markets group. The SPE pays the asset cash flows to the bank arranger's swap desk as one leg of a swap payment. The bank arranger provides the structured coupons due to the investors under the EMTN issue.

EMTN Has Structured Coupons Backed by Single Asset

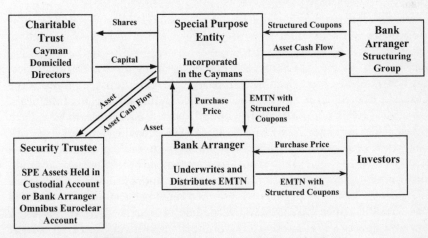

FIGURE 3.3 Cayman Domiciled SPE Cash Flows

Cayman SPEs do not require audited accounts. No financial or managerial reporting is required in the Caymans. The bank arranger or a third party acceptable to the EMTN investor is the swap counterparty to all derivatives transactions with the SPEs. The bank arranger may handle the back office for the SPEs, leaving nothing for the SPEs to administer. The bank arranger is the calculation agent and issuing and paying agent for the EMTNs issued by the SPEs. The SPEs receive the swap confirms, but do not generate confirms or negotiate terms. The bank arranger in the role of paying agent makes the payments on the SPE-issued EMTNs.

The security trustee, on behalf of the SPE, administers the security interest over the underlying asset/s for benefit of the swap counterparty and the EMTN investor. To keep this arm's length, especially if an early termination event is triggered, an institution separate from the bank sponsor acts as security trustee.

REPACKAGINGS TO SATISFY INVESTOR DEMAND

A diverse group of investors will probably purchase EMTNs issued by these SPEs. These include insurance company funds, independent funds, bank-sponsored funds, corporations, insurance companies, commercial banks, merchant banks, investment banks, savings banks, regional banks, and U.S. investors eligible to purchase 144A assets.

The reason the bank arranger sets up the vehicles is to satisfy various investor needs. The SPE offers more competitive note issuance, because it can take advantage of a more advantageous funding cost relative to the bank's funding cost. The following are some of the repackaging uses of an SPE:

- The SPE repackages asset swaps and issues floating rate EMTNs.
- The SPE can issue repackaged tranches of synthetic CDOs in note form.
- The SPE can issue notes linked to individual loans or clusters of loans for investors who cannot service loans or purchase loans outright.
- The SPE can issue freely transferable notes, even if the underlying asset is a securitization of funding agreements, with limited tradeability.
- The SPE can issue notes linked to a portfolio of trade receivables.
- The SPE can buy an asset denominated in one currency and issue an asset denominated in the investor's preferred currency.
- The SPE-issued note can embed derivatives in the note for investors with regulatory restrictions, or who lack capacity to enter into derivatives transactions.

- Investors can do business even if they do not have an ISDA documentation in place with the bank sponsor, and may prefer the simpler EMTN documentation.
- The SPE-issued note can embed derivatives for investors for whom the bank sponsor doesn't have credit lines or for which it doesn't want to use up credit lines. This is particularly useful for transactions that embed a high degree of counterparty exposure. Examples include long dated transactions and highly leveraged transactions.
- From the investor's point of view, the SPE-issued note is different from a credit-linked note issued by the bank sponsor, because the investor has no exposure to the bank sponsor (assuming that bank sponsor collateral is not used for synthetic repackagings). The note is securitized by collateral purchased by the SPE and frequently—but not always—selected by the investor.
- If the bank sponsor enters into a credit default swap (CDS) agreement with the SPE, the SPE can purchase 0 percent or 20 percent Bank for International Settlements (BIS) risk-weighted, highly rated collateral, which will satisfy the required CDS payments if a credit event occurs.

CLNs AND FUNDING COSTS

A typical AA bank issuer has a funding cost of London InterBank Offered Rate (LIBOR) flat or even sub-LIBOR for maturities less than three years. If eligible collateral from a single A-rated bank with a higher funding cost is used, the collateral can generate more implied income on the EMTN issue. This income may be passed on to the investor. Eligible collateral is any collateral that can be held by the SPE and is also specified in the EMTN documentation.

An unwary investor may agree to any highly rated underlying collateral, but may not be sensitive to the nuances. SPEs can purchase an asset of high credit quality that generates coupon income of LIBOR+45 to 50 basis points (bps). For example, combining the AAA tranche of a synthetic CDO paying 50 bps with an AA-rated bank deposit at LIBOR flat creates hybrid underlying collateral with a coupon of LIBOR+50 bps. This coupon is then used as the floating payment in a structured swap or to enhance the coupon of a further CLN repackaging. For instance, the hybrid collateral can now be combined with a CDS referencing the BBB tranche of another synthetic CDO. If the CDS referencing the BBB tranche pays a premium of 275 bps for credit protection, one would think a repackaging with this hybrid collateral would pay somewhere between LIBOR+275 and LIBOR+325 bps, but at any rate more than LIBOR+275. It seems logical that at least part of the benefit of using hybrid collateral would be passed on to the investor. This isn't necessarily the case. Some bank arrangers pocket all of the additional spread if the investor is unaware. The investor may have assumed that a bank deposit returning only LIBOR flat was used as collateral. Figure 3.4 shows a schematic of the cash flows where the bank arranger captures the excess spread.

One bank arranger, who employed this strategy, asked me the following question: "If I want to create a par asset swap package, and make sure the investor gets par back before maturity, how can I do that?"

"Well, you could create a put-able asset swap and charge a fee. The premium could come out of the coupon you pay on the asset swap," I replied.

"Yes, I like that," he said. Then he paused and added, "But I don't want the investor to have the right to put this whenever he wants. I just want him to be able to put the asset swap on a certain date."

"You mean, you don't want the investor to have an American option. You want to give him a European put, with a one-time exercise," I clarified. I realized I was asking the next question a little late, but now I was curious. "What is this for?"

He said in a rush, "Well, I can buy the AAA privately rated equity from a synthetic arbitrage deal and get a fixed coupon that I can swap to floating. I will then add that to a bank deposit to create a floating rate note. The problem is that the asset swap package matures after a synthetic BBB tranche risk I'm selling to an investor, and I want to use the asset swap package as collateral."

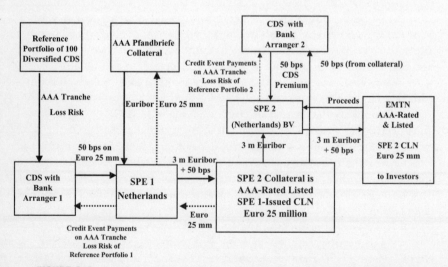

FIGURE 3.4   Synthetic Repackaging with Synthetic Repackaged Collateral

"The investor is happy with this?" I asked. I knew the answer already, but I wanted to hear him say it.

Instead he asked another question.

"Do I have a fiduciary relationship to my investor?" He frowned at the thought that he might.

"You mean because you aren't disclosing to him that you are not passing along the extra 50 bps per annum?" I asked, urging him on.

"Well, yeah. He's a sophisticated portfolio manager." He said this with an encouraging tone. He seemed to be feeling better already now that he had halfway persuaded himself he was out of the woods.

"Well, I'm not a lawyer, you should really check with one on that point, but my inclination is that no, you don't have what one would normally define as a fiduciary relationship with a sophisticated institutional investor."

"That's what I thought." He seemed greatly relieved.

"I believe you have an obligation to disclose, however."

"The *50 bps per annum*?" He was visibly agitated.

"Not strictly. The agreed price is just that, and a bank arranger might include some compensation for additional repackaging. Of course, most aware investors would ask for at least a portion of that 50 bps per annum benefit."

"*Not strictly*, you say." He had found his loophole and was smiling now.

"The documents should reflect the potential risk, however," I added.

"Risk?" He was frowning again.

"Suppose the equity tranche is exhausted and a further default requires a payment from the holder of the BBB tranche risk," I explained. "Suppose also that the AAA-rated tranche referenced by the credit derivative is downgraded. Its spread would widen, and the collateral couldn't be liquidated at par. We've seen this sort of thing happen recently. Who takes that risk in this transaction?"

"It's unlikely that would happen . . . ." He wavered.

"Perhaps," I said. "But let's consider another scenario. What if the investor wants to sell before maturity? You look for bids in the market for the underlying collateral, the credit default swap referencing the AAA in particular, and find it has widened to 60 bps and there are 3 years remaining to maturity. Who eats the present value of 10 bps per annum for 3 years?"

"The investor has to take that risk," he said.

"Okay, even though the investor gets nothing extra for that risk. He thinks he's getting the risk of the short-term bank deposit, and now he has the greater potential risk of liquidation of the asset swap package at a nonpar price. Somewhere in the documentation you have to disclose what constitutes eligible collateral and the fact that the price risk upon liquidation is borne by the investor."

"Right," he agreed. "But he'll probably never read the documents that thoroughly anyway, and even if he did, he probably wouldn't figure out that he's taking additional risk due to *this* collateral. Thanks. You've been a big help." He was confident the investor wouldn't challenge his skimming off the additional 50 bps per annum.

To paraphrase Jeff Goldblum's character in *The Big Chill*: Rationalizations are more important than sex. We can live a day without sex, but have you ever tried to go a day without rationalizations?

I was tempted to let it go at that, but I couldn't resist—I continued the discussion.

"If this investor realizes that he's being given hybrid collateral without any additional compensation, do you think he'll do business with you again? Think about this from your own perspective. Are you indifferent between the risk of an AA-rated bank deposit versus the risk of that deposit combined with the risk of the AAA-rated equity tranche? If you aren't, why would you accept an identical interest payment for the different types of collateral?" I asked mildly.

"I'll cross that bridge when I come to it," he said. He played the short game.

Even the shorter form documentation used for these transactions can be daunting. They are usually about as much fun to read as the back of a peanut butter jar, but if you know where to look, you can find the comic section.

The documentation might state that eligible collateral is rated single A or higher, or it may state that eligible collateral must be rated AA or higher. It may specify that securitized assets and ABSs, among other types of collateral, are eligible. How many types of assets can you squeeze into those innocuous-sounding definitions?

Investors have control of the process when the SPE is an MIE. The collateral is not a blind pool. The investor can negotiate the type of collateral and the compensation for the collateral. Investors should ask detailed questions; it pays economic rewards. To remove all doubt, an investor can specify that the underlying collateral for his note be restricted to specific types of collateral, or even a specific bond with a specific Committee on Uniform Securities Indentification Procedures (CUSIP) number.

If an investor is happy with having a hybrid asset as the underlying collateral, that is fine. The idea is that the investor should be aware that is the case, and aware of the risks. Furthermore, it seems reasonable that any aware investor who is happy with this collateral would attribute part of that happiness to a higher spread earned on the EMTN. Investors usually have a price for taking additional risk, but it usually isn't zero.

STRUCTURED FLOATERS

We saw that some investors cannot engage in interest rate swaps, caps, or floors, and thus cannot normally buy asset swap packages. These investors can often buy a floating rate note (FRN) issued by an SPE with an asset swap package as the underlying asset. The coupons on these EMTN issues are usually generic floating rate coupons. Extra income can be created in a number of ways. For instance, if the investor can accept an interest rate cap, the deal arranger can create more current income for the investor versus a generic floating rate note by creating a capped floating rate note as shown in Figure 3.5.

PRINCIPAL PROTECTED NOTES (PPNs)

Bank sponsors may use SPEs to enhance the distribution of noninvestment grade CDO tranches. SPEs are used to repackage equity tranches of collateral loan obligations (CLOs) or collateralized bond obligations (CBOs) combined with highly rated zeros to create principal protected EMTNs. Often, only the principal portion of these notes will be rated. This structure is popular in Europe. If 144A tranches are issued, U.S. investors can also participate. Figure 3.6 illustrates this application.

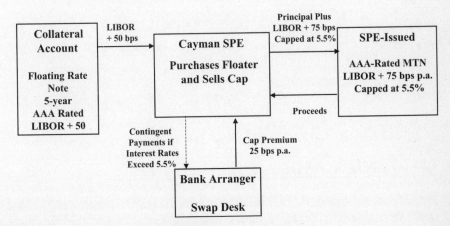

FIGURE 3.5 Capped FRN

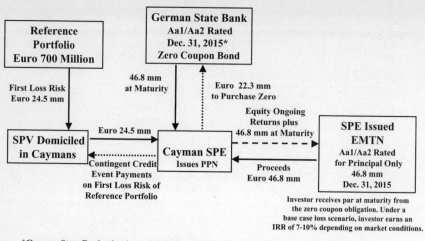

*German State Banks that issue debt before 2005 and maturing before December 31, 2015, enjoy the benefit of the state guarantee on the debt.

FIGURE 3.6 Principal Protected Rated EMTN: Zero plus Equity

LOAN REPACKAGINGS

Other investors cannot buy loans, but can purchase securities. Loans can be repackaged and sold to investors in note form. Another variation is to repackage a credit derivative referencing the loan with underlying collateral purchased by the SPE to create a CLN.

European investors often want access to loans to leveraged borrowers. Many funds cannot purchase loans, but can purchase loans repacked in the form of an EMTN. These are usually defined as loans with coupons of LIBOR +250 bps. The EMTN's underlying assets would be leveraged loans, and the EMTN passes all the risk of the underlying asset to the investors. The historically high recovery rate of the loans make this a desirable alternative to high yield bonds. The bank sponsor usually marks the EMTN to market for the fund and services the loan. Of course, the loan credit risk can also be transferred in the form of a CDS or a total return swap (TRS). Figure 3.7 shows an example using CDSs to transfer the credit risk.

FIRST-TO-DEFAULT NOTES

Other investors may seek leverage in the form of first-to-default baskets. A credit derivative referencing the first-to-default risk of a preselected basket is embedded in the EMTN and purchased by the investor as shown in Figure 3.8.

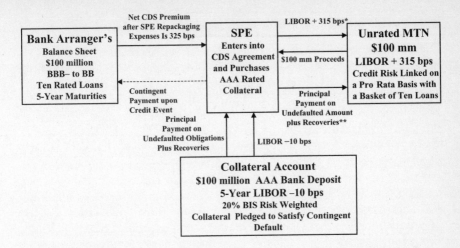

* Investor receives coupon payment on the remaining principal balance of undefaulted bank loans in the reference portfolio.

**Investor receives $100 million at maturity (plus coupon) if there are no defaults in the reference portfolio.

FIGURE 3.7 MTN Collateralized with Bank Loans

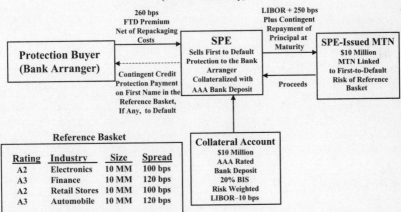

* Contingent Payment = 10 MM × (Original Price – Recovery Value). The protection seller's obligation terminates after the first name defaults and the protection payment is made. Most transactions are cash settled, and recovery value is market price of an allowable reference obligation for the reference obligor that is the first to default.

FIGURE 3.8 Repackaged First-to-Default Risk

MISMATCHED MATURITIES

Funds, banks, and other investors may have a maturity restriction on investments. If these investors can accept price and principal risk at maturity of the EMTN, a longer dated asset can be embedded in an EMTN, which meets the investor's maturity requirement. This is especially useful for amortizing assets with a short average life, but long dated legal final maturity. For example, many funds with a maturity constraint of three years are willing to buy five-year maturity assets repackaged to a three-year maturity provided the yield of the assets is sufficiently high and they have a positive view of the underlying credits. The SPE purchases a five-year maturity asset and issues an EMTN with a three-year maturity. The SPE passes through all of the benefits and risks of the asset to the investor. At the three-year maturity of the SPE, the underlying asset is sold at market, and the proceeds are paid to the EMTN investor. Any price change is knowingly borne by the investor as in Figure 3.9.

Sometimes a repackaging is not driven by investor demand, but is driven by the bank sponsor's need to lay off risk in the form of a repackaging. The bank sponsor will repackage risk on its own balance sheet, underwrite the EMTN, and distribute the EMTN through its salesforce. For instance, it is sometimes cheaper to lay off credit risk in the form of a CLN than it is to buy credit default protection in the credit derivatives market. Theoretically, the bank could sell the underlying asset outright, but that may not be a politically acceptable alternative. For instance, the bank may prefer not to sell the asset outright for confidentiality reasons. This usually happens when the asset is a loan.

LIQUIDITY

The liquidity of the EMTN varies. The investor has the right to sell an EMTN at any time. The secondary market for many of the issues of an SPE

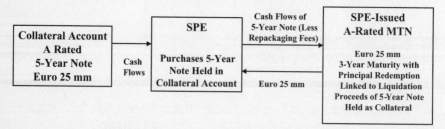

FIGURE 3.9   Mismatched Maturity Transaction

may be limited, so the SPE may seek the help of the bank sponsor, as market maker, to unwind the transaction. In absence of a default of the underlying asset, the investor typically solicits bids from dealers for the asset and derivatives transactions (if any) and compares this with the bank sponsor provided mark-to-market. If the investor finds a more favorable price in the dealer market for the underlying asset, this price is used for the unwind.

SETUP COSTS

The SPE setup requires some sunk costs as well as ongoing fixed costs, variable costs, and semi-variable costs. The upfront setup costs are sunk costs and are usually between $250,000 to $500,000. Rated programs may incur further charges. The cost will depend on the complexity of the structure and the number of changes the bank inevitably requires during the setup process. There is also an annual fixed cost for the maintenance of the SPEs. Each time the SPE issues an EMTN, it will incur a variable cost. Each tranche may incur incremental costs as necessary depending on specific investor requirements. Listing, rating agency fees, U.K. tax and legal opinions, Cayman legal opinions required for rating agencies, other venue legal opinions required by rating agencies, pledge opinions, true sale legal opinion, U.S. 144A opinion, and investor tax opinions can be among the causes of additional costs to issue a particular EMTN.

The cost of setting up two SPEs, one for rated tranches and one for unrated tranches, can be as low as only $50,000 more than the cost of setting up a single program. The documents required for both programs are very similar, which reduces the cost. The benefit of setting up separate issuing entities is that it will be possible to issue unrated tranches quickly, cheaply, and with flexibility. Separate legal opinions per tranche are required by the rating agencies for all tranches issued by SPEs with any outstanding-rated tranche. These costs are avoided by dedicating one of the SPEs to issuing only unrated product.

UNWIND TRIGGERS LINKED TO
DERIVATIVES TRANSACTIONS

The following refers to noncredit default derivative contracts such as interest rate and currency swaps and options. The bank swap provider has potential market risk exposure due to the fact that it is providing a hedge to the SPE. This exposure is the sum of the mark-to-market exposure on the swap, plus the potential value move of both the underlying asset price and the swap mark-to-market between notice of liquidation and close out. The bank swap provider will often attempt to arrange its obligation to make payments to the SPE under the swap agreement conditional upon the performance of the underlying assets dedicated to the specific EMTN.

A default of the underlying assets triggers an early redemption event for the EMTN. The underlying assets secure the EMTNs and the swap, and are held in either a bank custodial account (for non-Euroclear eligible assets) or a custodial omnibus Euroclear account. If the unwind is triggered, the security trustee sells the assets at prevailing market prices and the proceeds are passed to the EMTN investors and to the bank swap provider in order of the seniority set up in the note agreement. Other unwind triggers are possible, and we'll address these later.

In the event of default of the underlying asset, the security trustee liquidates the underlying asset by soliciting dealer bids from a prespecified set of banks and provides the mark-to-market on the derivatives transaction. The security trustee pays in order of seniority. For instance, if the seniority is *pari passu*, the EMTN investor and the bank swap provider will get a pro rata payment based on the par value of the EMTN and the positive mark-to-market on the swap. If there is a negative mark-to-market on the swap, the proceeds usually remit to the bank swap provider, although the disposition of this payment is sometimes negotiable.

The bank swap provider often has the option (but not the obligation) to trigger liquidation of the underlying asset and unwind the swap once prespecified conditions are met. These conditions are known as the *unwind triggers*. The unwind trigger will ensure the early termination of the EMTN, to prevent the possibility that a combination of market movement and price decline of the underlying asset might fail to cover the positive mark-to-market value (if any) to the bank swap provider. As mentioned before, the security trustee administers the unwind of the EMTN, which includes liquidation of the underlying asset and payment of any positive mark-to-market.

Unwind triggers may vary by repackaging. Unwind triggers are set to liquidate the underlying assets to cover the expected potential market risk exposure of the bank swap provider. A dynamic trigger is the most common type, but riskier transactions may have multiple unwind triggers. A key factor in determining unwind triggers is the degree of liquidity of the underlying asset. Illiquid assets may require different trigger strategies and trigger levels. The documentation of each EMTN series provides full disclosure of all unwind triggers.

A dynamic trigger comes into effect when the mark-to-market of the swap reaches a prespecified percent of the market price of the asset. This prespecified trigger is usually set to 80 percent to 90 percent of the market price of the asset for liquid investment grade assets, because this is the usual worst-case overnight move in underlying assets. This is known as the *gap margin*. This trigger will be set based on several factors: credit quality of the underlying asset, maturity of the transaction, size of the transaction, price volatility of the asset and derivatives transaction, and perhaps even endogenous and exogenous factors related to the quality of the underlying asset and swap. As an added fail-safe feature, this dynamic trigger can be scaled to decline as the public credit rating of the underlying asset declines.

Static triggers come into effect when a prespecified boundary condition is met. These are also called *knock-in* unwinds. Default of the underlying asset, regardless of price, is an unwind trigger. Another type of static trigger may be used in which the unwind trigger is set for the condition when the underlying asset price equals a prespecified estimated recovery value of the underlying asset in the event of default.

DAX-LINKED NOTE WITH TRIGGERS

A U.K. corporation's fixed rate vanilla secondary paper with a one-year remaining life trades at par. The SPE purchases the U.K. corporation's secondary paper and restructures the coupon cash flows via a swap with the bank sponsor. The bank sponsor receives the fixed sterling cash flows and pays Euros linked to the Deutsche Aktienindex or German stock index (DAX) for one year.

The bank sponsor has risk when there is a major price decline in the underlying secondary paper *and* when the Euro depreciates sharply against sterling. For purposes of assessing mark-to-market movements, the interest rate risk of the one-year underlying U.K. corporate paper is a minor effect relative to the currency effect.

The bank sponsor estimates the underlying U.K. corporate asset will not decline by more than 20 percent during a 5-day liquidation period. Furthermore, the bank sponsor believes that downward moves in the Euro will be orderly declines rather than extreme overnight gaps. The bank sponsor chooses a dynamic trigger based on this assumed maximum market price decline during the liquidation period. Since it believes 20 percent is a safe gap margin for this asset, it sets the trigger so an unwind will occur if the positive mark-to-market of the swap reaches 80 percent of the asset market bid price. The asset and swap are marked-to-market daily and compared with the trigger.

The bank sponsor also makes the gap margin dynamic. The gap margin is scaled to change with the rating of the underlying security. The U.K.

corporation is rated A2 at the outset of the transaction. The gap margin is 80 percent of the asset market bid price at the current rating, but scales down to 60 percent of the asset market price if the rating drops to BBB+ or BBB flat. If the rating drops below BBB flat, it is an automatic unwind trigger.

The bank sponsor also sets static triggers. The bank sponsor's estimated recovery rate for the U.K. corporation's senior debt is 40 percent, so it sets a static trigger condition when the underlying bond price declines to 40 percent of the original par value. Another static trigger condition is met if there is a credit event defined as the U.K. corporation fails to pay any debt obligation or is declared bankrupt, or has its debt rescheduled. Because of the automatic unwind trigger if the U.K. corporate credit rating drops below BBB flat, the bank is willing to take the risk of the remote (in its view) possibility that the asset would default before this trigger is met and if so, that the positive mark-to-market on the swap would exceed 40 percent of the par value of the asset. Figure 3.10 summarizes the cash flows and triggers.

When dealing with emerging market securities, or when dealing with soft currencies, certain considerations need to be emphasized. When determining mark-to-market exposure, correlation between the mark-to-market of the swap and the underlying asset is a factor.

Right-way-around swaps are those in which a bank sponsor receives the soft currency and pays a hard currency. The bank sponsor exposure is likely to be very low. The soft currency is unlikely to appreciate after a default of the underlying sovereign asset. In the event of a default of the underlying sovereign asset, the swap will probably have a negative mark-to-market to

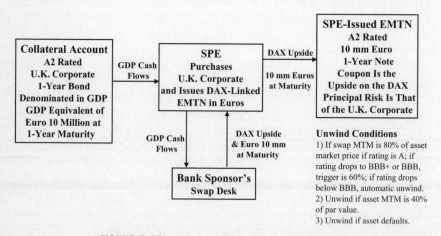

FIGURE 3.10 DAX-Linked Note with Triggers

the bank sponsor. This means the bank sponsor will not *be* owed money under the swap agreement, rather the bank sponsor *will owe* money under the swap agreement. This is a mitigating risk factor for sovereign assets.

Wrong-way-around swaps are those in which the bank sponsor receives a hard currency and pays a soft currency. The bank sponsor is likely to have more exposure and the liquidity and the credit quality of the underlying asset is of much more concern. Not all assets will be sovereign assets, however. Single currency swaps in hard currency have less exposure than the same type of swap in a soft currency, and there is often little correlation between the swap mark-to-market and the underlying asset quality.

RATINGS

One of the SPEs in the example above will issue rated EMTNs. The rating agencies review all new rated issues to ensure the new issues will not impact the rating on existing securities. The rating agencies typically require that such language be embodied in the rated SPE's articles of incorporation. If the bank swap provider holds a senior position to the noteholders, the rating agencies will usually not allow an EMTN issue to have a rating higher than that of the bank swap provider. There are a few exceptions, such as when the cash flow stream is relatively negligible and there are strict substitution clauses (should the bank provider's rating deteriorate) in the documentation.

A deal arranger may employ a credit wrap on either the swap or the underlying assets to enhance the overall rating of an EMTN series. Reinsurance companies and highly rated banks are all providers of credit wraps, for a fee.

MASTER TRUSTS

Master trusts are the most important asset-backed trust structure developed in the 1990s. This innovation enhanced investor appeal of securitizations of short-dated assets such as credit card receivables, and long-dated assets such as European mortgage backed securities (MBSs). Credit card receivables have been the dominant asset for master trusts, but others are gaining popularity. The master trust can issue multiple series from the same trust, and each series is backed by the trust's entire asset pool. The advantage is that if a series has a target maturity date, principal payments can be made from any asset in the trust.

Besides allowing synergies in legal and administrative costs, the master trust structure allows the creation of a variety of cash flow structures. Inevitably some new terminology was developed along with the master trust structure:

- As we know, the pass-through structure simply passes through principal and interest payments. This is also known as an *uncontrolled amortization* or *fast pay* structure.
- A *controlled amortization* prespecifies the amount of collected principal that will be passed through on a payment date.
- *Revolving term securitizations* have a *revolving period* followed by a controlled amortization period also known as the *payout period*. At the end of the preset revolving period, the excess cash flow is used to amortize or retire debt, and the principal is repaid in equal scheduled repayments. During the revolving period, net excess cash flow after meeting interest and other liabilities is used for the purchase of new receivables. The nonamortizing revolving period followed by an amortization period is used most frequently for credit card receivables, although the next structure is more popular.
- A *soft bullet* structure aims to pay back principal on an expected maturity date. There is an initial revolving period, but principal payments after the revolving period are collected in a principal funding account and reinvested to be paid back in a lump sum at an expected, but not guaranteed, maturity date. For securitization of short-term assets such as credit card receivables and trade receivables, the soft bullet is currently the most elegant and popular solution available.
- The *hard bullet* or *bullet* structure has a guaranteed principal repayment at a preset maturity date. The guarantee is usually accomplished by purchasing third party liquidity enhancement. The added certainty and added cost are not deemed necessary by most investors.

The U.K. has adopted the master trust structure as an elegant solution for residential mortgage backed security (RMBS) and CLOs in the European market. Investors like the soft bullet structure. Originators like the economies of scale in the legal and administrative costs and the flexibility provided by the revolving period.

OWNER TRUSTS

Owner trusts are used to securitize nonmortgage, nonrevolving assets and provide more cash flow flexibility than grantor trusts. As a result, they are gaining in popularity, even for auto, student, and equipment loan securitizations. This structure allows seniority tranching and different maturities for bonds.

In securitizations of assets where a residual value of the asset is involved, such as auto lease receivables, it is more difficult to achieve debt-for-tax treatment with the owner trust structure than with a revolving structure. For tax purposes, the equity piece is structured to look like a bond. The tax benefits all devolve to the equity piece. The tax benefits can therefore either be retained by the originator/seller or sold to an outside investor, who can also realize the tax benefits. The documentation states that if somehow the entity becomes taxable, it would convert to a partnership and pass income and expenses through to the partners, thus avoiding the entity level tax.

GRANTOR TRUSTS

Grantor trusts issue senior and subordinated interests in pass-through certificates and are pass-through structures. As such, they do not attract entity-level taxes. In other words, they are passive tax vehicles.

The grantor trust's limited ability to reinvest cash flows or purchase additional receivables is a drawback for short-dated receivables such as credit cards and long-dated receivables such as RMBS, but these are usually not severe drawbacks for auto, student, and equipment loan securitizations.

Grantor trusts have other general drawbacks. Investors receive principal and interest on a pro rata basis. No time tranching is allowed, although the trust can tranche senior and subordinated bonds. Since the payments occur over the life of the transaction, the wide payment window of the grantor trust structure has limited appeal to many investors. The owner trust structure has the ability to create greater cash flow certainty and is gaining in popularity versus the grantor trust structure, especially for auto loan receivables.

REMICs

REMICs are a U.S. phenomenon allowed by part of the Internal Revenue Code of 1986. Only assets secured by real assets can be used in a REMIC structure. These are term transactions and allow all of the flexibility of collateralized mortgage obligation (CMO) tranching technology, including tranching of the cash flow payments and timing of cash flows. This structure avoids entity level taxation. A REMIC has the tax certainty of a pass-through entity and the investor classes are treated as debt for U.S. federal income tax purposes. The equity class of the REMIC is the residual interest, more commonly called the *residual*. The residual must be owned by a taxpaying entity. The transfer must be done in such a way to ensure that taxes associated with the residual interest will be paid. Due to projected cash flows of the REMIC, at some time during the REMIC life, one can expect the residual to become a noneconomic residual interest (NER). The NER's present value of net expected tax liabilities is greater than the present value of expected distributions. To transfer this asset, the owner makes a payment for the tax loss along with the transfer of the asset. Another investor with a tax loss offset could become the low bidder and avoid paying tax on the residual interest. If the transfer is not done correctly, it may be disregarded for tax purposes, and the original owner becomes responsible for the residual interest tax liabilities. To be absolutely sure that the transfer won't be disregarded, the transferor should comply with the regulations of 1992, and further regulations added in 2002, that ensure *safe harbor* against disregard of the transfer. Since these regulations are subject to change, they should be rechecked at the time of the transaction.

FASITs are another U.S. structural phenomenon and are similar to REMICs. They are rarely used because gains, if any, on the sale of assets to a FASIT are taxable at the time of the sale.

MULTISELLER AND SINGLE SELLER CONDUITS

Conduits are SPCs set up so that the entire vehicle is funded and rated. *Multiseller* conduits buy interests in pools of assets (mainly receivables) from a number of different sellers and issue indivisible obligations, usually asset-backed commercial paper (ABCP). Banks or finance companies that generate a large number of receivables—bank sponsored credit card programs, for instance—sometimes set up *single seller* conduits, but they are cost-effective only for generators of high volumes of assets. Banks set up most conduits, although a few fund groups have also done so. These SPCs are more numerous in the United States, but are now growing in use in Europe.

Unlike the MIE we examined earlier, conduits primarily use short-term funding with a claim against the entire pool of assets owned by the conduit. *Mind the gap*. Even though short-term funding rates for the diversified pool of assets is usually lower than for the longer-term assets in the pool, that may not always be the case. Conduits use an interest rate hedge overlay for the entire program life to minimize gap risk.

Assets must meet the credit requirements of the conduit. If the assets do not meet them on their own, the conduit may require seller-level enhancement, which applies only to that specific seller's sold assets. The seller might be asked to overcollateralize, to sell a senior portion and retain the subordinated piece, or to allow limited recourse back to the seller. The good news from the seller's point of view is that the credit requirements of the conduit are usually only the equivalent of a low investment grade rating. An explicit rating usually isn't required, so the seller can avoid rating agency costs.

Unlike the other long-term structures we've examined, the sponsor banks usually administer conduits. A trustee is required only if the SPE selling the ABCP is set up as a trust. Since bank employees are often administering the conduits, they often have influence over the sponsor bank's willingness to provide liquidity. They often receive pressure to introduce assets of bank customers into the conduit. The asset securitization groups of banks with poor underwriting and distribution capabilities sometimes set up conduits to pool unsold assets. Diversification depends on what the group is securitizing. Investment banks with strong distribution capabilities frown on the use of conduits for this purpose.

From a common sense standpoint, one would want to minimize the influence an internal group can exert on the assets purchased by the conduit administrator. As a practical matter, it is often difficult to ensure objectivity. Investors in conduit ABCP should take this into account when evaluating various conduits.

Conduits also use program-level credit enhancement, which applies to the entire asset pool. This includes credit wraps in the form of surety bonds and a letter of credit (LOC) from the sponsoring bank. Credit enhancement providers must have ratings at least as high as that of the conduit's commercial paper.

Liquidity facilities are employed to bridge the gap between timing of asset cash flows and the commercial paper cash flows. There is often more than one source of liquidity, and liquidity providers must have a short-term rating equal to or higher than the conduit's rating. Since banks are currently not required to hold risk-based capital against obligations shorter than 365 days, these facilities are usually 364 days long. These have to be renewed, and the renewal cost, or *repricing risk*, is always a factor.

Conduit sponsors sometimes represent that liquidity lines are virtually risk-free. They aren't meant to be an additional means of credit enhancement and are not meant to cover defaulted assets. The lines are not risk-free to the providers, however. A commercial paper market disaster could result in drawn liquidity lines without immediate means of repayment. Changing capital regulations often threaten to make liquidity lines too expensive for

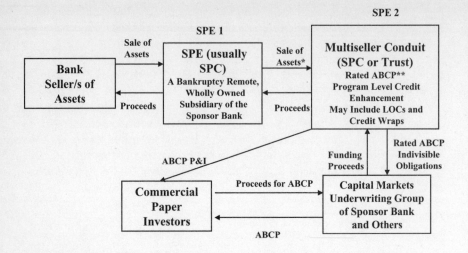

FIGURE 3.11   Multiseller Conduit

banks to supply. Bank managers have noticed that the lines are not risk-free and seesaw in their willingness to provide them. Some banks will not provide liquidity lines for outside conduits.

Figure 3.11 shows the cash flows and credit enhancement for a multiseller conduit. The size of the program varies depending on the timing and volume of the receivables of the various sellers.

DOMESTICALLY DOMICILED CORPORATIONS

Special purpose corporations can be set up onshore in certain venues. Some corporations are not meant to issue bonds, but provide a means for investors to take degrees of credit risk through either equity shares or loans. For example, in the German market, a Gesellschaft mit beschränkter Haftung (GmbH) corporate structure is sometimes employed. The GmbH issues obligations, which are backed by a diversified portfolio of noninvestment-grade corporate bonds. The GmbH has both lenders and shareholder(s). The investors who are lenders are limited partners (Kommanditists), and are only

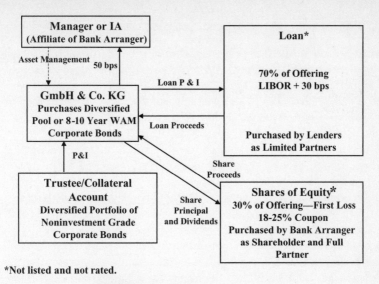

FIGURE 3.12 GmbH Securitization

liable to the extent of their capital investment. The shareholder(s) (Komplementär) are fully liable partners. The shareholder is often the bank arranger. Figure 3.12 shows a typical GmbH Securitization.

A bank arranger–affiliated asset manager usually handles portfolio management and credit research for a fee of around 50 bps per annum. A bank arranger–affiliated trustee usually handles administration services for the GmbH for a fee of around 5 bps per annum. The costs of setting up the structure are usually cheaper than for an offshore SPE. Applications are more limited and the first-loss piece is generally larger, resulting in a higher regulatory capital charge relative to other structures, if the bank arranger retains this piece.

The lenders loan money to the corporation and have a higher credit quality risk than the shareholders. The credit risk of the loan is investment-grade equivalent risk. The shareholders in the corporation are analogous to equity investors and take the equivalent of noninvestment-grade first-loss risk.

These investments are not listed and are not rated. Listing is a requirement for debt investment in Germany, but that doesn't apply to shares. There is also no need for an offshore securitization vehicle. Local corporate tax regulations apply, and from this point of view, the transaction may appear more transparent to German participants.

BANKRUPTCY REMOTE?

In order for investors to have the highest priority claim against the assets in a securitization, they must have protection from bankruptcy of the original owner of the assets or the "seller," or any creditor lien including a government lien involving taxes. If a bank is the seller of the assets, then protection from bankruptcy of the original owner is usually not an issue, at least in the United States. We're already aware that this protection is usually accomplished via a *true sale at law* of the assets to an SPE. The SPE is a specially created corporation or trust that is *bankruptcy remote* from the original seller of the assets.

Accountants usually verify that the financing gets off-balance sheet treatment. Usually this means that the SPE must be legally independent of the seller. For instance, the SPE cannot be a wholly-owned subsidiary of the seller, or the assets of the SPE would have to be consolidated on the seller's balance sheet under U.S. generally accepted accounting principles (GAAP).

Sellers want to avoid creating a taxable event by the sale of assets. For tax purposes, the seller wants to characterize this transaction as a financing. Tax laws are independent of bankruptcy treatment and accounting treatment. The securitization is usually structured as seller debt for tax purposes, but as a sale for bankruptcy purposes.

While the above conditions are opinions issued by accountants and lawyers, they may not protect the investor's economic interests. The financial institution sponsoring an asset-backed transaction has made representations and warranties. In the event of bankruptcy, the investor may find these representations are in breach. After all, the financial institution didn't go bankrupt because it was well managed, did it?

If the financial institution is also the servicer of the transaction, the bankruptcy court may not want you to replace the servicer, and yet the rating agencies may view this as a potential credit event. CDOs attempt to account for this by documenting that a servicer must be replaced if the servicer's rating declines below a certain credit rating. If the deterioration is very swift, however, there may not be time for replacement before the bankruptcy court gets involved.

Different countries take different positions on bankruptcy law. It is important to review the price that the assets are sold to an SPE under *true sale at law*. In some venues, if a financial institution is in a shaky state, and if it sells assets at a discount, the sale could be voided if the financial institution goes bankrupt. For example, in the United States, this might be viewed as a *fraudulent conveyance*, and the sale could be voided. Of course, rated deals will have opinions as to the legality of the transfer of assets and the fair price transfer of the assets. These are only opinions, however. Sound financial institutions usually don't cut corners. It is usually when a financial institution isn't doing well that it cuts corners or is tempted to engage in transactions that are in the gray zone. Opinions can be overruled.

Many venues have rules against *preferential payments*. In the personal finance arena, the equivalent would be paying off your Rolls Royce just before declaring bankruptcy. If you received deal payments from an issuer, or if you received support agreement payments from a credit wrap provider who subsequently declares bankruptcy, these payments might be deemed to be preferential. Payments made in the *ordinary course* of business are exempt from preferential status, and a legal opinion showing that the payments satisfy a series of conditions can be issued. That is only a legal opinion, however, and if something goes amiss with the deal or the financial institution, all of the deal documentation will be reviewed.

In the United States, banks and thrifts are not subject to the bankruptcy code and are not subject to the same preference risk, at least theoretically. In the case of proven fraud, however, the Federal Reserve could potentially step in and reverse the transaction. Their mandate is to protect the banking system, not investors in fraudulent transactions. The Federal Reserve would be reluctant to do this, because securitization is a key tool of U.S. banks, but it doesn't pay to get complacent if it appears something is amiss in the documentation of a deal for which a bank is a sponsor. In any case, under financial duress, a bank sponsor would be asked to stop making payments that might be viewed as favorable to a creditor's interest at the expense of another, once the financial difficulty is known.

Structural protections work for many of the payments due to investors. As we saw earlier, first perfection of collateral security interest protects investors from preferential treatment of collateral cash flows. Some conduit structures will have a *clawback* letter of credit that allows investors to claim reimbursement if any of their payments are reversed because they are ruled preferential.

Rules may change, so there is no substitute for checking with lawyers in each venue to maximize the probability that a deal will always be viewed as bankruptcy-remote from the sponsoring entity.

Even when a deal is bankruptcy-remote, the investor may make decisions that result in bankruptcy risk. One obvious trap is to invest proceeds in the collateral of the sponsoring entity. The collateral is subject to bankruptcy risk of the sponsor. Investors can protect themselves by insisting the documentation asks for nonsponsor collateral. You already have the documentation risk to the sponsor, so why add additional risk for a given deal?

J.P. Morgan estimated they had about $100 million in unsecured exposure to Enron, who acted as servicer of a "bankruptcy-remote" SPE for which J.P. Morgan acted as administrative agent. Enron sold receivables to the bankruptcy-remote SPE, but invested the cash in Enron commercial paper. J.P. Morgan claims Enron didn't inform them of the composition of the assets in the SPE. It's hard to be sympathetic if the documentation didn't exclude investment of cash from receivables in Enron paper in the first place.

CHAPTER 4

Credit Derivatives and Total Rate of Return Swaps

RISKS TO PORTFOLIO VALUE

There are three types of credit risk. The first is risk of a downgrade in credit quality of an asset. On a purely statistical basis, the rating agencies each publish their own *transition matrices*. This shows the probability of a single asset being upgraded or downgraded based on historical corporate data. Table 4.1 is an example of a transition matrix.

With these probabilities, we could use a simple binomial tree to calculate a horizon price in one year. This would then allow us to calculate a horizon value and an expected return for the asset. Similarly, we could do this analysis for a portfolio of assets (see Figure 4.1).

The second risk is a general widening in credit spreads, which will cause the price of the asset to decline. The third risk is the risk of default by the obligor. Standard & Poor's publishes data on the cumulative default rates based on historical corporate data. Table 4.2 is an example for the period 1983–2000. If you look at data for another time period, the default rates will differ somewhat from those shown in the table.

The portfolio also has market risk. If the general market level of interest rates increases, the price of a fixed rate bond will decline. If the general market level of interest rates decreases, the price of a fixed rate bond will increase. If the portfolio is a multicurrency portfolio, the portfolio may also have currency risk relative to the investor's benchmark currency.

Of course, it is also possible that an asset can be upgraded or that credit spreads can tighten. It is also possible that interest rates and currency rates move in a direction that enhances portfolio value.

Just as we looked at the horizon value of a bond due to rating transition, we can incorporate all of the above factors, taking into account the

TABLE 4.1 Rating Transition Matrix

Current Rating	Rating in One Year								
	AAA	AA	A	BBB	BB	B	CCC	Default	NR*
AAA	89.37	6.04	0.44	0.14	0.05	0.00	0.00	0.00	3.97
AA	0.57	87.76	7.30	0.59	0.06	0.11	0.02	0.01	3.58
A	0.05	2.01	87.62	5.37	0.45	0.18	0.04	0.05	4.22
BBB	0.03	0.21	4.15	84.44	4.39	0.89	0.28	0.37	5.26
BB	0.03	0.06	0.40	5.50	76.44	7.14	1.11	1.38	7.92
B	0.00	0.07	0.26	0.36	4.74	74.12	4.37	6.20	9.87
CCC	0.09	0.00	0.28	0.56	1.39	8.80	49.72	27.87	11.30

Source: Standard & Poor's Risk Solutions CreditPro® 6.2 as published in *Corporate Defaults Peak in 2002 Amid Record Amounts of Defaults and Declining Credit Quality—Hazards Remain (January 23, 2003).*
*NR means not rated.

corresponding estimates of volatility, to model the horizon value of a portfolio.

Synthetics such as credit default swaps (CDSs), total rate of return swaps (TRORSs), and credit spread options (CSOs) can mitigate risk in a portfolio or can add risk to a portfolio.

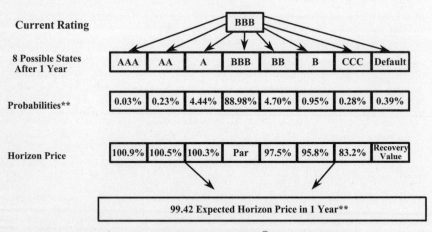

*Source: Standard & Poor's Risk Solutions CreditPro® 6.2 as published in
   *Corporate Defaults Peak in 2002 Amid Record Amounts of Defaults and Declining
   Credit Quality—Hazards Remain (January 23, 2003).*
**Adjusted for assets not rated after one year.

FIGURE 4.1 Price Change of BBB Bond due to Rating Migration

TABLE 4.2 Standard & Poor's Cumulative Average Default Rates Expressed as Percent of Total

Jan. 1 Rating	Years after Static Pool Formation									
	1	2	3	4	5	6	7	8	9	10
AAA	0.00	0.00	0.03	0.06	0.10	0.17	0.25	0.38	0.43	0.48
AA	0.10	0.03	0.08	0.16	0.27	0.39	0.53	0.65	0.75	0.85
A	0.05	0.15	0.28	0.44	0.62	0.81	1.03	1.25	1.52	1.82
BBB	0.37	0.94	1.52	2.34	3.20	4.02	4.74	5.40	5.99	6.68
BB	1.38	4.07	7.16	9.96	12.34	14.65	16.46	18.02	19.60	20.82
B	6.20	13.27	19.07	23.45	26.59	29.08	31.41	33.27	34.58	35.87
CCC	27.87	36.02	41.79	46.26	50.46	52.17	53.60	54.36	56.16	57.21
Inv. Grade	0.13	0.34	0.57	0.87	1.20	1.52	1.83	2.13	2.41	2.72
Spec grade	5.17	10.27	14.81	18.46	21.31	23.67	25.71	27.36	28.83	30.07
All ratings	1.67	3.36	4.86	6.12	7.14	8.02	8.80	9.47	10.07	10.64

Source: Standard & Poor's Risk Solutions CreditPro® 6.2 as published in *Corporate Defaults Peak in 2002 Amid Record Amounts of Defaults and Declining Credit Quality—Hazards Remain (January 23, 2003).*

CDSs

The credit derivatives market weathered a number of high profile defaults in 2001 and 2002, and most market participants were satisfied with the payments made on their CDS contracts. As market participants discovered their CDS contracts were honored even while some insurance contracts were disputed, the confidence level for using credit derivatives increased. This bodes well for the future of CDSs as the hedge instrument of choice for credit event risk.

A CDS is a transaction in which the credit protection buyer pays a fee, usually called a *premium*, to a credit protection provider in exchange for a payment if a credit default event of a reference asset(s) occurs. The protection buyer is the seller of default risk. The protection seller (also called the protection provider) is a buyer of credit risk. The protection seller is often called the *investor* and makes no payment unless a credit default event occurs. The protection seller and the protection buyers are called CDS *counterparties.* CDSs are sometimes called credit default options, but market professionals usually use the former.

Figure 4.2 shows a generic CDS.

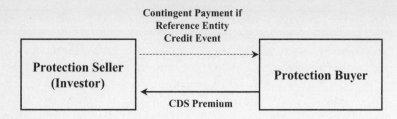

The protection seller receives a periodic premium from the protection buyer in exchange for a contingent payment if there is a credit event of the reference entity. The contingent payment is determined based on prespecified settlement terms.

FIGURE 4.2   Generic CDS

ARE YOU HEDGED?—THE REGULATORY VIEWPOINT

If CDSs only address credit default risk, why does the United States allow a bank to mismatch the maturity of a CDS with a banking book asset, yet still allow the same regulatory relief as for a matched maturity hedge? Canada and Germany don't allow it. France and the United Kingdom only give a 70 percent risk weighting credit to this hedge. Australia recognizes a percent of the maturity matched. Japan waffles. It may be that because banks do not yet mark their balance sheets to market, the United States views default risk as the source of all credit risk for hedging purposes. Needless to say, the trend will probably evolve to a common agreement on how to recognize the hedge across venues.

A key feature of a credit derivatives contract—unlike an insurance contract—is that the protection buyer does not have to suffer loss as a result of a credit event in order to get paid under the terms of a credit derivatives contract. In the United Kingdom, this feature exempts credit derivatives from the necessity to get authorization under the Insurance Companies Act of 1982, because a credit protection buyer under a credit derivative does not have to hold an underlying obligation in order to get paid. In some venues, insurance companies can raise other issues as a defense against paying out under the terms of an insurance contract. (See also Chapter 8: "Enron, J.P. Morgan, and Offshore Vehicles.") It is much more difficult to raise a defense against payment under a credit derivatives contract than an insurance contract.

Investing in a CDS is similar to going long the credit risk of a cash asset, except that a CDS isn't funded, it is purely synthetic. These are over-the-counter (private confidential dealing) negotiated contracts. The terms and conditions can be modified.

Credit derivatives are bilateral financial contracts that isolate credit risk from financial instruments. A financial institution can transfer—or take on credit risk—in a trading book. When trading books are used, credit derivatives are off-balance sheet transactions. Even if one isn't transferring risk from a trading book, one can transfer credit risks without transferring underlying reference assets. For instance, a bank can use a CDS to transfer credit risk of a loan, and does not need to notify the borrower. The bank retains legal ownership of assets while hedging default risk. This is particularly useful when assets are under water (below their initial book value), because a sale of the loan would require the bank to recognize a loss.

A structurer can use a CDS to transfer an assets credit event risk to a collateralized debt obligation (CDO), and can negotiate features rather than use "market template" documentation. As we will see, the United States and Europe often use different language in generic CDS contracts. CDO structurers and synthetic deal managers should use the flexibility of this market to their advantage. Structurers can tailor credit risk in terms not available in cash markets. Structurers can also create arbitrage opportunities not available in cash markets. Finally, structurers can hedge any type of credit exposure, even *anticipated* exposure.

Just about any contract imaginable can be created. The key issues in the CDS market revolve around pricing and contract language:

- Definition of the credit event (potential source of basis risk).
- Determination of the default protection fee.
- Determination of the reference asset or the allowable deliverables (potential source of basis risk).
- Determination of the default payment (potential source of basis risk).

In the current market, fees are usually paid like swap payments—quarterly in arrears—but any negotiated payment structure is feasible. The premium can be thought of as the credit spread that an investor would demand to take the default risk of a par asset swap package or a par floating rate note (FRN).

Default protection can be purchased on any notional stream of cash flows. For instance, it can be purchased on an asset swap package, a loan, a bond, receivables, tranches of CDOs, sovereign risk due to cross border commercial transactions, or even on credit exposure due to a derivative contract such as counterparty credit exposure in a cross-currency swap transaction. Credit protection can be linked to an individual credit or to a basket of credits.

By *notional*, I mean a counterparty doesn't have to own—or ever intend to own—the underlying reference asset in order to buy protection. Suppose an investor wants to own the risk of a corporate loan, but the investor is not allowed to buy loans. The investor can sell credit protection (buy credit risk) on the loan, and use cash settlement. The credit protection buyer can even buy credit protection on a notional exposure, such as the exposure an interest rate swap desk might have to a counterparty in an interest rate swap. Conversely, a protection seller does not ever have to take delivery on a defaulted asset. The settlement can be a cash settlement referencing the loss on an asset or on a notional exposure.

Figures 4.3 and 4.4 show the cash flows of investment in a par FRN versus a generic CDS, which provides credit default protection for the protection buyer, who owns a par floater, the reference asset. In this example, the CDS uses physical settlement if a credit default occurs. In physical settlement, the protection seller purchases the floater at par, and takes delivery of the floater, which is now only worth its current market price, or recovery value. In cash settlement, the protection seller does not take delivery of the asset, but makes a net contingent payment equal to par minus the market price.

The *market price* is the postdefault price, or the *recovery value*, of the reference asset and is usually determined by a dealer poll. Par minus the market price equals the loss on the reference asset, so the protection buyer is made whole on the initial value of par. Notice that either one of these counterparties can be called an "investor," so it is safer to identify a counterparty either as the *protection buyer* or as the *protection seller*.

The credit default option or swap is a contingent option. The protection seller makes a termination payment only if a credit event occurs. If the credit event does not occur, the default protection seller has no obligation.

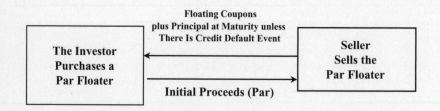

The Seller receives par.

The Investor receives the floating coupons and receives par at maturity unless there is a credit default event. If there is an event, the asset is worth the current market price, or recovery value.

FIGURE 4.3   Par Floating Rate Bond Purchase

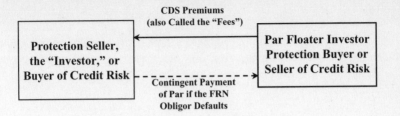

The protection seller (investor) receives a periodic premium from the protection buyer.

If the FRN obligor defaults, the protection seller pays par for the floater and takes delivery of the FRN, which is worth only the current market value, or recovery value.

FIGURE 4.4   Par FRN Investor Buys Credit Default Protection

The CDS premium may increase, but it is never actually in the money until a credit default event occurs, as defined by the confirm language. That seems like a knock-in option or a knock-in swap, which is a type of barrier option. The *knock-in* is triggered by either a credit default or a *credit event*. If the option knocks-in, then and only then is the option in the money.

Any negotiated payout in the event of default is feasible. The most common market structure is the *par value minus market price* [also called the "(100 − market value) × notional"] structure. It can leave a position of premium bonds partially unhedged or can overhedge a position of bonds trading below par.

DIGITAL CASH PAYMENT—ALTERNATE TERMINATION PAYMENT

A *digital* or *binary* termination payment is a fixed percentage of the notional principal. Settlement is usually cash. There are two types of digital payouts.

The *all-or-nothing* (also known as the *zero-one*) payment is equal to the entire notional amount. The investor loses the entire notional amount—not merely coupon and some principal loss—if there is a default event. I believe there is no need to offer credit protection on the entire notional amount for a CDO, since recovery rates are usually greater than zero. Using this payout structure for most corporate credit introduces significant basis risk into a CDS. For other structured finance products, however, the digital payout may be a useful tool. For instance, if the underlying obligations are trade receivables, the structurer may feel that if payment isn't made within an allowable grace period, none will be made at all.

The second type of digital payment is a pre-agreed cash payment in the event of default. For instance, in the Swiss Bank Corporation (SBC) Glacier Finance Ltd. deal, some payouts were set at 51 percent of par, the average recovery value for senior unsecured obligations according to the Moody's standard at the time. SBC used this termination device when there was no specific reference asset. For example, this might occur if the credit exposure is due to a cross-currency swap with a reference obligor. The reference is the notional exposure of the cross-currency swap. It might also occur if SBC doesn't have that particular risk, but wants to create capacity to take on some credit risk at a later date.

Pre-agreed fixed cash payments also make sense in other scenarios. If a credit event occurs, daily price volatility can be enormous. Emerging market debt spreads are often highly volatile. As most credit default contracts look for settlement within a month of an event, a daily price fluctuation can work against the default protection buyer. If the protection buyer wants to protect itself against this possibility, it may make sense to agree in advance on a fair default payment.

Another scenario is one in which the protection seller doesn't want to get tagged with the exercise of a "cheapest to deliver" option. From the protection seller's point of view, the pre-agreed payment completely avoids this risk, but also closes out the possibility of a recovery value higher than the pre-agreed payment.

INITIAL VALUE × (PAR − MARKET VALUE): ALTERNATE TERMINATION PAYMENT

Another termination payment calculation used in the market today uses the following formula:

$$\text{Initial Value} \times (\text{Par} - \text{Market Value})$$

This may be particularly useful for arbitrage CDOs that use both cash and synthetic securities. The CDO can sell credit default protection on a specific bond or loan. The initial value is equal to the full value or total cost of the specific reference asset. When the reference asset is trading well above or well below par, this settlement calculation is a better option. When assembling a portfolio, a CDO structurer or CDO manager should try to incorporate this language when a reference asset is trading below par. (The CDO portfolio is long the credit protection seller and receives the fee.)

When a desired reference asset is trading well above par, and when other assets of the same reference obligor trade well above par, it may be useful to employ a different strategy. It might be worthwhile to execute a standard CDS and agree to pay only par minus market value on an allowable set of deliverables. Investors should look at the language of deals to see if an attempt was made to get the most favorable terms on synthetic exposures.

If a bond trades above par, and if the generic contract isn't available, the calculation amount should decrease to the equivalent of a par price over time. Most credit derivatives desks feel this is too complicated. Rather, they adjust the calculation amount of the transaction in an attempt to compensate the default protection seller for the potential additional termination payment. The default protection buyer pays a fee based on a higher calculation amount adjusted to reflect the initial price of the bond. For instance, for a bond with a $10,000,000 face amount trading at 105, the calculation amount would be $10,500,000 instead of $10,000,000.

NORMALIZED PRICE METHOD—ALTERNATE TERMINATION PAYMENT

To be fair to both the default protection buyer and seller, one should account for the initial price of the reference asset and recognize that the price will change over time. The price *decreases* to par if the reference asset initially trades *above* par. The price *increases* to par if the reference asset initially trades *below* par. The reflected price should be adjusted to screen out price changes due to market moves and changes in the term structure of credit spreads.

Creating a fictitious asset with the same maturity and coupon as the reference asset can normalize the price of the reference asset. The spread of the reference asset to a risk-free asset, such as an AAA treasury security, is input into a bond pricing calculator. That way, as the reference asset approaches maturity, the price of the shorter maturity proxy bond can be used as the reference price to calculate the termination payment.

This method is almost never used because most practitioners do not want to draft the language, but there may be times when it pays to do this.

HEDGE COSTS IN CASH AND SYNTHETIC CDOs

Synthetic structures sometimes fold hedge costs into termination payments. Suppose a buyer of protection asks for credit default protection on a par asset swap package. The buyer may ask for a par minus market value payment plus accrued interest plus hedge costs. The hedge costs are the costs of unwinding the swap in the asset swap package. Since the reference asset may not be priced at par, the price difference from par is reflected in the hedge cost. It is important to note that the seller of protection does not usually get a rebate if there is a net market gain in the hedge. If there is a net market loss, however, the hedge cost will most likely reflect all costs to make sure the buyer is made completely whole. In credit linked note (CLN) structures, issuers often incorporate the hedge costs of a swap from fixed to floating coupons as part of the termination payment. This is tricky for the seller, because the theory is that the hedge costs make up for any price difference from par of the reference asset. This practice is even used in multicurrency structures in which an issuer may hedge a nondollar asset to dollars. This is fine if the intention of the default protection seller is to hedge all of the risks for the buyer on a dollar basis. That cost, however, should be factored into the seller's price of protection.

CDOs of cash assets often require currency hedges. For example, a bond denominated in U.S. dollars with a fixed coupon may have to be swapped to Euros with a floating coupon. Sometimes a manager will ask a deal arranger to provide a hedge so that if the underlying reference asset defaults, the arranger will unwind the hedge at no cost to the deal. If the arranger agrees, a credit contingent option to unwind a cross currency swap at no cost to the deal is added. Often this isn't effectively priced into the overall deal cost, and it is, quite simply, a mistake.

DELIVERABLES: CDOs AND THE "CHEAPEST TO DELIVER" OPTION

Structurers at banks and investment banks attempt to exploit the "cheapest to deliver" option at the expense of CDO investors whenever possible. Synthetic arbitrage CDOs, for example, provide credit protection to the structuring bank or structuring investment bank that arranges the deal. The arranger will attempt to incorporate the broadest delivery language possible into a synthetic CDO or synthetic first-to-default baskets. When the arranger sells protection, however, the arranger will attempt to limit deliverables to the most expensive to deliver possible. As you've probably deduced, the arranger keeps the difference in value whenever possible.

It's reasonable for CDO investors to either insist on limiting deliverables, or to ask for a higher spread for each tranche to reflect the added risk of the cheapest to deliver option.

In the previous example, we calculated the termination payment referencing a single specific reference asset, but financial institutions may have a variety of credit exposures from a given reference obligor. The reference obligor is also known as the reference entity. We call this cluster of exposures *reference obligations*. In the current market, it is popular to reference *borrowed money*, which usually means bonds and loans. Many dealers will try to say this is the standard contract and therefore more liquid. So what? In times of high volatility in a given credit sector, the contract may be easier to trade, but you won't necessarily like your execution.

If you sell a bank credit protection on a loan, you don't want undue basis. The basis risk results from the option of the credit protection buyer to produce the *cheapest to deliver*. The credit protection buyer may own a loan, but under the terms of the contract can buy a discounted bond in the marketplace and deliver this instrument, thus getting a higher payout under the CDS.

The seller of credit protection does not have to accept whatever the market wishes to dish out. In fact, I would encourage protection sellers to differentiate between types of deliverable assets, and price the fee for the credit protection differently depending on the reference asset.

Convertible bonds pose a unique set of challenges to delivery in the credit derivatives market, because investors can purchase them as convertibles or can buy strips of the risk of the convertible bonds.

CONVERTIBLE BONDS AND ASSET SWAPS

Convertible bonds or *converts* are corporate securities that can be exchanged for a fixed number of common equity shares at a prespecified price at prespecified times at the bondholder's option. Many convertible bonds issued today are combinations of zero coupon bonds and warrants, but the debt portion does not necessarily have to be a zero coupon bond. The shares are usually the shares of the issuer of the convertible, but not always. In general, convertibles can be either debentures or preferred shares (convertible into common shares), but we'll focus on convertible bonds.

If the stock price rises, convertibles behave like equity and their price move is almost the same as the equity. The embedded option to convert into shares of stock is deep in the money and the price movement of the convertibles approaches one-to-one with the stock. When the stock price plummets, the option moves out of the money and has less value. The fixed income characteristics of the convertible dominate its price behavior.

The issuer has the right to call most convertibles. If the convertible has a *conversion price* above par, the issuer will try to minimize the value of the bond and call the issue at par. The investor, on the other hand, wants to maximize the value of the bond, and has an economic imperative to convert the bonds to shares and capture the value above par, rather than receive only par on the call date. This is a *forced conversion*.

The *conversion ratio* allows the investor to calculate the number of common equity shares into which the bond is convertible. For instance, a bond with a face value of $1,000 is convertible into 50 shares of common stock in the same company. The theoretical *conversion price* for the common stock is represented by X in the calculation below and is calculated as follows:

$$\frac{1 \text{ bond}}{25 \text{ shares}} = \frac{\$1,000}{X} \qquad X = \$40$$

The conversion price is $40. An investment of $10,000,000 face value in bonds of this corporation's convertible bonds would be convertible into 250,000 shares of stock at the conversion price of $40. If the price of the stock is only $30, the *conversion parity* is 25 shares $\times$ $30 or $750 per $1,000 face value investment. For a $10,000,000 face value investment, the conversion parity is $7,500,000.

For instance, convertible bonds with a face value of $10,000,000 that trade at $9,500,000, but have a conversion parity of $7,500,000, trade at a high conversion premium. The conversion premium is $9,500,000 − $7,500,000 or $2,000,000. The *percent of conversion premium* is calculated as follows:

$$\text{Percent of Conversion Premium} = \frac{\$9,500,000 - \$7,500,000}{\$7,500,000 \times 100} = 26.67\%$$

This is the percent conversion premium over conversion parity. Notice that this is a high percentage. When convertible bonds trade at a premium to conversion parity, they trade at a *conversion premium*. A low conversion premium means that the convertible's price behavior will track the market value of the underlying stock. A high conversion premium means the convertible price behavior will be similar to that of comparable fixed income bonds.

Convertibles may have a variety of other features, which make them challenging to price. The following is a summary of some of the variations:

■ If the convertible is callable at a certain date at certain prices, the call is an *unprotected call*.

- If the convertible can only be called if the stock price is above a certain barrier, the call is *a barrier option*, and the call is a *protected call*.
- Convertibles may be put-able by the investor, and this increases their value.
- Conversion is sometimes into a combination of shares and cash instead of shares only.
- *Conversion numbers*, the number of shares and/or amount of cash into which the bond can convert, may vary over time.
- Convertibles may have *step-up coupons,* which are prespecified increases in coupons.
- Convertibles may be convertible into shares of different issuers in different countries, thus exposing the investor to currency risk.

Dividends and dilution are other considerations. Stock dividends affect the price of convertible bonds, because they affect the price of the shares into which the convertible may convert. If an investor converts and receives newly printed shares, the company now has more shares for the debt-adjusted capital base, thus creating a *dilution effect.*

All of the above considerations will determine when it is financially advantageous for an investor to convert to stock. Nonetheless, sometimes investors fail to convert. Sometimes this is *rational* behavior and sometimes it is *irrational* behavior. Rational behavior includes tax considerations, or perhaps the investor was attending to more attractive financial opportunities and had conversion further down his list of things to do. Irrational behavior usually occurs because someone miscalculated or simply forgot.

Efficient market theory suggests that options should never be irrationally exercised, or remain irrationally unexercised. But it happens all the time. The philosophical camp says that forgetting, or making cognitive errors, is part of human nature, and therefore is consistent with efficient market theory. In other words, the market is as efficient as human beings. For my part, I simply view this as irrational behavior. Pricing models are easy to construct in comparison to trying to understand the complications of human nature, at least for me. Others may be able to incorporate this feature into their models, and if so, I look forward to learning more about myself.

Convertibles are deliverable obligations in many credit derivatives contracts. Many CDOs limit the percentage of the original portfolio against which convertibles would be deliverable in the event of default. The rating agencies pay attention to the ability to allow the delivery of convertibles as well. Moody's, for instance, will add stress tests to the cash flow model of a CDO that allows convertibles as deliverables.

Convertible arbitrageurs consist of hedge funds and specialized structurers at banks and investment banks. It's estimated that arbitrageurs buy more than 50 percent of new issue convertibles. New issues tend to embed cheap equity call options. These long-dated call options are known as *warrants*, and are a source of cheap equity volatility.

The arbitrageurs sometimes purchase the convertible and hedge the credit risk by buying credit protection in the form of a credit derivative. The characteristics of convertibles in their whole form shouldn't be confused with *stripped convertibles*, however. Alternatively, the arbitrageur strips out the option to convert into the equity shares. The arbitrageur is left with an inexpensive equity warrant and a deeply discounted zero coupon bond. They repackage and sell the bond as a *callable par asset swap*.

Normally, when the equity warrant is stripped from the convertible bond, the right to force conversion is also purchased by the arbitrageur, the holder of the equity warrant portion of the convertible bond. Investors in the callable asset swap should anticipate efficient exercise of the option by the arbitrageur. The par asset swap investor has sold the arbitrageur a call option on the bond at any time before maturity or put date of the contract. The convertible asset swap matures either on the first put date, if any, of the underlying convertible, or on the maturity date of the original convertible bond.

Since the arbitrageur can call the asset swap package immediately, the structure usually includes a six-month *clawback* so the buyer of the convertible asset swap package is guaranteed to receive the spread for at least the minimum equivalent of a six-month period. The clawback includes a compensation for the break funding costs, if any. The clawback is also called a *make whole provision*. The specified period—six months in our example—is more commonly called the *lockout period*. The lockout period is negotiable. Most of the early convertible asset swap packages were sold without this feature, but most investors currently demand a lockout of at least six months.

The option to call back the bond is a CSO. The call option on the bond is the same as a put option on the spread. As the spread decreases, the bond trades at a higher theoretical price, and the right to call the bond becomes more valuable.

Many banks buy the stripped convertible par asset swap and buy a CDS as a hedge against the company's credit risk. Since the bonds are callable, there is a potential mismatch between the CDS protection and the par asset swap.

In a par asset swap package that includes a CDS, the convertible bond's fixed income strip value is calculated by netting out the value of the CSO. Many banks use a forward starting duration weighted option to value the bond portion using bond spreads. Binomial models are simpler and more transparent than more complicated models, and a model with simplifying assumptions can be constructed in a short time frame.

CSOs are used to hedge against or make a bet on credit spread changes. A generic CSO contract specifies a reference asset, or even an index. It will also specify a strike spread at each payoff period. Often the payoff period will be the maturity date of the option. The gross spread is the difference between the credit spread and the strike price.

Convertible asset swaps have an embedded American CSO. The investor pays an up-front premium. The option payoff profile is asymmetric with changes in the credit spread.

Credit spread options can be puts or calls. The payoff for the put occurs when credit spreads tighten, and is represented by the following formula:

$$P_i = \text{Notional} \cdot \text{Max (DWOE (S}-\text{FCDS),0)}$$

where P_i = the put payoff at time i, which is just at the end of the
lockout period
Notional = the notional amount of the par asset swap
DWOE = the duration weighted optimal exercise
S = the strike spread or recall level
FCDS = the forward credit default swap at optimal exercise

Since the put option is priced at the end of the lockout period, the value can be discounted to the present using the following formula:

$$P_0 = P_i \cdot e^{-r \cdot t_I}$$

where P_0 = the put payoff at time 0 (now)
r = the risk free rate
t_I = the number of time increments in the period (e.g., 260
trading days)

Earlier we discussed the fact that duration is not sufficient to describe the price behavior of bonds. Second order terms such as convexity, and even higher order terms, are often necessary to model bond price behavior. I ignore them here to make the example easier to follow. In this case, ignoring convexity understates the option value. If the credit spread tightens, the present value is greater than expected, because the underlying CDS has negative convexity and the option's value will increase more than the option model predicts.

Furthermore, CDS prices tend to track bond prices, but not always, as we've seen earlier when demand causes pricing distortions. The CDS price change is included in this formula, however, as if it is proportional to the duration of the bonds. I've made a further simplifying assumption that the duration of the bonds doesn't change at exercise. I've also ignored the change in duration of the bonds at optimal exercise. I've assumed optimal exercise occurs when one third of the time to maturity elapses. In actual practice, this is often the case. Now we can restate DWOE as follows:

$$ \text{DWOE} = (1 + r)\frac{t_e}{t_I} \cdot 3 $$

where r = the risk free rate
   t_e = the time to exercise or 1/3 of elapsed time to maturity beyond the lockout period (e.g., one-third of the number of trading days left to maturity at the end of the lockout period)
   t_I = the number of time increments in the period (e.g., 260 trading days)

Rating agencies are often concerned about delivery of the stripped portion of the convertible. Recent history shows that the amount paid in the event of default on a deeply discounted convertible is comparable to the net liability on a generic par bond in the event of default. When Enron defaulted, the deeply discounted stripped convertible recovery value was calculated off the implied accreted price for the deeply discounted bond, and protection providers paid amounts only slightly higher than protection providers who made the calculation from bonds that were originally par generic bonds. Nonetheless, the rating agencies are still cautious about the potential for calculation differences and view these deliverables as potentially creating a higher liability in the event of default.

DEFAULT AND RECOVERY RATE

Two of the key determinants of value of a credit derivatives contract are the probability of default and the recovery rate. These are based on historical data. Estimates are available from databases kept in the public market as well as proprietary databases. We'll see later how historical data can let us down, but for now, we'll examine how the market employs this data. The major rating agencies maintain tables, which show the probability of default for bonds with given ratings. This data includes mainly U.S. and European credits, and data is often used to estimate default probabilities for any bond with the same rating.

Moody's (in a proactive strike to improve their data relative to Fitch and S&P) recently purchased KMV Corporation, which offers one of the best-known proprietary default risk models, with fundamental balance sheet analysis. Stephen Kealhofer, John McQuown, and Oldrich Vasicek founded KMV Corporation in 1989. Their focus is on corporate credit-risk measurement and management. The KMV analysis takes a fundamental balance sheet approach to analyze credits and correlations between credits. KMV also claims to be able to identify relative strength between same-rated credits.

Data is limited especially for Asian markets and sovereign bonds. Sovereign defaults tend to be both event- and credit-related. Sovereign risk requires a macroeconomics analytical approach, and one must pay attention to global economic and political events.

Default risk may vary over time. Rating agencies keep data that measures the cumulative risk of issuer default over the term of an obligation. For discrete time periods within the term of an obligation, rating agencies also measure the marginal risk of default, which shows the change in the default probability of the issuer over time. During the term of an obligation, it is wise to refresh this data to incorporate current data and revised predictions on the credit prospects of an issuer.

Recovery rates pose another problem. The major rating agencies also compile data on public and rated securities and their recovery rates, but the data isn't always available. For instance, in Europe, where recovery rate data is sparse, rating agencies may arbitrarily assign a percentage recovery rate to the corporate obligations of an entire country. In 2002, about 60 percent of Moody's revenues in Europe came from rating CDOs, yet this crude method is what the rating agencies use. Recovery rates in the United States show a wide variance, as we shall see later.

Credit officers at many institutions may do individual name analysis based on their experience and on the fundamentals of the company. A bank with a long lending relationship may have access to data that is difficult to obtain in the public market, and that may be the best source of a recovery value estimate. KMV keeps an extensive database on recovery rates for individual names, which can also be used in a credit default price analysis.

Relative recovery rates—even if one doesn't successfully guess the absolute recovery rate—among reference assets of the same reference obligor are very important to a seller of credit default protection. Seniority of the obligation and the capital structure of the issuer(s) (reference obligors) are key factors in recovery rate estimates.

TABLE 4.3 Moody's Recovery Analysis 1983–2000

Seniority/Security	Median	Average	StDev	Min	Max	1st Quartile	3rd Quartile
Senior/Secured Bank Loans	72.00	64.00	24.40	5.00	98.00	45.30	85.00
Senior/Unsecured Bank Loans	45.00	49.00	28.40	5.00	88.00	25.00	75.80
Senior/Secured Bonds	53.80	52.60	24.60	1.60	103.00	34.80	68.60
Senior/Unsecured Bonds	44.00	46.90	28.00	0.50	122.60	25.00	66.80
Senior/Sub-ordinated Bonds	29.00	34.70	24.60	0.50	123.00	15.10	50.00
Subordinated Bonds	28.50	31.60	21.20	0.50	102.50	15.00	44.10
Junior/Sub-ordinated Bonds	15.10	22.50	18.70	1.50	74.00	11.30	33.00
Preferred Stock	11.10	18.10	17.20	0.10	86.00	6.40	24.90

Source: Moody's *Historical Default Rates of Corporate Bond Issuers, 1983–2000.*

Loans have a higher recovery rate than bonds. Senior secured debt usually has a much higher average recovery rate than even senior subordinated debt. Table 4.3 summarizes Moody's data from 1983 to 2000.

The table shows average recovery estimate was 64 percent for senior secured bank loans versus 52.6 percent for senior secured bonds. Loans have a much higher median value of 72 percent versus 53.8 percent, respectively. The standard deviation of the average recovery value was 24.4 percent for senior secured bank loans versus 24.6 percent for senior secured bonds. Due to the high volatility of the recovery values, there is a lot of overlap in the recovery values among these categories as well as all the classes of debt.

In normal trading, loans are more price robust than fixed rate bonds because loans have a floating rate coupon. If the coupon could adjust instantaneously, and if credit spreads remained the same as at the beginning of the loan agreement, the loan would always trade at par. As market rates moved, the loan's coupon would instantly readjust. In reality, there is some lag in the loan coupon, but this market readjustment tends to help even in a default situation where the market coupon readjustment of defaulted bonds adds another element of confusion to the price of defaulted bonds.

A notable exception is corporate bonds with coupons that step-up if the credit of the reference obligor deteriorates, usually reflected by a rating downgrade. This is especially true if the coupon is floating.

The major advantage for the price robustness of loans is that loans are negotiated agreements between banks and the borrower. Loans have a hierarchy. Those secured by current assets have higher average recovery values than loans secured by plant and equipment. The bank may have a longstanding business relationship with the borrower and have access to extensive financial data. Often banks are advisors and bank officers may be on the board of directors of the borrowing institution. Loans are often restructured and have customized workout periods. Loans have an "inside" nature.

Once you've guesstimated the default probability and loss in the event of default (or its complement, the recovery value), the next step is to calculate the expected loss for the issuer. In its simplest form, expected loss is defined by the following formula:

$$\text{Expected Loss} = [\text{Default Probability} \times (1 - \text{Recovery Rate})] \times \text{Loss Exposure}$$

This is an average number, an average expected credit loss. If one wanted to examine a worst-case scenario, one could look at the worst-case default probability and worst-case recovery rate for a given loss exposure to calculate an expected loss.

The International Swap and Derivatives Association (ISDA) has incorporated new successor definitions for bonds that can be substituted into a reference entity pool. There are threshold tests on the size of the issuance to address liquidity issues and rules for substitution. The ISDA Supplement to the 1999 Credit Event Upon Merger allows delivery of convertible bonds in standard CDS contracts. Zero coupon bonds are deliverable in standard CDS contracts, and the supplement clarifies how payable amounts are calculated for zero coupon bonds. Credit Suisse First Boston (CSFB) and Nomura Securities are currently disputing whether convertible bonds are deliverable under older CDS contracts that were written without the Supplement. The new language is an attempt to avoid this type of ambiguity.

Moody's will penalize a synthetic CDO deal, which allows for unlimited delivery of convertible bonds, even though they agree owners of Enron convertible bonds had about the same loss experience as generic bondholders. They envision a scenario in which delivery of convertible bonds will cause a credit protection provider to suffer a greater loss. Zero coupon bonds can also be problematic. The solution is to modify the CDS to eliminate the possibility of delivery of a convertible, but this isn't always possible. An alternative is to allow a fixed percentage, usually 10 percent, into the potential deal pool.

From the rating agency perspective, a CDS can be structured to fit the agency's recovery assumptions. Moody's defines the loss severity as the difference between par and recovery rate. Moody's uses the market value of defaulted instruments about 30 days after default for the recovery rate estimate.

THE DEFAULT PROTECTION SELLER: CREDIT AND CORRELATION

Who is the most desirable credit default protection seller? If prices were the same, a default protection seller with a triple A credit rating—if you can find one—and negative correlation with the asset the credit protection buyer is trying to hedge would be the most desirable. A default protection seller with these characteristics should be the high cost provider, but the current market is inefficient. You'd be hard pressed to find a highly rated entity with the exact criteria you desire, but you'll probably find several suitable providers. There are also unsuitable providers, however.

Theoretically, the premium paid on a CDS should be sensitive to the credit quality of the credit default protection provider. The premium should also be sensitive to the correlation between the protection provider and the reference obligor on which one is buying the credit default protection.

DEFAULT LANGUAGE FOR SOVEREIGN DEBT

The generic credit default market ceases to appear generic after we deviate from the most basic definition of credit default. The market now differentiates between suitable language for a sovereign credit risk versus a corporate credit risk.

For sovereign debt, one reasonable way to define the default event is to use similar language to that in the prospectus for the reference obligations one is trying to hedge. For example, for non-U.S. sovereign dollar denominated bonds, the default is usually defined with some minimum standards to objectively determine default. Conditions usually include the following: materially prejudicial to the bondholders' interests; an acceleration in excess of a high preset amount, for instance, $25 million or equivalent; failure to make payment on public external debt in excess of a high preset amount; declaration of a moratorium of payment of principal or interest on public external debt; or the sovereign's denial of its obligations.

If you are trying to hedge a different sort of sovereign risk, you and your counterparty may want to create your own language. You may wish to include war or coup d'état as a credit event.

DEFAULT LANGUAGE FOR NONSOVEREIGN DEBT: CONTROVERSY AND CDOs

In the fourth quarter of 2000, the credit derivatives dealer community was up in arms about settlement of termination payments on Conseco CDSs. The banking community restructured Conseco loans and triggered a credit event under the ISDA restructuring definition. Delivery in the event of a credit event could be either a bond or a loan. This was common language in credit derivatives documentation.

The credit event was the deferral of the loan's maturity by three months, and this was an allowable event according to ISDA's restructuring definition. The slight extension may have been disadvantageous to the banks in a minor way, but the restructuring also included features very advantageous to the banks: an increased coupon, a new corporate guarantee, and additional covenants in favor of the lenders. The senior unsecured rating was only downgraded to B1, which is not the rating of debt in default or bankruptcy. This is now known as a *soft default*. Moody's did not consider this to be a *diminished financial obligation* or a *distressed exchange* default. The market didn't seem to think that there was any harm done, either. In fact, just the opposite. The restructured loan prices *increased*.

Protection buyers delivered long-dated, deeply discounted bonds—instead of the robustly priced loans—to the credit default protection providers. The long-dated bonds were susceptible to both market risk and credit risk. Furthermore, as we discussed earlier, long-dated bonds often trade at drastically reduced prices to short-dated bonds under workout situations. The price disparity between long-dated bonds and loans was pronounced. The credit default protection providers had to pay the difference between par and the market price of the discounted bonds.

Protection sellers felt burned two ways. They felt the banking community was closer to the Conseco situation. After all, the banks were the loan underwriters. Protection sellers knew that the banks had significant control over the restructuring. Secondly, protection sellers felt that by delivering the deeply discounted bonds, banks that were protection buyers were not acting in good faith.

If counterparties embed a cheapest to deliver option into credit default documentation, the protection seller should get paid for the embedded option. Granted this option is difficult to price, but the protection seller should at least attempt to value it. In the Conseco transactions, most protection sellers were caught completely unaware of their additional basis risk.

Some credit default contracts are now written excluding restructuring as a credit event. Banks hedging loans cannot use those CDOs, however. When banks buy credit default protection against their loan portfolios, restructuring must be specified in the credit default protection contract; otherwise, the banks cannot get regulatory capital relief. The banks in the Conseco transaction that took the short-term opportunity nearly closed the door for themselves for future credit hedging transactions.

To eliminate gaming from the settlement procedure, counterparties can craft their own language for allowable deliverables. Language changes in ISDA contracts have already occurred in response to the Conseco controversy. The Loan Syndications and Trading Association (LSTA) and ISDA have formed a joint working group to advise ISDA's credit derivative documentation group on issues that arise in connection with the physical delivery of a loan as settlement for a credit derivatives transaction.

ISDA introduced new *modified restructuring* language that is used in most U.S. CDS contracts, but not in Europe. (ISDA confirmation language is available from the ISDA web site: www.isda.org.) ISDA introduced language to limit the maturity of deliverable obligations for physically settled swaps after the occurrence of a restructuring event triggered by the credit protection buyer. The maturity of the deliverables is limited to the earlier of 30 months after the restructuring date or the latest final maturity date of any restructured bond or loan. Furthermore, if the restructuring event occurs on a five-year default swap in the first year of the contract, protection buyers would be able to deliver physical securities with maturity dates equivalent to the termination of the swap date, but the limitation cannot be set earlier than the swap termination date. The obligations must be fully transferable, and no bilateral loans can be used to trigger a credit event. The obligations must be multiholder obligations.

When the reference obligations are bonds, modified restructuring is fine. It's trickier when loans are included as reference obligations. The proposed Basel accord on capital adequacy standards calls for some form of restructuring to be recognized in a CDS in order for banks to get regulatory capital relief, and there is no clarity on just how far the language must go to satisfy this requirement.

Moody's has been very vocal about how this rating agency views non-credit related risk introduced by ISDA language. They are clear that they cannot account for this in rating CDO transactions. Their data was never meant to capture this kind of risk. Moody's feels this is a potential conflict of interest or moral hazard risk. The sponsoring bank determines when a loss event has occurred and the bank can control the payout by manipulating the deliverable.

Obligation acceleration is another credit event prone to abuse. Whenever the protection buyer has the right to accelerate, there is the potential for moral hazard. Suppose a bank purchases protection on a loan. Suppose further that the borrower has suffered some credit deterioration, or violated some covenants, but is not in immediate danger of defaulting on any payments. The bank knows it will get all of its money back if it accelerates the loan; it does so and declares a credit event. Then the bank gets bids on the remaining outstanding debt and produces the "cheapest to deliver" (the bond trading at the lowest price) under a CDS in which the bank has bought credit default protection on the borrower. If bonds trade at 80 percent, the bank gets 20 percent of the contract notional amount in loss compensation, but the bank has suffered no loss whatsoever.

Repudiation and moratorium were included in many corporate CDSs, but now are usually dropped. These terms apply to sovereign risk and shouldn't be included in a corporate CDS.

CDO structurers often need deals rated, and Moody's prefers language that differs from ISDA documentation. Particularly in arbitrage CDOs meant to mirror the bond market, rating agency language protects investors in the tranches of CDOs. Wherever possible, it is a good idea for investors in arbitrage CDOs to ask for deals that match Moody's preferences as closely as possible. Buyers of CDO tranches should be especially wary of unrated deals. CDOs, which include only bankruptcy, failure to pay, and modified restructuring give the best protection. Even then, however, there are differences in Moody's preferred language and in language proposed by ISDA. The following are examples:

■ *Bankruptcy*: ISDA allows swap counterparties to terminate early due to credit problems with a counterparty, even before a default occurs. Planning for or considering a bankruptcy filing might be in furtherance of bankruptcy, and can trigger an ISDA default, but would not generally be considered a bankruptcy event by Moody's. This is because ISDA originally meant to protect counterparties in interest rate swaps in which a payment failure can occur even when the counterparty is a worthy credit risk. Here's a scary thought. If you checked with the back office of any interest rate swap desk, you would find several counterparties who have failed to make payments on their swaps. Sometimes the amounts owed are very large. This is usually due to a counterparty back office problem or a miscalculation. Failure to make payment could potentially be viewed as a credit event. Why should an investor in a CDO accept this condition as a potential credit event?

■ *Failure to Pay*: ISDA allows a broader category of reference obligations than Moody's recommends. Moody's also recommends higher payment thresholds.

■ *Restructuring*: Moody's preferred restructuring is defined to be the result of deterioration of the obligor's creditworthiness or financial condition. Distressed exchange involves a *diminished financial obligation* or exchange that helps the borrower avoid default. Moody's does not consider some voluntary restructurings credit events.

There are broad implications to the CDO market. Synthetic collateralized loan obligations (CLOs) that have this embedded language risk in the credit default documentation may have to be re-examined. Newly structured arbitrage CDOs should incorporate language that serves the interest of potential investors. Figure 4.5 tracks some of the recent language changes with respect to credit events.

When the deal is a CDO of CDOs with asset backed security (ABS) underlyings, special language is required. When does a default occur, what is deliverable, and how is the loss given default determined? The definitions may vary depending on the underlying assets.

Old Paradigm

New Paradigm

Old Standard ISDA Swap Confirmation

- Bankruptcy
- Failure to pay
- Obligation acceleration*
- Repudiation or moratorium*
- Restructuring

Menu of Additional Events
- Downgrade
- Credit event upon merger
- War
- Coup d'état
- Obligor is past due for more than 90 days on any credit obligation (Basel proposal)

Recommended CDO Credit Events

- Bankruptcy
- Failure to pay
- *Modified* restructuring or no restructuring
- Additional events for sovereigns including repudiation and moratorium
- Special definitions for ABS

*Contracts entered into after 2002 usually exclude these definitions.

FIGURE 4.5   Credit Event Definitions for Rated Arbitrage CDOs

COMMENTS ON CDS PRICES

Credit default protection should logically trade near the spread of the reference security to a risk-free asset. For instance, if a 10-year maturity bond trades at a spread of 100 basis points (bps) to the 10-year U.S. treasury, the amount of spread due to credit risk is about 100 bps. Some of the 100 bps may be due to liquidity. CDSs, however, tend to trade at a level that is benchmarked to the asset swap market. This is because most banks benchmark their funding costs based on a spread to London InterBank Offered Rate (LIBOR) and look at the net spread they can earn on a given credit relative to their funding costs.

Most modelers of credit derivatives build models to predict the possible payoffs. The simplest model is little more than a binomial tree with a few key variables to predict the potential payoff under preset scenarios. The result will be modified for soft variables including supply and demand.

Key inputs include the following:

- Credit quality of the obligor (or obligors in the case of baskets).
- Credit quality of the default protection provider.
- Correlation among the obligor(s).
- Correlation of the obligor(s) with the credit protection provider in the CDS contract.
- Probability of default (and volatility of the data) of the obligor(s).
- Probability of default (and volatility of the data) of the credit default protection provider.
- Joint probabilities of default in the event that the obligor(s) and credit default protection provider are correlated.
- Recovery rate in the event of default of an obligor.
- Recovery rate in the event of default of the credit protection provider (replacement value of the CDS).
- The leverage of the structure.
- Maturity of the deal.
- Settlement provisions in the event of default.
- Supply and demand for the credit default protection.
- Economic research that may change my view of the credit quality.
- Urgency of the need to reduce my credit exposure.
- Special documentation considerations.
- If applicable, Bank for International Settlements (BIS) risk weighting of the default protection seller.

Supply and demand often drives CDS prices, and even the best models cannot accurately predict the effects. For example, we know that new issuance of convertible bonds creates demand for credit default protection on the issuer. In December 2001, Fiat brought a $2.2 billion convertible bond issue to market. The bonds paid a coupon of 3.25 percent, and were convertible bonds into common shares of General Motors (GM). Arbitrageurs bought protection in anticipation of this issuance, and the price of protection in the form of CDSs increased from about 130 bps to about 190 bps in just over 1 week. Cash instruments were locked up in buy-and-hold portfolios, and their spreads remained the same. This caused a dramatic widening in the spread between CDS levels and the spread of Fiat fixed income securities in the same maturity (e.g., the benchmark Euro Fiat issue maturing in 2006). The *positive basis* widened.

The effects are not wholly predictable, however. As we saw earlier, convertibles often have short-dated puts or maturities earlier than five years. The most actively traded and most liquid CDSs have five-year maturities. When arbitrageurs buy large amounts of protection in the short end of the curve, for example, the two-year area, the CDS curve tends to invert for this reference credit. Furthermore, it is often possible to buy a normal five-year par asset swap, purchase five-year credit default protection, and lock-in a positive spread. In other words, one can put on a *negative basis trade*.

TOTAL RATE OF RETURN SWAPS (TOTAL RETURN SWAPS)

Total rate of return swaps (TRORS) are also called *total return swaps* (TRS). I usually refer to these transactions as TRORS to highlight a minor distinction that may occur in the cash flows of these transactions, which we will discuss in a minute. For now, let's define a TRORS.

A TRORS is primarily used as a financing tool, but it is also a complete hedge of market and credit risk of an asset. A TRORS is a bilateral financial contract between a total return payer and a total return receiver. The total return payer pays the total rate of return of a reference security and receives a form of payment from the receiver of the total rate of return. The receiver's payment is usually a floating rate payment. The payment is usually a spread to a floating rate index such as U.S. dollar (USD), LIBOR, or Euribor; but any index can be used, including a fixed rate index, an equity index, or a bond performance index. The reference assets themselves can be indexes, corporate bonds, sovereign debt, bank debt, mortgage-backed securities (MBSs), loans (term or revolver), equities, real estate receivables,

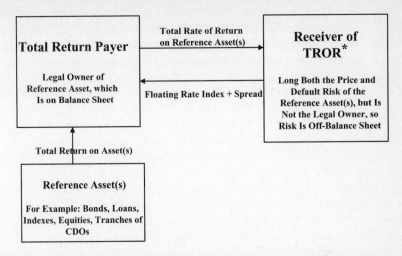

*Receiver of the TROR hedges both the price and default risk of the reference asset for the legal owner. Price risk can be due to credit spread widening, credit downgrade, or changes in market levels of interest rates.

FIGURE 4.6 Generic TRORS

lease receivables, or commodities. Virtually any asset can be a reference asset in a TRORS.

Figure 4.6 shows a generic schematic of the cash flows of a TRORS.

Notice that the timing of the reference asset(s) cash flows do not have to match the payment of the total rate of return to the total rate of return receiver. For instance, a particular reference asset may have a monthly coupon, but the payments on the TRORS may be set for quarterly periods or even annual payments. This means that the coupons must be reinvested according to a pre-agreement between the receiver and payer. There may be some reinvestment risk of the cash flows. Likewise, settlement structure in the event of default may introduce some cash flow mismatch. To highlight this point, I refer to these transactions as TRORS. Others may prefer to say TRS. Use whichever terminology resonates best for you, as long as you are clear about the terms of the transaction.

The *total rate of return payer* is the legal owner of the reference asset(s), and holds the reference asset(s) on the balance sheet. The total rate of return payer has created a short position in the market risk, and a short position in the credit risk of the reference asset(s) until the maturity of the swap.

The *total rate of return receiver*, also called the *investor*, is not the legal owner of the reference asset(s). The TRORS is an off-balance sheet transaction for the receiver who has a synthetic long position in the market risk and a synthetic long position in the credit risk of the reference asset(s). The TRORS documentation is negotiable, and often the total rate of return receiver will want the option to purchase the reference asset at the then prevailing market price at the maturity of the swap. Note that this feature is independent of settlement structure in the event that there is a default of the reference asset(s).

In the event of a reference asset(s) default, the total rate of return receiver makes the total rate of return payer "whole" for the market risk and credit risk of the reference asset. The total rate of return receiver makes a net payment of the difference between the price of the reference asset(s) at the beginning of the transaction or at the latest price reset if this comes later, and the price of the reference asset(s) at the time of default. Alternatively, the total rate of return receiver may take delivery of the defaulted reference asset and pay the initial price or last reset price, if later, of the reference asset(s) to the total rate of return payer. This settlement terminates any obligation to the other party, and the TRORS for the relevant reference asset(s) terminates.

Just like CDSs, the documentation for a TRORS is negotiable. The observations we made earlier regarding ISDA documentation with respect to rated CDOs applies for TRORS. We want to be careful how we specify credit default events if we want to use a TRORS in a rated CDO.

PRICING TRORS ON LEVERED CDO TRANCHES

There is no standard method for pricing TRORS. Let's focus on the pricing from the point of view of a bank that is providing financing for a counterparty. The bank buys an asset and pays the total rate of return to the counterparty in exchange for periodic payments of a spread over LIBOR on the notional amount of the asset.

One reasonable lower bound for pricing is the rate the bank would charge to provide an unfunded revolver of the same maturity to this counterparty. This seems to be the absolute lower bound, however. An unfunded revolver is essentially a standby loan. The loan will probably have a lower expected loss than the asset used as the reference obligation in the TRORS. Furthermore, a revolver will usually reflect relationship pricing.

The upper bound is whatever the market will bear. Generic TRORS tend to trade at a level that allows the bank providing the financing to earn a positive spread to its funding costs and an adequate return on economic and regulatory capital. The counterparty receiving the financing will compare the offered level for the financing to calculate the all-in return on the transaction. The TRORS should be comparable with the return on floating assets or asset swaps of similar credits (although funded obligations should trade at a premium because the counterparty is using much less capital and getting an off-balance sheet transaction and a leveraged return). TRORS have been done on MBSs, for instance, in the range of LIBOR + 10 to LIBOR + 25 bps in maturities of 3 months to 5 years. These are high credit quality assets. BBB assets have been financed at rates from LIBOR + 25 to LIBOR + 50 bps for maturities under 3 years. It is difficult to generalize. Pricing varies with supply and demand factors. TRORS for low spreads must be done in large size to make the documentation and capital considerations work for the bank providing the financing. Often, outside counterparties will attempt to arbitrage the bank's various financing desks: the TRS desk and the traditional financing desk.

The upper bound is whatever the market will bear. One hedge fund representative, who asked me about market pricing of TRS on mezzanine tranches of CDOs, felt the pricing was too high for his financing on a TRS he was offered by one of my competitors. I didn't work for an institution that offered a TRS on these products, but pointed out that there was a limited supply of banks that would take his credit, and they would charge a premium to take his credit risk. He was very irritated with my response.

"Don't fulminate. *Negotiate*," I advised.

"How do I do that?" he fulminated.

When there are a limited number of counterparties, and they are essentially offering you financing, you may have few options for negotiation. The best one can do is to prepare the best case possible.

The first step is to try to determine where the market is in general for the type of transaction you want to do. Mezzanine tranches of CDOs can be structure-specific, but at least try to determine the market for mezzanine tranches of the same underlying collateral. There will be a limited number of suppliers, and it is useful to get to know them all. If the suppliers will not supply information on pricing in the absence of a live transaction, then it is time to consider how one would look at the upper bound of a more generic TRORS.

To determine the market value of any security, there are certain rules of value. Everything trades off the next most certain bond or asset. For a TRORS, one would look at floating assets or assets of a similar credit. Compare the potential return on unfunded equity transactions relative to the TRORS on the mezzanine tranche. Compare the potential return on an equity transaction in which a hedge fund posts treasury collateral and earns the excess spread on a portfolio of high yield bonds overcollateralized with the injection of the treasury collateral. We'll discuss these equity transactions in a later chapter on equity structures.

This is still a blind market for mezzanine TRORS pricing, so in the end, the hedge fund will have to decide whether the return for the credit risk is worth it, relative to its traditional investments.

TRORS VERSUS REPOS

Both TRORS and repurchase agreements are used as CDO structuring tools. Why do a TRORS instead of buying an asset? The reason is that the receiver of the TRORS gets *leverage*. Because of leverage, hedge funds like to be the receivers in TRORS.

Repurchase agreements are also a type of financing. What is the difference between a TRORS and a repurchase agreement? In a repurchase agreement, also called a *repo,* the owner of an asset, the "seller," *repos* or sells the asset to a "buyer," and agrees to repurchase the asset at a fixed price on a fixed date. The asset seller agrees to pay the buyer a prenegotiated rate of interest, the repurchase rate, also called the *repo rate.* The "buyer" lends the "seller" money for the period of the agreement at the repo rate implied by the difference between the asset sell price and the asset repurchase price. At the maturity of the agreement, the "seller" is obligated to repurchase the securities at the prespecified repurchase price.

In a TRORS, the total rate of return receiver is not obligated to purchase the reference asset at the maturity of the transaction. There is no pre-agreed fixed price for the reference asset at the maturity of the transaction. The TRORS receiver is obligated only to exchange payments based on the market value of the reference asset at the maturity of the transaction.

When the maturity of the TRORS is much less than that of the reference asset(s), the price risk due to market value fluctuations in the absence of default can be substantial. Some TRORS receivers, the protection sellers, will not participate in mismatched maturity transactions. TRORS receivers, who do engage in these transactions, like the ability to invest in a reference asset for a shorter period of time than is available in the market, and they are happy to take the additional element of market risk.

How do we determine market price? In between the inception and the maturity—due to default or expiration—of the TRORS, the receiver may be content with prices provided by the seller. In the event of default of the reference asset, or if the TRORS matures before the reference asset, market value is often determined by a dealer poll. The calculation agent calls three to five market makers—the names are often prespecified in the documentation—in the reference asset and takes the average price. The calculation agent may be one of the dealers offering a price. An auction method is preferable for very non-liquid assets that are difficult to price. Because of the market value risk, the receiver of the TRORS usually retains the option to take physical delivery of the reference asset and pay the difference between the initial price (or last reset price, if later) and the dealer poll price or auction price.

MORAL HAZARD WITH BANK LOAN REFERENCE ASSETS

TRSs have the same moral hazard risk as CDSs when it comes to bank loans. If a bank originates a loan and is paying the total return of an on-balance sheet loan, how much financial information is the bank required to disclose to its protection seller counterparties? Does the bank have an obligation to the original borrower to keep confidential its knowledge of the corporation's nonpublicly disclosed financial information? Does the lending bank have insider information, an unfair advantage over its counterparties? Does the lending bank have control over the credit event trigger?

The bank, as legal owner of the loan, retains voting rights when the bank pays the total rate of return on a loan or when a bank buys credit default protection on a loan. There is usually a "gentleman's agreement" that the bank will vote according to the wishes of the total rate of return receiver, or the credit default protection provider. If the bank cannot contact the counterparty, however, it is usually assumed that the bank will vote with the majority of the other lenders. This may or may not be in the best interests of the bank's counterparty. There is the further issue that the lenders may have better information than the counterparty, which may influence the majority vote.

CDS VERSUS TRORS

Besides the difference in applications described above, it seems the chief difference between a CDS and a TRORS is that in addition to default risk, a TRORS also hedges market risk. Some regulators have correctly pointed out that while a CDS will hedge credit default risk, it will not exactly hedge credit spread widening risk, completely confer the benefits of credit spread narrowing, completely hedge credit quality deterioration, completely confer the benefit of credit quality improvement, or hedge other changes in value due to other market risk factors. For this reason, some regulators will give only partial regulatory capital relief, if any, for bonds and loans hedged with a CDS.

It seems reasonable to hedge the credit risk of investments held to maturity with a CDS. It also seems reasonable to recognize the CDS provides at least a partial hedge of credit migration and credit spread moves, because CDS spreads tend to move in tandem with these events. There is no current consensus on regulatory relief across venues.

CHAPTER 5

Cash versus Synthetic Arbitrage CDOs

The chief cause of the phenomenal growth in the collateralized debt obligation (CDO) market is the use of synthetics in both arbitrage and balance sheet CDO structures. Other reasons include new structures, regulatory capital arbitrage, economic effects, and organizational idiosyncrasies. Let's examine some of these reasons by comparing and contrasting the peculiarities of a managed cash arbitrage CDO and a managed synthetic arbitrage CDO during every step of deal creation.

COMPARISON OF MANAGED ARBITRAGE CDO FEATURES: CASH VERSUS SYNTHETIC DEALS

Both deals are cash flow deals. This means that the assets themselves, not the total return generated from active management of the portfolio, are the primary source of repayment of the liabilities. The liabilities are the deal expenses and tranche payments.

We'll discuss balance sheet CDOs and special regulatory considerations later. I start with the arbitrage CDO market since most of the key economic considerations are exemplified by this comparison. This initial comparison of cash and synthetic arbitrage CDOs uses senior unsecured bonds and generic credit derivatives as assets, respectively. I choose to use this comparison because most people are familiar with bond cash flows. Of course, a credit derivatives contract can reference any type of underlying asset, but the structural challenges of the credit derivatives contracts are most easily understood when compared with a well-understood benchmark instrument. Figures 5.1 and 5.2 show a typical structure of a managed cash arbitrage CDO and a managed synthetic arbitrage CDO.

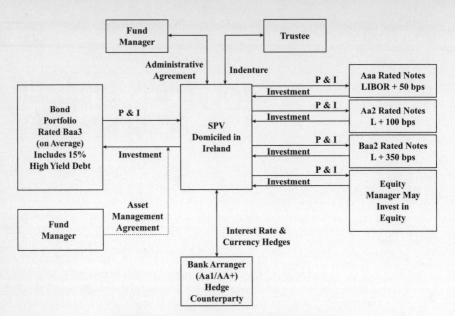

FIGURE 5.1 Managed Cash Arbitrage CDO

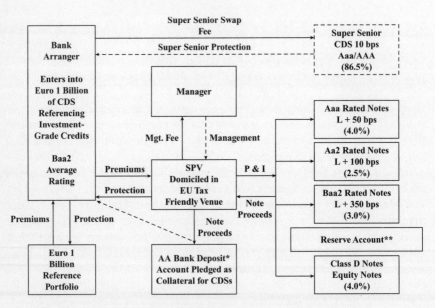

* Subject to price restrictions and Arranger Bank maintaining a minimum AA− rating.
** Excess Spread and accumulated loss tests trigger cash trapping.

FIGURE 5.2 Managed Synthetic Arbitrage CDO

It is redundant to say the cash arbitrage CDO is managed, because that is always the case. However, synthetic arbitrage CDOs can be either managed or unmanaged, and in our example, it is managed.

The tranching of the cash and synthetic CDOs looks similar but has important differences. The percentages of the same-rated tranches are different. The portfolio of the cash deal has an average Baa3 rating, and the synthetic portfolio has an average rating of Baa2. The synthetic deal does not have a market risk hedge counterparty. On the other hand, the synthetic deal has a super senior tranche, and the cash deal doesn't.

Both deals have an overall investment grade rating, and both are Euro 500 million in size. *One key advantage of synthetic arbitrage CDOs versus cash arbitrage CDOs is that it is easier to bring a synthetic deal in larger total deal size.* As we will see later when we talk about deal economics, there are economies of scale in bringing a deal to market. In this example, we're comparing deals of the same size so we can look at the relative economic effects due to differences in tranching.

Several steps in the process of structuring a CDO will occur during overlapping time frames. The following summary of key steps is in the general order in which they occur.

THE ARRANGER AND THE MANAGER

Bank arrangers look for a good track record versus fixed income benchmarks when choosing the manager. They also look for a name with a high degree of market recognition, and portfolio managers with longevity at the firm. A manager's willingness to retain part or all of equity and mezzanine tranches is a factor. Prior success with CDO management is an enormous plus in selection of a manager. Managers with these qualities have a long line of investment banks courting them to do deals. For synthetic securitizations, knowledge of the credit default swap (CDS) market is a plus, especially when the rating agencies do their due diligence.

Managers have their own criteria when choosing to work with a bank arranger on an arbitrage deal. Managers will want to know the proposed management fee and will also want to know the percentage of the fee that is senior in the deal cash flow waterfall. Managers also look for other qualities from a bank arranger. These are:

- Successful prior experience in closing and distributing managed CDOs.
- Strong distribution capability, especially for mezzanine and equity pieces.
- Strong trading capabilities.

- Willingness to absorb warehouse funding and hedge costs.
- Willingness to provide a liquidity facility for the deal.
- Ability to provide multiple hedge choices at various prices.
- Responsiveness in providing market information and mark-to-market information for the portfolio.
- Deal modeling assistance.

Some of the better-known CDO managers include AXA, Barclays Capital, The Blackstone Group, Mass Mutual, Merrill Lynch Investment Management, New England Asset Management, Pimco, Prudential Investment, TCW, WAMCO, and the Zais Group.

Just about every fund manager, however, wants to manage CDOs to earn the 40 to 50 basis points (bps) per annum fees for a cash deal or the 12 to 25 bps per annum fees for a synthetic deal. Just as the quality of fund managers varies, so does the ability to manage CDOs. The ability to manage a portfolio and the ability to manage a CDO don't always go hand in hand, but both are necessary for successful CDO management.

In our examples, the managers will both take 51 percent of the equity investment.

MANDATE AGREEMENT

The manager and arranger will agree on broad general terms in a mandate letter. This letter includes an estimate of the deal economics and the deal timeline. At a minimum, both parties will usually agree not to engage in transactions that will create a conflict of interest for the contemplated CDO. Often the deal type is given as an exclusive for a fixed time period, especially on the part of the manager. It is not uncommon for arrangers to work on several deals at the same time. This poses no problem if the arranger has adequate staff and can handle the trading and distribution of the deals in the pipeline.

DEAL ASSEMBLY

Around the time the mandate agreement is signed, portfolio selection will begin. If it hasn't been done already, the arranger and manager will choose a law firm to draft documents. The arranger will usually propose the venue and administration for the special purpose entity (SPE). Either the arranger or manager will nominate the trustee, custodian, and reporting accountants.

If third party credit enhancement is contemplated, the arranger may contact monoline insurance companies around this time.

The arranger may begin premarketing the deal, especially if the arranger needs to place any equity or mezzanine tranches. In our examples, the arranger will sell 49 percent of the equity and all of the mezzanine tranches. Feedback from potential investors may persuade the arranger and manager to change certain features of the structure.

The arranger will begin modeling the deal. The arranger usually provides the analytics for marketing the deal and for negotiating ratings with agency ratings. The manager will use portfolio management software to monitor the deal on an ongoing basis. The arranger and manager may share certain analytical tools so investors and trading desks can support the CDO throughout the life of the deal.

Document drafting begins now, including the warehousing agreement (not required for a synthetic deal), management agreement, and a very preliminary deal prospectus.

CDS LANGUAGE FOR THE SYNTHETIC CDO

Crafting the CDS language using state-of-the-art interdealer language gives the CDO investor the optimal advantage. In this case, state-of-the-art means language that gives the maximum benefit to the credit protection seller. The credit protection seller is the SPE from which the investors buy notes, so the investor ultimately benefits from better language. From the point of view of the CDO tranche investor, this language should avoid unnecessary technical defaults.

Credit events include only 3 triggers: bankruptcy, failure to pay (with a Euro equivalent minimum of 1 million), and modified restructuring. The default trigger also includes a hurdle of a Euro equivalent of U.S. dollar (USD) 10 million. The language includes the supplemental successor definition.

Allowable deliverables are senior unsecured debt, except for a potential allowance of 10 percent of subordinated bank paper.

The investors take no currency risk, since the basis for recovery is calculated from an original Euro amount of 10 million, and all payments are in Euros.

SELECTING THE PORTFOLIO AND IMPACT ON RATING

This may be the most important part of any arbitrage CDO. A static arbitrage CDO doesn't have a manager, and will be rated on diversification of the portfolio, among other criteria. Most of the early static deals were unrated, but today many static deals are rated. Managed deals are almost always rated, and that is the case for the deals in our example.

Whether or not a deal should be managed is a very controversial issue. Investors are polarized and vehement in their opinions.

Diversification is important, and rating agencies view this as a key input to the ultimate credit rating. Some investors feel this rigid thinking may obscure the value of a good manager in a deal. A competent manager may avoid obligors and entire sectors that may have systemic risk. That's what a manager is paid to do. Furthermore, a competent manager may find relative value in a sector he knows well, but avoid sectors about which he knows little. This is contrary to diversification, but often key to avoiding loss in value or loss due to default. Why should a manager diversify into sectors about which he knows nothing?

Moody's will penalize a deal if a manager doesn't have a good track record. Moody's will not give a deal credit, however, if the manager has a great track record. There is no way in the rating framework to factor in the possibility of a lower portfolio diversity score due to competent management choice.

On the other hand, many investors scorn managed deals. They feel managers may introduce incompetence for a fee, or even worse, may introduce moral hazard when the manager has a claim to equity cash flows. Even when these investors are being charitable, they sound harsh. They feel that even at their best, managers wouldn't have dodged a bullet like Enron or Railtrack. These investors feel they shouldn't pay extra for managed deals. Instead, they prefer to have input to the initial selection of the portfolio for a static deal.

If views are this polarized, one might turn to ratings to provide accurate guidance. One might think that rating agency criteria will at least be objective and will produce results that can be replicated across deals. But this would be a mistake, as we'll see later when we look at rating agency criteria.

For cash deals, the arranger's trading desk provides feedback on the availability of bonds. For an investment grade cash deal, around 25 percent noninvestment grade debt may be allowed in order to improve the arbitrage. It is difficult to find rated European high-yield debt, however, so managers will often look to the U.S. market for high yield bonds. If the deal is Euro-centric, investment grade bonds may be difficult to find in the size desired by the manager, and diversification is often difficult. Most of the European investment grade bond issuance for reasonably good spreads is concentrated in the telecom and automotive sectors. Bonds are sometimes difficult to find in the U.S. market, but to a much lesser degree.

CDSs can reference virtually any obligation of a desired reference credit. The arranger doesn't have to scour the market for a specific bond issue that may be tied up in a reference portfolio as often happens for a cash deal. It is much easier to source a portfolio of credits using CDSs than bonds.

RATING CRITERIA AND RESTRICTIONS

Structurers impose portfolio standards in an attempt to protect the integrity of the deal tranches and maintain deal ratings. Moody's, Standard and Poor's (S&P), and Fitch International Bank Classification Agency (IBCA) issue long-term credit ratings for various corporate and government credits. A summary of their ratings indicators is given in Table 5.1.

Credit ratings in the lower portion of Table 5.1 are considered below investment grade. This means that a Moody's rating below Baa3, an S&P rating below BBB−, and a Fitch IBCA rating below BBB− are considered

TABLE 5.1 Summary of Ratings Indicators

Long-Term Credit Ratings		
Moody's	S&P	Fitch IBCA
Aaa	AAA	AAA
Aa1	AA+	AA+
Aa2	AA−	AA−
Aa3	AA−	AA−
A1	A+	A+
A2	A−	A−
A3	A−	A−
Baa1	BBB+	BBB+
Baa2	BBB−	BBB−
Baa3	BBB−	BBB−
Ba1	BB+	BB+
Ba2	BB−	BB−
Ba3	BB−	BB−
B1	B+	B+
B2	B	B
B3	B−	B−
Caa1	CCC+	CCC+
Caa2	CCC−	CCC−
Caa3	CCC−	CCC−
Ca	CC	CC
C	C	C
	D	D

below investment grade by each of the respective rating agencies. Ratings at or above those levels are considered investment grade by each of the respective rating agencies.

It would seem logical that the rating agency ratings can be directly mapped onto one another, but they cannot. It is important to note that the rating agencies often do not agree on the quality of a rating assigned by another rating agency. For instance, a reference entity considered to be investment grade by S&P or Fitch IBCA may not be considered investment grade by Moody's. Ratings assigned by the various agencies are almost always within a couple of notches of each other, but this isn't always the case. In addition, some entities, especially in Europe, do not have ratings by any of the rating agencies.

CDO structuring makes the rating agency issues even more interesting. For instance, Moody's and Fitch IBCA may supply ratings on cash flow structures for which S&P will refuse to provide a rating, because it doesn't fit into the S&P framework. For example, S&P will not rate raw equity cash flows, no matter how robust.

One would think that rating agencies would at least be internally consistent. But that isn't necessarily so. Even within the same rating agency, portfolio tests and restrictions may vary by deal, and some deals are better protected than others. Different structurers within a rating agency may choose different stress scenarios when evaluating cash flows for an ultimate rating, for instance.

The rating agencies also use different modeling approaches. Each of the rating agencies publishes information about their data and models, and the magnitude of the differences from the varying approaches differ by deal type and collateral. To a limited extent, it is possible to arbitrage the rating agencies. For instance, one might tranche a synthetic corporate deal using S&P methodology because it results in less subordination to get an AAA-rated tranche than Moody's methodology.

Many investors prefer deals that are rated by at least two rating agencies, but many synthetic CDOs have been issued with a rating by only one agency or even with no rating whatsoever.

The various rating agencies have slightly different industry classifications. Moody's first introduced this concept and has classifications for 33 different industries. Bloomberg lists this information when one looks up an obligor's bond by the Committee on Uniform Securities Identification Procedures (CUSIP) number. Each obligor can be mapped to the appropriate industry classification, and the relevant rating agency may be consulted when there is doubt. Table 5.2 gives an example of the industry summary for the cash arbitrage CDO.

TABLE 5.2 Industry Summary for Cash Arbitrage CDO

Moody's Industry Codes	Moody's Industry Designations	Number of Obligors	Obligors as % of Total
1	Aerospace and Defense	0	0
2	Automobile	1	2
3	Banking	3	6
4	Beverage, Food, and Tobacco	5	10
5	Buildings and Real Estate	5	10
6	Chemicals, Plastics, and Rubber	1	2
7	Containers, Packaging & Glass	2	4
8	Personal & Nondurable Consumer Products (Mfg Only)	0	0
9	Diversified / Conglomerate Manufacturing	2	4
10	Diversified / Conglomerate Service	0	0
11	Diversified Natural Resources, Precious Metals & Minerals	0	0
12	Ecological	0	0
13	Electronics	1	2
14	Finance	4	8
15	Farming & Agriculture	0	0
16	Grocery	3	6
17	Healthcare, Education & Childcare	2	4
18	Home & Office Furnishings, Housewares & Durable Consumer	1	2
19	Hotels, Motels, Inns, and Gaming	0	0
20	Insurance	0	0
21	Leisure, Amusement, Motion Pictures, Entertainment	3	6
22	Machinery (Nonagriculture, Nonconstruction, Nonelectronic)	1	2
23	Mining, Steel, Iron, and Nonprecious Metals	0	0
24	Oil and Gas	2	4
25	Personal, Food & Misc. Services	0	0
26	Printing, Publishing, and Broadcasting	0	0
27	Cargo Transport	2	4
28	Retail Stores	0	0
29	Telecommunications	4	8
30	Textiles & Leather	3	6
31	Personal Transportation	0	0
32	Utilities	4	8
33	Broadcasting & Entertainment	1	2
	Total	50	100%

TABLE 5.3 Diversity Score for Number of Obligors in the Same Industry

Number of Firms in Same Industry	Diversity Score
1	1.00
2	1.50
3	2.00
4	2.33
5	2.67
6	3.00
7	3.25
8	3.50
9	3.75
10	4.00
>10	Individually Determined

After the obligors have been mapped to an industry, one uses Table 5.3 to calculate the portfolio diversity score.

The initial diversity score for our cash arbitrage CDO is 33.8. The concentration by individual reference obligation is also important. In our cash asset portfolio, the initial concentration per obligor is 2 percent, and the maximum concentration per obligor allowed is 2 percent.

Our cash managed arbitrage CDO invests in a portfolio with an average investment grade rating of Baa2, but is allowed to have up to 15 percent high yield assets in the portfolio and up to 10 percent asset backed securities (ABS). Unlike synthetic CDOs, for cash arbitrage CDOs, a percentage of high yield is almost always necessary for the cash arbitrage to work. There are further restrictions. The high yield securities must have a rating of at least BB−, and the ABS must have a rating of at least BBB−. No emerging market credits are allowed in this particular portfolio. The lower volatility of defaults for investment grade collateral on most of the pool, combined with skilled management, should offer more stable equity ("first loss") returns relative to CDOs with only high yield collateral. The hope is that this deal will offer good relative value for the risk versus cash managed deals that invest exclusively in high yield collateral.

Default volatility for single B assets is nearly *10 times* the default volatility of BBB assets. Although the cash arbitrage CDO is investment grade, it includes high yield collateral. The manager must *barbell* the portfolio by including higher rated investment grade assets to get an average rating of investment grade. The lower rated assets contribute to higher default volatility for at least a portion of the portfolio. Figure 5.3 illustrates how default volatility exponentially increases as one goes down the credit spectrum.

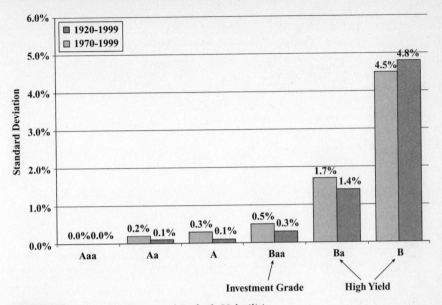

FIGURE 5.3 Moody's Historical Default Volatilities
Source: Historical Default Rates of Corporate Bond Issuers, 1920–1999; Moody's Investors Service, 2000.

The cash arbitrage CDO's initial portfolio has a Moody's *weighted average rating factor,* or *WARF,* of 319, which falls between the Baa1 and Baa2 band of 260 to 360. The manager must maintain a minimum average rating of Baa3 (equivalent to an S&P rating of BBB−) throughout the life of the deal. This means the maximum Moody's target WARF band is 360 to 610, with a maximum WARF of 610. Our deals are rated by Moody's only, but it is important to keep in mind that rating conventions vary by rating agency and rating factors vary between Moody's and Fitch. Table 5.4 shows the rating factor conventions for Moody's and Fitch.

At purchase, the minimum allowable rating is Ba3, but only 25 percent of the assets can be rated below Baa3. Due to downgrade, 5 percent of the assets can be rated below Ba3. The initial portfolio rating distribution is as shown in Table 5.5.

Notice that the S&P ratings are largely irrelevant, because only Moody's is rating the deal. Nonetheless, they are included here because we allowed for 5 percent of the deal to include obligors that are not rated by Moody's, but are rated by S&P. The obligor could be rated by S&P, or by both S&P and Fitch, and still be eligible for the 5 percent inclusion. Moody's maps the rating to a Moody's rating. Usually Moody's does this by simply deducting two notches from the exogenous rating agency's rating.

TABLE 5.4 Moody's and Fitch Rating Factors

Moody's		Fitch	
Rating	Factor	Rating	Factor
Aaa	1	AAA	1.30
Aa1	10	AA+	2.00
Aa2	20	AA	2.30
Aa3	40	AA−	3.30
A1	70	A+	4.00
A2	120	A	5.00
A3	180	A−	7.50
Baa1	260	BBB+	10.00
Baa2	360	BBB	14.00
Baa3	610	BBB−	20.00
Ba1	940	BB+	37.00
Ba2	1350	BB	43.50
Ba3	1780	BB−	46.50
B1	2220	B+	50.00
B2	2720	B	52.20
B3	3490	B−	65.00
Caa	6500	CCC	90.00
Ca	1000	CC	100.00
C	1000	C	100.00

The cash arbitrage portfolio must maintain a minimum weighted average spread of 150 bps over Euribor, per the minimum weighted average spread test. Investment is only allowed in entities located in the United States, Canada, or Europe. The maximum exposure to a single country risk is limited to 50 percent of the portfolio, and the maximum exposure to a nonEuro currency (USD) is limited to 40 percent. Maximum exposure to European countries that are not members of the European Union (EU) is limited to 10 percent. There are no criteria for these limits other than the hypothetical cash manager's areas of expertise or modeling sensitivities. For instance, a high concentration of non-EU European countries might influence Moody's to give the deal a lower rating due to concentration in riskier venues. The initial country risk distribution is shown in Table 5.6.

The cash arbitrage portfolio must maintain a minimum diversity score above 30, and as we saw earlier, the initial diversity score is 33.8. The minimum weighted average life is seven years from the issue date. The maximum industry concentration is 12 percent, and only one industry may be at this level. Only 2 obligor industries may be at the 10 percent level; all

TABLE 5.5 Cash Portfolio Ratings Summary

Moody's	#	Notional	%	S&P	#	Notional	%
Aaa	0	—	0	AAA	0	—	0
Aa1	0	—	0	AA+	0	—	0
Aa2	0	—	0	AA	0	—	0
Aa3	1	10,000,000	2	AA−	1	10,000,000	2
A1	2	20,000,000	4	A+	1	10,000,000	2
A2	6	60,000,000	12	A	4	40,000,000	7
A3	8	80,000,000	16	A−	7	70,000,000	13
Baa1	14	140,000,000	28	BBB+	16	160,000,000	39
Baa2	6	60,000,000	12	BBB	4	40,000,000	7
Baa3	5	50,000,000	10	BBB−	6	60,000,000	11
Ba1	2	20,000,000	4	BB+	3	30,000,000	5
Ba2	6	60,000,000	12	BB	3	30,000,000	5
Ba3	0	—	0	BB−	1	20,000,000	4
B1	0	—	0	B+	1	—	0
B2	0	—	0	B	0	—	0
B3	0	—	0	B−	0	—	0
Caa	0	—	0	CCC	0	—	0
Ca	0	—	0	D	0	—	0
NA	0	—	0	NA	3	30,000,000	5
Total	50	500,000,000	100	Total	50	500,000,000	100

Source: All assets are rated by either Moody's or S&P or both.

TABLE 5.6 Geographic Summary for Cash Arbitrage CDO

Country	#	Notional	%
Britain	11	110,000,000	22
Finland	2	20,000,000	4
France	3	30,000,000	6
Germany	3	30,000,000	6
Italy	1	10,000,000	2
Singapore	2	20,000,000	4
Sweden	3	30,000,000	6
Netherlands	5	50,000,000	10
Spain	1	10,000,000	2
United States	19	190,000,000	38
Total	50	500,000,000	100

others must be at a maximum concentration of 8 percent. Maximum exposure to subordinated debt in a corporate structure is 10 percent.

Historically, investment grade collateral has both a lower default rate and lower volatility of defaults than high yield collateral. The synthetic managed arbitrage CDO uses exclusively investment grade collateral. This should offer an advantage versus the cash deal.

A look at the Moody's 5-year idealized loss rates shown in Figure 5.4 illustrates this point.

The synthetic arbitrage deal manager can invest in investment grade assets, but may hold up to 5 percent of the portfolio in assets rated below BBB− due to downgrades. The assets must be matched off or liquidated if the rating falls below BB−, since no assets rated below BB− are allowed in the portfolio. A maximum of only 5 percent may be nonrated by Moody's. The portfolio may take the risk of subordinated bank debt, but only up to a limit of 10 percent, and no corporate subordinated debt is allowed. No asset-backed assets are allowed, because our hypothetical manager has no expertise in ABS.

The synthetic arbitrage deal starts out with a WARF of 236, which is between a Baa1 and an A3 rating. The minimum weighted average spread test is only 90 bps. The manager must maintain a minimum average rating of Baa1 to Baa2 throughout the life of the deal. The Moody's minimum allowable WARF is 290 (between Baa1 and Baa2). At the deal inception, the diversity score is 45, and the minimum allowable diversity score is 40. Industry concentration is limited to a maximum of 10 percent, and only 2 industries may be at this level. All other industries have a maximum concentration limit of 8 percent. There are further restrictions on the maximum

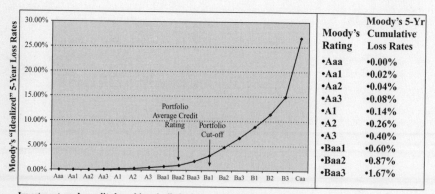

Investment grade credits have historically had very low cumulative loss rates.

FIGURE 5.4 Moody's "Idealized" 5-Year Loss Rates
Source: Moody's Investors Service.

country exposure of 35 percent, no emerging market—defined in this example as rated below A– and/or gross domestic product (GDP) per capita less than 17,000 Euros—exposure is allowed. No corporate subordinated debt is allowed, but up to 10 percent subordinated bank debt is allowed. Each CDS initially has a 5-year maturity from the issue date, but subsequent CDS may be entered into to match the final maturity of the CDO.

SUBSTITUTION AND REINVESTMENT CRITERIA

Notice that the minimum weighted average spread test for the cash deal is higher than for the synthetic deal. For cash deals, there will also be a minimum spread requirement for assets that are eligible for reinvestment during the reinvestment period.

For the synthetic deal, substitution and reinvestment of recovery value is usually allowed, and the minimum spread test is equal to the average portfolio spread at the deal inception. The deal manager may substitute up to 10 percent of the portfolio per annum, but there is no limit for credit-impaired substitutions. All substitutions must be rated investment grade by Moody's or S&P (up to 5 percent total, although the deal itself is only rated by Moody's). Substitutions can be made to a lower rated name if the name has a positive or stable credit watch outlook.

WAREHOUSING ASSETS

Usually no warehousing agreement is needed for synthetic securitizations. Under normal conditions, hedging or funding is required. For this example, we'll use an all Euro synthetic deal. The warehouse is the credit derivatives trading desk, because the speed of assembling assets is much greater than for a cash deal. The warehousing period for cash deals is usually 2 to 6 weeks for an investment grade arbitrage collateral bond obligation (CBO). Either the manager or the arranger must provide funding and absorb hedge costs.

Structured product-backed CDOs usually require a longer warehousing period than even high yield transactions, often as long as 2 to 3 months with a further ramp-up period of 2 to 3 months, because it is so difficult to assemble the necessary collateral. The overall market is smaller, and the individual issue sizes are smaller. Analysis of structured products is also more difficult, since it is deal specific. The exception to this long incubation period is when the structured products are in a bank's investment portfolio, but that isn't the case for our deal. The arranger of the cash deal sources assets from the market at the direction of the manager.

PRICING AND CLOSING

Pricing usually occurs within a week of the closing period. The closing date defines the end of the warehousing period, and the special purpose vehicle (SPV) is the owner of the bonds. The SPV purchases the collateral at the arranger's acquisition price.

RAMPING-UP THE PORTFOLIO

Ramp-up is the period in which the remaining required portfolio assets are acquired. Some assets can be very difficult to source. For a cash deal, the ramp-up period can be 4 to 6 weeks or more. For a CDO backed by ABS (including tranches of CBOs), the ramp-up period may last several months. There is a danger with hard-to-find high yield and highly leveraged loan deals in particular. Full ramp-up may not be feasible in the allowed time period, or it may not be feasible at all. Some of the early highly leveraged loan deals failed to fully ramp-up in the specified deal period. The deals were scaled back. Investors agreed to the reduced size, but the portfolio characteristics (such as diversity score) did not seem to be impaired. If the portfolio diversity score or other parameters are not met, this could be a severe problem and result in a failed deal with penalties.

At a minimum, the deal must be scaled back. At the end of the ramp-up period, if the manager has been unable to purchase sufficient securities, there is a partial liquidation of the notes great enough to pass the portfolio tests as outlined in the indenture.

Synthetic arbitrage deals are either fully ramped-up at closing, or are ramped-up within a few days of closing. Trading desks often retain risk, either because they know they can quickly hedge the position, or because they have a view and are using the long protection position as a trading position. CDS traders can do this with more confidence than bond traders, because the market is more liquid than the cash markets, where it may be difficult to find a specific bond of limited issue size.

REINVESTMENT PERIOD

Cash arbitrage deals have reinvestment periods. If short-dated assets mature, they can be replaced with longer-dated assets during a reinvestment period. Recovered value from a defaulted asset is also reinvested. All principal collections from principal repayments, however they arise, are reinvested in new collateral according to the investment criteria outlined in the indenture agreement. Interest is paid as coupon to investors, and excess interest is a residual payment to equity investors.

A typical reinvestment period is five years, and that is what we will specify for our cash arbitrage CDO. This means the average life and expected final maturity may change slightly throughout the reinvestment period. Because of this feature, the deal documents will specify the acceptable average life range and acceptable expected final maturity range. The manager must stay within those guidelines.

The reinvestment period extends the average life of the deal and tends to increase equity returns. This applies to investment grade and high yield CDOs. Cash asset-structured product CDOs often do not have a reinvestment period.

The managed synthetic arbitrage CDO, in contrast, has no reinvestment period. It has a bullet 5-year maturity. The manager trades either to avoid losses or to exploit gains.

NON-CALL PERIOD

Cash CDOs usually have a non-call period, and ours will have a typical non-call period of five years. Equity investors may prefer this because it gives them a minimum time to earn a floor return on their investment. If interest rates go down and if there is a gain in price in the underlying portfolio, they may also prefer to liquidate the portfolio and take gains. Investors in the senior tranches will have an interest in the call not being exercised. Usually the equity investors control whether or not a call is exercised. In our deal a majority, or more than 50 percent of the equity investors, must choose to exercise the call, or the deal cannot be called. Since in our deal the manager buys 51 percent of the equity, the manager can exercise the call without consensus from the other holders. Similarly, if the manager does not want to exercise the call, the other equity investors cannot exercise the call even if they can organize a vote to call with all of the other holders.

After the non-call period, the tranches are callable, but at a slight premium. The premium is equal to half of the annual coupon for each tranche. If the tranches are not called, they will pay par at maturity.

After the non-call period, there is an exception to the premium call for a tranche. When a tranche balance is below 10 percent of the original investment—due to bonds maturing after the reinvestment period—the tranche can be called at par. This is known as a *clean-up call*. The cost of servicing this tranche begins to outweigh the arbitrage advantage at these small principal balance amounts.

Synthetic CDOs are often structured without a call, and for our example, the CDO is not callable.

PAY DOWN PERIOD

After the reinvestment period, the notes of the cash arbitrage CDO pay down sequentially, in order of seniority. Principal collections are no longer reinvested, but are passed through to investors to pay down principal. During this period, the manager is restricted to trading to avoid losses or exploit gains within specific limits.

The synthetic arbitrage CDO requires no special pay down period, just as it requires no reinvestment period, because it has a bullet final maturity.

WEIGHTED AVERAGE LIFE AND EXPECTED FINAL MATURITY

For the cash managed arbitrage CDO, the expected final maturity is in the range of 8 to 10 years, and the weighted average life of the deal varies between 7 to 9 years for each tranche.

For the managed synthetic arbitrage CDO, the weighted average life of the deal equals the expected final maturity. This is exactly five years, the initial maturity of the CDSs that make up the collateral of the CDO.

EARLY TERMINATION

The cash arbitrage CDO can be terminated early based on several triggers. If key prenamed members of the management team leave, and there are no acceptable substitutes, the deal can be terminated early. Failure to comply with deal covenants, failure to make timely payments on the Aaa and Aa2 classes, bankruptcy of the manager or of the CDO's issuing entity are other triggers. The purpose of the triggers is to safeguard the return of principal to the Aaa and Aa2 investors. Often the class Baa2 investor is not as well protected with respect to early termination triggers.

LEGAL FINAL MATURITY

For cash-managed arbitrage CDOs, the legal final maturity is the date on which the longest-dated asset can mature, or a prespecified date. In our example, the legal final maturity is 12 years.

For our synthetic managed arbitrage CDOs, the legal final maturity is 5 years and 90 days. If no defaults occur near the expected maturity date of 5 years, the maturity will be exactly 5 years. The 90 days allows for potential settlement time needed if an asset defaults just prior to the 5-year mark.

TRANCHING AND THE SYNTHETIC ARBITRAGE ADVANTAGE

The portfolio is tranched into risk classes. As we observed earlier, the subordination is a form of credit enhancement for the senior notes. The *super senior* tranche, feasible only in synthetic CDOs, is a *delevered* position and bears the risk of *extreme systemic risk* to the credit markets. The *equity* tranche, or *first-to-default* risk, bears the *name risk* or the *idiosyncratic risk* of the portfolio. The *mezzanine* tranches are between these two extremes. The subordination of the equity tranche (and junior mezzanine tranches, if any) protects them from some of the name-specific risk, but these tranches are less delevered than the super senior tranche.

Table 5.7 shows the difference in the tranching of our managed cash arbitrage CDO versus our managed synthetic arbitrage CDO.

Notice that the size of the equity tranche for the cash deal is larger than that of the synthetic deal. This is due to the lower average rating and the tendency for the ratings of the cash collateral to be distributed around the lower allowable rating. It is also due to more stringent stress tests required by the rating agencies for high yield collateral. The manager must be more aggressive about the credit risks than the synthetic manager to make the arbitrage work. As a result, the amount of subordination required to get to the AAA level is higher than for the synthetic deal.

TABLE 5.7 Managed Cash CDO vs. Managed Synthetic CDO

	Cash CDO*		Synthetic CDO**	
Grade	Tranche Size	Percent of Portfolio	Tranche Size	Percent of Portfolio
Super Senior			432,500,000	86.5%
Aaa	439,500,000	87.9%	20,000,000	4.0%
Aa2	11,500,000	2.3%	12,500,000	2.5%
Baa2	14,000,000	2.8%	15,000,000	3.0%
Equity	35,000,000	7.0%	20,000,000	4.0%
	500,000,000	100.0%	500,000,000	100.0%

* Baa3 average portfolio rating. Up to 15% high yield and 10% asset backed.
** Baa2 average portfolio rating. Exclusively investment-grade portfolio.

Synthetic deals have more highly rated assets including more double A-and single A-rated assets than cash deals. A smaller equity tranche is sufficient, and the amount of subordination required to get to the AAA level is lower than for the cash deal, although structures may vary. In most static deals, when the first loss occurs, the equity notional is written down by the loss amount and the recovered amount is used to write down the AAA and super senior tranches. Managed deals may make a provision for reinvestment of recovered amounts, however.

WATERFALLS FOR CASH VERSUS SYNTHETIC ARBITAGE CDOs

Interest proceeds for the cash arbitrage CDO include all interest received on the underlying assets plus interest earned on any cash in reserve accounts. It also includes all amendments, waivers, consent fees, and commissions. All payments from hedge counterparties are also considered interest proceeds. A small reserve account is maintained and replenished from future interest proceeds, if necessary. Equity cash flows can be diverted in the first year of the deal to fund this account, if required. The purpose of the reserve account is to insure that the notes above the equity tranche receive timely interest payments.

For the cash arbitrage CDO, principal proceeds include all principal prepayments from the portfolio assets, optional redemptions (due to calls, for instance), payments at maturity, mandatory sinking fund payments, exchange offers, all principal proceeds received from asset sales other than certain realized trading gains, and tender offers. Call premium and realized trading gains from asset sales and recoveries on defaulted assets are considered principal proceeds.

The interest and principal waterfalls for the cash arbitrage CDO are shown in Figures 5.5 and 5.6.

Notice that this deal incorporates interest and principal coverage tests, even though the portfolio initially has an investment grade rating. These tests will vary by deal, and are stated in the deal prospectus. Our deal uses tests typical of cash CDOs currently in the market.

The overcollateralization ratio or *O/C ratio*, also known as the *par value test*, for this deal is calculated as follows for tranche X:

O/C Tranche $X =$

$$\frac{\text{Total Collateral} + \text{Cash in Reinvestment Accounts}}{\text{Remaining Principal Amt Tranche } X + \text{Remaining Principal Amounts of Tranches Senior to } X}$$

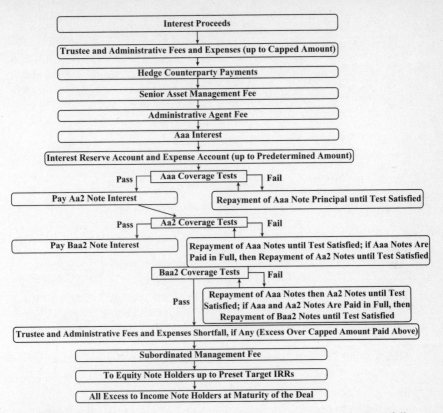

FIGURE 5.5 Managed Cash Arbitrage CDO: Interest Proceeds Waterfall

The principal amount for a cash flow deal is the par amount of the bonds, irrespective of their market values. The principal amount for a market value deal is the mark-to-market principal value of the bonds.

The interest coverage ratio or *I/C ratio* for this deal is calculated as follows for Tranche X:

I/C Tranche $X =$

$$\frac{\text{Collateral Interest Proceeds} + \text{Hedge Proceeds}}{\text{Senior Expenses} + \text{Hedge Costs} + \text{Interest on Tranches Senior to } X + \text{Interest on Tranche } X}$$

The coverage tests are lower than they would be if the portfolio consisted exclusively of high yield collateral. The coverage tests for the various tranches are shown in Table 5.8. For a portfolio with an average rating that

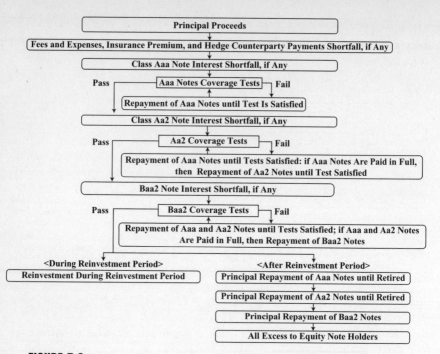

FIGURE 5.6 Managed Cash Arbitrage CDO: Principal Proceeds Waterfall

is noninvestment grade, the coverage tests would be about 20 percent higher across the board.

As we can see from the interest waterfall for our cash deal, when the coverage tests are violated, interest is not paid on the subsequent tranches, and principal on the senior tranches is paid down instead. This continues until the coverage tests are satisfied.

Principal is diverted to pay down senior tranches, even during the reinvestment period, if coverage tests are violated.

TABLE 5.8 Coverage Tests for Various Tranches

	Overcollateralization Trigger	Interest Coverage Trigger
Aaa	106	110
Aa2	103	105
Baa2	100	102

It is easy to see that cash flow modeling for this deal is complicated, and becomes even more complicated for scenario analyses in which coverage tests are violated.

In contrast, the waterfall for the synthetic arbitrage CDO is relatively straightforward. Due to the abundant excess interest spread in the synthetic deal, the reserve account provides the most important structural protection for the Aaa and Aa2 tranches.

The positive difference between (1) the default swap premium and the interest on the collateral security, and (2) the coupons payable on the notes, is excess income, which is placed in the reserve fund. The reserve fund amount is invested in eligible investments (A-1+/P1 collateral). The reserve account accumulates for the benefit of netting trading losses up to 50 percent of the original class D amount, and then for the benefit of the Aaa and Aa2 noteholders, if needed, to make coupon or principal payments. At the maturity of the deal, the excess reserve fund amount beyond the needs of the Aaa and Aa2 tranches, if any, reverts to the equity investor.

Losses due to (1) default and (2) trading gains and losses are netted from the class D note amount. Trading must stop when losses exceed 50 percent of the class D amount, and up to 50 percent of the original tranche D amount in trading losses can be netted from the reserve account if the original class D investment amount has been exhausted. When the original class D investment amount is exhausted, no further payments are made to the equity investors until maturity, and then a payment will occur only if excess reserve funds are available after satisfying payments due the Aaa and Aa2 investors.

If accumulated losses exceed the class D first loss (or equity) original investment, the Baa2, Aa2, and Aaa notes will be written down in reverse order of seniority by the new loss amount. It is unlikely the Aaa and Aa2 tranches would experience any loss, because excess spread in the reserve account is available to pay any losses they would otherwise incur, and if the reserve account makes up the loss, there is no write-down of the senior notes. If any of the Baa2 tranche is written down, the average coupon payable on the notes is reduced, and the cash flow is further enhanced because all cash flow has been diverted from the equity investors at this point. An added boost to this deal is that cash settlement of the transactions allows for quicker recovery and reinvestment of recovered amounts. There are no payment-in-kind tranches in the synthetic deal.

As we compare the waterfall for the synthetic arbitrage CDO (see Figure 5.7) with the earlier interest and principal waterfalls for the cash arbitrage CDO, we see that the waterfall for the synthetic deal is much easier to follow and model. The cash flow protection for the senior tranches of the synthetic deal structured in this fashion is also much greater than for the

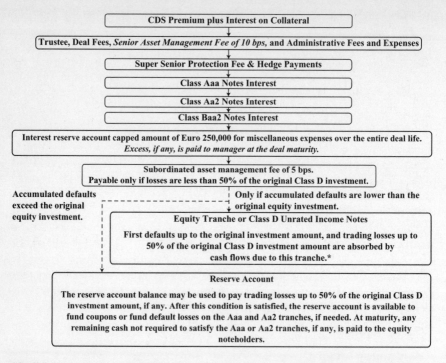

*Credit losses greater than the class D investment amount will be written down from the Baa2, Aa2, and Aaa notes in reverse order of seniority, albeit the reserve account may mitigate Aaa and Aa2 tranche losses, if any. Trading losses, if any, are absorbed by the residual cash flows and limited to 50% of the original class D investment, and trading must cease if this condition is met.

FIGURE 5.7   Managed Synthetic Arbitrage CDO: Waterfall for Unrated Equity

cash deal, as we will see later when we discuss the arbitrage advantage of synthetic CDOs. Note, however, that not all synthetic CDOs are structured in this manner. Later we will discuss structures that give no reserve account benefit to senior noteholders.

PAYMENT-IN-KIND (PIK) TRANCHES

Payment-in-kind or *pay-in-kind (PIK)* corporate bonds have been in the market since the late 1980s. A corporation has the option of paying the corporate coupon, or increasing the principal amount of the bond, a payment-in-kind. Future coupon payments are calculated off the new principal balance and the principal balance owed at the final maturity is increased to the new principal amount. Corporations that first issued PIK bonds were lower-rated corporations. The PIK was meant to allow cash flow–strapped corporations to avoid default.

Some cash deals allow for PIK tranches, which are said to be *pickable*. Instead of making a coupon payment, the principal amount of the relevant tranche is increased by the amount of the unpaid coupon amount. The PIK tranche can pay either the current coupon calculated from the new principal balance, or can pay-in-kind depending on the cash flow availability in the deal. This mechanism is meant to prevent default of a tranche payment and to avoid triggering an early termination of the deal.

PIK tranches are structured primarily in high yield bond and high yield loan (highly leveraged transaction or HLT) deals, especially in a high default environment. Some investment grade cash deals also use this device, especially those with 25 percent high yield bonds in the collateral pool.

Notice that in comparison, the synthetic deal with reserve account support for the senior tranches is much more straightforward. Investors can more easily examine cash flows under stress tests, investors can more easily model the CDO, and investors can more easily determine the rating criteria.

PSYCHIC RATINGS: RATING AGENCY TREATMENT OF PIK TRANCHES

The lack of standardization among rating agencies with respect to PIK tranches can make it difficult to compare deals. Moody's uses an expected loss approach to rate these tranches. The expected loss approach uses the probability of loss and the potential severity of loss as the criteria for mapping a rating to a specific tranche. According to these criteria, if the tranche PIKs, but eventually pays all accrued interest and interest on accrued interest, if applicable, there is no loss. The timely return of interest is not an issue for Moody's for purposes of this rating. Moody's will allow PIKing in all tranches, including the Aaa rated tranche. This is a recent innovation for Moody's, however, who did not allow PIKing above the A2 level in deals rated before the summer of 2002, because they didn't want to treat interest on accruals the same way they treated accruals. CDO buyers may prefer deals rated prior to that time. This internal inconsistency is disturbing to many investors.

This is not true of the other rating agencies. S&P allows PIKing at the BBB level or below, and allows PIKing for tranches rated single A only if there is clear disclosure that interest can be deferred. Even so, if a bond rated A−, A, or A+ PIKs for more than a year under a stress test, S&P considers it a default. This same event is not considered a default for tranches rated BBB+ or lower. S&P doesn't allow PIKing for tranches rated higher than A+. Their logic is that investors in higher rated products expect timely payment of interest.

Fitch takes what seems to be the most reasonable approach, specifying exactly what its rating means. If a CDO tranche pays timely principal and interest under the relevant default and recovery scenarios, Fitch will rate the tranche for timely payment of principal and interest. If the tranche only accrues coupon and eventually pays it off along with interest on accrued interest, Fitch will rate the tranche for timely payment of principal, and for *ultimate* payment of interest.

Investors focus on internal rate of return (IRR), but they also focus on timing of cash flows. In any security, timing, frequency, and certainty of cash flows are all part of determination of value from an investor's point of view. I can spend cash, but I can't spend IRR, and I can't spend yield. I can be rich in net worth, but poor in cash. For instance, funds that need to make interest distributions to investors may need reliable cash flows, and for them the various rating agency approaches can be misleading. The investor bears the burden of interpreting the rating agencies' psychic ratings for PIK tranches.

THE SUPER SENIOR ADVANTAGE

Notice that the super senior tranche is 86.5 percent of the synthetic deal, and the combined super senior and Aaa tranches are 90.5 percent of the deal. For the cash deal, the Aaa tranche is only 87.9 percent of the deal. In addition, the cash deal's liabilities below the Aaa level are more expensive than those of the synthetic deal. But the largest difference in cost comes from the liabilities above the Aaa attachment point. The super senior tranche of arbitrage deals backed by corporate obligors has been priced as low as 6 bps over the past few years, but I'm using 10 bps in this example. The *per annum* difference in cost due to this factor alone is 1,665,000 Euros. Table 5.9 shows the cost advantage for our managed synthetic arbitrage CDO example.

The chief arbitrage advantage of the synthetic arbitrage CDO over the cash arbitrage CDO is due to the large super senior tranche in the synthetic CDO. I believe this is the reason for the surge of synthetic CDOs issued in recent years.

CDS VERSUS CASH ASSET SPREADS

If we want to compare the cash flow of our two deals, one way to do it is to look at the CDS spreads versus asset swap spreads of the assets in the

TABLE 5.9 Arbitrage Advantage of Synthetic CDOs (per annum cost of liabilities at the AAA and higher levels*)

| | Cash CDO | | Synthetic CDO | |
Grade	Tranche Size	Tranche Costs	Tranche Size	Percent of Portfolio
Super Senior			432,500,000	432,500
Aaa	439,500,000	2,197,500	20,000,000	100,000
TOTAL	439,500,000	2,197,500	452,500,000	532,500
	Savings of Synthetic vs. Cash		1,665,000 p.a.	

*This example assumes the Aaa rated tranche is priced at LIBOR + 50 bps, and the super senior tranche is priced at 10 bps.

cash portfolio. For readers unfamiliar with interest rate swaps and assets swaps, the following is a simplified review of the basic concepts.

SIMPLIFIED EXAMPLES OF INTEREST RATE SWAPS AND ASSET SWAPS

It is the morning of September 14, 2008, and you are given the following term deposit rates and Eurodollar futures prices. All value dates are business days, and this is not a leap year. The initial value date is 9/18/08. Refer to Table 5.10. How would you determine the values shown in bold?

The number of days is calculated from value date to value date for deposits with terms of three, six, and nine months. The initial value date for 9/14/08 would be 9/18/08. Subsequent value dates would simply be 12/18/08, 3/18/09, and 6/18/09. Terminal wealth in each case is calculated as $1 + (\text{Rate}/100)(\text{Days}/360)$, and I have rounded them to five decimal places.

We need to know how to calculate forward rates if we want to bootstrap a swap curve, so I show an example in Table 5.11.

$$E_0 R(3, 6) = \left[\frac{1 + R(0, 6)\left(\dfrac{d_{0,6}}{360}\right)}{1 + R(0, 3)\left(\dfrac{d_{0,3}}{360}\right)} - 1 \right]\left(\frac{360}{d_{3,6}}\right)$$

I use the well-known formula for calculating forward rates to fill in the second table. The forward from month 3 to 6 is $= (((1 + (.0725 \cdot 181/360))/(1 + (.07 \cdot 91/360)) - 1) \cdot 360/(181 - 91) = 7.372\%$

TABLE 5.10 Deposit Rates

Term (Months)	Bid (LIBID)	Ask (LIBOR)	Days in Deposit Period	Future Value Factor (At the Bid)	Future Value Factor (At the Ask)
3	7.000	7.125%	91	1.01769	1.01801
6	7.250	7.375%	181	1.03645	1.03708
9	7.500	7.600%	273	1.05688	1.05763

An alternative method for calculating the forward rates is to take the ratio of the future value factors from the deposit table above and convert them to an annual rate. For example, the 3-month forward rate of 7.372 is calculated as follows: $((1.03645/1.01769) - 1) \cdot (360/(181 - 91)) = 7.372$.

Since we calculated the implied futures rates above, I'll digress for a moment to look at a classic futures analysis to determine if futures are rich or cheap relative to implied forward rates (see Table 5.12).

The implied futures rates represent the futures markets pricing of the offered side of the forward deposit market. For the sake of simplicity, I have used the fair values of the forward offered rates calculated for the table even though the dates do not line up exactly with the value days for Eurodollar expirations. There isn't enough information to determine the fair value of the June forward rate. This analysis is useful because when we trade interest rate swaps (or forward rate agreements), we want to know whether the implied rates are telling us whether futures contracts, our short-term hedge instruments, are rich or cheap.

We wanted to calculate the future value factor because this represents the terminal wealth factor for each period. A dollar invested today will have a future value in the relevant period of $1 times the terminal wealth factor (or future value). A zero coupon bond priced today to have a terminal wealth factor of 1.00 at a future date will have a price today of 1/(terminal wealth factor) for the relevant period. Table 5.13 shows the zero coupon

TABLE 5.11 3-Month Forward Deposit Rates

Months Forward	Bid	Ask
0	7.000%	7.125%
3	7.372%	7.493%
6	7.711%	7.755%

TABLE 5.12 Eurodollar Futures Prices (Market Price vs. Implied Prices)

Contract Month	Market Futures Price	Implied Futures Rate	Fair Futures Price	Futures Rich or Cheap? (Number of Basis Points)
Sep '08	92.87	7.125%	92.87	fairly priced at expiry
Dec '08	92.75	7.493%	92.51	24 ticks rich
Mar '09	92.15	7.755%	92.24	9 ticks cheap
Jun '09	91.00	—	—	—

prices that correspond to the terminal wealth factors (future values) for various future dates, given the futures prices.

From these prices, we can determine the fixed rate in September 2008 on a one-year fixed/floating interest rate swap that pays fixed and floating quarterly on International Money Market (IMM) value dates.

The fixed rate for a swap that pays fixed and floating quarterly would satisfy the following equation,

$$(C/4) [0.98261 + 0.96433 + 0.94522 + 0.92533] + 100 \times 0.92533 = 100$$

which simply sets the sum of the cash flows on a hypothetical 1-year fixed-rate note equal to par. The floating side of the swap by definition is worth par if it pays an initial rate of 7.00 percent. The fixed coupon in this case would be 7.82 percent.

Using similar—but much more complicated—methodology a swap trader will build a curve using appropriate benchmarks of futures and cash government bonds, and will bootstrap a zero curve and calculate the fixed swap rate corresponding to a relevant benchmark floating rate (for example, USD, LIBOR, or Euribor).

TABLE 5.13 Eurodollar Futures Summary

Contract Month	Futures Price	Implied Futures Rate	Days in Contract Period	Terminal Wealth (Future Value)	Zero-Coupon Prices (DF)
Sep '08	93.00	7.00%	91	1.00000	1.00000
Dec '08	92.50	7.50%	91	1.01769	0.98261
Mar '09	92.00	8.00%	91	1.03699	0.96433
Jun '09	91.50	8.50%	91	1.05796	0.94522
Sep '09	91.00	N/A	N/A	1.08069	0.92533

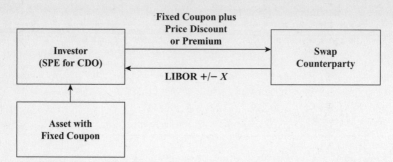

The asset may be trading at a premium or discount to par, or at par. The difference from par, if any, is amortized over the life of the swap and incorporated into the floating rate coupon.

Note that an asset swap can also swap floating coupons to fixed.

The swap can be single-currency or from one currency to another currency.

FIGURE 5.8 Generic Par Asset Swap Cash Flows

Now that we can calculate a fixed floating swap rate, how do we construct an asset swap? Figure 5.8 is a schematic of a generic asset swap.

Suppose you own a 5-year maturity USD denominated corporate bond. The bond is trading at par with a semiannual coupon of 7.00 percent. You want to do a par asset swap and you want to swap the coupon to 3-month LIBOR. The 5-year swap is trading at 46/50 versus 3-month USD LIBOR and the 5-year treasury is trading at 6.5 percent. The swap quote means that if the interbank dealer market is going to pay a fixed rate versus receiving 3-month LIBOR, they will pay the 5-year treasury rate plus 46 bps. In this case the fixed rate the swap dealer would pay versus receiving 3-month LIBOR is 6.5 percent plus 46 bps or 6.96 percent. This is the *bid side* of the market.

For our asset swap, we will pay a fixed rate versus receiving USD LIBOR. The trader will quote us the *offer side* of the market, which is 6.5 percent plus 50 bps or 7.0 percent. The trader wants to receive 7.0 percent versus paying 3-month LIBOR. Conveniently, our bond pays a 7.0 percent semiannual bond equivalent yield (BEY) coupon, and this is the same way that the U.S. market quotes its interest rate swaps. Furthermore, let's assume our bond pays its coupon on the exact day the trader wants the first fixed swap payment on the swap. The cash flows are shown in Figure 5.9, where we are the investor and the owner of the bond. From the investor's point of view, this is similar to owning a par floater with a coupon of USD LIBOR flat. Notice that in this example, the swap provider faces the investor who owns the bond, so the rating on the bond is irrelevant from

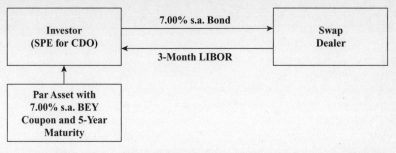

The asset is trading at par and the asset's fixed coupon matches the 5-year swap fixed offer rate of 7.0% s.a. BEY. The coupon date also matches the fixed payment date in the swap.

The investor now has a par asset with a coupon equivalent 3-month LIBOR.

FIGURE 5.9   Par Asset Swap Cash Flows with Par Asset

the point of view of the investor's swap counterparty. Only the creditworthiness of the investor matters for our example. We'll talk about asset swaps and currency swaps in more detail in a moment when we look at hedging the portfolio cash flows.

If we look at the cash portfolio swapped to a par asset swap level in Euros, it is as if it is a portfolio of par floaters (see Figure 5.9). We can now compare the spread level and the cash flows to a portfolio of synthetic asset swaps. Assuming for the moment that the tranches of each of the deals will trade at the same levels for same rated tranches, we can more easily see the difference in the arbitrage. Let's look at a credit like IBM. Figure 5.10 captures the 5-year CDS premium versus the 5-year asset swap spread for IBM for the period from April 1999 to November 2000. The top line is the CDS

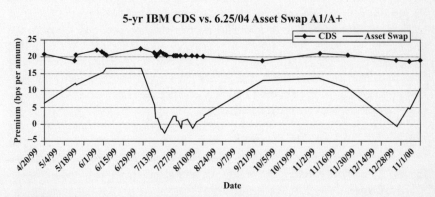

FIGURE 5.10   CDS vs. Asset Swap Spreads for IBM (April '99–November '00)

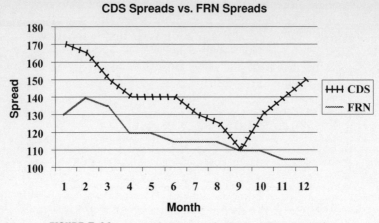

FIGURE 5.11   Typical Pattern of CDS vs. FRN Spreads

spread. For this period, the CDS spread was close to constant while the asset swap spread showed some volatility. Despite the asset swap spread's volatility, the CDS spread was always wider.

Is this typical? Do CDS spreads always trade wide relative to the cash markets? Unless a new convertible or large bond issue is involved, there is a tendency for CDS spreads to trade wider. Figure 5.11 shows typical behavior of the CDS market versus floating rate spreads for the same credits. CDS spreads tend to be wider and more volatile than asset swap spreads or floating rate note (FRN) spreads.

Is the CDS market a high beta market? You beta believe it.

The CDS market tends to be slightly more volatile than the cash market, although the correlation between the markets is estimated to be around 90 percent for the few years in which CDS prices have been tracked relative to the cash markets. The difference between the spread of CDSs over the spreads in the cash markets, or the *basis*, is also correlated with market direction. As credit spreads widen, the basis widens. As credit spreads narrow, the basis narrows. Of course, there are exceptions in which the basis becomes negative due to supply and demand pressures as we saw in our earlier example of convertible bond issuance.

We've already seen the advantage of the synthetic arbitrage due to the super senior tranche. The synthetic portfolio enjoys another advantage as well. For a portfolio of identical maturities with the *same WARF*, also known as the *probability factor*, the synthetic portfolio will have a wider arbitrage spread than the cash portfolio.

Adding even more fuel to the advantage is that cash deals have a lower average portfolio quality and require more subordination, thus reducing equity leverage. For synthetic deals, not only is there more cash available for the arbitrage, the portfolio quality tends to be higher when comparing an investment grade cash deal versus an investment grade synthetic arbitrage CDO.

HEDGING THE CDO PORTFOLIO CASH FLOWS

For the cash arbitrage CDO, the challenge of hedging the portfolio cash flows is much more complicated than for the synthetic CDO. Earlier we looked at an example of a par asset swap. We would have to be incredibly lucky to find an asset in the currency we desire trading at par with the exact coupon required to meet the swap dealer's quote. Usually there is a mismatch in the cash flows that must be accounted for in a pricing model.

For a portfolio of cash assets, how much can the hedge affect value? What if a hedged asset defaults? What if the manager wants to trade a hedged asset prior to maturity? Would the potential loss on the hedge make a manager think twice about trading an asset that he thinks will deteriorate in credit? How much can this affect the value of a CDO?

Managers of cash portfolios hedge interest rate and currency risk. Let's take a simplified example where the manager purchases a fixed rate bond in dollars and wants a par asset swap package. The following analysis is an approximation of the coupon on the bond. Even when one has a rigorous swap quote using a model and a proper swap curve, it is a good idea to have an approximation of the answer. The models are usually standard, but often users make input errors. Having a good idea of the answer enables a manager to get corrections made immediately.

The bond is trading at 101 with a semiannual coupon of 7.00 percent (7.00 percent BEY) and has a 5-year maturity. You want to do a par asset swap and you want to swap the coupon to 3-month LIBOR. The 5-year swap is trading at 48/50 versus 3-month LIBOR and the 5-year fixed rate treasury is trading at 6.5 percent. Since you are doing a par asset swap, the swap dealer is financing the 1-point premium for you, the buyer. You only pay par, and you assign the asset coupons to the swap dealer. A 1 point premium is 1/100 = .01. One bp is .0001 so a 1-point premium is equal to 100 bps. The swap dealer will amortize the premium over the life of the swap and subtract it from the floating payment on the asset swap. You purchase the asset swap at the offer side of the swap market, or 7.00 percent. The slightly higher offer rate (versus the bid side) means that the swap dealer

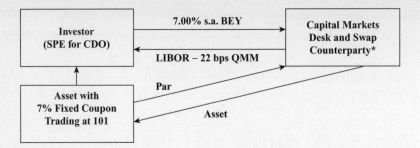

The asset may be trading at a premium or discount to par, or at par. The difference from par, if any, is amortized over the life of the swap and incorporated into the floating rate coupon.

In this case, the asset is trading at 101, a 1-point premium. This is amortized over the life of the swap at the 7.00% swap rate for an approximate 22 bps (QMM basis) reduction in the floating rate coupon.

*Swap counterparty offers to receive fixed at 7.00% s.a. bond basis vs. 3-month LIBOR QMM basis.

FIGURE 5.12   Par Asset Swap Cash Flows with Premium Asset

subtracts a higher amortized value of the premium from the coupon payment than if the dealer used the bid-side rate. One hundred bps amortized over 5 years at 7.0 percent is 22.79 bps, but these are bond bps, so the floating coupon will be about LIBOR − 22 bps, and this is only an approximation. Figure 5.12 illustrates the cash flows.

Similarly, if the bond were trading at 101 and had a coupon of 9 percent, the par asset swap would have a coupon of about LIBOR + 175 bps.

If the asset defaults after one day, the manager has to pay the bid/ask spread on the hedge unwind, but that is usually only 2 to 4 bps. Economically, the manager has lost a par asset with a coupon of LIBOR − 23 and suffers the hedge unwind cost. If market credit spreads remain the same, and if the asset maintains its credit rating, then theoretically, changes in the hedge cost should offset potential changes in the asset price due to interest rate fluctuations. If the manager wants to sell the asset in the future, the manager must only absorb the bid/ask spread in the hedge unwind. If credit spreads change adversely or if the credit quality of the asset declines, the loss on the asset is theoretically the same as it would have been if the asset were unhedged. The hedge isn't perfect, however. Later we'll look at typical exposure due to mark-to-market differences in the swap versus the asset for interest rate moves.

When the asset is in the same currency, the analysis is fairly straightforward. When more than one currency is involved, the hedge is more complicated. Currency swaps can be structured in three ways:

1. Floating to floating,
2. Fixed to fixed, or
3. Fixed to floating.

In a currency swap there may or may not be an initial and final exchange of principal, but for our CDO, all of the currency swaps must have both an initial and a final exchange of principal. I once worked with a structurer who didn't take into account the final exchange of principal, which is the chief component of mark-to-market value. He was under the mistaken impression that if one did a par asset swap in USD to create a par floater structure, one could just swap the coupons to Euros on a floating to floating basis, and have very minimal basis risk. As a result he told a client that the hedge cost for the CDO and the ongoing unwind risk would be very low. He was unpleasantly surprised when the error was pointed out. When structurers have only a bond background and no background in the currency or swap markets, this is a common mistake.

If bond professionals have trouble with this concept, bond fund managers who are single currency investors may have difficulty, too. A quick review of currency swaps illustrates this point.

In addition to the interest rate component, currency swaps have a foreign exchange component. The day count and payment period conventions vary for different currencies. In a Euro swap, the fixed rate basis is paid annually on a 30/360 basis (annual bond), and floating payments are on an actual/360 basis. In the sterling swap, the fixed rate is paid semiannually on an actual/365 day basis, and the floating rate is paid on an actual/365 day basis.

Suppose we are buying a 5-year new issue sterling bond. The bond pays sterling LIBOR + 25 bps. We are swapping the bond to a floating rate Euro bond so we can include it in our Euro portfolio. I'm using fictitious swap rates and coupon rates for the illustration. Figures 5.13 through 5.15 illustrate the cash flows from the perspective of the investor in the sterling asset swapped to Euros.

At issue here is an initial exchange of cash flows. The initial sterling amount owed to purchase the bonds must be swapped to Euros, since our CDO will pay Euros. On an ongoing basis, the coupons of the sterling bond are swapped to Euros, so the CDO receives Euro coupons. At the 5-year maturity, the sterling payment on the bonds must be swapped back to the same amount of Euros as we initially invested.

Sometimes you will hear the currency swap shown in the figures incorrectly referred to as a *dual currency swap*. That is incorrect. It's possible that because people see two currencies involved, they think it should be called dual. A dual currency swap is a different transaction: The counterparty

Issue Settlement Date

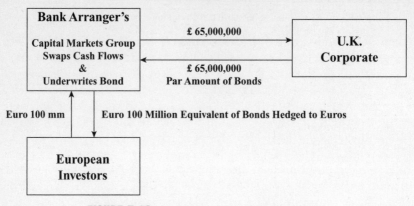

FIGURE 5.13 Initial Exchange of Cash Flows

receives one currency, pays coupons in another currency, and has a final exchange of principal in a third currency. Borrowers often perform this swap when they want to lower their all-in borrowing costs by taking on more currency risk.

I realize this terminology is untidy, but the only solution, if you feel there is a misunderstanding, is to have the speaker outline the cash flows.

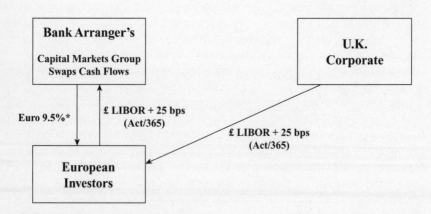

*Coupon payments are annual 30/360 basis.

FIGURE 5.14 Coupon Payments in Euros

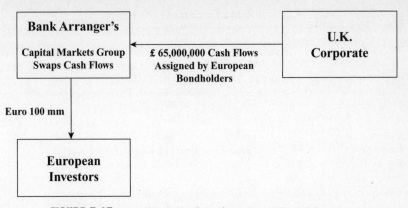

FIGURE 5.15   Final Principal Exchange at 5-Year Maturity

Don't assume market professionals know the correct terminology. Ask for the cash flow structure in writing so you can examine the cash flows to see if they are consistent with the terminology as you understand it.

The value of a swap hedge changes by its mark-to-market value depending on changes both in interest rates and foreign exchange rates (if applicable). The change in value can be modeled for different exchange rate movements and interest rate movements. The mark-to-market exposure changes, based on the interest rate and exchange rate scenarios one models, and is a function of the volatilities the modeler assumes. Table 5.14 shows typical mark-to-market exposure patterns for a USD fixed/floating swap, and for a Great Britain pound (GBP)/Euro currency swap. I've highlighted the relevant exposures for our transactions for a 5-year period.

From the table, we can make some useful generalizations about single currency and cross currency swaps.

Notice that the single currency fixed/floating swap exposure diminishes as we approach maturity, and in general, is lower in magnitude than the currency swap. Currency swap exposure becomes greater as time passes, and becomes greater in magnitude as we approach maturity. If we did a 10-year currency swap, the exposure would continue increasing in size.

This suggests that in the event of default of an asset, which has been swapped from sterling to Euros, there is potentially a great deal of exposure. That exposure can work to the benefit of the CDO, or it can work against it, depending on which way swap rates and currency rates have moved since the onset of the transaction.

In comparison, our managed synthetic arbitrage CDO has a much easier time of it. There is no interest rate risk or currency rate risk to

TABLE 5.14　Swap Mark-to-Market Exposure Comparison

Currency	USD Fixed/Floating Swaps		Currency	Currency Swaps	
Tenor	5 Years		CDO Pays	GBP	Euro
CDO Pays	Fixed	Floating	CDO Receives	Euro	GBP
Time			Time		
0	0.00	0.00	0	0.00	0.00
2 weeks	1.85	1.79	2 weeks	3.99	4.15
1 month	2.74	2.62	1 month	5.89	6.25
2 months	3.99	3.72	2 months	8.27	9.00
3 months	4.99	4.57	3 months	9.92	10.99
4 months	5.83	5.27	4 months	11.47	12.91
5 months	6.63	5.90	5 months	12.79	14.60
6 months	7.37	6.46	6 months	14.02	16.22
9 months	9.52	7.39	9 months	17.41	18.91
1.0 year	11.24	8.51	1.0 year	20.00	22.62
1.5 years	13.22	9.18	1.5 years	24.43	27.54
2.0 years	14.23	9.24	2.0 years	27.93	31.98
2.5 years	14.44	8.88	2.5 years	30.80	36.18
3.0 years	14.20	8.23	3.0 years	33.23	40.20
3.5 years	13.15	7.19	3.5 years	35.37	44.03
4.0 years	11.11	5.77	4.0 years	37.34	47.66
4.5 years	8.04	4.06	4.5 years	39.05	51.15
5.0 years	4.27	2.05	5.0 years	40.74	54.39

hedge. For example, the CDO might earn a Euro premium for selling Euro 10 million of protection on a reference obligor that normally issues sterling debt. If the obligor defaults, cash settlement is based on the then Euro 10 million amount of debt and the recovery is based on that benchmark amount. Notice we constructed our deal to be cash settled. In a physically settled deal, the disposition of the currency risk must be carefully outlined, especially if a long workout period is allowed. As we'll see later, balance sheet deals referencing multicurrency portfolios also pose special problems.

For many deals, the bank arrangers will not provide hedges that have no unwind cost in the event of default. For other deals, the cost of a hedge is deemed to be too much, leaving too little excess cash for the equity investor to find investment attractive. Common methods of lowering hedge costs are as follows:

■ The collateral is swapped based on a fixed amortization schedule set up at the start of the deal. This is usually employed for cash deals in which the tranches are to be issued as floating rate tranches, but the assets are primarily fixed rate. All or part of the portfolio that requires a hedge may be included in the swap. Sometimes managers like to keep a portion of the portfolio unhedged, since they feel they can use the extra flexibility to their advantage. In either case, as assets mature, default, or are reinvested, the hedge amount required may vary, albeit the schedule is fixed. Some investment banks may offer this swap for multicurrency assets. Other types of swaps require that the assets first be hedged to a single currency before entering into the larger portfolio swap.

- Each asset may have its own individual currency swap, the portfolio can be hedged with currency options, or the portfolio can be completely unhedged with respect to currency. Managers may have to make a case to rating agencies about their ability to manage multicurrency portfolios if they leave a portion unhedged. Some consultants provide *currency overlays* in which they charge a hedge fee for managing the currency risk. A CDO manager essentially subcontracts the currency hedge by purchasing the currency overlay.

- Interest rate caps are sometimes used instead of a swap to hedge interest rate risk. The cap is paid for with an upfront fee, and this cost is incorporated into the initial deal economics. If fixed rate assets are used in a floating rate deal, a cap will hedge the risk of rising Euribor rates. A cap is a series of calls on the underlying interest rate index, which is Euribor in our example. The manager specifies a strike price for the cap. The payment dates for the cap match the coupon payments on the CDO. For example, the payment, if any, on payment date t is calculated as follows:

$$f \times N \times (\max[0, R_{t-m,t} - S])$$

where
f = payment frequency
N = notional face value/principal
S = strike or fixed cap rate
$R_{t\text{-(period)}}$ = t-period floating rate set at time $t - (1\ \text{period})$

- Payment basis swaps account for timing mismatches in the deal. The swap desk agrees to take in deal cash flows and pay agreed coupons on the correct payment dates. Alternatively, the manager may decide to reinvest all cash flows and manage the timing of payments.

The above hedges are merely choices for the manager. Rating agencies do not mandate any of the above, but the more certain the cash flows, the easier it is to rate a deal.

Cash asset based CDOs, especially multicurrency deals, have a much greater degree of complexity in hedging currency and interest rate risk than synthetic CDOs.

SETTLEMENT IN THE EVENT OF DEFAULT OR CREDIT EVENT

In the event of a default in the cash CDO portfolio, the manager will try to maximize recovery on the asset. In cash deals, the manager's expertise in workout situations is one of the criteria in management selection. Investors should ask the following questions. Did the manager get experience in the banking industry? In how many workout situations has the manager participated? The workout can sometimes last up to two years. Foregoing the present value from sale of the defaulted asset might be worth it if the manager can recover more. If a default occurs near the expected final maturity of an affected tranche, the investors may want some voice in deciding whether to extend the workout process. This is particularly true of equity investors.

In the synthetic CDO, cash settlement occurs within 90 days. When a credit event occurs, the purchaser of credit protection from the CDO, usually the bank arranger, provides the CDO (the trustee) with a *credit event notice* and *notice of publicly available information*. These notifications satisfy the *conditions to payment*. The *cash settlement amount* is the difference between the relevant par value amount of the reference obligation and the market price. As soon as this occurs, coupon interest stops accruing on the cash settlement amount (the loss amount on the reference obligation). The cash settlement amount is still unknown, however, so it is estimated and retroactively adjusted, if necessary.

Several business days prior to the *valuation date*, the *calculation agent* (usually the bank arranger) gets bids on the reference obligation from five dealers that are active market makers in the CDS market. In today's market, this could include dealers such as Credit Suisse First Boston International, Morgan Stanley International, J.P. Morgan Chase, Citigroup/Salomon, Goldman Sachs International, Merrill Lynch, and Deutsche Bank AG, among others. The calculation agent uses the highest bid of at least two full quotations obtained on the same business day within three business days of the valuation date to calculate the cash settlement amount. The cash settlement amount is paid three business days after the valuation date.

What if the calculation agent can't get two full quotations? After all, this obligation just defaulted and the market may be irregular. In that case, the calculation agent will attempt the process again or attempt to obtain a weighted average quotation for up to five business days after the valuation date.

After all that, in the unlikely event the calculation agent is unsuccessful, the calculation agent will request a disinterested dealer in this type of reference obligation to use this same determination method for up to an additional five business days. If the disinterested dealer is unable to obtain the *final price*, the calculation agent will determine the final price on the date following the end of the five-day period. The calculation agent will promptly notify the CDO manager and trustee of the basis for its determination. Figure 5.16 shows a typical cash settlement process.

Different dealers may have slightly different cash settlement timelines. This is based on their interpretation of the International Swap and Derivatives Association (ISDA) language governing physical settlement of the CDS, written to hedge the CDS they have with the CDO. When an arbitrage deal is executed, the bank arranger hedges by buying credit default protection from the CDO and selling credit protection in a trade that is matched as much as possible. Most market transactions call for physical settlement. The bank arranger as protection buyer will not want to deliver notice until it receives notice from the counterparty to which it sold protection. The

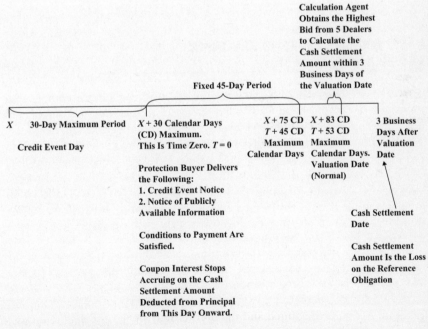

FIGURE 5.16 Typical Timeline for Cash Settlement of CDS

above timeline is based on my and Allen Overy's interpretation of ISDA documents in early 2002. These slight variations will not add or subtract significantly from the cash settlement timeline.

This may sound more complicated than a workout situation, but it is actually more streamlined. The process is much faster and the recovery amount is available for reinvestment in another CDS or to accrue interest in the reserve account. Investors in this CDO must determine whether they feel they will get the best recovery value in the event of default. The hope is that by judiciously choosing the portfolio and manager in the first place, a default will be a rare event.

DOCUMENTATION

After all the discussion about CDS language, it would be easy to conclude that the documentation for a synthetic arbitrage CDO must be more voluminous than that for a cash synthetic arbitrage CDO. Actually the opposite is true. The cash arbitrage CDO requires much more detailed information about how the deal will be managed, triggers, and other aspects of the cash transaction. The documentation of the transaction is generally several times more massive than for a synthetic arbitrage CDO.

CASH VERSUS SYNTHETIC ARBITRAGE CDO EQUITY CASH FLOWS

The cash arbitrage CDO documentation is longer and more complicated than that of the synthetic CDOs. The hedges are much more complicated for cash arbitrage CDOs than synthetic CDOs, and in both cases, the equity investor bears the risk if hedge counterparties default. There is more risk in ramping-up the portfolio for a cash arbitrage CDO than for a synthetic CDO. The portfolio of a cash arbitrage CDO includes high yield assets, whereas the synthetic arbitrage CDO does not. It would seem to follow that greater complexity results in greater reward. It would also seem to follow that greater risk results in greater reward. But it isn't true. At least it isn't true at this time for these products.

The return on the synthetic arbitrage CDO's equity often exceeds the return on the cash arbitrage CDO. In the fall of 2002, the spreads of CDSs gapped out. They were so wide that the returns on equity exceeded the returns available in the cash market by as much as 20% and more. This was an anomaly, but it illustrates the point that investors can earn higher returns for comparable risks.

The type of equity structure we've used for our synthetic arbitrage CDO is very clean and advantageous to the equity investor. As we'll see later, other structures are not as advantageous, so the stated returns on those structures will offer a less favorable deal relative to cash arbitrage CDOs. As investors become more aware of the differences, they will ask for structures similar to the one we've outlined in our example, which is why I chose it.

Equity distributions are often made annually. There is usually a target objective under the no-loss and Moody's base case historical loss scenarios. In the cash arbitrage CDO, the excess proceeds are the sum of interest collections, and certain fees, less expenses (including debt expenses, asset management fees, CDO set up costs, and administrative expenses). At maturity, after repayment of all indebtedness and expenses, the equity investors receive the remainder of the CDO's assets as a final payment based on the percentage of the equity investment.

The equity payments are the obligation of the SPE that issues the CDO, and is in no way the obligation of the manager. These are buy and hold investments, and equity investors understand that these are very non-liquid investments. The only difference between the synthetic arbitrage CDO and the cash arbitrage CDO equity cash flows in our examples is that there is a possibility that when losses exceed the initial equity investment, cash flows are diverted for the benefit of Aaa and Aa2 noteholders, if required. This is a structural

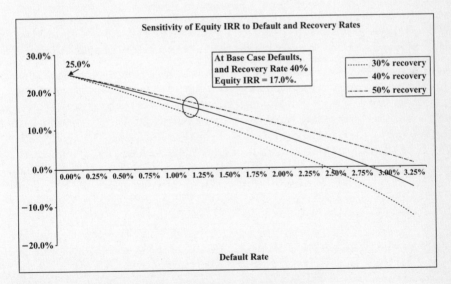

No Default Scenario IRR Is 25.0%; Base Case Default Scenario IRR Is 17.0%.

FIGURE 5.17 Equity Returns—Sensitivity Analysis

enhancement from the senior noteholder's point of view, and the likelihood this cash flow would be needed is very small. The unused accumulated cash flow reverts to the equity investors at the end of the transaction.

Figure 5.17 shows the equity IRR sensitivity analysis graph for various recovery values and default rates. The graph is representative of the returns for our managed synthetic arbitrage CDO example during an economic scenario when initial CDS spreads are relatively wide as they were during the late fall and early winter of 2002. IRR returns are shown for the no default scenario, the Moody's historical base case scenario, and for defaults up to three times the base case default scenario.

Most investors focus on the base case default scenario. It is important to note that this scenario is based on Moody's *historical* data for assets with the same WARF as our CDO portfolio. We'll examine this assumption in more detail later, and make recommendations about alternative ways of looking at equity returns.

TABLE 5.15 Typical Expenses for Synthetic Arbitrage CDO

Period Begin Date	Language Mismatch Premium 0.0005	Structuring Fee 50 bps −2,500,000	Underwriting Fees −1,022,500	BkArrgr Admin −250,000	Rating Agencies −250,000	Trustee/ Collateral Ad/Counsel −375,000	Legal Fees −520,000
11/2/02							
2/2/03	−62,500	−138,538	−56,662	−13,854	−13,854	−20,781	−28,816
5/2/03	−62,500	−138,538	−56,662	−13,854	−13,854	−20,781	−28,816
8/2/03	−62,500	−138,538	−56,662	−13,854	−13,854	−20,781	−28,816
11/2/03	−62,500	−138,538	−56,662	−13,854	−13,854	−20,781	−28,816
2/2/04	−62,500	−138,538	−56,662	−13,854	−13,854	−20,781	−28,816
5/2/04	−62,500	−138,538	−56,662	−13,854	−13,854	−20,781	−28,816
8/2/04	−62,500	−138,538	−56,662	−13,854	−13,854	−20,781	−28,816
11/2/04	−62,500	−138,538	−56,662	−13,854	−13,854	−20,781	−28,816
2/2/05	−62,500	−138,538	−56,662	−13,854	−13,854	−20,781	−28,816
5/2/05	−62,500	−138,538	−56,662	−13,854	−13,854	−20,781	−28,816
8/2/05	−62,500	−138,538	−56,662	−13,854	−13,854	−20,781	−28,816
11/2/05	−62,500	−138,538	−56,662	−13,854	−13,854	−20,781	−28,816
2/2/06	−62,500	−138,538	−56,662	−13,854	−13,854	−20,781	−28,816
5/2/06	−62,500	−138,538	−56,662	−13,854	−13,854	−20,781	−28,816
8/2/06	−62,500	−138,538	−56,662	−13,854	−13,854	−20,781	−28,816
11/2/06	−62,500	−138,538	−56,662	−13,854	−13,854	−20,781	−28,816
2/2/07	−62,500	−138,538	−56,662	−13,854	−13,854	−20,781	−28,816
5/2/07	−62,500	−138,538	−56,662	−13,854	−13,854	−20,781	−28,816
8/2/07	−62,500	−138,538	−56,662	−13,854	−13,854	−20,781	−28,816
11/2/07	−62,500	−138,538	−56,662	−13,854	−13,854	−20,781	−28,816

SAMPLE CASH FLOWS

A synthetic arbitrage CDO is much simpler to model than a cash arbitrage CDO. Usually direct feeds of interest rates provide data from which to build a forward curve of interest rates used to discount and amortize cash flows in the deal. The spreadsheet shown in Table 5.15 is not meant to be a rigorous model, but is meant to provide transparency to understand what is happening to the cash flows.

The first schedule shows the cash flows for the deal expenses, not including the management fees. Some of the fees and expenses occur periodically, and some occur up front. In this instance, the bank arranger pays the upfront fees and expenses, where applicable, and amortizes the cost over the life of the deal. These costs are recovered in the reduction of net CDS premium paid to the SPV for protection on the names in the portfolio and would be factored into any unwind of a CDS contract with the SPV.

Offshore Counsel Fees	SPE Start-Up Costs	Accountant Fees	SPE Trustees 4-Tranches	SPE Admin 4-Tranches	SPE Calc. & Wire Fees	Luxembourg Listing Fee	Total Fees & Costs
−110,000	−50,000	−80,000	−77,500	−25,000	−60,000	−15,000	−7,162,814
							0
−6,096	−2,771	−4,433	−4,295	−1,385	−3,325	−831	−358,141
−6,096	−2,771	−4,433	−4,295	−1,385	−3,325	−831	−358,141
−6,096	−2,771	−4,433	−4,295	−1,385	−3,325	−831	−358,141
−6,096	−2,771	−4,433	−4,295	−1,385	−3,325	−831	−358,141
−6,096	−2,771	−4,433	−4,295	−1,385	−3,325	−831	−358,141
−6,096	−2,771	−4,433	−4,295	−1,385	−3,325	−831	−358,141
−6,096	−2,771	−4,433	−4,295	−1,385	−3,325	−831	−358,141
−6,096	−2,771	−4,433	−4,295	−1,385	−3,325	−831	−358,141
−6,096	−2,771	−4,433	−4,295	−1,385	−3,325	−831	−358,141
−6,096	−2,771	−4,433	−4,295	−1,385	−3,325	−831	−358,141
−6,096	−2,771	−4,433	−4,295	−1,385	−3,325	−831	−358,141
−6,096	−2,771	−4,433	−4,295	−1,385	−3,325	−831	−358,141
−6,096	−2,771	−4,433	−4,295	−1,385	−3,325	−831	−358,141
−6,096	−2,771	−4,433	−4,295	−1,385	−3,325	−831	−358,141
−6,096	−2,771	−4,433	−4,295	−1,385	−3,325	−831	−358,141
−6,096	−2,771	−4,433	−4,295	−1,385	−3,325	−831	−358,141
−6,096	−2,771	−4,433	−4,295	−1,385	−3,325	−831	−358,141
−6,096	−2,771	−4,433	−4,295	−1,385	−3,325	−831	−358,141
−6,096	−2,771	−4,433	−4,295	−1,385	−3,325	−831	−358,141
−6,096	−2,771	−4,433	−4,295	−1,385	−3,325	−831	−358,141

The bank arranger may charge a periodic fee for making sure that the synthetic CDO uses the most favorable language for the investor. When the bank arranger hedges itself in the European market, it may not be able to get terms such as modified restructuring. This creates a language mismatch between the protection bought from the CDO and the protection sold in the market. The bank arranger will charge a small negotiable fee to hedge the language mismatch for the specific contracts involved. For the purposes of this spreadsheet, I assumed that all of the contracts are hedged, although in practice, some or all of the contracts will not require a hedge. I arbitrarily set a mismatch fee of 5 bps, but mismatch fees as low as 2 bps are sometimes available.

Structuring fees, legal fees, and rating agency fees are paid up front, but for purposes of looking at net cash flows I'm amortizing the fees over the life of the deal at a rate of 4.0 percent. This is arbitrary. The higher the assumed rate, the higher the costs reflected in the amortized cash flows. To be a bit perverse, I've assumed that collateral interest and reserve account interest is only 1 percent, thus penalizing the deal relative to the amortized costs. In practice, an actual rate curve can be used to determine the interest rate to use to amortize each period's costs or to calculate each period's interest.

The cash flow to the SPE before management fees is calculated for the no-loss scenario simply by multiplying the total notional amount of the deal by the premium available in the marketplace. In this example, the gross spread for the entire portfolio is 198 bps, or 1.98 percent. The net cash flow to the SPE after subtracting deal costs is shown in Table 5.16.

Of course, our synthetic arbitrage CDO has management fees of 12.5 percent, and each tranche pays interest, which is the liability cost. Notice that the Aaa rated tranche was to be offered at LIBOR + 50 bps. In the spreadsheet, I've used 55 bps to show that in a typical deal, some room is usually allowed so that the underwriters can sell the tranches cheaper, if necessary. If the tranches are sold at 50 bps, the 5 bps may be passed on to the equity holder, or may be retained by the underwriter. This is negotiated between the manager and underwriter when the fees and level at which the tranches are underwritten is discussed.

Notice that the IRR on the equity is around 30.60 percent in the no-loss scenario (see Table 5.17). Based on the Moody's loss rates for this portfolio, I'll use a base case constant annual default rate (CADR) of 0.25%, and a 35 percent recovery rate. I'll assume the first default occurs immediately, and recovery occurs six months after default and is cash settled. At this base case CADR, the equity residuals suggest an IRR of 27.92 percent (see Table 5.18).

We can also stress test the cash flows for a 1.00 percent CADR, and the equity residuals are 16.9 percent. Notice that taking into account recoveries, the losses do not yet exceed the original investment in the equity. Once

TABLE 5.16 Cash Flows to SPE

Year Fraction	Month	Period Beg. Date	Days in Period	Notional Balance	Cumulative Notional Losses	Notional Cash Flow A/360 in arrears 1.980%	Total Fees & Costs −7,162,814	Net Premium Paid to SPV 174.49 bps
0	0	11/1/02	0	500,000,000	0	0	0	2,171,859
0.255556	3	2/1/03	92	500,000,000	0	2,530,000	−358,141	2,089,359
0.247222	6	5/1/03	89	500,000,000	0	2,447,500	−358,141	2,171,859
0.255556	9	8/1/03	92	500,000,000	0	2,530,000	−358,141	2,171,859
0.255556	12	11/1/03	92	500,000,000	0	2,530,000	−358,141	2,171,859
0.255556	15	2/1/04	92	500,000,000	0	2,530,000	−358,141	2,116,859
0.250000	18	5/1/04	90	500,000,000	0	2,475,000	−358,141	2,171,859
0.255556	21	8/1/04	92	500,000,000	0	2,530,000	−358,141	2,171,859
0.255556	24	11/1/04	92	500,000,000	0	2,530,000	−358,141	2,171,859
0.255556	27	2/1/05	92	500,000,000	0	2,530,000	−358,141	2,089,359
0.247222	30	5/1/05	89	500,000,000	0	2,447,500	−358,141	2,171,859
0.255556	33	8/1/05	92	500,000,000	0	2,530,000	−358,141	2,171,859
0.255556	36	11/1/05	92	500,000,000	0	2,530,000	−358,141	2,171,859
0.255556	39	2/1/06	92	500,000,000	0	2,530,000	−358,141	2,089,359
0.247222	42	5/1/06	89	500,000,000	0	2,447,500	−358,141	2,171,859
0.255556	45	8/1/06	92	500,000,000	0	2,530,000	−358,141	2,171,859
0.255556	48	11/1/06	92	500,000,000	0	2,530,000	−358,141	2,171,859
0.255556	51	2/1/07	92	500,000,000	0	2,530,000	−358,141	2,171,859
0.247222	54	5/1/07	89	500,000,000	0	2,530,000	−358,141	2,089,359
0.255556	57	8/1/07	92	500,000,000	0	2,447,500	−358,141	2,171,859
0.255556	60	11/1/07	92	500,000,000	0	2,530,000	−358,141	2,171,859

TABLE 5.17 Residual Equity Cash Flows—No-Loss Scenario

Net Premium Paid to SPV 174.49 bps	Management Fee 0.125%	Account 1 Collateral Interest 1.00%	Account 2 Collection & Operating 1.00%	A-1 Super Senior 0.10% 432,500,000	A-2 Aaa 0.55% 20,000,000	A-3 Aa2 1.10% 12,500,000	B Baa2 3.50% 15,000,000	Cash Flow Total Ex-Equity	Interest On Equity Collateral 1.00%	Residual Cash IRR 30.60% 20,000,000 1.00%
	−625,000			0	0	0	0	−625,000		−20,000,000
2,171,859	0	118,750	2,290,609	−110,528	−28,111	−35,139	−131,250	1,627,441	48,438	1,675,878
2,089,359	0	118,750	2,208,109	−106,924	−27,194	−33,993	−131,250	1,550,607	48,438	1,599,045
2,171,859	0	118,750	2,290,609	−110,528	−28,111	−35,139	−131,250	1,627,441	48,438	1,675,878
2,171,859	−625,000	118,750	2,290,609	−110,528	−28,111	−35,139	−131,250	1,002,441	48,438	1,050,878
2,171,859	0	118,750	2,290,609	−110,528	−28,111	−35,139	−131,250	1,627,441	48,438	1,675,878
2,116,859	0	118,750	2,235,609	−108,125	−27,500	−34,375	−131,250	1,576,219	48,438	1,624,656
2,171,859	0	118,750	2,290,609	−110,528	−28,111	−35,139	−131,250	1,627,441	48,438	1,675,878
2,171,859	−625,000	118,750	2,290,609	−110,528	−28,111	−35,139	−131,250	1,002,441	48,438	1,050,878
2,171,859	0	118,750	2,290,609	−110,528	−28,111	−35,139	−131,250	1,627,441	48,438	1,675,878
2,089,359	0	118,750	2,208,109	−106,924	−27,194	−33,993	−131,250	1,550,607	48,438	1,599,045
2,171,859	0	118,750	2,290,609	−110,528	−28,111	−35,139	−131,250	1,627,441	48,438	1,675,878
2,171,859	−625,000	118,750	2,290,609	−110,528	−28,111	−35,139	−131,250	1,002,441	48,438	1,050,878
2,171,859	0	118,750	2,290,609	−110,528	−28,111	−35,139	−131,250	1,627,441	48,438	1,675,878
2,089,359	0	118,750	2,208,109	−106,924	−27,194	−33,993	−131,250	1,550,607	48,438	1,599,045
2,171,859	0	118,750	2,290,609	−110,528	−28,111	−35,139	−131,250	1,627,441	48,438	1,675,878
2,171,859	−625,000	118,750	2,290,609	−110,528	−28,111	−35,139	−131,250	1,002,441	48,438	1,050,878
2,171,859	0	118,750	2,290,609	−110,528	−28,111	−35,139	−131,250	1,627,441	48,438	1,675,878
2,089,359	0	118,750	2,208,109	−106,924	−27,194	−33,993	−131,250	1,550,607	48,438	1,599,045
2,171,859	0	118,750	2,290,609	−110,528	−28,111	−35,139	−131,250	1,627,441	48,438	21,675,878

TABLE 5.18 Residual Equity Cash Flows—Base Case Scenario: 0.25% CADR / 35% Recovery

Month	Period Beg. Date	Days in Period	Notional Balance	Cumulative Notional Losses Due to Default	Notional Cash Flow A/360 in Arrears 1.980%	Net Premium Paid to SPV 174.08	Residual Cash IRR 27.92% 20,000,000 1.00%
0	11/1/02	0	500,000,000	0	0		−20,000,000
3	2/1/03	92	498,750,000	1,250,000	2,523,675	2,165,691	1,044,866
6	5/1/03	89	498,750,000	1,250,000	2,441,381	2,083,397	1,593,239
9	8/1/03	92	499,187,500	812,500	2,525,889	2,167,850	1,671,970
12	11/1/03	92	499,187,500	812,500	2,525,889	2,167,850	1,043,845
15	2/1/04	92	497,937,500	2,062,500	2,519,564	2,161,681	1,662,833
18	5/1/04	90	497,937,500	2,062,500	2,464,791	2,106,908	1,612,931
21	8/1/04	92	498,375,000	1,625,000	2,521,778	2,163,840	1,666,031
24	11/1/04	92	498,375,000	1,625,000	2,521,778	2,163,840	1,037,906
27	2/1/05	92	497,125,000	2,875,000	2,515,453	2,157,671	1,656,893
30	5/1/05	89	497,125,000	2,875,000	2,433,427	2,075,646	1,581,628
33	8/1/05	92	497,562,500	2,437,500	2,517,666	2,159,830	1,660,091
36	11/1/05	92	497,562,500	2,437,500	2,517,666	2,159,830	1,031,966
39	2/1/06	92	496,312,500	3,687,500	2,511,341	2,153,661	1,650,954
42	5/1/06	89	496,312,500	3,687,500	2,429,450	2,071,770	1,575,823
45	8/1/06	92	496,750,000	3,250,000	2,513,555	2,155,821	1,654,152
48	11/1/06	92	496,750,000	3,250,000	2,513,555	2,155,821	1,026,027
51	2/1/07	92	495,500,000	4,500,000	2,507,230	2,149,652	1,645,015
54	5/1/07	89	495,500,000	4,500,000	2,425,473	2,067,894	1,570,017
57	8/1/07	92	495,937,500	4,062,500	2,509,444	2,151,811	1,648,213
60	11/1/07	92	495,937,500	4,062,500	2,509,444	2,151,811	17,145,088

accumulated losses exceeded the original equity investment of EUR 20,000,000, cash flows would divert to the reserve account. Table 5.19 shows the cash flows for the stress case scenario.

Earlier we discussed economies of scale. If this deal were EUR 1,000,000,000 in size, or double the current size, the deal economics improve dramatically. The no-loss scenario equity IRR would be 37.7 percent, the base case scenario of a CADR of 0.25 percent per annum with a 35 percent recovery rate would be 35.4 percent, and the stress case with a CADR of 1 percent per annum with a 35 percent recovery rate would be 26.4 percent.

But wait a minute, I was using a 35 percent recovery rate for these calculations. Shouldn't I use the industry standard of 40 percent? Most investment grade deals in the European market were marketed with a 50 percent recovery rate at the beginning of 2001. That was indefensible then and is indefensible now. Even 40 percent may seem too high to many buyers, although this is a very popular way to market these deals. In practice, I would also do sensitivity analyses over a wide range of recovery rate scenarios. Table 5.20 shows the effect of doubling the deal size as well as the effect of a 5 percent change in the recovery value assumption for this particular deal from 35 percent to 40 percent.

Sensitivities will vary by deal. One can, however, develop a feel for the order of magnitude of the effects. Spreadsheets like this are useful, because they can instantaneously calculate sensitivities. Many simulation models take a much longer time to calculate sensitivities. They may be more precise, but they are often not more accurate. Many sophisticated models are not transparent, making them difficult to troubleshoot. For all of these reasons, spreadsheets provide a good cross-check of results.

Whatever the model, the structure of the CDO is the real key to the value of a CDO investment. Model refinements are wonderful, but a small error in a model is insignificant compared to accepting a structure that does not give one the proper claim to cash flows in the deal, as we'll discover in the next chapter.

Since the Moody's CADR is a standard method for modeling and for showing results across a wide variety of deals, I use this for our example. The CADR assumptions shown above are what investors will find in most marketing and research pieces published by the street. The reality is that these numbers often do not capture the *granularity* of actual portfolios. You'll recall that each obligor makes up 2 percent of my portfolio. Historical probabilities indicate that a smaller percentage of my portfolio would default on a per annum basis, but in fact when a single default occurs, it will affect 2 percent of my investment portfolio. The argument is that it would be unfair to tag the portfolio with a prerecovery default of 2 percent right away, because it is unlikely this would happen. The theory is that if

TABLE 5.19 Residual Equity Cash Flows—Stress Case Scenario: 1.00% CADR/35% Recovery

Month	Period Beg. Date	Days in Period	Notional Balance	Cumulative Notional Losses Due to Default	Notional Cash Flow A/360 in Arrears 1.980%	Net Premium Paid to SPV 172.85	Residual Cash IRR 16.90% 20,000,000 1.00%
0	11/1/02	0	500,000,000	0	0		-20,000,000
3	2/1/03	92	495,000,000	5,000,000	2,504,700	2,147,184	1,026,828
6	5/1/03	89	495,000,000	5,000,000	2,423,025	2,065,509	1,575,820
9	8/1/03	92	496,750,000	3,250,000	2,513,555	2,155,821	1,660,246
12	11/1/03	92	496,750,000	3,250,000	2,513,555	2,155,821	1,022,746
15	2/1/04	92	491,750,000	8,250,000	2,488,255	2,131,146	1,623,696
18	5/1/04	90	491,750,000	8,250,000	2,434,163	2,077,053	1,577,756
21	8/1/04	92	493,500,000	6,500,000	2,497,110	2,139,782	1,636,488
24	11/1/04	92	493,500,000	6,500,000	2,497,110	2,139,782	998,988
27	2/1/05	92	488,500,000	11,500,000	2,471,810	2,115,107	1,599,938
30	5/1/05	89	488,500,000	11,500,000	2,391,208	2,034,504	1,529,377
33	8/1/05	92	490,250,000	9,750,000	2,480,665	2,123,743	1,612,731
36	11/1/05	92	490,250,000	9,750,000	2,480,665	2,123,743	975,231
39	2/1/06	92	485,250,000	14,750,000	2,455,365	2,099,068	1,576,181
42	5/1/06	89	485,250,000	14,750,000	2,375,299	2,019,002	1,506,156
45	8/1/06	92	487,000,000	13,000,000	2,464,220	2,107,704	1,588,973
48	11/1/06	92	487,000,000	13,000,000	2,464,220	2,107,704	951,473
51	2/1/07	92	482,000,000	18,000,000	2,438,920	2,083,029	1,552,423
54	5/1/07	89	482,000,000	18,000,000	2,359,390	2,003,499	1,482,935
57	8/1/07	92	483,750,000	16,250,000	2,447,775	2,091,666	1,565,216
60	11/1/07	92	483,750,000	16,250,000	2,447,775	2,091,666	3,552,716

TABLE 5.20 Managed Synthetic Arbitrage CDO Economies of Scale: Equity IRRs

Scenario	35% Recovery Deal Size		40% Recovery Deal Size	
	500 Million	1 Billion	500 Million	1 Billion
No Loss	30.60%	37.70%	30.60%	37.7%
Base Case[a]	27.92%	35.39%	28.1%	35.52%
Stress Case[b]	16.90%	26.42%	17.96%	27.24%
Discrete Default Case[c]	21.22%	29.72%	22.07%	30.41%

[a]Base Case CADR is 0.25% per annum.
[b]Stress Case CADR is 1.00% per annum.
[c]Discrete Default Case is one immediate obligor default and another default just before month 36.

we show the lower CADR based on historical defaults happening right away, we should probabilistically capture this effect.

A sensitivity analysis should include tagging the portfolio with immediate discrete defaults. The last row of Table 5.20 captures this. I've inserted a scenario in which one obligor defaults immediately, and another defaults just before month 36. I used a scenario in which I didn't have to divert equity cash flows to make this easier to follow. In practice, a scenario analysis would include the case where the original equity investment is exhausted and cash flows are diverted.

Most deal presentations will not include discrete default scenarios, and it is up to the investor to review this. Given the high degree of defaults in synthetic portfolios in the past two years, it is difficult to understand why this type of sensitivity analysis is not included in standard deal presentations, for instance, showing one default per annum, but that is simply not the case. On the other hand, standard marketing presentations for cash deals do not show this degree of stress testing, either.

As we mentioned before, there are economies of scale in bringing a CDO to market. Legal costs, rating agency fees, and structuring fees have a large upfront fixed component. In comparison, the ongoing maintenance fees are minimal. For the analysis above, I simply assumed that the initial portfolio was upsized to 1 billion, which means each obligor would have increased in value from EUR 10 million to EUR 20 million. I used this simplifying assumption so that I wouldn't have to retranche the portfolio and could compare deals in a consistent manner.

Unlike cash asset arbitrage CDOs, it is much easier to increase the size of a synthetic CDO by adding more obligors. Instead of increasing the obligor size from EUR 10 million to EUR 20 million, we simply could have increased the number of obligors from 50 to 100. This means we'd have 100 obligors with a notional size of EUR 10 million each. Now it is much easier to get a much higher diversity score for the underlying portfolio. It is also much easier to decrease the size of the equity tranche relative to the total deal.

In other words, instead of having an equity tranche that is 4 percent of the deal, we could create a smaller equity tranche on a percentage basis, as low as 2 percent to 3 percent in some transactions, and deals have come to market with even lower percentage equity tranches. This increases the leverage on the equity tranche and therefore dramatically increases the returns. For instance, for the deal shown above, if I decrease the size of the equity tranche to 2 percent of the deal, the equity IRR for the 1 billion Euro deal using the no-default scenario and a 35 percent recovery rate, increases from 37.5 percent to 78.2 percent. Of course, this isn't a strictly valid comparison. I didn't actually create a new portfolio, solve for the new tranching, calculate the new portfolio gross spread, and so forth. Nonetheless, it gives you a feel for the order of magnitude of the benefit. In this case, it is more than double the IRR. The increased leverage also makes the equity tranche more vulnerable in scenario analysis, but the smaller granularity of the portfolio works to the benefit of the investor.

Another observation about creating a spreadsheet for a synthetic deal is that it is very easy to follow the cash flows, troubleshoot calculations, and observe the effects of a sensitivity analysis. It is easy to see possibilities for refinements and possibilities for further analysis.

Cash deals are much more complicated to model. A portfolio of fairly straightforward bonds may include callable bonds or sinking funds. Furthermore, each bond's principal and interest must be modeled. Each bond has a different maturity and coupon, so the cash flows aren't nice and even. Now reinvestment assumptions become more critical, because the investor must be able to reinvest the proceeds of maturing bonds at a minimum spread for the deal economics to continue working. Furthermore, principal and interest coverage tests are more difficult to calculate. PIK tranches further complicate the spreadsheet. Hedges also add a degree of complexity. When the assets include ABSs or mortgage backed securities (MBSs), a program such as Intex might be required to model the deal's cash flows. Dedicated, skilled quantitative analysts are required to model these deals. Often a good programmer cannot anticipate the type of analysis a CDO structurer requires, or cannot anticipate structural innovation. Each deal usually has its own dedicated program to account for its structural anomalies. It is much harder to troubleshoot the cash flow economics and sensitivity analyses.

TABLE 5.21 Comparison of Cash and Synthetic CDOs

Cash Arbitrage CDOs	Synthetic Arbitrage CDOs
• Size limited to around $500 million	• Much easier to create larger size deals
• Large AAA tranche	• Large Super Senior above small AAA
• Long documentation	• Documentation is brief
• Higher funding cost	• Lower funding cost
• Complicated waterfall	• Relatively simple waterfall
• PIK-able tranches	• No PIK-able tranches
• Rating agency inconsistency	• Ratings more straightforward
• Substantial sourcing risk— limited european universe	• Reduced sourcing risk— wider universe
• Physical assets required	• Can securitize nontransferable assets
• Difficult execution, note placement	• Fewer notes
• Funded	• Unfunded or partially funded
• Managed	• Static or managed
• Management fees 50–75 bps p.a. typical	• Management fees 10–30 bps p.a.
• 10–15% high yield	• 100% investment grade
• Baa3/BBB– average rating	• A2/A to Baa3/BBB– typical
• Interest & currency risk	• No interest & currency risk
• 7–9 year A.L.; 10 year final maturity	• 5-year bullet (slightly longer legal final maturity)
• Transfers assets to trust or SPV	• No asset transfer required
• Less leverage. Equity is 8–20% of the deal.	• More leverage. Equity is 1.5–4.5% of the deal.

SUMMARY OF CASH ARBITRAGE CDOs VERSUS SYNTHETIC ARBITRAGE CDOs

Table 5.21 summarizes the key issues exemplified by our comparison of cash and synthetic CDOs.

CHAPTER 6

Cash Flow Caveats

If you don't understand what is going on with your cash flows, you are in serious trouble. As we saw in the previous chapter, it is important to understand under what conditions assets will pay expected cash flows. In this chapter we'll explore how to view cash flows in the context of a securitization.

First, let's take a step back for some caveats. We won't launch into a rigorous analysis of models. It's more useful to review some very simple examples of calculations that market practitioners routinely get wrong. These crop up again and again in various forms, and they cost both investors and capital markets groups extraordinary amounts of money.

Even when Monte Carlo engines have been well designed and sound methodology for random number generators have been used, the mistakes are made. The models are often precise, but not accurate. Incredibly, market professionals committed all the examples of conceptual errors I highlight below. The math in the following examples is simple, but people tripped over concepts. If one can't visualize the cash flows, how does one model them?

Cash flows matter. Timing, frequency, magnitude, and probability of receipt of cash flows are the four elements that determine the value of an asset. These are also the four elements that determine the value of a structure.

Before I go further, I'd like to clarify a few points. I'm often asked why I mention both timing and frequency. Isn't this redundant? I do this for absolute clarity. It is not sufficient to state that I will get all of my cash back within the year. This is merely the timing of my ultimate receipt of cash flows. I want to know the frequency. Will I receive the cash flow in one lump sum towards year-end, in equal monthly payments, or in a varied stream of payments over the course of the year? I'm not indifferent. This is why I emphasize timing and frequency.

Frequency of cash flows will imply different value to different investors. One reason is that different investors often have different reinvestment rates and different tax and accounting rules. One of the key factors that any investor should scout for in valuing a securitization is what assumptions are made for reinvestment of cash flows, both within a deal and in representing the deal's return to the investor. Everyone knows this, or do they?

What would the rate of interest be if you borrowed $500,000,000 from a bank and paid it back at the rate of $46,000,000 per month for a year? Okay, I know you don't know off the top of your head, but what would you guess it would be? You are paying back $552,000,000, which is 10.4 percent more than $500,000,000. Many smart people would guess the rate of interest is in the neighborhood of 10.4 percent.

They would be wrong.

The problem is that you don't have the full use of your money over the course of the year. The actual rate of interest is slightly more than 20.35 percent. That is very different from having full use of your money for the entire year and paying back $552,000,000 at the end of the year.

You will recall from corporate finance the internal rate of return (IRR), which makes the 12 stream of monthly $46,000,000 cash flows equal to $500,000,000, is 1.55598 percent. This is expressed on a monthly basis, however. Annualizing this rate: $(1 - (1 + .0155598)^{12}) \cdot 100 = 20.35\%$.

Of course, you saw this immediately. No one could be fooled by this type of financial optical illusion!

Oh, but they could.

Lenders to car buyers and white goods buyers perpetrated just this sort of financial optical illusion on American consumers until the law required lenders to state effective annual interest rates on loans. Many of those American consumers were bankers and Wall Street professionals.

One marketer of collateralized debt obligations (CDOs) for an American investment bank informed me that it wasn't necessary for him to know too much about the cash flow details. Marketing is marketing. In fact, he said accusingly, I was probably one of those people who can correctly calculate his own taxes. He was right. It allows me to correctly employ tax advantages, free and legal, from your respective governments! I didn't mention this last bit because I suspected he'd ask me to do his. Perhaps he's right about marketing, too. His approach might even work for marketing used cars, but would you accept a financing rate from this man?

CONVENTIONAL WISDOM

One has to know the calculation conventions for the financial instruments one models. Ignorance can cost money. Mistakes can cost money. Perversely, mistakes are rarely in one's favor.

Recently, an investment banker from one of the top five U.S. banks was arranging bond issuance for a northern European bank. The deal economics were agreed and the bond was to have a stated coupon at a set semiannual bond equivalent yield (BEY). The U.S. bond market convention uses a 30/360 day count basis and a semiannual BEY. For instance, if the agreed rate for the bond is a semiannual BEY of 8.806 percent, the coupon is paid semiannually or twice a year. The coupon rate is 8.806 percent divided by 2 or 4.403 percent. It doesn't need to obey rules of logic. It's just a convention.

The investment banker, who graduated from a good U.S. East Coast business school (the University of Chicago is in the Midwest), said that some of the investors wanted a quarterly coupon. To keep the economics the same, he told them he would pay them a quarterly coupon of 2.2015 percent, or 4.403 percent divided by 2. I pointed out to him that the economics were not the same. This is because 2.2015 percent times 4 would imply a quarterly bond equivalent yield of 8.806 percent and that equated to a higher bond semiannual BEY than 8.806 percent. In fact it equated to just a bit more than 8.9029 percent.

Despite all his time in the market, he was lost. The quarterly bond rate he needed to quote was 8.71 percent, or a payment of 2.1775 percent 4 times per year. Rather than face the fact that he would have to call his investors and correct his earlier statement, he tried to argue why it didn't make any material difference. He persisted until I showed him the numbers. For the 12-year $250,000,000 bond deal the error made a payment difference of $60,000 per quarter. Every quarter. For 12 years. Would he offer to personally make up the difference?

Another common error occurs when comparing fixed coupons with floating coupons. A rate of 10 percent calculated on a bond basis is not the same as 10 percent calculated on a money market basis. Similarly, the number of basis points (bps) under London InterBank Offered Rate (LIBOR) calculated on a bond financing is not the same as bond bps.

One bond bp is not equal to a LIBOR or money market bp. Conventionally, conversions are done on a bond basis. If we change the frequency and go from quarterly money market (QMM) to semibond, we must first convert QMM to a quarterly bond basis, and then convert to semibond.

Example:
3-month LIBOR is at 5 percent. You achieve a financing cost of LIBOR − 25 bps. What is the semiannual BEY?

$$5.00 - .25 = 4.75\% \text{ QMM}$$

$$((1 + 4.75 \cdot (365/360) / 4 \cdot 100) \wedge 2 - 1) \cdot 200 = 4.84\% \text{ s.a. BEY}$$

Note that 5 percent QMM = 5.10 semiannual BEY and the difference between 5.10 percent and 4.84 percent is 26 bps on a semiannual BEY basis.

This difference is not a constant, and discrepancies are larger for higher levels of interest rates.

These are only a few pitfalls. Structurers write programs to deal with the day count conventions of various instruments in various countries. In addition, structurers write programs to account for different ways of calculating interest rates. But not everyone gets it correct, so it is useful for investors to check the cash flows themselves. At the minimum, an occasional spot check is in order.

ACCRUING ERRORS

When asked to make the following simple calculation by hand, many people get an incorrect answer. If you don't believe me, and want to have a little fun, ask a friend to solve the following:

Refer to Table 6.1. Using just a pencil and paper, create a two-bond portfolio using bonds A and C to duration match and proceeds match bond B.

The solution is as follows:

The market value of B = 0.6 × $1,000,000 = $600,000

Since the duration of B is halfway between that of A and C, half of the dollars must be invested in A and half of the dollars must be invested in C. Therefore, I must purchase $300,000 of A and $300,000 of C.

The required par amount of A = $300,000/0.75 = $400,000

The required par amount of C = $300,000/0.5 = $600,000

The key is that I'm investing the proper amount of dollars in each bond so that I get the expected change in dollar amounts on my hedge. In order

TABLE 6.1 A Simple Calculation

Bond	Modified Duration	Full Price	Par Amount
A	4	75	$400,000
B	5	60	$1,000,000
C	6	50	$600,000

to make this work, I have to normalize the par amount I purchase by the full prices of the bonds. Of course, everyone knows how to do the math, but when attention flags, it is easy to use the wrong basis in formulating the calculation.

Mistakes in interest calculations and mistakes in forward price calculations affect CDO warehousing calculations, portfolio cash flow calculations, and structured product calculations.

Let's assume that interest rates have moved higher from the levels at year end 2002, and the yield curve is steeper. I can borrow money for 14 days at a rate of $7\frac{1}{8}\%$ on an actual/360 basis. Let's also assume that I can purchase a U.S. treasury (UST) bond with a coupon of $11\frac{1}{4}$ at a dollar price of $104^{10}/_{32}$ (a current yield of approximately 10.8 percent).

The bond pays coupons on the fifteenth of the month each six-month period in May and November of every year. It is now August 1, and I am financing this bond until August 15, for 14 days. Furthermore, I do not mark-to-market.

On August 1, the flat price of the bond is $104^{10}/_{32}$, so I would pay $1,043,125.00. The accrued interest is $23,845.11 (accrued from 5/15 to 8/1: 78/184 days). The full price of the bond is $1,066,970.00 (106.6970).

I own the bond on August 15 and do not mark-to-market. Therefore, in 14 days, my flat price is still 1,043,125.00 and the accrued on the bond is now $28,125. My income over the fourteen-day period is $4,279.89. My borrowing cost is $(\$1,066,970.11 \cdot .07875 \cdot 14)/360 = \$3,267.60$. This means I have a *positive carry* of $1,012.29.

In an *arbitrage free* world, I cannot borrow to buy and earn this kind of excess cash, so the market would tell me that the forward price must be such that I have *zero positive carry*.

To satisfy the arbitrage free condition, if I wanted to sell this bond forward, the forward price would be such that I could not make a profit. The accrued interest remains the same, so the forward flat price of the bond must change to meet the arbitrage free condition.

The *forward flat price* would have to be as follows:

$$\$1,043,125 - \$1,012.29 = \$1,042,112.71 \ (104.211271)$$

Note that the forward flat price is lower than the price on August 1. This is known as "the drop."

The forward price doesn't always have to be lower, however. Suppose interest rates have moved even higher and the yield curve is *inverted*. I can borrow money for 14 days at a rate of 15 percent on an actual/360 basis. Let's further assume that I can purchase a UST bond with a coupon of

12.5 percent at a dollar price of $105^{10}/_{32}$. This bond pays coupons on the fifteenth of the month each six-month period in May and November of every year. It is now August 1 and I am financing this bond until August 15, for 14 days. Furthermore, I do not mark-to-market.

What is the *flat price* (the ex-interest price) of this bond on August 1? The flat price is simply $105^{10}/_{32}$ or a dollar amount of $1,053,125.00. The *accrued interest* is $26,494.57 (accrued from 5/15 to 8/1: 78/184 days). The *full price* of the bond is $1,079,619.56 (quoted as 107.961956). The full price of the bond is the amount that I have to pay for the bond.

I own the bond on August 15 and do not mark-to-market. Therefore, in 14 days, my flat price is still $1,053,125.00, but the accrued on the bond is now $31,250.00. My income over the 14-day period is $4,755.43. My borrowing cost is ($1,079,619.56 · .15 · 14)/360 = $6297.78. This means I have a *negative carry* of $1,542.35.

The forward price is higher than the spot price. The forward flat price would be 1,053,125.00 + 1,542.35 = 1,054,667.35 plus accrued of 31,250.00, so the full price of the bond is 1,085,917.35 or 108.591735.

If you are long a forward commodity contract, you have an obligation to purchase the commodity or give its cash equivalent on the pre-agreed delivery date. The value of a long forward contract is calculated as follows:

$$f_L = (F_0 - D_L)e^{-rT}$$

where F_0 = the forward price of contract today
D = the delivery price on settlement date
r = the continuously compounded interest rate applicable for period from trade date to settlement date
T = time from trade date to settlement date

If you are short a forward commodity contract, you have an obligation to sell the commodity (or you will receive its cash equivalent) on the pre-agreed delivery date. The value of a short forward contract is calculated as follows:

$$f_S = (D_S - F_0)e^{-rT}$$

where F_0 = the forward price of contract today
D = the delivery price on settlement date

r = the continuously compounded interest rate applicable for
period from trade date to settlement date
T = the time from trade date to settlement date

Petroleum-related forward contracts often exhibit *normal backwardation*. This means *the future price is lower than the spot price* and the futures prices tend to decline as maturity increases, so the price curve is negatively sloped. Keynes's theory of normal backwardation is based on the premise that production is planned and consumption is flexible. Consumers of the commodity can buy it from many sources, but producers commit to production, and sometimes consume some of the commodity in the process of production. Hedgers who produce and are long the underlying commodity tend to go short futures, and speculators tend to go long futures. Keynes theorized speculators require a positive risk premium, meaning they must earn a positive abnormal expected return to take on the risk that the hedgers are trying to avoid.

For most nonpetroleum-related commodities, the forward price curve is in *contango*, meaning that the *forward price exceeds the spot price*. Keynes's theory ignored long hedgers, and the fact that speculators can make money off incompetent or unlucky speculators. Nonetheless, the petroleum markets tend to exhibit backwardation, but none of the Enron trades, which consisted of natural gas and oil contracts, seemed to exhibit backwardation.

I can almost hear the wails of protest. But no one gets accrued interest wrong! No one gets forward price calculations wrong!

But they do. They get it wrong and they get it wrong frequently.

In fact, a simple error in accrued interest calculations brought down the house. At least it brought down the house of Kidder Peabody (see the section titled "Structured Finance and Kidder Peabody").

These calculations can also be used to disguise chicanery. Enron and J.P. Morgan were involved in odd prepaid forward transactions, and the courts are trying to determine whether the transactions were actually disguised loans. (See the section titled "Enron, J.P. Morgan, and Offshore Vehicles").

PROBABILITY OF RECEIPT

The probability of receipt of cash flows appears so simple that it seems it doesn't bear mentioning. Yet this is a key risk that most residual cash flow investors or CDO equity investors assess when they buy these securities. Errors in assessing this risk can be of such orders of magnitude that they swamp the cash flow risks mentioned previously.

Much depends on tolerance for potential losses. For instance, suppose I'm asked to make a bet of $100. There is a 50 percent chance I will win $300 immediately and a 50 percent chance I will lose the entire $100 immediately. I will take the bet. I don't mind losing $100, and the expected return is $150(0.5 × $300 + 0.5 × $0).

Now suppose I'm asked to make a bet of $20 million. There is an 80 percent chance I'll win $30 million and a 20 percent chance I'll lose $20 million. I will probably decline the bet, because I don't want to lose $20 million, even though the expected value is $24 million. The downside risk is too catastrophic. Expected value is another financial optical illusion. Probability of receipt or loss of cash flows is important, and so is magnitude of the cash flows.

Let's further suppose I'm a hedge fund or an investment group of a reinsurance company, and I want to buy equity that has a payoff profile similar to the previous example. I don't want to put any money up front, but I want someone to finance the losses as they occur. I also want the transaction to be done in the form of a credit default swap (CDS), and I want a bank to provide me with financing until the maturity of the transaction. This would mean that the bank would pay any credit losses, and I would be charged a finance rate for the money paid to cover the losses. This money is essentially a loan to me, which I must repay at the maturity of the CDO. Does the bank know how many of these transactions I've engaged in already? Should the bank lend me the money to make my bets?

It gets even more interesting if we change the payoff profile. Say I bet $20,000,000 for a 25 percent chance of winning $30,000,000; a 25 percent chance of getting back only $15,000,000; a 25 percent chance of getting back only $5,000,000; and a 25 percent chance of getting back nothing. Now my expected return is only $12,500,000. I would avoid this bet even if I were asked to bet only $100 because the expected payoff is lower than my initial bet. Yet this is what happens to people who play against house odds at a casino, even though the odds are more in favor of the player at a casino. CDO equity investors are making a more complicated bet with a more complicated payoff profile. Yet many equity investors unwittingly set themselves up for probable returns that were lower than their original investments even at the inception of their trade. How did that happen?

EQUITY STRUCTURES

All equity tranches are not created equal. Besides portfolio selection, the largest variability among deals stems from the structure of the equity cash

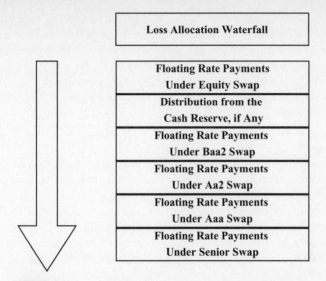

FIGURE 6.1   Loss Allocation in Reverse Order of Seniority

flows. Portfolios can either be actively managed, have limited right of substitution, or be completely static. Equity can be either rated or unrated. The investment in equity can be either funded or unfunded. There is also a wide variety of ways that cash flow is made available to the equity investor and to the senior tranches.

For example, in synthetic deals, we're familiar with the loss allocation diagram in Figure 6.1.

Losses are allocated first to the equity investor. That isn't the whole story, however. CDOs vary in terms of how much of the stream of residual cash flow the equity investor can claim. Another key issue is the amount of loss that can be allocated to the residual cash flow stream above and beyond the initial equity investment. The equity investor determines whether or not he is getting the best deal possible for the risk he takes, based on these structural features.

The more cash flow the equity investor gets, the less someone else gets. The following summarizes some of the common structures currently in the market:

■ The equity investor has the right to a return of original principal plus a fixed coupon only. One type of structure actively marketed in 2001–2002 offered fixed coupons in the neighborhood of 15 to 25 percent. The coupon is paid on the remaining equity balance only. This means that if the original equity investment is used to absorb losses due to default, the coupon is calculated only on the net balance. The remaining excess cash flows are paid to the bank arranger.

- The equity investor has the right to a return of original principal plus a fixed coupon only, but all of the residual cash flows are made available to pay the principal plus fixed coupon to the equity investor. Once this pre-agreed amount is satisfied, the remaining cash is paid to the bank arranger.

- The equity investor has the right to a portion of the equity residual cash flow and the bank arranger retains a small strip of the residual equity cash flows.

- The equity investor has the right to the residual cash flows, but only if losses remain below a certain threshold. This threshold is usually set at 50 to 100 percent of the initial equity investment. For instance, for a 50 percent threshold, residual cash flows will be diverted to the reserve account once portfolio losses exceed $10 million, if the original equity investment is $20 million. The reserve account funds are made available to the Aaa and Aa noteholders in the unlikely event the funds are needed to meet coupon payments. Funds are also available for the unlikely event they are needed to repay principal, because losses threaten the return of principal to these highly rated tranches.

- The equity investor may invest funds that are used to purchase highly rated collateral, such as treasuries. This highly rated collateral serves to overcollateralize the portfolio, and the equity investor earns the residual cash flows. The overcollateralization reduces the equity leverage. This device is used primarily for deals using lower rated collateral such as highly leveraged transactions (HLTs) or high yield bonds. The former Chase Secured Loan Trust (CSLT) deals used this type of structure.

- The equity investor gets maximum leverage and has the exclusive right to all of the residual cash flows. Loss is limited to the original investment in the equity. That is the worst type of deal from the point of view of investors in the other tranches, but it is the best type of deal for the equity investors. As we'll discover later, if the portfolio is managed and not static, this structure has the highest degree of moral hazard.

This last structure is not exactly the same as the structure used for our earlier cash CDO deals, because cash CDO deals include structural protection for the senior investors. Overcollateralization (O/C) ratio test, interest coverage (I/C) ratio tests, and trading constraints worked to the benefit of the senior tranches. Senior noteholders should not be indifferent to the payout structure to the equity investor.

EQUITY EARNS ALL RESIDUALS, BUT LOSS IS LIMITED TO ORIGINAL INVESTMENT

In many cash managed CDOs and certain synthetic managed arbitrage CDOs, the equity investor claims all of the residual cash flows. Earlier, we saw how these cash flows waterfalled in a typical cash managed arbitrage CDO. The equity investor enjoys a payout of all of the residual cash flows as they occur, and the equity investor absorbs losses up to the amount of the initial equity investment only. Once the losses exceed the initial equity investment, accumulated cash flows above this amount are paid as they occur exclusively for the benefit of the equity investor. Any cash remaining at the maturity of the deal is paid out exclusively for the benefit of the equity investor.

If the equity holder manages this type of structure, the moral hazard is that once losses exceed the initial equity investment, the manager has an incentive to create a portfolio with as much spread income as possible. Any further losses are borne by noteholders above the equity level. The next tranche in seniority is in peril. The only protections the other tranche investors have from this behavior are trading restrictions and cash flow triggers. If a trading desk is managing the deal and holding the equity tranche, it will attempt to pass on as many structural risks to the other tranche holders as it can.

When trading desks hold the equity of static synthetic CDOs, their first priority is to claim all of the residual cash flows.

EQUITY INVESTOR INJECTS CASH AS OVERCOLLATERALIZATION

Let's look at an example we haven't used before. In some structures, the equity investor invests a cash amount, which serves to overcollateralize a portfolio as a means of added credit enhancement for the senior investors. The equity cash flows are usually unrated, but it is possible to get a rating from Fitch or Moody's for a segment of the equity cash flows that would have the same probability of loss as an investment grade rated security. The entire residual cash flow stream due to the equity investor is not rated, but

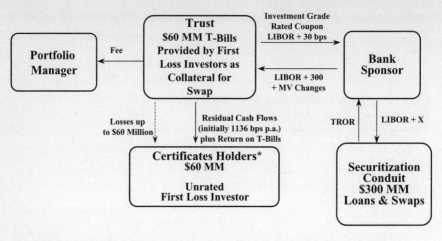

*Noteholders and certificate holders have pari passu cash flow priority. Profit and loss is magnified by leverage.

FIGURE 6.2   CDO Equity Investors Receive Unrated Residual Cash Flows

a probable return of a preset amount of cash flow is rated. Usually the return of principal and ultimate (not timely) return of an investment grade equivalent coupon is rated.

Figures 6.2 and 6.3 show a funded equity tranche in which the investor gets all of the residual cash flows. The second structure shows a

*Noteholders and certificate holders have pari passu cash flow priority. Profit and loss is magnified by leverage.

FIGURE 6.3   CDO Equity Investors Receive Residual Cash Flows: Part of Equity Cash Flow Is Rated

rated portion of the first loss cash flows plus an unrated portion. In this structure, equity investors have varying degrees of leverage, but they both have first loss risk.

Of course, the equity doesn't have to be rated. Both cash and synthetic arbitrage CDOs often have unrated first loss tranches. The leveraged nature of the equity tranche means that as credit spreads widen, the equity investor receives a leveraged benefit from the widening as a new deal is assembled. Rating agency tranching is required for the rated senior tranches, and this determines the size of the unrated first loss tranche. Rating agency tranching remains constant when credit spreads widen due to causes other than downgrades. Credit spreads may widen due to supply and demand conditions as sometimes happens in the CDS market.

In 2002, new issue arbitrage CDOs on investment grade corporates saw base case equity IRRs gap out from lows of 10 to 15 percent to as high as 50 to 60 percent in the fall of 2002.

Figure 6.4 shows a principal protected Schuldschein (PPS) structured from a static synthetic arbitrage CDO with a 2.5 percent equity tranche

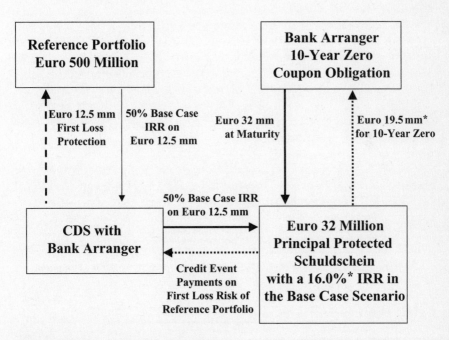

*Note: Base case scenario IRRs were as low as 8% in the spring of 2001. Widening spreads made these structures much more attractive by the fall of 2002.

FIGURE 6.4 Unrated Equity Repackaged as 10-Year Principal Protected Schuldschein

from a well-diversified portfolio 500 million Euros in size. The equity base case IRR is 50 percent and the base case IRR on the PPS is 16 percent. In the spring of 2001, investors were happy to receive a base case PPS IRR of only 6.5 to 8.0 percent depending on the underlying collateral. In the fall of 2002, 16 percent and more was achievable.

RATED EQUITY EARNS STATED COUPON APPROPRIATE TO RATING

Moody's has provided a Aaa rating for the equity of managed synthetic arbitrage CDOs. It's rare, but possible. The equity has a fixed coupon consistent with a Aaa rated bond in the neighborhood of 5.5 to 6 percent for a Euro asset. Moody's and Fitch rate the timely return of principal and the ultimate payment of the stated note coupons. Ratings to date have been private ratings. Since a rating of this type is inconsistent with Standard & Poor's (S&P's) methodology, S&P does not provide ratings on equity tranches, no matter what the cash flow structure. At least, this was their position in the fall of 2002.

The equity investor absorbs losses up to the entire equity investment only, but all residual cash flows are made available to absorb losses. Any accumulated cash flows remaining at maturity belong to the deal manager. The deal manager adds value to the deal by absorbing portfolio trading losses, if any, in return for potential deal upside if there are any remaining cash flows after all of the tranche holders are paid off. This type of deal gives the manager an incentive to attempt to achieve trading gains, and also gives the manager an incentive to avoid losses throughout the life of the deal.

Figure 6.5 shows the equity cash flows from the special purpose vehicle (SPV) and deal tranches. The waterfall in Figure 6.6 shows how the deal management fee might be structured to give the manager a further performance incentive. A subordinated management fee is paid only if losses are less than 50 percent of the original equity investment. The subordinated management fee gives the manager an incentive to keep the losses to the equity investor—and therefore the rest of the investors—to a minimum.

RATED EQUITY: STATIC DEAL

Static synthetic arbitrage CDOs by definition are unmanaged. Therefore, there are no management fees to contribute to the deal costs and fees. Since

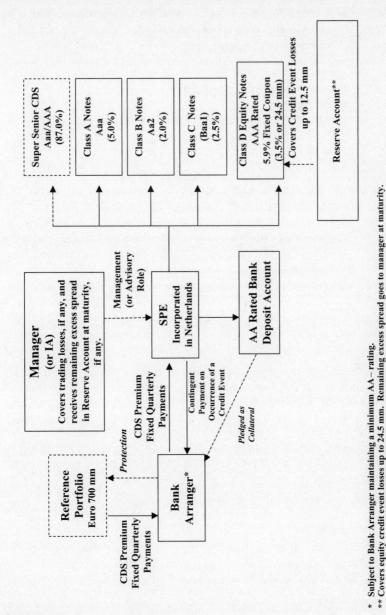

FIGURE 6.5   Managed Synthetic Arbitrage CDO: Rated Equity Cash Flows

* Subject to Bank Arranger maintaining a minimum AA− rating.
** Covers equity credit event losses up to 24.5 mm. Remaining excess spread goes to manager at maturity.

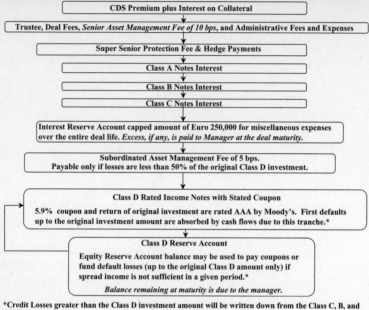

FIGURE 6.6   Managed Synthetic Arbitrage CDO: Waterfall for Rated Equity

there is no trading of the original portfolio, there are no potential trading losses. This means there is more cash flow available under every scenario to increase the probability of the return of the equity investor's original investment plus a stated coupon consistent with an investment grade rated tranche.

For a well-diversified portfolio of investment grade credits, it is much easier to get an investment grade rating on a stated coupon first loss note, than it is for a managed deal. Rating agencies do not have to take into account trading losses and management fees when they stress test the cash flows. The static deal equity structure and cash flow waterfall are shown in Figures 6.7 and 6.8.

In the static deal illustrated in Figures 6.7 and 6.8, who receives the benefit of excess cash flows, if any, once the rated notes are paid off?

Incredibly, this is negotiable. Some equity investors will accept that as long as they receive the rated cash flows, they will not ask for the potential additional upside of the remaining residual cash flows. The deal arranger will keep the excess.

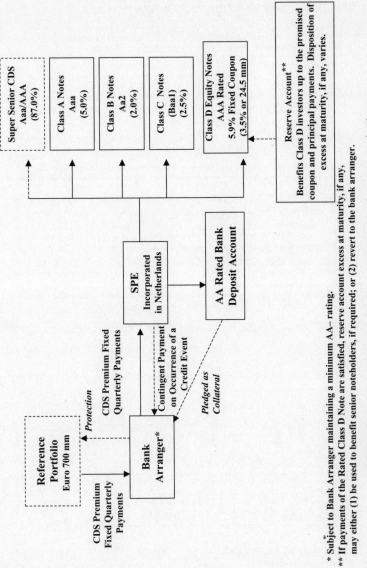

Reference Portfolio Euro 700 mm

CDS Premium Fixed Quarterly Payments

Protection

Bank Arranger*

CDS Premium Fixed Quarterly Payments

Contingent Payment on Occurrence of a Credit Event

SPE Incorporated in Netherlands

Pledged as Collateral

AA Rated Bank Deposit Account

Super Senior CDS Aaa/AAA (87.0%)

Class A Notes Aaa (5.0%)

Class B Notes Aa2 (2.0%)

Class C Notes (Baa1) (2.5%)

Class D Equity Notes AAA Rated 5.9% Fixed Coupon (3.5% or 24.5 mm)

Reserve Account** Benefits Class D investors up to the promised coupon and principal payments. Disposition of excess at maturity, if any, varies.

* Subject to Bank Arranger maintaining a minimum AA– rating.

** If payments of the Rated Class D Note are satisfied, reserve account excess at maturity, if any, may either (1) be used to benefit senior noteholders, if required; or (2) revert to the bank arranger.

FIGURE 6.7 Static Synthetic Arbitrage CDO: Rated Equity Cash Flows

187

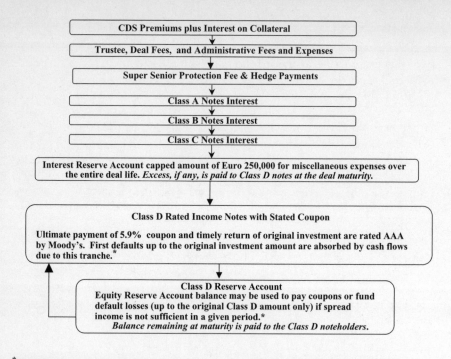

FIGURE 6.8   Static Synthetic Arbitrage CDO: Waterfall for Rated Equity

Some investment banks create a rated equity note to broaden distribution of the first loss tranche to investors who would otherwise not be able to invest in equity. Some investors can purchase BBB rated notes, but cannot buy unrated equity. By offering a AAA rated equity tranche with potential upside, they can reach new investors. All of the excess residual cash flows will be made available to these investors.

EQUITY INVESTOR EARNS A STATED COUPON ON THE REMAINING EQUITY INVESTMENT

Most of the initial static synthetic CDOs promised to pay a coupon on the remaining equity balance. The equity was unrated. Suppose the initial equity tranche size is Euro 25 million. The CDO paid a stated fixed annual coupon of 20 percent. Any cash flows in excess of the amount needed to make the liability payments for the CDO benefit the bank arranger.

This is also the structure employed in portfolio swaps, which is a term used to describe a product that can be as simple as a 50-name portfolio with two tranches. In general, a portfolio swap can refer to any CDS of any portfolio, including the reference portfolio for a CDO.

If the portfolio experiences 6 million in losses, the 20 percent coupon is paid only on the remaining balance of Euro 19 million. There is usually excess cash flow above and beyond what is needed to pay the coupon on the remaining equity balance. This excess cash flow benefits the bank arranger. The cash flow in Table 6.2 is adapted from our previous example.

Notice that there are significant excess cash flows that will be paid to the bank arranger at the termination of the deal, if losses occur according to the historical constant annual default rate (CADR) of 0.25 percent. We recall that the equity IRR stated under the no-loss scenario is 19.089 percent, but this is a semiannual BEY. Stated on an annual basis, this is 20 percent. Likewise, the equity IRR under the 0.25 percent CADR scenario is 13.775 percent on a semiannual bond equivalent basis, which is 14.25 percent on an annual basis.

The equity doesn't need to be as straightforward as in the example above. In fact, the cash flows as constructed above don't give the equity investor the best possible deal. The previous structures give the equity investor access to more of the cash flows of the deal and access to a larger payout. Many equity investors were unaware of this fact.

Several German insurance companies bought this type of equity structure embedded in PPS. Since the return of principal is supplied by a zero coupon bond embedded in this structure, the equity cash flows are used to pay current income on the PPS.

Because the principal is protected, if the IRRs of the combined structure look good under the no-loss and base case CADR scenarios, it is easy to ignore the fact that the equity investor does not have a claim to all of the residual cash flows. Most investors did not question the structure of the equity tranche. It was also interesting that these investors were usually shown scenario analysis assuming a 50 percent recovery rate.

The attraction of the PPS structure is that German insurance companies do not have to mark-to-market a Schuldschein. Nonetheless, there is no reason not to get the best deal possible on the cash flows embedded in the structure.

Since the equity investor absorbs the first loss, investors should look at the likely loss experience throughout the life of the deal. Stress testing is also a good idea. Of course, the loss calculation is affected by our assumptions about recovery. As we saw earlier, we can do some sophisticated calculations to determine equity performance under scenarios. That is always a good idea. A very simple and straightforward technique is to look at the

TABLE 6.2 Equity Investor Earns Stated Coupon on Remaining Balance—Equity Is Unrated

Month	Equity Remaining Balance No Defaults	Investor's Equity Payout Residual Cash IRR 19.09%	Net Cash Available No Default Scenario	Equity Remaining Balance Due to Defaults	Investor's Equity Payout Residual Cash IRR 13.77%	Net Cash Available 0.25% CADR 40% Recovery
0	20,000,000	−20,000,000	19,375,000	20,000,000	−20,000,000	19,375,000
3	20,000,000	0	21,050,878	20,000,000	0	21,044,866
6	20,000,000	0	22,654,113	20,000,000	0	22,642,279
9	20,000,000	0	24,338,189	18,750,000	0	23,072,718
12	20,000,000	4,000,000	17,401,475	18,750,000	3,750,000	16,629,233
15	20,000,000	0	23,082,420	19,250,000	0	22,548,002
18	20,000,000	0	24,716,345	19,250,000	0	24,171,191
21	20,000,000	0	26,405,576	18,000,000	0	24,601,845
24	20,000,000	4,000,000	19,474,031	18,000,000	3,600,000	18,458,575
27	20,000,000	0	25,160,157	18,500,000	0	24,227,935
30	20,000,000	0	26,773,665	18,500,000	0	25,826,338
33	20,000,000	0	28,468,040	17,250,000	0	26,257,523
36	20,000,000	4,000,000	21,541,651	17,250,000	3,450,000	20,414,785
39	20,000,000	0	27,232,946	17,750,000	0	26,035,052
42	20,000,000	0	28,851,635	17,750,000	0	27,634,490
45	20,000,000	0	30,551,205	16,500,000	0	28,066,587
48	20,000,000	4,000,000	23,630,024	16,500,000	3,300,000	22,524,764
51	20,000,000	0	29,326,540	17,000,000	0	27,996,325
54	20,000,000	0	30,950,464	17,000,000	0	29,597,182
57	20,000,000	0	32,655,281	15,750,000	0	30,030,578
60	20,000,000	24,000,000	6,364,360	15,750,000	18,900,000	9,665,058

survival rate of tranches for a given number of defaults. To do this, we create a table of the number of discrete obligor defaults, and assume a recovery rate. Then we determine when each tranche takes its first loss and when each tranche is finally exhausted due to losses.

Tables 6.3 and 6.4 show the effect of losses on the remaining equity balance for 2 assumed recovery rates: 50 percent and 40 percent, respectively.

In the context of actual recoveries experienced in the period from 1999–2002, a recovery rate of 50 percent seems ridiculously high. The benefit of simple tables like these is to show the sensitivity to recovery rates to a number of discrete defaults.

Tables like these are straightforward when the equity is structured as discussed above (coupons are calculated from the remaining balance), and when the amount invested in each obligor is the same. They are more difficult to put together when equity cash flows are constructed differently and when the timing of the occurrence of defaults matters to the net equity cash flows. Similar tables can still be constructed for specific scenarios, however.

Investors in the senior tranches also look at tables like these. Super senior investors in particular may want to know how many losses the deal can sustain before the super senior investor would experience a loss.

At first glance earning a stated coupon on the remaining equity balance looks as if it is the same as the previous rated equity structure, but it isn't. This equity is unrated. The stated coupon is paid from interest on the original investment amount, plus the deal cash flows. As losses occur, the equity is written down up to the amount of the original investment and the coupon amount is calculated on the lower balance.

Unlike the previous rated equity structure, once losses occur, the equity investor has no claim to further cash flows beyond the remaining balance and coupons on the remaining balance. The investor has no claim on excess residuals beyond this. The equity investor has a much lower probability of recovering the initial investment plus a coupon. The stated coupon is usually much higher than for rated structures that include all residuals, but the coupon still doesn't reflect all of the potential residual cash flows of the deal.

We recall that if the equity investor isn't entitled to all of the residual cash flows, and if the senior noteholders do not benefit from the excess residual cash flows (if required), the deal arranger keeps the remaining cash flows. The exception to this is when the manager agrees to accept potential trading losses in return for a claim to excess residual cash flows not required to satisfy a rated equity tranche. Equity investors should not give away residuals to arrangers or managers who don't have either first loss risk or trading loss risk.

TABLE 6.3 Effect of Default Rate on Equity—Recovery Rate, 50%; Equity Tranche, 4%

Class	Subordination	Defaults to Experience First Euro Loss (50% Recovery)		Defaults to Experience Full Principal Loss (50% Recovery)	
		# Defaults	Cum. Default Rate	# Defaults	Cum. Default Rate
SS	16%	16	32%	50	100%
A1	11%	11	22%	16	32%
A2	8%	8	16%	11	22%
B1	4%	4	8%	8	16%
E	NA	NA	NA	4	8%

Euro 500 Million Portfolio. Each Obligor is Euro 10 million.
This CDO is structured so that the equity investor earns a stated coupon on the remaining initial investment less accumulated losses, if any. Accumulated losses for this calculation cannot exceed the amount of the initial equity investment.

TABLE 6.4 Effect of Default Rate on Equity—Recovery Rate, 40%; Equity Tranche, 4%

Class	Subordination	Defaults to Experience First Euro Loss (40% Recovery)		Defaults to Experience Full Principal Loss (40% Recovery)	
		# Defaults	Cum. Default Rate	# Defaults	Cum. Default Rate
SS	16%	13.3	26.6%	50	100.0%
A1	11%	9.2	18.3%	13.3	26.6%
A2	8%	6.7	13.3%	9.2	18.3%
B1	4%	3.3	6.7%	6.7	13.3%
E	NA	NA	NA	3.3	6.7%

Euro 500 Million Portfolio. Each Obligor is Euro 10 million.
This CDO is structured so that the equity investor earns a stated coupon on the remaining initial investment less accumulated losses, if any. Accumulated losses for this calculation cannot exceed the amount of the initial equity investment.

CONFLICT OF INTEREST BETWEEN THE RESIDUAL HOLDER AND SENIOR TRANCHE INVESTORS

If a deal manager has a claim on the equity cash flows, there may be a conflict of interest between the manager and senior noteholders. Investors should be particularly wary of deals in which four structural conditions are met, which can tempt managers to behave against the interest of the noteholders. The first is that losses are allocated in reverse order of seniority, and losses deductions are limited to the initial investment of each tranche investor. The second condition is that excess spread does not accrue to the benefit of any of the noteholders and is not available to absorb losses. The third condition is that the manager does not have adequate restraints on his ability to cause a deterioration in the quality of the underlying portfolio. The fourth condition is that the manager has a claim on the excess spread. Figure 6.9 shows an example of this type of structure.

When losses exceed the initial equity investment, all of the residual cash flows are diverted to the benefit of the manager. The manager now has an incentive to trade out of good credits into credits on negative credit watch or even into lower rated, but higher spread credits, if there are no constraints prohibiting this. In any case, a manager must have some latitude to make judgment calls, but now the temptation will be to make judgment calls that result in higher spread, even if this means the portfolio will deteriorate.

Notice that once the equity is gone, the next most senior noteholder bears additional losses. If that is a BBB noteholder, any new losses reduce the BBB principal amount, and the high coupon payment is now calculated off a lower principal amount. The deal liabilities are decreasing, and the manager earns more excess spread.

You might be thinking to yourself that this is so reprehensible that it could never happen. But it has happened. In fact, a large "yankee bank" (the U.S. branch of a non-U.S. bank) in New York invested in a single A rated tranche of a deal brought by a major investment banking firm, and this is exactly what happened. The deal tranches experienced multiple downgrades. The investors forcefully complained to the manager, with no result. The originally investment grade portfolio was actively traded down in credit quality and became a noninvestment grade portfolio, a *junk* portfolio.

The yankee bank was in danger of losing some of its original principal investment. They brought the matter to one of the rating agencies who said it was statistically impossible for an investment grade portfolio to reach the junk status this deal's portfolio achieved in that period of time. The rating

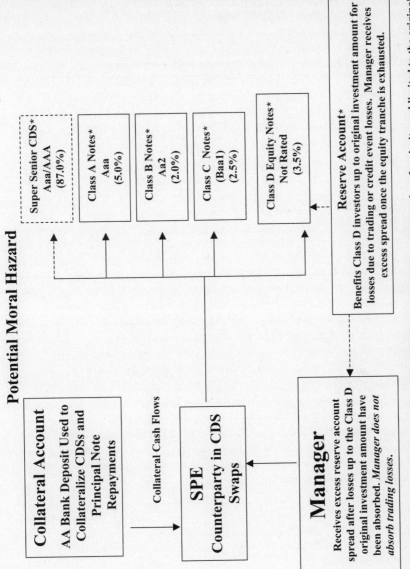

Potential Moral Hazard

Collateral Account

AA Bank Deposit Used to Collateralize CDSs and Principal Note Repayments

Collateral Cash Flows

SPE
Counterparty in CDS Swaps

Manager

Receives excess reserve account spread after losses up to the Class D original investment amount have been absorbed. *Manager does not absorb trading losses.*

Super Senior CDS*
Aaa/AAA
(87.0%)

Class A Notes*
Aaa
(5.0%)

Class B Notes*
Aa2
(2.0%)

Class C Notes*
(Baa1)
(2.5%)

Class D Equity Notes*
Not Rated
(3.5%)

Reserve Account*

Benefits Class D investors up to original investment amount for losses due to trading or credit event losses. Manager receives excess spread once the equity tranche is exhausted.

* All reference portfolio credit event losses and trading losses are allocated in reverse order of seniority and limited to the original tranche investment.

FIGURE 6.9 Potential Conflict of Interest Between Manager and Investor

195

agency was wrong. Perhaps if you assumed a random sampling of investment grade credits, the rating agency was correct, but the manager was working hard at investing in risky high spread credits.

The yankee bank contacted their lawyers in an attempt to get the investment bank to make amends. They even considered leaking their story to the *Wall Street Journal* in an attempt to embarrass the investment bank. They didn't, and I believe that was a wise idea. It's possible that an institutional investor may embarrass himself if he attempts to paint himself as a naïve victim of a sharper bank. The yankee bank might have asked itself why it didn't ask for more structural protections in the first place. It was enticed by the illusion of a slightly higher original coupon, but ignored the structural risk.

UNFUNDED EQUITY INVESTMENTS— ULTIMATE LEVERAGE

Equity risk can be transferred synthetically, just like any other risk. In most cases the investor, as the credit protection provider, must pay the loss amount on the settlement date for credit events, if any, covered by the first-loss protection. In between the deal closing and a credit default settlement date, the only money that changes hands is the premium payment to the investor under the terms of the CDS shown in Figure 6.10.

Who are the investors in unfunded equity? As you might imagine, the investors are usually hedge funds or the offshore subsidiary of a reinsurance company. Saying an investor is "an offshore subsidiary of the reinsurance company" sounds good to bank management and bank credit officers, but these subsidiaries that sell first-loss protection are essentially *hedge funds*. Because these are off-balance sheet transactions, the investors usually don't want to disclose how much of this risk they have taken on. They also usually don't want to disclose the exact deals, with the exact reference portfolios, in which they've invested.

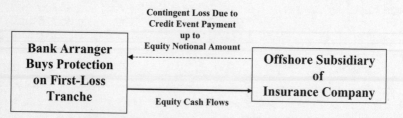

FIGURE 6.10 Unfunded Equity Risk Transfer

These investors want *leverage*. One would think that buying equity risk in unfunded form would be leverage enough. These investors ask for even more leverage. They ask the bank sponsor to *fund the losses*. This means that if the portfolio experiences a loss, the subsidiary of the reinsurance company (or a hedge fund) wants the CDO bank arranger to make the required payment to the CDO's special purpose entity (SPE). The CDO bank arranger must have an open credit line to the subsidiary of the insurance company or to the hedge fund, and must allow this to be drawn in the event of a default. The sponsoring bank is usually asked to charge only LIBOR + 25 for this funding.

The problem with this is that most of the CDOs for which this has been done are synthetic CDOs with 5-year maturities. The liabilities will all come due about the same time. In five years, the investors will have to come up with a big chunk of cash, and these are the investors that didn't want to put up cash in the first place. Of course, they don't have a 5-year track record with this type of investment, and are reluctant to disclose the degree of leverage they already have. They may have a solid investment grade rating, but rating agencies cannot keep up with the activities of these entities.

Structurers eager to get deals done have rammed deals like this through their institutions. Often the equity investor drives the deal, and in 2001 and 2002, some investment banks and banks had trouble finding enough mainstream equity investors. They turned to these willing "investors" instead.

Of course these investors are interested. Sky high returns and no money up front. In fact, investors make no loss payments for five years, and earn income in the interim. The investors can use the CDS premiums to pay the interest on the loans the banks give them to fund the equity losses, if any. What a deal!

These "investors" hate questions. One of my favorite questions is: "How are you guys compensated?" They especially hate that question.

My point is that the personnel are usually very new. Does their contract pay them on current revenues and ignore future liabilities? How are they reporting this deal internally? Are they exploiting some internal accounting glitch to get high bonuses today and move on before the potential losses need to be paid (and thus have no bonus that year)? The usual retort is that it is none of your business. I disagree. If you are relying on this investor to make the payments, you want to understand the investor's commitment to the survival of this business.

These "investors" may have a point, however. If you are a structurer, and you are compensated for current deal fee income, the long run may not matter to you, either. Most financial institutions have had rapid turnovers in personnel due to layoffs or other attrition. These departments often have rivals within the institution who want to take over their business. Everyone is under pressure to report high current fees. Under such circumstances, management is spending most of its time trying to survive or to jockey for position. They won't put in the time to understand these products or these issues. It's an accident waiting to happen. If structurers want to stuff a bank trading book with risk in order to earn high current fees, they won't be too picky about their equity "investors."

For every strategy, there is a counterstrategy, however. Let's say you want to do one of these deals, but you also want to survive a competent internal deal review. If you are dealing with the subsidiary of a reinsurance company, it may be possible to buy credit default protection on the subsidiary. In five years' time, when payment for the losses comes due, and if they begin defaulting on obligations, you are covered. The premium for the CDS should be folded into the deal economics. For instance, the subsidiary of the reinsurance company could receive a lower net premium on the equity. This strategy may make your deal less competitive in the eyes of the subsidiary, however, because CDS premiums are usually quoted in hundreds of bps per annum for these subsidiaries. For example, in fall of 2000, one subsidiary had a AA rating, but the credit default protection on the subsidiary traded at 400 bps (4 percent) per annum. At the time, equity returns on investment grade synthetic static portfolios were in a range of 16 to 22 percent per annum.

ACTIVELY TRADED AND LIMITED SUBSTITUTION SYNTHETIC ARBITRAGE CDOs

When the bank arranger has a claim to part of the residual cash flows, they may also have the right to actively trade the portfolio or to perform limited substitution of names in the portfolio. This is especially true for synthetic arbitrage CDOs.

Many investors do not see the point in having a manager. They feel the manager earns a fee, which reduces overall cash flows available for the deal. They feel the manager wouldn't avoid losses due to event risk such as Railtrack or fraud such as Enron. They also fear that if the bank arranger has the right to trade the portfolio, once losses do exceed the original equity investment, the portfolio is up for grabs. The bank arranger will have every incentive to dump deteriorating credits into the portfolio to pump up the excess cash flows. Meanwhile the tranche investors up the line will absorb any extra losses due to default.

Investors who choose to participate in these deals should take this as fair warning. The best defense is good structural protection within the documentation. Documentation may call for limited substitution only. This may limit the number of obligors that may be substituted in a given period. It may also limit the ability to substitute obligors that have not traded wider than a certain threshold amount relative to its peer group or to its historical spreads. We saw some of these restrictions earlier when we discussed the managed synthetic arbitrage CDO. These restrictions included limiting names traded to 10 percent of the portfolio per year, and rating and outlook restrictions for each substituted name.

Note that the previously mentioned manager did not have a stake in the equity cash flows. If the bank arranger acts as manager, even more severe restrictions should be included in the documentation. The senior tranche investors—particularly an outside super senior investor—may include right of refusal of names substituted in the portfolio.

INTEREST SUBPARTICIPATIONS (ISPs): WHEN EQUITY ISN'T FIRST LOSS

In Europe, the ISP structure has been used in many balance sheet CDOs issued by many banks located in Germany and the Netherlands. Banks in these venues are exploiting a regulatory capital regulation loophole. Normally, equity attracts a one-for-one regulatory capital charge. This means that for every Euro 10 million of equity, the bank must take a Euro 10 million capital charge. If a bank has a return on regulatory capital target of 18 percent, the bank must get a stable return of 18 percent or Euro 1.8 million on the equity to meet this target. In some venues, such as Germany, future interest does not require any capital charge at all. In other words the capital charge is *zero*. The ISP structure is meant to allow a bank sponsor to appear to be securitizing the equity risk of a portfolio of assets, but in reality the bank retains the first-loss risk.

There is a possibility that the ISP might not get a 0 percent capital treatment, but may still only attract a 100 percent times 8 percent Bank for International Settlements (BIS) risk weighted charge. For a Euro 10 million first-loss tranche, this amounts to 100 percent times 8 percent times Euro 10 million or only Euro 800,000. Now to achieve an 18 percent return on capital, the bank only needs to earn Euro 144,000 (see Table 6.5).

Figures 6.11 and 6.12 show both funded and unfunded ISPs of a bank balance sheet CDO.

The ISP entitles the investors to an ISP in the future interest income of the reference pool. If the CDO allocates a loss to the "equity" investor, the investor in the ISP receives a payment equal to the loss amount. *The issuer* makes this payment to the investor in the ISP tranche.

TABLE 6.5 Equity and Potential ISP Treatment

	Equity	Potential ISP Treatment
Regulatory Capital Charge	1:1	100% times 8%
Size of Investment (Euros)	10,000,000	10,000,000
Capital Charge (Euros)	10,000,000	800,000
Earnings for 18% ROC*	1,800,000	144,000

*Return on capital.

The available interest income is the total amount of interest payments paid on the entire reference portfolio during the ISP period. If the accumulated losses exceed the current calculation amount available, it is possible to recover the losses later as the total accumulated interest on the reference portfolio continues to build over time, up to the maturity of the ISP note.

You may be wondering about these interest payments. Aren't the other tranches of the deal higher in the waterfall, and aren't interest payments used to pay the coupons on these notes first? Yes, of course. How is it possible that the holder of the ISP tranche potentially receives a payment equal to the entire interest accrued up to the payout time?

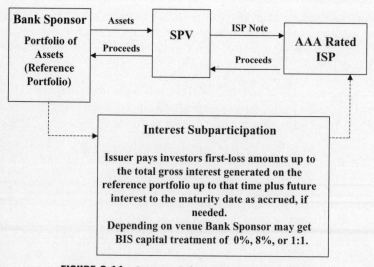

FIGURE 6.11 Interest Subparticipation (Funded)

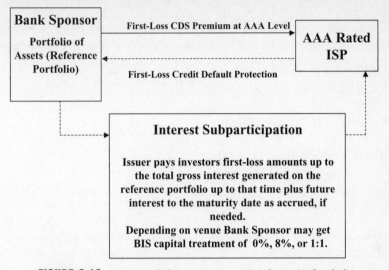

FIGURE 6.12 Interest Subparticipation (Synthetic Unfunded)

The answer is that the payment does not come from the interest on the reference portfolio. The payment comes from the issuer's own funds, even though the calculation amount is based on the interest earned by the reference portfolio. This is merely a calculation device to make sure there is a very high likelihood that the holder of the ISP note will get paid. It is unlikely that the accumulated losses will exceed the entire interest paid on the reference portfolio assets during the life of the ISP notes.

This means that the issuer has in effect retained first-loss risk under most probable scenarios. One could imagine an extremely high default scenario in which accumulated interest is insufficient to cover first loss on the ISP tranche, but it is very unlikely. In fact, it is so unlikely that ISP pieces achieve private ratings as high as AAA, or AA, although some have had ratings as low as single A.

The amount of the protection the issuer provides for first-loss events is usually much greater than required. The benefit will depend on the gross interest of the portfolio and the size of the equity tranche. For instance, if the portfolio gross interest is 8 percent, and the first-loss tranche is only 2 percent, the first-loss coverage is four times the amount needed.

European bank portfolio managers have invested in ISP notes as if they are rated floaters that offer enhanced coupons. The extra coupon income usually paid on the ISP note compensates the investor for the time it takes to understand the structure. When these structures first appeared a few years ago, investors could earn a premium to same-rated floaters of 20 to 40 bps. By 2002, often there was no enhanced coupon for the ISP structure because it was much better understood by a much wider investor base.

PARTICIPATION NOTES (PNs)

Investors who must invest in rated notes, yet want income upside potential versus current market coupons, will consider investing in a PN. PNs are rated, but either with respect to return of principal only, or with respect to return of principal plus the ultimate return of a small coupon. Ratings on PNs vary from AAA to Ba2. The rating will depend on whether (1) principal plus coupon is rated, (2) principal only is rated, (3) the rating of the rated tranche is used in combination with the equity, and (4) the ratio of equity to the rated tranche is used in combination with the equity.

PNs allow an investor to own a portion, or *participate*, in the equity cash flows on a pro rata basis with the other equity investors. For example, using a single CDO, I can combine Euro 8 million of the AAA tranche and 2 million of the equity tranche. The equity return is 15.5 percent and the AAA is priced at Euribor + 50. The participation note will have an expected rating of Aa2, but only for return of principal and for payment of a coupon of Euribor − 120 bps. However, the expected coupon on the note is Euribor + 120 bps. The upside potential on the coupon is due to the participation in the unrated equity tranche, most of which cannot be commingled in the rating. In the same market environment, a Aa2 trades at only Euribor + 80 bps.

Figure 6.13 shows an example of a PN. Notice that a vertical slice of the equity tranche is used to create the PN. This means that in terms of seniority, the equity investment is the same as the equity investment of the other equity holders. Therefore, this portion of the equity investment participates on a pro rata basis in the equity cash flows with the other equity investors.

PNs can be structured at the same time as the CDO. That won't necessarily work for all investors. When the deal is being marketed, an investor may request that some of the equity be combined with a AAA tranche after the fact. In that case, the tranches can be combined in an SPV and the return of principal and a submarket coupon of the SPV issued Euro medium term note (EMTN) can be rated. It is usually slightly more expensive to create a PN after the deal has been tranched and rated.

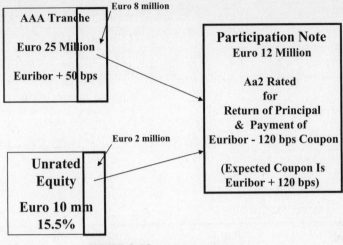

FIGURE 6.13   Participation Note

CAPPED PNs

PNs that use a senior slice of the equity tranche, combined with a rated tranche from the same CDO, often have a cap on the upside to the participation noteholder. The equity investment is no longer pari passu with the other equity investors. The loss is borne first by the junior equity investors and then by the equity portion of the PN investment. The senior equity investment has a preset yield and the coupon on the PN is, therefore, capped.

COMBINATION NOTES (CNs)

CNs or *combo* notes combine two *rated* classes of notes from the same CDO, but will not include an equity tranche (even rated equity). Ratings on CNs vary about as much as PNs. Usually CNs are rated BBB and above, but it is possible to have a lower rating on a CN.

Not all CNs look attractive when compared to alternatives. Figure 6.14 shows a CN of a CDO. The CDO's AAA rated tranche has a coupon of Euribor +50 bps and the Baa2 tranche has a coupon of Euribor + 285 bps. The CN combines a Euro 6.66 million investment in the AAA tranche and a Euro 3.34 million investment in the Baa2 rated tranche. The resulting CN is rated A2 for timely payment of both principal and coupons, and has a

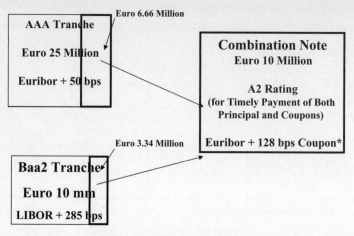

*At the time this was not attractive versus A2 rated CDO tranches at Euribor + 155 bps.

FIGURE 6.14 Combination Note

coupon of LIBOR +128. In the same market environment, A2 rated tranches of CDOs with comparable collateral will trade at around LIBOR +155 bps. This particular CN does not look attractive to potential investors, given the alternatives.

A CN can be structured at the time the CDO is structured, or any time before closing. If the deal has already closed and an investor is interested in a CN from the existing rated tranches, a portion of the tranches can be combined in a multi-issuance SPV and an EMTN CN can be issued from the SPV.

INVESTOR MOTIVATION

Both CNs and PNs allow more investors to participate in a deal's cash flows in a specific way. Investors who normally cannot buy unrated equity can do so in the form of a rated PN. In the United States, insurance companies get favorable capital treatment for notes rated above single A. This was the motivation for creation of the lower leveraged equity tranche in the secured loan trust structure we saw earlier. The National Association of Insurance Commisioners (NAIC) rates these securities NAIC 1, their highest rating, and insurers hold less capital against these holdings. Since these securities are created as one note with one Committee on Uniform Securities Identification Procedures (CUSIP) number, they probably will not be separated out into rated and unrated components for capital purposes.

Banks and funds that require rated securities for investment portfolios are also buyers of these notes. Banks may have renewed interest in these rated securities with upside potential when BIS II comes into effect. Highly rated notes will get favorable capital treatment relative to lower rated notes, and of course, will receive much more favorable capital treatment than equity.

PRINCIPAL PROTECTED STRUCTURES

As we saw earlier, principal protected structures can be issued directly by a highly rated issuer. In that case, the investor looks to the issuer for principal repayment. It is possible to get the principal rated the same rating as the highly rated issuer by a rating agency. If the issuer has a BIS risk weighting lower than 100 percent, there may be advantages to certain investors who can utilize the lower BIS risk weighting and who are able to consider the note as having the BIS risk weighting of the issuer. For instance, certain sovereigns have a 0 percent BIS risk weight. In Europe, Organization for Economic Cooperation and Development (OECD) banks have a 20 percent BIS risk weight.

Equity is usually repackaged with zero coupon bonds issued by highly rated entities. An SPE issues a note with proceeds adequate to buy the zero coupon that accretes to par at maturity to pay off the principal on the note. The remaining note proceeds are used to purchase equity, which provides cash flows for interest payments on the note. Figure 6.15 outlines the cash flows. In this instance, the note uses the zero coupon bond of a AA1 rated OECD bank. Although the equity has a 5-year maturity, the zero coupon bond has a 10-year maturity. The residual cash flows can be smoothed and reinvested to make a steady stream of coupon payments in the equity no-loss scenario. Alternatively, the investor may choose to receive all residual cash flows as they are paid by the underlying CDO and either liquidate the note at the 5-year maturity or hold it until the 10-year maturity and receive par at maturity. Longer dated maturities on the underlying zero allow for a lower price for the principal protection and a larger participation in the equity cash flows.

Figure 6.16 shows the expected IRR for an investment in the equity residual cash flows without principal protection. The IRR is shown for various annual default rates. Notice that the IRR of the equity declines as the default rate increases. If the default rate approaches 3 percent per annum, the IRR of the equity investment becomes negative for this particular deal.

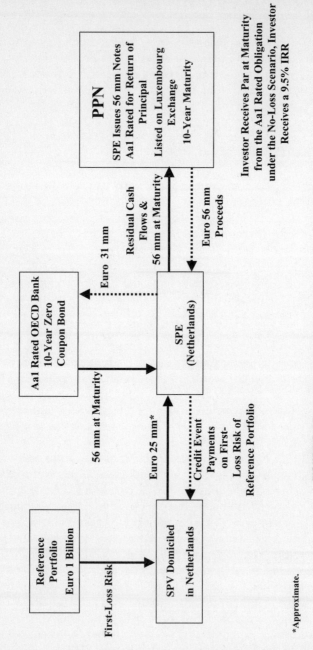

FIGURE 6.15 Principal Protected Note—Equity Repackaging

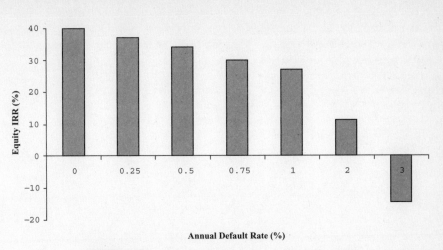

FIGURE 6.16 Effect of Default Rate on Equity IRR

The IRR of the principal protected note (PPN) starts out lower than that of the equity investment, but does not go negative due to the assumption of principal protection. The principal risk is that of the Aa1 rated issuer, and we are assuming it has not defaulted and it is not a reference credit for the CDO from which the equity has been created. A default of a

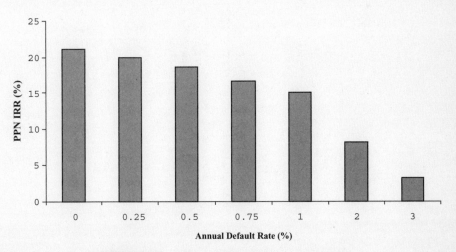

FIGURE 6.17 Effect of Default Rate on PPN IRR

reference credit of the CDO will not have an effect on the principal repayment of the note (see Figure 6.17).

As we mentioned earlier, German insurance companies prefer PPS structures because they do not have to mark a Schuldschein to market. The economics of the structure are similar to the PPN.

CHAPTER 7

Balance Sheet CDOs

Consumer loan securitizations are balance sheet collateralized debt obligations (CDOs). As we saw earlier, the technology for these deals originated in the United States in the 1980s. New product development has centered on applying the lessons learned to nonconsumer loans.

The introduction of synthetics allowed new product development in the dollar market. The introduction of the Euro gave an added boost to balance sheet securitization, since Euro denominated assets found a new, broader investment base than was possible with the currency Tower of Babel that existed before 1999. A critical mass of technology, assets, and currency acceptability contributed to innovations in the U.S. market and product development in the European market. While new products appeared in 2002, the full menu of the following products is currently in use in the CDO markets.

Among the key distinctions we'll examine are funding cost and documentation differences. Another key distinction is that most synthetic balance sheet CDOs have *regulatory calls*. This means that when the Bank for International Standards (BIS) II regulatory capital rules come into effect, the issuers may call these CDOs. We'll discuss this in more detail at the end of this chapter.

TRUE SALE ("FULLY FUNDED"): DELINKED STRUCTURE

The first rated collateralized loan obligation (CLO) backed by U.S. bank loans was brought to market in 1990. The first deals were arbitrage CLOs, mainly securitizations of smaller size loans. The return on the equity tranche is the sole driver of an arbitrage CLO. The collateral manager's goal is to maximize the return on the equity tranche, the difference between the spread on the investment assets and the deal liabilities (coupons on the nonequity tranches and deal expenses). Arbitrage CLOs sometimes use sponsor collateral and also use collateral purchased in the secondary market. The deal arranger might not have an underwriting or servicing relationship with many of the loan obligors.

The bank originator/seller/sponsor is usually not motivated by a potential arbitrage. The bank originator that has assets on balance sheet is motivated by regulatory capital relief and wants to fund the assets off-balance sheet, similar to the motives for a traditional consumer loan asset backed security (ABS) transaction. The bank originator has an underwriting and servicing relationship with the borrowers. The bank originator in a fully funded CLO has intimate knowledge of the credit characteristics of the underlying borrowers.

The following characteristics are typical of these cash flow CLOs. Cash flow from interest on the underlying collateral services the deal liabilities, including coupons on the various CLO tranches and fees. Excess spread is diverted to a reserve account to service the deal.

These transactions have a two- to four-year revolving period called the *lockout* period. During the lockout period, the deal doesn't amortize. The deal manager invests principal from maturing loans in additional loans, according to criteria set out in the deal prospectus. Although defined reinvestment is allowed during the lockout period, cash flow balance sheet deals usually restrict trading throughout the life of the deal.

The lockout period is followed by an amortization period. Both principal and interest are repaid on a sequential basis. The payment priority is based on tranche seniority and tranches have a predetermined target amortization schedule.

The CLO will amortize early if one of several unwind triggers is breached. There are several types of possible unwind triggers that can cause the early termination of a fixed level structure, or that can cause early amortization of an amortizing structure. These triggers include insolvency of the issuer, breaching a boundary condition for collateral maintenance, or reaching a certain level of defaults on the underlying reference obligors, among others.

Note that commercial and industrial (C&I) loans can be either *bilateral* or *multilateral*. A bilateral loan means that the sponsor bank is the sole lender or *underwriter* to the borrower or *obligor* for that particular loan. Many loans are syndicated among several bank underwriters to reduce total obligor exposure. These multiunderwriter loans are multilateral loans.

Because the loans are sold, this transaction reduces the size of the bank's balance sheet. One would normally think this would be an advantage, allowing the bank to originate new business. Incredibly, some financial institutions reject this structure because this efficient transfer of risk combined with funding doesn't appeal to them. They don't want to reduce the size of their balance sheets. For instance, officers of savings banks in Germany are compensated based on the size of their balance sheet. The last thing they want is a major reduction in balance sheet size.

In the United States, C&I loans may be either fixed rate or floating rate. The tranches of balance sheet CLOs normally pay a floating rate coupon indexed to the London InterBank Offered Rate (LIBOR). Floating rate C&I loans can be indexed to a number of floating rate indexes. Many loans allow the credit spread of the loan versus the index to increase or decrease as the borrower's financial condition deteriorates or strengthens, respectively. This basis risk and spread risk of the underlying loan coupons, versus the ultimate note coupons, is hedged by entering into an interest rate swap with a hedge provider.

CLOs have varied in size from $300 million to $5 billion, although larger sizes are usually synthetic, nontrue sale, structures. By selling the interests in the loans to a special purpose vehicle (SPV), the seller/originator/sponsor is *delinked* from the investor. For U.S. Federal Deposit Insurance Corporation (FDIC) institutions, this step is usually not required to achieve a bankruptcy remote structure. Figure 7.1 shows how traditional ABS technology employing an intermediate SPV and a master trust structure can be applied to a true sale CLO.

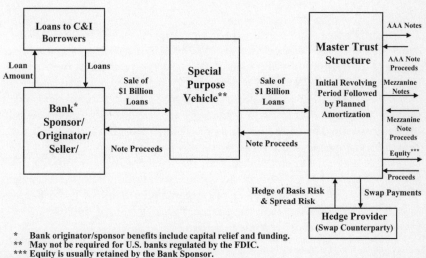

* Bank originator/sponsor benefits include capital relief and funding.
** May not be required for U.S. banks regulated by the FDIC.
*** Equity is usually retained by the Bank Sponsor.

FIGURE 7.1 True Sale ("Fully Funded") Balance Sheet, C&I Loan Cash Flow CLO (Seller Is *Delinked* from Investor)

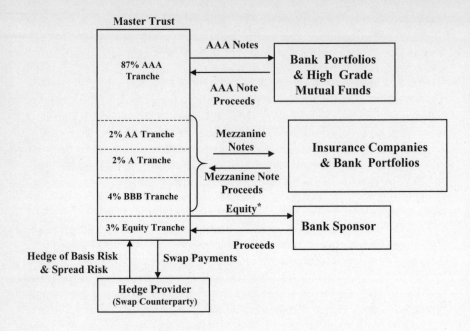

* Equity is usually retained by the Bank Sponsor.

FIGURE 7.2   True Sale CLO—Investor Perspective

As shown in Figure 7.2, it is possible to have a AAA rated tranche in a delinked structure, because the rating is based on having the appropriate degree of subordination for a given CDO structure and for a given portfolio of loans.

As we saw earlier in our discussion of SPVs, the experience and credit rating of the servicer is important to rating agencies, as is the ability to substitute servicers. The credit rating of the hedge provider is also important. (See the section in Chapter 3 titled "Bankruptcy Remote?")

BIS I regulatory capital charges for the loan portfolio are the lessor of (1) 100 percent times 8 percent times the entire loan portfolio (the unlevered amount), or (2) 100 percent of the remaining liability. If the liability capital charge is smaller than the charge on the unlevered portfolio, this is known as the low lever recourse requirement.

As shown in Figure 7.2, the bank's sponsor/seller/originator often retains the entire equity piece. To evaluate capital relief, let's use an example of a $1 billion CLO with a 3 percent equity tranche. Prior to securitization, the loans attracted a 100 percent BIS risk weight on the entire remaining loan balance. The regulatory capital charge is:

$$\$1 \text{ billion} \times 100\% \times 8\% = \$80,000,000$$

When all of the tranches are sold, but the entire equity tranche is retained, the new capital charge is calculated as follows:

$$\$1 \text{ billion} \times 100\% \times 3\% = \$30,000,000$$

The regulatory capital requirement is only 37.5 percent of what it was prior to securitization of the loan portfolio.

If the bank can exploit a regulatory regulation loophole, such as an interest subparticipation piece (ISP) structure, the required regulatory capital reduction may be even greater. Even more efficiently, if the bank can sell some of the equity to a third party, the reduction is dollar for dollar without the ISP documentation risk and without the ISP risk of regulatory capital clawback.

As we saw earlier, some investors are concerned with the moral hazard embedded in balance sheet CLOs. One school of thought is that the reputation of the seller bank is bound up with the CLO issuance. Another school of thought is that the bank may let the loan portfolio deteriorate once the loans are sold. Theoretically, if the bank retains servicing rights and an equity interest, the bank has an interest in solid performance of the loan portfolio. If things go wrong, however, some investors fear the bank may use the revolving period to dump shaky loans by selling them to the SPV. Subsequent events have shown that both schools of thought have merit. Structural protections can mitigate this risk, but can never completely eliminate it. One can protect against the moral hazard mentioned above, but it is difficult to protect against incompetence or fraud. Fortunately, this is rare.

The documentation for true sale structures is more intensive than for synthetic structures. The key documents are as follows: (1) the purchase agreements for the various note classes, (2) documentation for Reg S and rule 144A global notes, (3) the paying agency agreement, (4) the trust deed, (5) the cash bond administration agreement, (6) asset sale agreements, and (7) the servicer agreement. Deals that employ an interest subparticipation tranche have additional documentation outlining this agreement.

LINKED NONSYNTHETIC STRUCTURES

In 1996, National Westminster Bank (NatWest, now part of Bank of Scotland) brought the $5 billion Repeat Offering Securitization Entity (R.O.S.E.) Funding No. 1 CDO to market. NatWest retained legal ownership of the loans, but transferred the loan risk in the form of subparticipation interests in the loans. Subparticipation interests do not have loan voting rights, so deciding how to administer those rights in the context of the structure wasn't an issue. The collateral consisted of revolving corporate loan facilities. This was a *linked* transaction, because the deal was linked to NatWest's credit risk. The collateral consisted of C&I loans. This deal was the first large-scale nonarbitrage CLO. The deal had no AAA rated tranche, because the highest rating possible for any tranche was NatWest's rating, which was below AAA. This is a significant drawback of linked transactions. Figure 7.3 shows the generic structure.

The benefit to NatWest was that it got funding and regulatory capital relief. The collateral was investment grade rated, and the equity tranche size was only 2 percent of the CDO, which meant that NatWest held only $100 million in capital against the equity tranche versus $400 million required before the securitization. This was a 4:1 capital reduction.

While this was a seminal deal at the time, from the investor point of view the recent rash of bank credit rating downgrades makes a delinked structure desirable. From NatWest's point of view, the CLO wasn't cost efficient. This deal had no AAA tranche. At the time, NatWest's rating was Aa2/AA, and that was the highest rating possible for any tranche in this CDO. The Aa2/AA tranche size was about 95.9 percent of the transaction. If this deal were delinked and tranched, the Aa2/AA tranche would probably

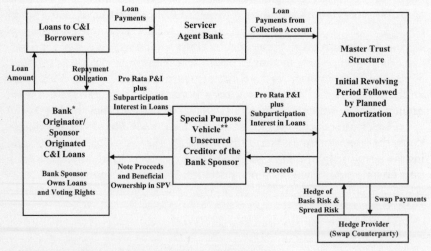

* Bank originator/sponsor benefits include capital relief and funding.
** May not be required for U.S. banks regulated by the FDIC.

FIGURE 7.3   Generic Funded CLO linked to the Bank Sponsor

have been about 2 percent of the deal, and the AAA tranche would have made up about 94 percent of the deal. This means that the liability cost of the largest tranche increased by the difference in per annum spread between a AAA tranche and a AA2 tranche! R.O.S.E. by any other name would still stink from the point of view of cost efficiency.

As we look at more recent structures, we'll see the objective is to find a balance between capital efficiency and all-in deal costs to the bank sponsor.

LINKED BLACK BOX CREDIT LINKED NOTE (CLN) CDOs

CLOs up to 1997 could transfer credit risk of a bank's loan portfolio, but what if a bank wanted to transfer credit risk on an enterprise-wide basis? For instance, what if you had swap counterparty exposure and wanted to transfer this credit risk? On September 10, 1997, the then Swiss Bank Corporation (SBC) made the first attempt to do this using CLNs. Rated AA+/AA1 at the time, SBC launched Glacier. This first of its kind deal proved so popular that SBC upsized the deal from $1.5 billion to $1.75 billion at its launch. It is, however, another linked structure.

Glacier Finance is a master trust structure special purpose entity (SPE) domiciled in the Grand Caymans. The portfolio consists of SBC issued CLNs. At the time of issue, the maximum achievable rating on the senior notes was AA+/AA1, capped at SBC's rating, but the amount of subordination was only 8.25 percent to get to the AA+/AA1 rating threshold. This suggests that the AAA tranche, if it had been feasible, would have been very large, probably around 90 percent of the total deal size.

SBC gave a lot of thought to international issues in the deal structure. While the CDO appears cost inefficient, there were added economic benefits to SBC. It issued the medium term notes (MTNs) from its New York branch because funding is an expense item for tax purposes in New York.

Glacier uses a blind pool also known as a *black box*. Investors do not know the composition of the risks to which the CLNs are linked. Swiss banking laws require high client confidentiality standards. Penalties include a 15-year prison term for violation of client confidentiality. To preserve this confidentiality, SBC embedded the client credit risk in CLNs, MTNs issued by Swiss Bank's New York branch. Figure 7.4 outlines the structure.

Credit risk is transferred on an enterprise-wide basis from investment and commercial banking businesses: loans, derivatives, securities, and project loans. The maturity of the underlying credit risks does not need to match the maturity of the notes issued by the SPV. The CLNs also vary in maturity and do not necessarily match the maturity of the notes issued by

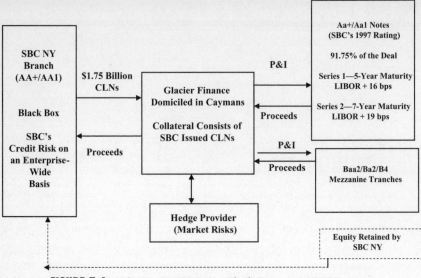

FIGURE 7.4   Glacier CLN CDO—Black Box (at 1997 Issuance)

the Glacier entity. The CLNs are callable by SBC on any interest payment date, and SBC can revolve credits embedded in the CLNs into and out of the SPV. As CLNs in the SPV mature, the SPV uses the cash to purchase other CLNs. Unlike the CLOs issued previous to this deal, the Glacier senior notes are bullet notes with bullet maturities of five years and seven years for each credit tranche. At the time of issue, the senior 5-year tranche was priced at LIBOR + 16, and the senior 7-year tranche was priced at LIBOR + 19.

The investors invested in a black box structure, but the structure is also a black box for SBC's now Union Bank of Switzerland's (UBS) relationship managers and line credit officers. They do not know whether their client's credit is embedded in CLNs used as collateral for the SPV. Only a few key credit officers have this information.

SBC mapped their internal bank rating system to the ratings of Moody's and Standard & Poor's (S&P). This allows SBC to continually revolve collateral in the SPV. SBC can call its CLNs and substitute others. This vehicle allows SBC's trading department to manage credit exposures. The rating agencies do not see the individual obligors.

SBC defines the credit events for the MTNs it issues. The investors have recourse to the CLN, not to the underlying credit risks. If there is no credit event, SBC pays par at the maturity of the CLN. If there is a credit event, SBC calls the CLN and redeems it at the recovery value. The recovery value is determined by the senior unsecured debt obligation of the underlying reference credit. The SPV would receive a payment after 18 days of the determined recovery value. If there is no reference security, the payout is preset at 51 percent, the average recovery value for senior unsecured obligations according to Moody's data at the time the deal closed.

SBC achieved its goal of regulatory capital relief because the regulators look at the resulting credit protection as cash collateralized exposure. CLNs, which embed full loan risk, are eligible for full regulatory capital relief. For the CLNs that reference a 51 percent recovery rate, 51 percent is cash collateralized and that portion requires no regulatory capital. SBC estimated that it achieved about a 5:1 regulatory capital reduction.

This deal sold well because, at the time, there was a dearth of product on the market. This deal was followed by the Triangle I deals, which had a very similar structure. For the first time, via the R.O.S.E., and Glacier and Triangle CDOs, investors had access to investments in huge diversified pools of bank portfolio loans. Like the R.O.S.E. deal, the linked nature of the Glacier and first Triangle deals has its drawbacks, as investors have seen in the current bank credit rating downgrade environment. Another drawback is the black box nature of the portfolio. Today, very few investors would accept either a linked structure or a black box structure.

SYNTHETIC STRUCTURE WITH SPE (BISTRO)

Portfolio managers use single name credit default swaps (CDSs) to lay off risk to individual obligors, but laying off the risk of a major portion of the portfolio requires a different strategy. Synthetic CLOs or synthetic collateralized bond obligations (CBOs) are the tools managers use to mitigate the credit risk of a diversified portfolio of assets. These are cash flow deals. These balance sheet deals may have revolving periods and lockouts, just as we saw earlier in the true sale structure.

The issuer usually retains the first-loss risk. In the United States, the originating bank almost always explicitly retains the equity tranche. In Europe, the ISP structure often makes it appear as if this risk has been sold to an investor, but the first-loss risk is actually retained by the originator.

It is possible to directly sell equity risk to an investor or a fund. As we'll see later, a modification of the secured loan trust structure may enable the transfer of equity risk. While this is a very good idea, most banks don't put in the required effort to accomplish it.

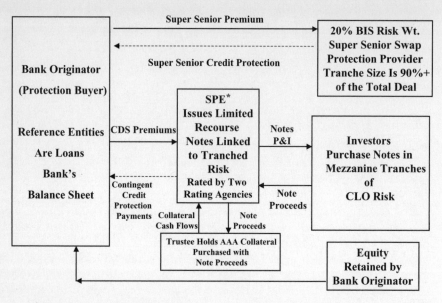

*SPE must be separately collateralized.

FIGURE 7.5　Synthetic Structure with SPE: Delinked Structure (BISTRO-Type Structure)

A synthetic structure can be partially funded using an SPE. Since the bank sponsor doesn't issue notes as collateral, the structure is *delinked* from the bank originator's risk. J.P. Morgan brought the first of many broad index secured trust offerings (BISTROs) to market in December 1997. It was the first CDO to exploit this type of synthetic structure. The transaction was both leveraged and delinked from J.P. Morgan.

For the first time, default risk of a pool of loans was transferred using CDSs. The super senior risk could be transferred purely in synthetic form, but J.P. Morgan liked to keep this tranche. The mezzanine risks were purchased by senior and junior noteholders in the form of CLNs. The mezzanine risk CDSs were repackaged in the BISTRO SPE and BISTRO issued the notes. The note proceeds were used to purchase AAA collateral.

Today, this is a widely used structure. Figure 7.5 outlines the generic structure.

The super senior swap counterparty is almost always a 20 percent BIS risk weighted entity. Depending on the venue, the counterparty may be an Organization for Economic Cooperation and Development (OECD) bank or a 20 percent BIS risk weighted financial institution or agency. The

20 percent BIS risk weighted counterparty may retain the risk in its trading book, or it may in turn lay off the risk with a monoline insurance company, a reinsurer, or a financial guarantor. Given the nervousness in the marketplace about nonmonoline insurance, protection bought from reinsurers will be closely scrutinized.

The equity is usually retained by bank originators.

Many balance sheet transactions allow for revolving periods and substitution of credits. The earlier deals are written with old CDS language.

Although this is the core structure, there are many variations, especially in the treatment of the equity tranche and transference of mezzanine risk from the SPE. Furthermore, this structure has now been adapted to synthetic arbitrage deals. Earlier we saw an example of a managed synthetic arbitrage CDO. Static synthetic arbitrage CDOs also use a variation of this structure.

Most balance sheet deals are rated by at least two rating agencies. Although the approaches of the agencies differ somewhat, in general they will look at the bank originator and assets very closely.

For the bank originator, and to a more limited extent for the bank arranger, the rating agencies consider the following: (1) the administration and organization of the bank, (2) credit policies and controls, (3) technology systems, (4) decision-making processes for adding assets, and (5) internal reporting procedures.

The rating agencies evaluate the asset pool using most of their standard criteria: (1) diversification of obligors including industry and regional diversification, (2) liquidation profiles, (3) delinquency and default data, and (4) recovery value data.

This structure allows only partial regulatory capital relief, and the equity is held on the bank's balance sheet and requires dollar for dollar capital. If 20 percent BIS risk weighted counterparties are used for the super senior, and if the collateral is 0 percent risk weighted, the capital will be calculated for these tranches accordingly, based on the size of each tranche.

European variations on this structure include marketing equity as an ISP tranche. Figure 7.6 shows how this tranche is incorporated into the overall structure.

Funding is limited to the tranches for which notes are issued, but the cost of bringing this deal to market is much lower than the cost of a true sale structure. These deals require much less documentation than true sale CLOs. The three key documents are (1) the terms and conditions of each of the note classes, (2) the CDS confirmations, and (3) the trust agreement. Deals that employ an ISP tranche have additional documentation outlining

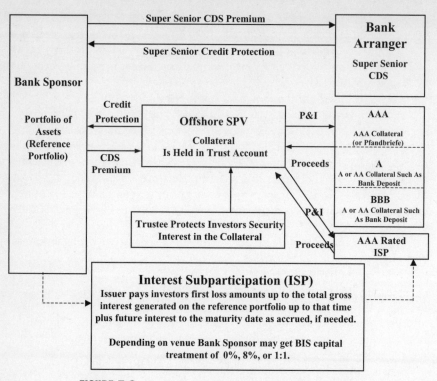

FIGURE 7.6 Partially Funded CDO with SPV and ISP

this agreement. In contrast to the documentation for the true sale structure we discussed earlier, this documentation is minimal.

PARTIALLY SYNTHETIC LINKED CDOs

Landesbank Kiel (LB Kiel) brought a Euro 1 billion balance sheet CDO to market in 2001. The underlying collateral consists of first and second residential mortgage loans. The deal is named FÖRDE 2000-1 and rated by Moody's and Fitch. At the time LB Kiel was rated Aa1 by Moody's, A1+ by S&P, and AAA by Fitch. Figure 7.7 shows that LB Kiel used many of the innovative elements of partially synthetic structures available at the time.

LB Kiel transferred the super senior risk in the form of a super senior swap. LB Kiel acted as issuer of CLNs for the other tranches. The equity

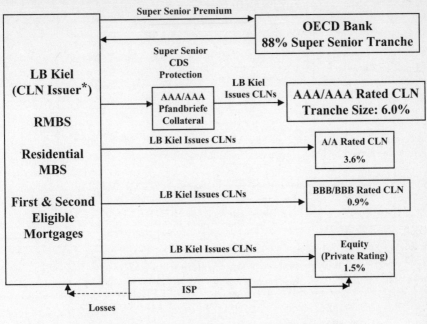

*Notes are rated by Moody's and Fitch and listed on the Luxembourg Stock Exchange.

FIGURE 7.7   Partially Synthetic CDO—FÖRDE 2000–1

tranche was sold in the form of a privately rated ISP. In order to get a AAA/AAA rating for the relevant CLN, LB Kiel had to use AAA Pfandbriefe collateral to back the principal repayment of the note.

FULLY SYNTHETIC CDOs

The SPV isn't necessary if other counterparties can be found for each of the CDSs. The bank originator, as protection buyer of the credit default protection, may require AAA collateral for the AAA rated tranche swap.

Figure 7.8 is a schematic of a fully synthetic balance sheet CLO.

Many arbitrage CDOs are fully synthetic, although mezzanine tranches may be repackaged. In this instance, the bank arranger's CDS trading desk, rather than a bank's balance sheet, provides the reference assets for the CDO. Figure 7.9 shows the reference portfolio.

Many investors are willing to take the tranched risk of a diversified portfolio of synthetic credits, but need the risk repackaged in note form.

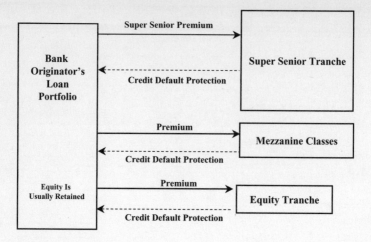

Losses are first absorbed by the equity piece, then mezzanine tranches, junior-most to senior-most, and finally to the Senior tranche.

FIGURE 7.8   Fully Synthetic CLO

This is usually done in one of two types of vehicles. A dedicated SPE can be set up for each deal. The SPE is prefunded with the purchases of limited recourse notes. We examined this structure previously when we compared managed synthetic versus managed cash arbitrage CDOs.

Alternatively, the CDSs can be repackaged in a rated multi-issuance SPE that can accommodate any number of deals, even though each tranche

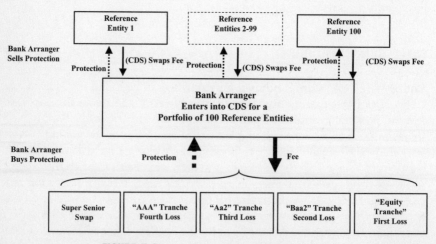

FIGURE 7.9   Synthetic Static Arbitrage CDO

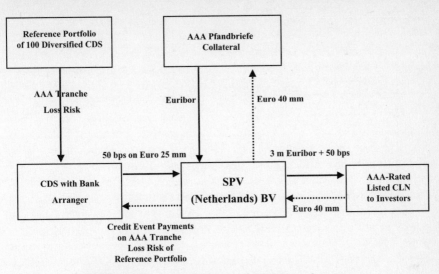

FIGURE 7.10 AAA Repackaged CDS Note Structure

is ring-fenced. The SPV usually requires AAA rated collateral, such as Pfandbriefe, for a AAA rated CLN, linked to the AAA CDS tranche of the reference portfolio. Investors often want the notes both listed and rated. Figure 7.10 shows the repackaged note structure.

SMALL TO MEDIUM-SIZE ENTERPRISES (SMEs)—EUROPE

Small to medium-size enterprises (SMEs) are often defined as companies with annual sales of less than Euro 250 million, but this definition varies by program. SME CDOs are backed by claims against SMEs. These claims are comprised of all types of debt instruments including loans, receivables, undrawn revolvers, and undrawn guarantees.

Most of these claims are unrated. Usually implied ratings vary from as low as BB+ to as high as single A. To get an idea of the rating agency implied rating on the underlying reference portfolio, an originating bank may map its internal rating criteria to rating agency criteria. If the origina-tor doesn't have a good internal rating system with a track record, the rating agencies may not accept this analysis. In that case, it is important for the originator to produce good records of historical default and loss data on the SME portfolio. When all else fails, a rating agency may apply an internal corporate rating model. The key issue with SMEs is the quality of the data and the stability of the portfolio characteristics so that conclusions based on good historical data are likely to apply to the future performance of the SME portfolio. Confidence in the stability of future SME loan character is particularly important for revolving portfolios. These rating challenges contribute to a longer lead time in bringing a rated SME CDO to market.

The first SME CDOs were funded transactions. Currently both funded and synthetic SME CDOs are brought to market, but synthetic CDOs dominate the market. SME CDOs can be either static or revolving. SME CDOs have been issued as part of promotional programs designed to stimulate economic growth, but they have also been issued as nonpromotional SME CDOs. The European Investment Fund and other organizations in Europe sponsor promotional programs that often include guaranteeing tranches of CDOs backed by SMEs. The programs and protection offered vary by sponsor.

In Germany, the Kreditanstalt für Wiederaufbau (KfW) initiated a promotional program for SMEs. The Federal Republic of Germany guarantees KfW's obligations. Therefore, all of KfW's primary obligations have a 0 percent BIS risk weighting and a AAA rating. KfW issues CDOs through the Program for Mittelstand-loan Securitization (PROMISE). KfW also has a sister program, PROVIDE, that has been used for nonPfandbriefe eligible residential mortgages to support the housing industry. KfW, often with the help of another arranger bank, consolidates loans from more than one German bank originator in order to increase the size of the transaction, if necessary. The reference portfolio is a revolving reference portfolio of SMEs.

KfW acts as the credit protection provider in a CDS with the banks that originated the loans. From the point of view of the originating banks, they are laying off credit risk, which currently has a 100% BIS risk weight, and getting credit protection from a 0 percent risk weighted provider. They not only receive the credit protection, they free up regulatory capital for additional bank business.

KfW transfers the credit risk in one of two ways. The first method transfers mezzanine risk to the SPV via KfW issued CLNs in the form of KfW certificates of indebtedness linked to the tranched mezzanine credit risk of the reference portfolio of SMEs. If there are no defaults at the relevant mezzanine level in the reference portfolio, the certificates repay principal with a AAA certainty. Therefore, the AAA tranched risk can get a AAA rating. The super senior risk is transferred with a super senior CDS. The first loss risk is also transferred via a CDS. The second method differs from the first in that the mezzanine risk is transferred to the PROMISE SPV using CDSs for the mezzanine tranches. The proceeds of the sales of the mezzanine notes are invested in KfW issued MTNs. The KfW MTNs are used as collateral for the CDSs. The MTNs are AAA rated, allowing the AAA tranched risk to achieve a AAA rating (see Figures 7.11 and 7.12).

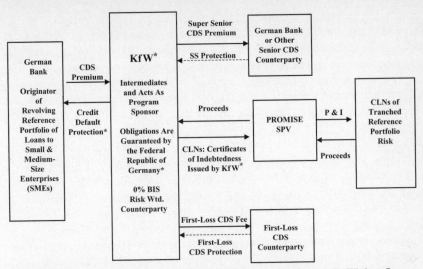

*The Federal Republic of Germany guarantees the obligations of the Kreditanstalt für Wiederaufbau (KfW). KfW as swap counterparty has a 0% BIS risk weight from the point of view of the German bank originator. The collateral for the SPV are KfW's certificates of indebtedness linked to the tranched mezzanine credit risk of the reference portfolio. If there are no defaults at the mezzanine level, there is a AAA certainty of payment of principal at maturity on the CLNs.

FIGURE 7.11 Promise SME CDO with CLNs

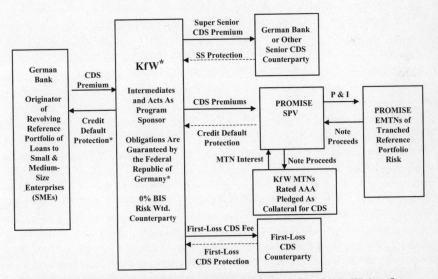

*The Federal Republic of Germany guarantees the obligations of the Kreditanstalt für Wiederaufbau (KfW). KfW as swap counterparty has a 0% BIS risk weight from the point of view of the German bank originator. The collateral for the SPV are MTNs issued by KfW and pledged as collateral for the CDSs.

FIGURE 7.12 Promise SME CDO with CDSs

Bank Austria Creditanstalt (BaCa), an Austrian subsidiary of HypoVereinsbank, became the first non-German user of KfW's PROMISE platform in December, 2002. The deal was called PROMISE-Austria 2002 Plc, and was rated by Moody's and Fitch. The Euro 1 billion synthetic CDO securitized Austrian SMEs. The Euro 90.7 million AAA/AAA rated tranche sold at 3-month Euribor + 38 bps, and had a 2.4 year average life, an expected maturity in 2011, and a legal final maturity in 2013.

In March of 2002, the European Commission approved the use of KfW's state-aid guarantees for specialized promotional activities and SME financing. KfW's securitization activities under the PROMISE and PRO-VIDE platform are promotional activities, and KfW may soon play a large role in European securitization. CDSs smooth over many of the difficulties of bringing deals in venues other than Germany. It is much simpler to handle the legal and practical issues of asset risk transfer with CDSs and this is evidenced in the greater speed and diminished documentation requirements of these deals.

In Spain, the Instituto de Credito Official (ICO) sponsors another promotional loan program with different structural features to other programs in Europe. For instance, unlike KfW, ICO does not act as an intermediary, although ICO acts as paying agent. The portfolio of SMEs usually includes a number of ICO sponsored loans, which have higher recovery rates than unrestricted Spanish SME loans. The Spanish treasury acted as a credit wrap provider for CLO transactions prior to 2002. The Kingdom of Spain guaranteed timely payment of interest and principal on the senior notes, and gave a partial guarantee to notes rated Aa and below on a sliding scale. In 2002, the Kingdom of Spain eliminated guarantees to the lower tranches, but continues to guarantee the senior tranche. The Kingdom of Spain was upgraded to Aaa from Aa2 by Moody's in 2001.

Deutsche Bank's CORE and CAST deals are examples of nonpromotional SME CDOs. Deutsche Bank used a true sale structure and a static SME reference portfolio for the CORE deal. For the CAST deal, Deutsche issued CLNs linked to the tranches of SME risk on its balance sheet. Like the Glacier deal, the credit risk of the CLNs included Deutsche's credit risk (as of this writing AA−) and the relevant tranched credit risk of the SME reference portfolio.

Banco Bilbao Vizcaya Argentaria S.A.'s (BBVA) SME CDO is another example of a nonpromotional SME CDO. BBVA referenced a revolving portfolio of SMEs and used a synthetic structure.

A few reinsurers have helped this market by seeking to invest in a diversified pool of European loans. They seek to avoid over-concentration in the actively traded names, and usually invest in medium-size enterprises, many of which do not have explicit ratings.

As an example, one French reinsurer guarantees the first-loss risk of diversified pools of European loans. They have individual size constraints and portfolio concentration limits within a single deal. They also have single obligor concentration limits in their macro portfolio. Since this reinsurer is single A rated and guarantees a first-loss tranche that is 30 percent of the deal, the credit rating of the senior tranches is investment grade for the grade of collateral they have accepted so far. As we shall see later, this structure may become very popular with banks after BIS II becomes official.

SMEs: UNITED STATES VERSUS EUROPE

In Europe, most loans are issued on a floating rate basis. Loans securitized by countries in the European Community have floating rate coupons paying at a spread to Euribor. The January 1, 1999, introduction of the Euro as a multicountry currency has given a boost to the securitization of small and medium-size loans in the European Community countries for consumption in the European market.

Prior to 2000, the U.S. Small Business Administration (SBA) securitized SBA loans into guaranteed loan pools certificates (GLPCs). Pooling was similar to the device used in the mortgage market. Capped loans were pooled separately from uncapped loans. A pool of 50 loans might make up a $5,000,000 GLPC. It was possible to sell GLPC in the Eurodollar (European U.S. dollar) market.

These loans are guaranteed by the full faith and credit of the U.S. government, currently rated AAA. The guarantee gives these securities a 0 percent BIS risk weighting. The U.S. government guarantees *timely* payment of both principal and interest. Unlike most ABSs, these CDOs are undercollateralized, because the loans trade at a premium to par due to their high credit rating and relatively high coupons.

GLPCs have maturities that range from 5 to 25 years. The coupons are variable rate coupons that adjust monthly or quarterly. The coupons can be either capped or uncapped. In a securitization, capped loans would not be securitized with uncapped loans, so that the pools are homogenous with respect to coupon cap character. This would normally be a plus in the European market, which often shuns U.S. fixed rate loans, but the GLPC coupons are indexed to the U.S. prime rate, not U.S. dollar (USD) LIBOR. Prime is the consumer lending rate used solely in the United States. USD LIBOR is usually acceptable to European banks that match fund on a floating rate basis and often have USD floating rate liabilities. The prime index is not as well correlated with their liabilities, however. This difference in the indexing, or basis, of the coupons versus the European market is a source of basis risk for many European investors.

In the U.S. market, these securities have many advantages. These investments can be held in a U.S. bank's portfolio. The index is well understood in the U.S. market. Many U.S. banks lend at prime, although they do not fund at prime, so the assets provide a hedge for potential liabilities. The pools have a 55-day delay, making it not usually possible to match assets and liabilities. In most cases, these assets can be pledged as collateral for public funds at the Federal Reserve.

The negatives for both the U.S. and European markets are that the loans may default or prepay, in which case the premium is prepaid at par. (The par amount is guaranteed by the U.S. government, as we saw earlier.) Most loans amortize at a scheduled principal repayment rate, but there is no penalty for prepayment of a loan. The prepayment risk due to default is minimized by securitizing a large pool of diversified loans. If one loan prepays, only the premium on that particular loan is lost.

The SBA International program eliminated the prime/LIBOR basis risk for investors. SBA International uses a grantor trust to securitize the loans and issues AAA rated "A" trust certificates, and the proceeds are used to purchase the premium GLPCs. The trust also has a subordinated tranche that takes most of the prepayment risk if constant prepayment rates (CPRs) increase. The protection is usually up to the 95 percent confidence band based on historical CPR data up to the time of issuance. The SBA International program warehouses loans and eliminates the 55 delay days, which is an additional benefit to investors.

The coupons can either be hedged or unhedged for basis risk. If investors don't hedge, they receive the difference between the spot prime/LIBOR spread and the swap strike price. These investors may initially get a higher coupon than investors that hedge, but they accept that in future the spread between prime and LIBOR can either move wider (in their favor) or narrower (against them).

Many European venues look through the grantor trust structure, unlike the special purpose corporation (SPC) structure, to the underlying collateral. An SPC would attract a 100 percent BIS risk weighting from European banks. The grantor trust with 0 percent risk weighted collateral will attract zero regulatory capital requirement from most European banks (see Figure 7.13).

SECURED LOAN TRUSTS

The first CLOs to use synthetics were the former Chase Manhattan Bank's secured loan trust structures. The maturity of these deals was around three

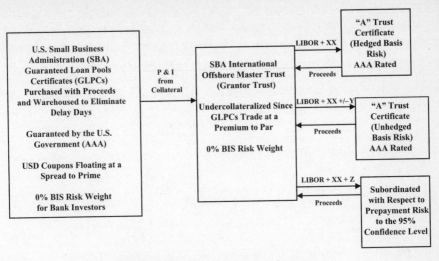

U.S. Small Business Administration (SBA) Guaranteed Loan Pools Certificates (GLPCs) Purchased with Proceeds and Warehoused to Eliminate Delay Days

Guaranteed by the U.S. Government (AAA)

USD Coupons Floating at a Spread to Prime

0% BIS Risk Weight for Bank Investors

P & I from Collateral

SBA International Offshore Master Trust (Grantor Trust)

Undercollateralized Since GLPCs Trade at a Premium to Par

0% BIS Risk Weight

LIBOR + XX
Proceeds

"A" Trust Certificate (Hedged Basis Risk) AAA Rated

LIBOR + XX +/–Y
Proceeds

"A" Trust Certificate (Unhedged Basis Risk) AAA Rated

LIBOR + XX + Z
Proceeds

Subordinated with Respect to Prepayment Risk to the 95% Confidence Level

FIGURE 7.13 SBA International Program

years. These arbitrage CLOs sometimes used loans from Chase's balance sheet, but additional loans were purchased in the secondary market to add diversity. For the most part, the loans were highly leveraged transactions (HLTs), with implied ratings of B to BBB. The coupons on these loans were at a spread of the low hundreds to LIBOR.

Secured loan trusts use total rate of return swaps (TRORS) to transfer first-loss risk, which is bifurcated for two types of investors. The bifurcated risks are pari passu, but one of them is more leveraged than the other. In Chase's structures, the less leveraged tranche often received a single A rating. Some structures had a BBB rated note rated by Duff & Phelps (now Fitch). The investor in the rated tranche is called the *noteholder*. The investor in the more highly leveraged tranche is called the *certificate holder*. Although they both have first-loss risk, the certificate holder is deemed to be the equity investor. Figure 7.14 outlines the basic cash flows of this structure.

In the structure illustrated in Figure 7.14, the noteholder and certificate holder are pari passu with respect to first-loss risk, but the noteholder is only leveraged 5:1, whereas the certificate holder is leveraged 8:1. The leverage depends on the portfolio and the structure, and in this example the note is only rated BBB. This investment grade rating is based on the return of the initial cash investment plus the return of a nominal coupon, not the return of the potentially high leveraged coupon.

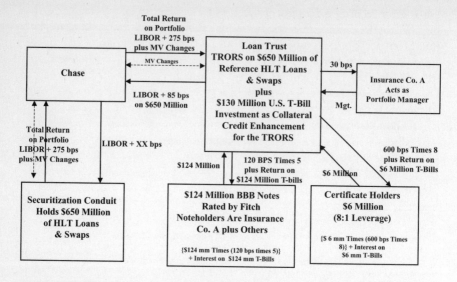

Chase and the portfolio manager have the option to unwind at any point. Payment of LIBOR + 85 bps is subordinate to management fees, noteholder and certificate holder interest payments. The noteholders and certificate holders are pari passu, although with different amounts of leverage.

FIGURE 7.14 Secured Loan Trust—Circa 1996 (Prematurity Cash Flows)

United States insurance companies were the investors who originally drove these transactions. The insurance companies acted as portfolio manager and investor in part of the first-loss risk. United States insurance companies are regulated by the National Association of Insurance Commissioners (NAIC), and theoretically cannot invest in high yield loans. If the less leveraged first-loss tranche receives a single A rating, it achieves a NAIC 1 classification. This is the highest asset classification and attracts the lowest asset capital charge. If the less leveraged first-loss tranche receives a BBB rating, it achieves a NAIC 2 classification, the second highest asset classification, and attracts the second lowest asset capital charge. The insurance companies received the leveraged return of an equity tranche while enjoying the reduced capital charge of an investment grade rated asset.

Hedge funds are willing certificate buyers. For this customer base, a rating is irrelevant. Ironically, hedge funds reluctant to disclose their own balance sheets prudently ask for full disclosure of the current portfolio. They also ask for models so they can perform stress tests to determine that the potential net reward will achieve their targets under their most important stress scenarios.

If possible, the hedge funds will try to get even more leverage. They may ask to receive the certificate cash flows in the form of a TRORS. A sponsor bank for a secured loan trust usually won't want to fund the hedge finance purchasing the certificate, so hedge funds ask yet another bank for the financing. From a U.S. tax perspective, it is often easier to net interest income and funding expenses in a swap form. Swap income is usually viewed as ordinary income. Equity income can be deemed to be either interest income or capital loss. There are other itemized deduction and state tax implications for equity income that can usually be avoided when recognizing swap income.

The bank sponsor receives a stream of floating rate payments from a TRORS backed by a significant amount of risk free collateral. With 30 percent collateral, this stream of cash flows would have an investment grade rating, even as high as AAA, or super senior risk depending on the collateral and unwind triggers. The bank sponsor is usually the primary structurer and has control over diversification criteria for the portfolio, the triggers, the amount of the initial collateral, and the structural features of the CLO. The bank sponsor books the TRORS in the bank's trading book, and has a back-to-back TRORS with the securitization conduit. The securitization conduit pays the TRORS on the loans and the bank sponsor pays a funding cost. The bank sponsor pays the TRORS to the loan trust, which is collateralized with AAA collateral. The bank sponsor charges the trust a higher funding cost than the funding rate it pays to the securitization conduit, thus earning annual income.

Counterparty risk is mitigated by frequently marking the TRORS to market. The bank sponsor is most concerned with its exposure to the loan trust. If the assets depreciate in value, the bank sponsor receives a make whole payment from the loan trust, which matches the make whole payment the bank sponsor must make to the securitization conduit. If there is a systemic rapid deterioration in the value of the HLTs, the TRORS will behave more like equity than debt. Unwind triggers can mitigate this risk. Since the loan trust is 30 percent overcollateralized, the secured loan trust (SLT) structure calls for the entire structure to unwind once the overcollateralization falls to the trigger threshold. The trigger level will depend on hedge exposures, diversification and credit quality of the portfolio, and the seniority of the bank sponsor in the event of unwind.

For regulatory capital purposes, the bank sponsor adds the mark-to-market value of the assets to the counterparty risk factor from a regulatory lookup table. This is a small fraction of the capital required to hold the loans on balance sheet. Economic capital required for the long position (receiving the TRORS from the securitization conduit) is offset by the short position (paying the TRORS to the loan trust). The true sale of the assets, combined with the low remaining capital charge, makes this an efficient way to reduce risk, and the transaction also reduces the size of the bank's balance sheet.

REGULATORY CAPITAL—THE MODEL ADVANTAGE

In July 1988, the Bank for International Settlements issued the Basel Capital Accord (BIS I). This accord defined the capital requirement for credit risk in all the world's major banking communities. It may even have worked for a picosecond. As soon as the rules were issued, each country set up its own capital guidelines for banks, often applying inconsistent interpretations of the BIS guidelines. As soon as that happened, banks began looking for ways to arbitrage the inconsistencies.

Examples of venue specific regulatory bodies that can interpret guidelines to fit into their respective regulatory frameworks are the Federal Reserve Bank (The Fed) in the United States, the Financial Service Authority (SFA) in the United Kingdom, the Office of the Superintendent of Financial Institutions (OSFI) in Canada, the French Commision Bancaire, the Bundesanstaltfür Finanzdienst-leistungsaufsicht (BAFin) in Germany, and the Ministry of Finance (MOF) in Japan.

When new products such as credit derivatives and synthetic CDO products were developed, the BIS I regulatory capital framework couldn't readily accommodate the new products. That left the products fair game for regulatory capital arbitrage. Even worse, BIS I created arbitrary noncredit related capital distinctions, such as a 0 percent risk weight for OECD sovereign risk. In a system meant to dole out credit-related regulatory capital, this was a major flaw.

BIS II is an attempt to fix all of that. The new rules are due to come into effect in 2005. The problem is that Basel is still trying to decide on the final rules. Basel keeps issuing working papers for comment and the first thing I do when I receive them is to reach for coffee—these papers are seriously boring—and look for the arbitrage opportunities.

First, it pays to take a step back and review the current rules to compare them with the still evolving proposed rules. After December 31, 1992, all banks were expected to meet a minimum ratio of qualifying total capital to BIS risk weighted assets of 8 percent. The amount of capital reserved against a risk-weighted asset is not necessarily 8 percent, however. The amount of capital reserved against an asset will depend upon its BIS risk weighting. The risk weight of a reference asset may vary by jurisdiction, however. This further complicates matters because central banks and ministries of finance have the right to set local standards for assets, which aren't clearly addressed by BIS. In general, however, BIS I is usually interpreted as follows:

- The sovereign debt member countries of the OECD will receive a 0 percent risk weight. This means that they are as good as cash. A bank does not need to reserve any capital against these assets.

- The senior debt obligations of OECD banks receive a 20 percent BIS risk weight. The amount of capital a bank must hold against this asset is 8 percent times 20 percent or 1.6 percent. This means that for a $10,000,000 investment, a bank would hold 1.6% × $10,000,000, or $160,000 in capital against this asset.
- Unfunded revolvers with a maturity greater than 1 year (for corporate credits) have a 50 percent BIS risk weighting. Banks hold 50 percent × 8 percent or only 4 percent capital against this asset.
- Unfunded revolvers with a maturity less than 1 year (for corporate credits) have a 0 percent BIS risk weighting. Banks hold 0 percent capital against this asset.
- If the revolver funds, the bank would assign a 100 percent BIS risk weight to the funded amount and hold 8 percent capital against this amount.
- For corporate debt and nonOECD sovereign debt, an OECD bank would assign a 100 percent risk weight to these assets and hold 8 percent regulatory capital in reserve.

For bank books with no value-at-risk (VAR) models, a default swap that is hedging a loan must meet the criteria for hedge accounting, which means that the seniority and legal entity of the reference asset must match the loan held in the portfolio, and the reference asset and loan must have cross default provisions. If these criteria are met, then the regulatory risk-based capital rules treat the default swap as a guarantee, so the counterparty risk replaces the obligor. Buying credit protection from another corporation or nonOECD bank provides *no* regulatory risk-based capital relief.

In 1998, many venues, led by the U.S. Federal Reserve, decided to treat credit derivatives like derivatives transactions. This meant they could be booked either in the bank book or in the trading book. Credit derivatives can use model-based capital treatment or can use regulatory lookup tables in most venues. Under these new market risk proposals, there are three components of risk:

1. *Counterparty risk* is the mark-to-market exposure for the credit derivative (a function of the underlying asset value) due to the possibility that the counterparty may default on their obligation or potential obligation under the terms of the credit derivative transaction.
2. *General market risk* arises from changes in the reference asset's value caused by broad market movements. It is the net exposure to interest rates, foreign exchange rates, commodity prices, and equity prices.
3. *Specific risk* arises from the changes in the reference asset's value *specific* to that asset, for example, credit quality. This is the risk of an adverse

change in price from factors related to the issuer of the reference asset due to nonmarket movements. One example would be changes in the credit risk of the reference asset. This can be accounted for by scaled risk weightings of 0 percent for government risks, 3 to 20 percent for investment grade risks, or 100 percent for noninvestment grade and other risks. Banks have the alternative of using standard specific risk add-on factors from models such as KMV Corporation's market risk models.

Only banks, which can prove they have models that can calculate exposures in a reproducible and consistent manner, can use this new capital treatment for credit derivatives. The whole point of purchasing credit default protection is to take advantage of the effect of the benefit of the reduction of default probability as evidenced by a reduced joint probability of default. Hence the extremely beneficial reduction in the required economic capital factors for low correlation obligor/counterparty transactions. The potential reduction in regulatory capital is enormous, and return on capital usually jumps threefold or more when model-based capital is applied to transactions.

Whether each of the three risk types requires regulatory risk based capital depends on the combination of long and short positions housed in the trading portfolio. These are summarized in Table 7.1.

General market risk capital is determined by a bank's internal VAR model and follows the same procedures as for cash instruments. The bank's internal model must use certain parameters set by the regulators. These too are sometimes arbitrary values depending on the specific asset, as we'll see later when we discuss BIS II in more detail.

TABLE 7.1 Risks for Type of Trading Position

| | | Risk Type | | |
Position	Definition	Market	Specific	Counterparty
Open	No offset	VAR	Reference Asset	Credit Risk
Matched	Longs and Shorts must reference identical assets	N/A	N/A	Credit Risk
Offsetting	Longs and Shorts with different maturities or legs (i.e., total return vs. default instruments)	VAR Residual Risk*	Reference Asset Residual Risk*	Credit Risk

*Residual risk depends on the degree of mismatch of maturity, reference asset basis, or type of credit protection.

TABLE 7.2 Specific Risk Capital Factors

Asset Category	Remaining Maturity	Capital
Government	—	0.00%
GSA, Investment grade	≤6 months	0.25%
	>6 mo and ≤24 mo	1.00%
	>24 mo	1.60%
Other	—	8.00%

Specific risk capital depends on the credit risk of the derivative's reference asset, as shown in Table 7.2. The factor is applied to the greater of the derivative notional or the market value of any cash asset hedging the derivative.

Determining *counterparty credit risk* capital begins by computing the swap's risk-weighted asset, which is the sum of two components. The first is the current, positive mark-to-market of the derivative. The second is an add-on for potential future mark-to-market and is determined by multiplying the swap's notional principal times the factor derived from Table 7.3.

The resulting risk weighted asset is then (1) multiplied by either 50 percent if the counterparty is a corporate or nonOECD bank or 20 percent for an OECD bank and then (2) multiplied by 8 percent to arrive at the risk-based capital for counterparty credit risk. Credit exposure is broken down by deal, maturity, counterparty, obligor, and reference asset type. Trading groups must send exposure reports to the bank's credit department.

Different VAR models will come up with different end results depending on their sophistication and degree to which regulators will ratify them and allow banks to move away from arbitrary add-on factors. Let's take a simple example. The trading book sells and buys a credit default option. The trading book assumes credit risk and purchases a hedge in the form of

TABLE 7.3 Federal Reserve Counterparty Add-On Factors

	Reference Asset	
Remaining Maturity	Investment Grade (Equity Factors)	Below Investment Grade (Commodity Factors)
≤1 year	6%	10%
>1 year to ≤ 5 years	8%	12%
>5 years	10%	15%

matching credit default protection (or shorts the reference asset). Matched positions encompass long and short positions in *identical* credit derivative structures over *identical* maturities referencing *identical* assets.

In the absence of a model, the bank must calculate the regulatory capital as follows:

Notional of the Credit Default Protection × Counterparty Risk Weight × 8%

The bank sells protection on a reference asset for 30 bps and simultaneously purchases credit default protection from an OECD bank selling protection for 20 bps. The net profit is 10 bps. Regulatory capital required is: 100 × 20 percent (for OECD bank counterparty) × 8 percent risk capital = 1.6 or 160 bps. The return on regulatory capital is 3.12 percent.

But if our counterparty, the credit default protection seller, is a nonOECD bank, the return on regulatory capital decreases by a factor of five. (Economic capital would remain the same, but economic calculations will also be unaffected by the change to BIS II.) The regulatory capital required is simply calculated as follows: 100 × 100 percent (for nonOECD bank counterparty) × 8 percent risk capital = 8.0 or 800 bps. The return on regulatory capital is now only 0.63 percent, or there is a 5-fold reduction in return on regulatory capital.

Under market risk guidelines, the calculation is different. This is a matched position and is captured under the market risk capital guidelines. Capital is held on the counterparty protection provider risk created by the purchased option. Each bank will have its own unique model. Most banks start out with a model that does not include a means of evaluating specific risk, that is, reference asset risk. These banks use the VAR model with the add-on number provided in Table 7.3. This is a type of modified VAR model, and is an interim step to a simulation model that can accommodate all of the risks, including specific risk. Table 7.4 shows the reduction in regulatory capital with the use of a modified VAR model.

First we calculate the on-balance sheet asset equivalent according to regulatory guidelines. This is then multiplied by the relevant risk weight of the counterparty protection seller to determine the counterparty risk capital.

The balance sheet asset equivalent is $1,160,000. We add the market value of the purchased option ($360,000) to the notional amount of the option ($10,000,000), and multiply by the percentage from Table 7.3 for the credit risk factor for the reference asset, in this case 8 percent for an investment grade asset with a maturity between 1 and 5 years.

This is then multiplied by the relevant category risk weight. In the case of an OECD bank, this is 20 percent to get the adjusted risk asset value of $232,000. This is further multiplied by the regulatory capital percentage of

TABLE 7.4 Market Risk Treatment for Regulatory Capital Trading Book Buys and Sells Matched Credit Default Protection

OECD Bank Counterparty		NonOECD Bank Counterparty	
Counterparty Risk*		**Counterparty Risk***	
Notional Amount of Option	$10,000,000	Notional Amount of Option	$10,000,000
Reg. Credit %age	8.00%	Reg. Credit %age	8.00%
M-T-M Purchased Option BP	$360,000	M-T-M Purchased Option BP	$360,000
Original Price of Option $	$300,000	Original Price of Option $	$300,000
Original Price of Option bps	30.00	Original Price of Option bps	30.00
On-Bal Sheet Asset	$1,160,000	On-Bal Sheet Asset	$1,160,000
Category Risk Weight	20%	Category Risk Weight	50%
Adj. Risk Asset Value	$232,000	Adj. Risk Asset Value	$580,000
Percent of Notional	2.32%	Percent of Notional	5.80%
× Reg Capital 8% =	0.19%	× Reg Capital 8% =	0.46%
Total Regulatory Capital	$18,560	Total Regulatory Capital	$46,400
Notional	$10,000,000	Notional	$10,000,000
Net Income (bps)	5	Net Income (bps)	5
Net Income in Dollars	$5,000	Net Income in Dollars	$5,000
Capital:	$18,560	Capital:	$46,400
Return on Capital:	26.94%	Return on Capital:	10.78%

*Counterparty Risk = f (Counterparty type, market value of buy option, notional amount of the option, investment grade/non inv.grade status of reference obligation, maturity of the option)

8 percent to get the required regulatory capital for the counterparty risk of $18,560.

While every bank will see a different degree of benefit, Table 7.5 shows the potential benefit of using just a crude first-generation VAR model for matched trades under BIS I regulations.

I deliberately used a small transaction of $10,000,000 with a small net profit of only $5,000. This transaction makes little economic sense, but makes sense on a return on regulatory capital basis.

Notice that it still matters whether our counterparty is an OECD bank, but the magnitude of the difference is less. While the nonOECD bank return on capital jumped 5 times when we switched to an OECD bank counterparty premodel, with the model it jumps around 2.5 times. This result is

TABLE 7.5 Regulatory Capital and Return on Capital Calculated without and with VAR Model

Hedge Counterparty Type	Regulatory Capital without VAR Model	Regulatory Capital with VAR Model	Return on Regulatory Capital without VAR	Return on Regulatory Capital VAR Model
OECD Bank	1.60%	0.19%	3.12%	26.94%
NonOECD Bank	8.00%	0.46%	0.63%	10.78%

specific to the type of model. There is still an enormous benefit for using the lower BIS risk weighted counterparty, however.

The major overall advantage comes from using the model. For the nonOECD counterparty, return on regulatory capital jumps 17 times. For the OECD counterparty, return on regulatory capital jumps 8.6 times.

This model-based capital benefit encouraged banks to set up trading desks for CDS, which in turn allowed banks to structure synthetic CDOs for other banks that had no models or had less sophisticated models. It also allowed banks to trade CDSs in a regulatory capital efficient manner for the sole purpose of creating synthetic arbitrage CDOs.

Some bank arrangers with poor capital markets distribution entered the synthetic CDO business knowing their only advantage was that they could reduce balance sheet regulatory capital for a customer, earn a fee, and park the assets in their trading books where the assets attracted much less regulatory capital. Many of the original transactions simply involved creating a structure to earn fees for the convenience of exploiting the regulatory capital arbitrage.

REGULATORY CAPITAL—BIS II

BIS II is still a work in progress. The details are available on the BIS web site, as are the working papers. After 2005, total regulatory capital will be calculated according to the following formula:

$$\text{Total} = \text{Capital Requirements for (Credit Risk} + \text{Market Risk} + \text{Operational Risk)}$$

We'll focus on the credit risk capital requirement, since changes in this capital requirement are the ones most relevant to ABS and CDO transactions.

Banks can use any one of the following, which incorporate both expected and unexpected losses:

- The standardized approach.
- A foundation model internal ratings-based approach (IRB).
- An advanced model internal ratings-based approach.

Under BIS II, the International Monetary Fund (IMF), the European Community (EC), and the European Central Bank (ECB) will continue to have 0 percent risk weights. All other credits will have a risk weight that depends on their external ratings. Under BIS I, all OECD sovereigns had a 0 percent risk weight. All OECD banks had a 20 percent risk weight. The risk weights will now reflect their creditworthiness. Or at least, that is the intent.

BIS I didn't address ABS, CDOs, or synthetic securitization. BIS II will attempt to design a regulatory capital framework for these products. So far, there have been numerous talking papers and working papers. It's no surprise that the Federal Reserve Bank's research has had a lot of influence on the thought process. As of this writing at the end of 2002, the most current draft is the following: *Basel Committee on Banking Supervision Second Working Paper on Securitization Issued for comment by December 20, 2002*, October 2002. The 45-page paper is available for download on the BIS web site. The Federal Reserve web site has papers outlining model-based approaches (see Bibliography).

The thought process on BIS II is still evolving. Rather than go into details, the remainder of this chapter summarizes the key features that will have the biggest impact on structured finance.

The standardized approach will result in the worst-case BIS risk capital charge. No one will develop a model that results in a larger capital charge if they are paying attention.

For the first time, BIS distinguishes between the bank originating a transaction and a bank investing in a transaction. The BIS risk weights for same rated securitizations can vary.

In Table 7.6, K_{IRB} is the ratio of the internal ratings-based capital requirement for the underlying exposures (using IRB standards as if the securitized exposures were held directly by the bank) to the notional amount of the credit exposures securitized. In other words, the *cap* of the capital charge is equal to that of the underlying exposures.

RBA means ratings based approach, SFA means supervisory formula approach, and IRB means internal ratings-based approach. For investment grade assets, banks that use IRB can use external ratings or the inferred rating equivalent to investment grade.

TABLE 7.6 Capital Treatment for Securitization

External Ratings	Risk Weights		
Long-Term Rating	Standardized Approach	IRB Approach Originating Bank	IRB Approach Investing Bank
Aaa	20% All	Exposures below K_{IRB}: Deduction	All positions: RBA
Aa	20% All		
A	50% All	Exposures above K_{IRB}: RBA	Maximum Capital Requirement: None
Baa1	100% All		
Baa2	100% All	Maximum Capital Requirement: K_{IRB}	
Baa3	100% All		
Ba1	350% Investing Bank Deduction: Org Bank	Exposures below K_{IRB}: Deduction	All positions: RBA
Ba2	350% Investing Bank Deduction: Org Bank	Exposures above K_{IRB}: RBA	Maximum Capital Requirement: None
Ba3	350% Investing Bank Deduction: Org Bank	Maximum Capital Requirement: K_{IRB}	
B+ and Below	Deduction		
Unrated	Deduction: All	Exposures below K_{IRB}: Deduction	All positions: Deduction
		Exposures above K_{IRB}: SFA or Deduction	Maximum Capital Requirement: None
		Maximum Capital Requirement: K_{IRB}	

The exception is unrated senior securitizations that can apply a look-through to the risk weightings of the underlying pool, but only if they are known.

The IRB approach requires capital calculation using the RBA or SFA, but only after the bank has approval from their relevant regulators to use this approach for the underlying exposures. Table 7.6 gives the guidelines when RBA or SFA can be used.

For most structures, an IRB will offer more regulatory capital relief than the standardized approach. Table 7.7 gives the ratings-based approach risk weight to be applied for ABS tranches with various Moody's ratings.

TABLE 7.7 RBA Approach for ABS

External Ratings	Risk Weights		
	Thick Tranches		
Long-Term	Highly Granular		Nongranular
Rating	Pools	Base Case	Pools
Aaa	7%	12%	20%
Aa	10%	15%	25%
A	20%	20%	35%
Baa1	50%	50%	50%
Baa2	75%	75%	75%
Baa3	100%	100%	100%
Ba1	250%	250%	250%
Ba2	425%	425%	425%
Ba3	650%	650%	650%
Below Ba3 (or Unrated)	Deduction	Deduction	Deduction

External Ratings	Risk Weights		
	Thick Tranches		
Short-Term	Highly Granular		Nongranular
Rating	Pools	Base Case	Pools
A1/P1	7%	12%	20%
A2/P2	20%	20%	35%
A3/P3	75%	75%	75%
Lower (or Unrated)	Deduction	Deduction	Deduction

Notice that BIS introduces new terms, *granularity* of pools and *thickness* of tranches.

A high degree of granularity requires a pool to have 100 or more obligors (N), and pools with 32 or fewer obligors are considered nongranular pools. For a tranche to be considered thick, the seniority of the position relative to the size of the pool (Q) must be greater than or equal to the following:

$$Q \geq 0.1 + (25/N)$$

By this definition a super senior tranche backed by a highly granular pool can make up no more than 35 percent of a CDO to be eligible for the 7 percent risk weight using the standardized approach. We've already stated that most super senior tranches are 85 to 95 percent of today's deals. This may mean that in the future, we will redefine what we mean by a super senior tranche.

The new rules are meant to encourage actual risk transfer and to discourage banks from bailing out failing deals. The deal should be "true sale" or meet certain tests for synthetic deals. Banks can only provide credit enhancement at the outset of the transaction.

Banks that originate deals with early amortization or banks that use revolvers in deals will get a maximum capital charge equal to either that required for the underlying assets or that required were the securitization exposures retained, whichever is greater. This is devastating news for this type of transaction, and investor banks also have risk-based capital guidelines for these structures that differ from bullet transactions.

Obviously, an originating bank cannot be responsible for credit enhancing the pool on an ongoing basis. For instance, substituting a good credit for a deteriorating credit at the originating bank's expense would not be allowed. Allowing the originating bank's equity subordination to increase would not be allowed. Fee or coupon step-ups as credit quality declines would also not be allowed.

An ISP would violate the spirit of BIS II. It also violates the spirit of BIS I, although that hasn't inhibited use of ISPs in some venues. The ISP loophole may soon be permanently closed, however.

Synthetic securitizations will have to follow various guidelines, not all of which have been defined as yet. New in the rules is that SPEs will not be recognized as eligible guarantors in a securitization framework, so that may limit the use of SPEs and the use of transformers. Since SPEs can be cash collateralized, or highly collateralized and dedicated to the specific securitization, it seems this rule is a knee-jerk reaction to abuses by Enron and others. This will be hotly debated, and perhaps changed, before BIS II is implemented.

Furthermore, synthetic securitizations can't use language that limits the actual transfer of credit risk, such as materiality clauses. Other restrictions are similar to "true sale" transactions. Among other restrictions, step-up CDS premiums or step-up coupon payments on the tranches are not allowed.

CHAPTER 8

Structured Finance and Risk

CREDIT RISK DUMPING GROUNDS: THE BANK'S BALANCE SHEET AND TRADING BOOKS

In May of 1999, Alan Greenspan spoke at a conference in Chicago about risks in the global banking system. At the time, many risk managers were very concerned about poorly understood derivatives contracts and the risks they posed to banks. Mr. Greenspan said that this risk was small in comparison to a much larger risk to the banking system. Mr. Greenspan asserted that the overwhelming risk facing the banking system was credit risk. Subsequent credit events and their terrific impact on bank balance sheets and credit ratings proved him correct.

In 1995, the Bank for International Settlements (BIS) estimated that the global notional value of all derivatives was about $41 trillion, but the loss to creditors if everyone stopped paying at once was only about $1.7 trillion, or 4.3 percent of the notional value. If I had $1 billion in interest rate swaps with Enron, I might have had only around $43 million of net credit exposure to Enron. If I had a $1 billion loan to Enron, I'd have had $1 billion in exposure to Enron. Which exposure should concern me more?

The system is critically flawed. The key issue is that banks—other than perhaps J.P. Morgan Chase—don't mark their balance sheets to market. Bank officers are tempted to remain in denial until either the newspapers advertise a critical problem, or until an obligor actually defaults.

What do banks' balance sheets have to do with securitization? Securitization has recently introduced new credit risks to bank balance sheets, and this could affect the future growth of the securitization business.

LOANS AND OTHER EXPOSURES

A traditional source of risk is the concentration risk that loan officers introduce to the balance sheet through large unsyndicated loans. "Low risk" high concentration exposures are the bane of the banking industry. Loan officers often argue it is fine to take the exposure because of the importance of the relationship and the "low risk" of default. A few years ago credit officers made this argument for a then perceived AAA credit risk, Long Term Capital Management. Recently, loan officers made that argument for Enron. At a German bank with close to $1 billion in Enron exposure, loan officers tripped over each other in their eagerness to claim a close relationship with Enron. Officers threw around names of Enron officers as if they were best friends. After Enron's collapse, the officers were quick to deny all responsibility for the bank's large exposure. Even if one loves a given risk, too much of a good thing can still produce an unacceptable expected loss.

New business development and "Tech Fever" led to huge exposures in Marconi, Adelphia Communications, Global Crossing, and WorldCom. The latter weren't even viewed as stellar credits. They were viewed as fast moving trains that banks needed to jump on board, that is until they crashed. Many banks had exposures of $500 million to close to $1 billion.

Figure 8.1 shows areas of exposure that should be of particular concern to bank managers, along with what I like to call the "blind spot." Usually credits that are known to be in trouble—even when the exposures are very small—are the subject of lengthy meetings, discussions, reports, and risk analysis presentations.

Enormous credit exposures that are deemed to be solid or good for business growth are not examined with the same jaundiced eye. This is true even

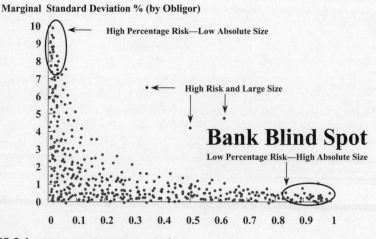

FIGURE 8.1 Exposure Size Versus Risk
Source: J.P. Morgan CreditManager™.

when the exposure is $1 billion or more. These exposures do not get the scrutiny they deserve. In fact, the possibility of risk is often strenuously denied.

You'll note that Figure 8.1 was generated with software developed by J.P. Morgan before it became J.P. Morgan Chase. J.P. Morgan knew what they were talking about, but even monkeys sometimes fall out of trees. They know better than to load up the boat with single name credit exposure. They've preached that gospel to the banking community for years. Yet the pressure to succumb to temptation is enormous. In December of 2001, just after Enron blew up, Marc Shapiro, vice chairman of J.P. Morgan Chase, defended the bank's *$2.6 billion* in exposure to Enron by referring to Enron's reputation just a few months prior: "Enron was a very solid investment grade company with a very positive reputation."

It's true Enron had a positive reputation, but it wasn't a "very solid investment grade" company. As any teenager knows, having a good reputation doesn't necessarily mean you are good. Sometimes it merely means you've been a bit clever, but not in the positive sense of the word.

By December 2002, J.P. Morgan Chase & Co. Inc., along with Citigroup Inc., were singing a different tune when Senator Carl Levin questioned them about structured finance transactions with Enron.

According to a Reuters report, Robert Traband, a J.P. Morgan executive, said: "We regret that we ever dealt with Enron." One of Citigroup's structuring heads told me Citigroup initiated a new policy in August, 2002, that would have prevented the types of transactions they engaged in with Enron.

In January, 2002, Global Crossing filed for bankruptcy. At the time it was the fourth largest bankruptcy in U.S. history. Gary Winnick, formerly one of Michael Milken's junk bond associates at Drexel Burnham, founded Global Crossing in the late 1990s. Global Crossing was accused of cooking its accounting books to show a profit, while they were actually experiencing heavy losses. Arthur Andersen LLP (Enron's accountant) was Global Crossing's accountant, and provided management consulting services.

John Legere, the chief executive officer of Global Crossing, said the problems were only due to competition and recession. But it seems Global Crossing overpaid for acquisitions while demand for its services—data and voice transmitting—declined. Furthermore, Congress and others are investigating Global Crossing's accounting practices. Once again, derivatives are coming under fire. Global Crossing swapped network wire capacity or underwater cable capacity with other network providers. Global Crossing claims they disclosed and properly accounted for the swaps.

Global Crossing's former vice president of finance, Roy Olofson, detailed deceptive accounting practices in an internal memo that was leaked to various media, but Global Crossing denies his allegations.

It's believed that Gary Winnick made more than $700 million trading his Global Crossing shares. But just as in the Enron situation, thousands of employees lost their jobs and retirement savings.

In the summer of 2002, WorldCom filed for bankruptcy. Bernie Ebbers, the former chairman and chief executive officer, is the focus of several investigations. In August of 2002, a U.S. grand jury indicted Scott Sullivan, WorldCom's chief financial officer, and Buford Yates, the former director of general accounting at WorldCom, on conspiracy and fraud charges. It was alleged they conspired to hide $8 billion in expenses to inflate WorldCom's earnings. Initially, both Buford Yates and Scott Sullivan pled not guilty to the charges.

On September 26, 2002, Buford Yates pled guilty to two felony charges that he conspired to commit securities fraud, and then committed securities fraud, by making adjustments to WorldCom's books at the request of his supervisors. In turn, David Myers, the controller and Buford Yates's supervisor, said he also conspired to falsify the books at the request of *his* supervisors. Like other nice guys throughout history, they were good at following orders.

WorldCom was the number two long-distance telephone service provider in the United States. Foreign and U.S. banks alike were happy to lend huge sums to WorldCom. Much of the loan exposures were unhedged. Several banks wrote down hundreds of millions in losses as a result of fraud at WorldCom. One large German bank had around $800 million in loan exposure to WorldCom. At the time they approved the loan, they didn't feel the need to diversify the risk, because they were committed to a strategy of lending to the higher margin telecom sector. They were proud they landed the business. They didn't even try to syndicate the exposure.

Syndication is a prudent way to spread the risk of a given obligor among a number of banks, but it isn't the final answer to diversifying risk. Its very prudence can disguise another credit trap. Banks tend to overconcentrate in an industry by being lulled into thinking that having a number of shaky obligors in a developing technology sector is less risky than concentrating the risk in only one shaky obligor. Unless the correlation between obligors is perfect, this is true, but the high correlation among the obligors in a developing industry sector may amount to nearly the same exposure risk as taking on an enormous loan to one obligor. When a bank has made a commitment to develop business in a sector such as telecommunications, examining the risks of each obligor and the correlation of the risky elements is very unpopular.

Raising a concern about these risks when everyone else is hell-bent on lending more money to one of these corporations is a career-cratering event for a middle manager. The top of the house has to take the reins to control the stampeding horses, but that's impossible when the leaders are among the herd.

In the equity markets, it is sometimes possible to take on large concentrations of risk and get rewarded for it. The debt markets are different. A lender cannot expect to be rewarded for taking on large concentrations of risk. Debt has no upside potential.

In 2001 and 2002, the markets cruelly drove home this point. Banks had large pockets of highly concentrated risk. Recovery rates were inversely correlated with annual default rates, and defaults—albeit relatively rare—reached highs that hadn't been seen in many decades. Not only were there more defaults on highly concentrated risk, when defaults occurred the banks recovered a lower percentage of their initial high concentrations.

NEW STRUCTURED FINANCE DEALS

Large loans aren't the only source of risk, however. Finance and securitization groups sometimes use the bank balance sheet as a dumping ground for deals they can't distribute through the bank's capital markets group. *Marquee deals* often make their way onto the bank's balance sheet.

This phenomenon is a perversion of the reasons securitization became popular in the first place. Banks used securitization as a balance sheet tool. Banks securitized credit card receivables and mortgage backed security (MBS), and in the process reduced their balance sheet exposure and gave investors worthwhile products. Banks then originated more MBS and credit card receivables, but didn't balloon the balance sheet.

Today, some finance groups securitize receivables, stuff them onto the bank balance sheet, and declare victory. Why not just call this activity what it is—secured lending—and pay the group the way the bank pays loan officers, a lot less? This may sound harsh, but it is probably not harsh enough. Banks must create disincentives for this behavior. At the very least, the bank should insist on prudent reserves that dent the group's perceived "profitability," and thus bonuses.

A German bank's senior officer asked me what I thought of an $800 million exposure the bank had to a securitized transaction arranged by its principal finance group. Revenues from fees for the rights to televise a sporting event backed the bonds. The bank co-led the deal with an investment bank. Upon issue, the investment bank discounted the bonds slightly, and thus earned lower net fees, in order to sell the bonds to its customers. The senior officer's bank couldn't distribute the bonds at full price through its salesforce. The bank's next most preferred choice would have been to sell the bonds to the conduit previously set up by the finance group for the purpose of buying their products. That wasn't possible, however, because the bonds did not have a high enough rating. The bank decided to buy the bonds and put them on the bank's balance sheet.

I pointed out that even if one loved the exposure, it was not prudent to have a high concentration of this risk. The bank wouldn't have considered taking down an enormous position in those bonds if they hadn't arranged the deal. If the bank saw the bonds in the general marketplace, the bonds wouldn't have the same halo effect. At a minimum, the senior officer might want to do some what-if scenarios: competitive threats, serious injuries to the key crowd draws, the public losing enthusiasm for the sport, or mismanagement (or fraud) in the franchise. What were the threats to the revenue stream backing the bonds?

The senior officer looked as if he had an orange stuck in his throat and protested that he liked the risk. There is a difference between having an open mind and believing something because you want it to be true. The chairman of the board had signed off on the deal and had signed off on the bank taking the position on balance sheet. This was a marquee deal. The bank got a lot of publicity and earned fee income. It was a watershed. The bank finally had a foothold in the principal finance business.

The senior officer did the politically correct thing in defending the decision. He suspected he had a problem, but he had to paddle up denial with everyone else. Shaken confidence triggers a craving for new converts. At this rate, the bank was in danger of doing another deal like this just to prove they were right the first time.

The senior officer had reason to worry. Market conditions had changed, and the bonds were looking even less liquid than when the bank brought the deal. Viewership was way down, and new competition threatened to produce competing televised sporting events, making the rights to televise potentially less attractive. One of the holders of a right to televise became embroiled in its owner's bankruptcy proceedings. Potential investors weren't keen to add this bond to their portfolios. The bank wouldn't be able to sell a major chunk of their position at the price it owned the bonds.

Meanwhile, the principal finance group reported the net revenues after funding costs as accruing profit and held *no reserves* against the position.

I like the idea of reserves. Even with the best of intentions, even with the best bright shining deal, things can go sideways.

FRAUD

Expect fraud.

We transact with human beings, and some of them weren't brought up with our own stellar values. Even when we expect it, we're capable of being stunned. Lenders were stunned when it was discovered that WorldCom, Global Crossing, and Enron cooked their books. Fraud on that scale is difficult to grasp, especially when a bank's individual exposure reaches into the high hundreds of millions or more.

Lack of due diligence has increased banks' vulnerability to loss in the securitization business, especially when banks put the entire position on their own balance sheets.

Steve Martin's character in *The Spanish Prisoner*, a movie about a confidence game, advised his mark: "Always do business as if the other person is trying to screw you, because most likely they are, and if they're not, you can be pleasantly surprised."

While I don't recommend that cynical view of the world, I do recommend that you at least consider the possibility that people and firms aren't necessarily what they seem. It's easy to believe something when we wish it to be true, because we're lured by the thought of a huge fee. That's why I believe a fraud analysis should be part of the analysis of any deal.

In the mid 1970s Paul Erdman wrote an entertaining fiction book: *Silver Bears*. The scam involved spreading rumors about a large silver discovery in the ancient Persian silver mines of Susa. No one actually checked the mines to see whether the alleged new silver supply actually existed. The limited amount of silver that was produced as evidence of the find came from trading contraband gold for legal silver to sources on the Indian subcontinent. The scammers shorted silver just before leaking rumor of the "find," and covered their shorts when the price of silver plummeted. Then the scammers went long silver just before they leaked news of the deception. The price of silver soared. They made a killing. The point was that *no one checked out the story*. Well-dressed educated people with a plausible story manipulated the market using little more than their vocal cords and a smart suit to pull it off.

Lance Poulson, the head of National Century Financial Enterprises, under investigation for the disappearance of reserve funds that supported NPF XII, its largest bond issue, ran Dinsmore Tire Centers, which filed for Chapter 7 liquidation in 1984. Most people didn't know about the liquidation. What they saw was the mansion Poulson lived in and the plane he lent for one of Governor Jeb Bush's campaign trips. Appearances can deceive.

One of the wealthiest people I know drives a secondhand car. He doesn't tie up cash in depreciating metals inventory. He dresses modestly. He doesn't fit the American preconception of a multimillionaire. He puts it this way: "It is a lot easier to get rich than to stay rich." He doesn't feel the need to impress people with his wealth, but uses his wealth to do really amazing things when he feels like doing them. As a result, he probably won't get the best table at an L.A. restaurant if he decides to negotiate a deal to buy a major film studio over dinner, but he doesn't care.

Robert Cialdini, Ph.D., wrote about how con men work in his book *Influence*. Bunco artists know that titles and trappings work forcefully on us. A study in the San Francisco Bay area showed that owners (or renters!) of prestige autos receive a special kind of deference from us. Furthermore, the tendency to lend money just because another bank has lent money is a phenomenon known as *pluralistic ignorance*. We look at what everyone else is doing to assess a situation, and if everyone else is OK with it, we go ahead. The trouble is, everyone else may also be assessing the situation, and noting our apparent calm, they think everything's OK, too. One by one we keep lending. Even worse, we tend not to like people who give us bad news such as: "Stop! Don't throw away more money!"

Fortunately, Dr. Cialdini gives us a simple antidote. All that is required is that we make a conscious decision to be alert to counterfeit social evidence. Question your preconceptions before they question you. By the way, did you even ask yourself in what field of study Robert Cialdini got his Ph.D.? It's in psychology. But if it had been in interior decorating, you'd be justifiably upset with me. It pays to question.

The German bank's principal finance group mentioned previously was burned in a metals fraud, which ensnared J.P. Morgan Chase, FleetBoston, Westdeutsche Landesbank, Hypovereinsbank, and Chinatrust Commercial Bank, among others. A network of related metals companies—RBG Resources, Hampton Lane, Allied Deals, and SAI Commodity—duped the banks. Where was the due diligence?

Initially, it appears the metals firms traded nickel and cobalt at a wash. For a few years, they bought the metals and sold them again at the same price or at a tiny profit. In this way they generated volume to continually increase credit lines in preparation for pulling off a large scam.

The principal finance group securitized RBG Resources' "receivables." They received the introduction through a broker, the financial business equivalent of a blind date. The head of RBG dressed well, drove expensive cars, wore expensive accessories, sat in plush offices, and lived in a mansion at a fancy address. Most of the veneer was rented, but it fooled a lot of people.

RBG wasn't what it seemed, either. Allegedly, affiliated companies used shell corporations that issued bills of lading and other papers for nonexistent metals. On the strength of this paperwork, banks authorized letters of credit to be drawn against trading credit lines. The metal didn't exist and the banks couldn't collect on their letters of credit.

The German bank's principal finance department's exposure to RBG was approximately $180 million. Most banks that had been roped into this scam immediately wrote down entire exposure. They felt if they were lucky enough to recover anything, it would be serendipity.

The bank branch manager did a post mortem analysis on the deal. He felt he couldn't blame the individual in the principal finance department who had arranged the deal: "I can't expect him to carry the can for that; it was fraud." It was admirable that he wasn't looking for a scapegoat. The employee had, after all, played by the bank's rules, or lack of them. Fingering a scapegoat wouldn't have solved the real problem, anyway.

The bank's "solution" was to suggest that reserves be held against the principal finance group's positions. They reasoned that the principal finance group's asset securitization business was a paper business. If the papers were in order, they went ahead with the deal. They accepted that people weren't going to do due diligence, no one was going to check the facts, so it would be prudent to take reserves against transactions.

Astounding. *No one is responsible*. The bank accepted that having guys sitting in a closet reviewing papers without kicking the tires was fine with them, because otherwise they might have to admit having a serious problem.

The bank only got it half right. Reserves are a good idea. Due diligence is a good idea. Due diligence combined with reserves is a *better* idea. In fact, it's a plan.

The bank's "solution" reminds me of what ice hockey players said after Teddy Green suffered a severe head injury in 1969. Players thought it was foolish not to wear a helmet; but they didn't, because the other guys didn't. They said if the league made them do it, they would, and nobody would mind. Individuals will often behave suboptimally and foolishly due to peer pressure or fear of ridicule. The only reason things changed is because the hockey league eventually made helmets mandatory.

Due diligence isn't a cure; it's only a defense. Even with due diligence, we can be fooled. Years ago Bernie Cornfeld thwarted lenders performing due diligence on his edible oil tank inventory. He simply poured a layer of oil over a tank full of water. When investigators plunged their dip sticks into the tanks to check the liquid level, the sticks emerged coated with a film of oil. They assumed the tanks were full of oil, and signed off on the loans. Bernie gave new meaning to corn oil.

If people work hard enough to deceive us, they will. To do any kind of business, there must be a certain level of trust, and that trust can leave us vulnerable to exploitation. We have a responsibility to make it difficult for people to exploit that trust. When they are successful, we need fraud reserves.

ENRON, J.P. MORGAN, AND OFFSHORE VEHICLES

When Enron declared bankruptcy on December 2, 2001, J.P. Morgan had $965 million in losses from payments due on oil and gas contracts with

Enron. J.P. Morgan thought the contracts were hedged with surety bonds. The surety bonds were advance payment bonds that guaranteed Enron's credit risk on prepaid oil and gas forward delivery contracts.

Surety bonds are a form of insurance. They protect against losses on specific assets. The insurance companies or *sureties* included Citigroup's Travellers Property Casualty, Liberty Mutual Insurance, and St. Paul companies among others. The insurers claimed J.P. Morgan and Enron used fraudulent inducement to cause them to enter into the contracts. They used this as a defense against not making immediate payments under the terms of the surety bonds. J.P. Morgan sued in an attempt to recover payments.

J.P. Morgan lost a pretrial bid in the Southern District of New York to get immediate payment from the insurance companies. As reported by Bloomberg news, in an affidavit filed in New York District Court, David Wilson outlined the gist of Enron's transactions. The following is a possible reconstruction of one of the transactions based on my interpretation of that account.

J.P. Morgan lent $330 million to Mahonia, an offshore corporation set up by J.P. Morgan in Jersey, one of the United Kingdom's Channel Islands. On December 28, 2000, Enron sold gas forward to Mahonia, and agreed to make a series of deliveries from April, 2001 to November, 2005. J.P. Morgan bought protection in the form of surety bonds on Enron's obligation to deliver the gas, but the insurers are challenging the contracts with Mahonia Ltd., which were "guaranteed" with surety bonds. Mahonia Ltd. got a 7 percent discount from Enron for the gas, and prepaid $330 million to Enron. Enron booked the upfront payment of $330 million from Mahonia for the forward sales as revenue. At the same time, Enron bought gas forward from Stoneville Aegean Ltd., another offshore corporation set up by J.P. Morgan in Jersey. In fact, Stoneville and Mahonia had the same address and the same board of directors, and it appears Stoneville was under the control of Mahonia. In exchange for a series of forward deliveries from Stoneville, Enron agreed to make a series of ongoing payments to Stoneville totaling $394 million.

Figures 8.2 and 8.3 show the cash flows of the transactions involving J.P. Morgan, Enron, Mahonia, and Stoneville.

It appears the $330 million J.P. Morgan lent Mahonia ended up at Enron. It further appears that the loan payments due from Mahonia to J.P. Morgan are originating from Enron. Furthermore, it appears Enron is booking what could be a $330 million loan as upfront revenue instead of booking it as a liability.

Mahonia prepaid the amount owed for the forward delivery of natural gas. Mahonia Ltd. and Stoneville Aegean Ltd. had the same address in Jersey and the same board of directors. The proposed deliveries of natural

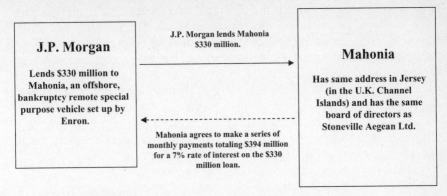

FIGURE 8.2 J.P. Morgan Lends Mahonia $330 Million

gas Enron owed Mahonia matched the proposed deliveries Stoneville owed Enron. It appears the contracts would be matched off, and there was never any intention to make delivery in the first place.

The surety bonds cover obligations by Enron on the series of forward deliveries to Mahonia, which are similar in value to the series of cash flows Enron owed to Stoneville. The upfront payment of $330 million Mahonia made to Enron appears to match the amount of the $330 million loan

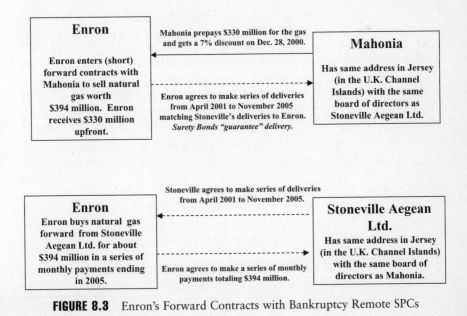

FIGURE 8.3 Enron's Forward Contracts with Bankruptcy Remote SPCs

J.P. Morgan made to Mahonia. The series of monthly payments owed by Enron to Stoneville seems identical to the series of monthly payments owed to J.P. Morgan by Mahonia. The cash flows Enron owed to Stoneville seem to be the present value of cash flows on a series of loan payments at 7 percent interest, which would equal the amount lent to Mahonia by J.P. Morgan. Although ownership of the offshore vehicles isn't disclosed, it is possible that Stoneville is 100 percent owned by Mahonia.

The insurers claimed the loan and the forward contracts were linked, and they were victims of a fraudulent scheme between J.P. Morgan and Enron. They claimed J.P. Morgan and Enron tried to disguise a loan from J.P. Morgan to Enron by using offshore vehicles and sham forward contracts. Surety providers cannot insure loans under applicable New York law, so they claimed that by entering into these transactions, J.P. Morgan and Mahonia could induce the surety providers to insure the loans. The insurers argued that since they provided the surety bonds based on fraudulent inducement and fraudulent concealment, they had a valid defense against having to perform under the surety bonds.

J.P. Morgan denies the forward contracts were a *de facto* loan and denies the transactions were linked. J.P. Morgan also denies knowing that Enron employed creative accounting and booked the forward sales as upfront revenue. It's possible they didn't know, but it reminds me of an incident that happened in my graduate school tax class. One of my classmates asked the professor a question.

"Professor, let's consider a scenario. What if I don't receive my 1099 (statement of interest on accounts issued by banks in compliance with U.S. tax law) from my bank on time, do I have to declare the interest on my tax return?"

The professor walked a couple of circles, shaking his head with an amused look on his face. Finally he turned to the student.

Barely able to disguise his mirth, the professor said, "I would love to be there to hear your defense to the Internal Revenue Service. What could it possibly be? You forgot you had a bank account? You didn't know you owed tax on the interest? You didn't know how to calculate the interest on the account? You mean to say that you have an MBA from the University of Chicago and your defense will be *ignorance*?"

The professor stopped for a moment because he couldn't stop himself from laughing. He composed himself and said, "Sir, *you are going down*!"

The transactions between Enron and the two offshore vehicles were odd. Futures contracts on commodities are exchange-traded contracts with standard terms. Futures contracts are standard, liquid, and allow for a number of delivery locations, but specify the delivery month. They specify a grade of commodity eligible for delivery, but allow for penalty and premium payments if the actual grade delivered is different from the specified grade. Futures contracts are usually netted out on a cash basis before delivery becomes an issue. Although delivery is rarely made on futures contracts, their standardization makes them a liquid method of exchange to hedge or speculate on commodity prices.

Forwards are over-the-counter contracts, and the terms of the contract are negotiated by the specific parties involved in the transaction. They are most frequently employed when physical delivery is expected. They are private nonstandard contracts. Settlement of the terms of the contract is either in the form of a physical asset or cash. It occurs on the negotiated settlement date. These contracts are often very detailed.

If you are long a forward commodity contract, you have an obligation to purchase the commodity or give its cash equivalent on the pre-agreed delivery date. The settlement terms will specify either the cash settlement amount or the grade of commodity you have to deliver on the settlement date, and the location of delivery.

If you are short a forward commodity contract, you have an obligation to sell the commodity (or you will receive its cash equivalent) on the pre-agreed delivery date.

When the parties enter into a forward contract, usually no money changes hands. *At-market* contracts have zero initial value and zero cash flow on the trade date. Usually cash only changes hands in an *off-market* contract. The cash flow would equal the discounted *expected net present value* (NPV) of the contract on the trade date and would be paid by the party for which the NPV is positive, to the party for which the NPV is negative. If you wish to create a nonstandard long forward, the purchaser of the commodity could choose to prepay the money in one upfront payment.

With forward contracts, you know the price you will pay or receive in advance. The pricing technology is straightforward. The parties to the contract build their forward interest rate curves, and for each date, they can plug their figures into formulas depending on whether they are long or short. (See the section titled Accruing Errors for more on forward price calculations.) It is highly unlikely the futures contracts would accidentally match a series of cash flows that would be so close in appearance to loan repayments.

The outcome of the offshore vehicles case is that J.P. Morgan Chase and the insurers agreed to a settlement just before the case was due to go to jury trial in January 2003. Instead of $965 million, J.P. Morgan Chase will get about $600 million and will take a fourth quarter pretax charge of about $400 million to recognize the net loss.

What would have been the outcome had the case gone to trial? Unfortunately we'll never know. The judge, Jed Rakoff, ruled that a senior

J.P. Morgan official's e-mail describing the transactions as "disguised loans" could be used in the trial. On the other hand, he dismissed claims that J.P. Morgan aided in Enron's financial fraud.

But J.P. Morgan still has civil suits pending related to its dealings with Enron. All of these issues may be reopened.

Suppose for a moment that these transactions were a convoluted way of hedging Enron credit risk. Why didn't J.P. Morgan just enter into a credit derivatives contract and hedge the credit risk? Credit derivative contracts were more expensive than surety bonds. Structurers overlooked the fact that insurers may have defenses against payment if the language of a surety bond isn't very tightly constructed. Institutions that hedged their Enron risk with credit derivatives may have paid more money for the protection, but all of them received immediate payment under their contracts.

Before the settlement, a J.P. Morgan spokesman said that the "good faith of insurance companies will be on trial." I don't agree. These transactions were highly unusual, and I believe the insurers would have been remiss if they didn't raise a legal challenge that is available to them under New York law. That's just good business sense. When one is being very clever, it is important to remember that the other people we do business with are also very clever. If we want to exploit form over substance opportunities, others may wish to do the same.

Game theory is the study of conflict between thoughtful and potentially deceitful opponents. In his *minimax theorem* John von Neumann mathematically proved there is always a rational solution to a precisely defined conflict between two players whose interests are completely opposed. When Enron declared bankruptcy, the interests of the insurers and J.P. Morgan were opposed. The insurers were merely making their logical move, and the documentation may have made the move available.

Were these transactions a good idea in the first place? What we consider clever finance today may be viewed as fraud tomorrow and vice versa. Tax avoidance is legal; tax evasion is illegal. Tax avoidance today may become tax evasion under tomorrow's public policy. Whenever someone is getting something for nothing, there is always that added risk.

In this series of transactions, it appears Enron received a loan and at the same time got to book it as immediate revenue. It appears the loan payments would be accounted for as forward liabilities. From a public policy point of view, use of special purpose corporations (SPCs) for this kind of benefit is on shaky ground. Anytime we use offshore vehicles to legally translate the character of cash flows, we need to be aware of public policy risk. Where were the clearer heads questioning how this transaction would look to a disinterested party?

Some good may come out of this dispute. Surety bonds are a good way to protect risk, and can be a good alternative to credit derivatives. Structurers may use surety bonds with more—rather than with less—confidence in the future. Lawyers will draft tighter language for surety bonds to bind the insurers to immediate payment on demand. Separately, if the surety bond providers believe fraud is involved, they can pursue a fraud claim or claim of breach of contract against the beneficiaries to recover their payments and damages.

PARTICIPATION NOTES

Some banks have unwittingly invested in equity risk of collateralized debt obligations (CDOs) in their bank portfolios in the form of participation notes. One New York branch of a European bank, a yankee bank, learned to their dismay that the income they thought they would receive on their portfolio of CDO tranche investments was lower than anticipated. Their portfolio manager had purchased participation notes (PNs). The PNs were rated Aa or better, but were rated only for return of principal. The coupon payments depended on the performance of the equity tranches of various CDOs.

Apparently the portfolio manager, bank management, and risk management miscommunicated. The portfolio manager felt that as long as investments were within the wording of the bank's guidelines, he could invest in this type of security. The PNs were held on the bank book, so he didn't have to mark the PNs to market.

When the equity portion of the deals deteriorated because they had to absorb credit losses, the income on the PNs declined. The bank managers were upset when risk management explained the dilemma.

The portfolio manager pointed out that the bank intended to hold the PNs to maturity, and therefore would not experience a principal loss. Since the bank didn't mark this portfolio to market, they wouldn't take writedown on the interim portfolio value, either.

The bank managers didn't expect to take this kind of risk in the bank portfolio on Aa rated investments. They expected that a rating of Aaa or Aa would apply to both the principal and interest. They didn't expect to invest money with the possibility of no income.

The bank had hidden risk, and now that the bank cannot liquidate the positions, it also has opportunity cost. The bank cannot free up the invested cash for other use before maturity without selling the securities and taking a loss.

EQUITY TOTAL RATE OF RETURN SWAPS (TRORS)— LOANS DISGUISED AS CAPITAL INJECTIONS

Disguising a corporate loan as a capital injection is accomplished by banks entering into an equity TRORS with a corporation desiring cash. (U.S. banks book this transaction in a foreign entity to avoid Glass-Steagall Act restrictions against banks trading equity, although the restrictions are changing.)

The bank buys the corporation's equity, receives London InterBank Offered Rate (LIBOR) plus a spread, and pays the corporation the total return on the equity. The cash is on-balance sheet as a capital injection, and the TRORS is off-balance sheet. The corporation usually enjoys a per annum spread to LIBOR of only 25 to 30 basis points (bps). A BBB rated corporation could raise cash at a cost of only 25 to 30 bps per annum over LIBOR versus a cost of around 200 bps more in the loan market. Of course, if the stock price goes down, the corporation is asked to put up more stock as collateral for the mark-to-market changes in the stock price that is owed by the corporation to the bank. The bank gets equity as collateral, the corporation gets a low-cost loan.

What could be the problem?

Given that credit risky corporations are eager to enter into this transaction because the cost of raising cash is lower than taking out a loan, the transaction raises several unpleasant issues. The opportunity to account for the cash paid for the equity as a capital injection raises an accounting red flag that only an Arthur Andersen auditor could ignore. As we saw earlier, TRORS are a financing tool. From the bank's point of view, if the price of the stock goes down due to a weakness in the corporation balance sheet, due to the economy, or due to a general depression in stock prices, the bank receives additional stock. This additional equity delivered to the bank may dilute the corporation's shareholder value at a time when the corporation can least afford it. Right about now it should occur to the bank that the floor price for equity is zero, especially if the bank is being delivered start-up technology stocks. In the past couple of years, many of the corporations that engaged in this activity saw their stock prices plummet.

This activity is a sweet deal for the head of total return trading desks. Often banks recognize the price risk of the equity collateral by asking for initial overcollateralization of the transaction, and corporations are happy to oblige by handing over more equity. Is it hard to find takers for this transaction? Finding takers for this kind of transaction is like waving a bankroll over your head in a Turkish bazaar. A lot of takers will be delighted to do business with you. The TRORS trading book earns fee income that is often recognized on an accrual basis. The traders have an incentive to put on as many trades as possible for as long as possible. Their bonuses are tied to the revenue generated on the trading desk.

Banks might want to ask themselves how they prefer to engage in lending activity. Does the bank prefer to perform lending activities from traditional lending groups that may ask for hard assets against a secured lending and get a higher fee? Does the bank prefer to participate in potential accounting games by lending money to corporations in the form of a financing from the total return trading book and earn less money in the process?

Ironically, hedge funds that lend money for stock are vilified for engaging in *toxic convertibles*. If stock prices decline enough, the amount of stock required to repay the loan may actually cause the control of the corporation to change hands. When banks do the same thing, they claim they're performing a public service.

THE TRADING BOOK PARKING LOT: REGULATORY CAPITAL ARBITRAGE

Many banks are eager to enter the securitization business, but few have the distribution reach to support it. As a result, structurers and traders will create convoluted justifications to get the bank to take risk in its trading books in order for structuring groups to earn fee income. Earlier we saw how risk ballooned on bank books, but when the risk is in a trading book, it can be virtually invisible to bank board members.

Let's take another look at the fully synthetic balance sheet trade we discussed earlier (see Figure 8.4). Until now, we focused on getting the risk off the bank balance sheet of the originating bank. We assumed the originating bank found an acceptable Organization for Economic Cooperation and Development (OECD) bank counterparty to get a 20 percent BIS risk weighting (or better if the counterparty is a government guaranteed entity). We also looked at the total reduction of regulatory capital in certain venues for the interest subparticipation (ISP) structure.

In the example illustrated by Figure 8.4, the originating bank's original regulatory capital charge is calculated as follows, assuming all of the assets are nonsovereign loans:

$$\text{Euro 1 billion} \times 100\% \times 8\% = \text{Euro 80 billion}$$

where 100% = BIS risk weighting for the assets
8% = regulatory capital charge

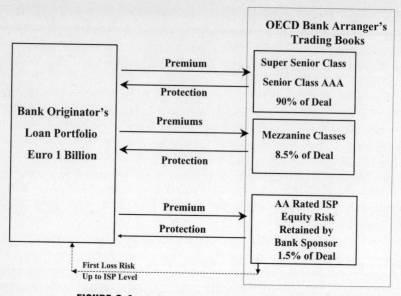

FIGURE 8.4   Fully Synthetic Balance Sheet CLO

After entering into the synthetic CDO with the OECD bank counterparty, the capital charge is calculated as follows:

$$\text{Euro 1 billion} \times 20\% \times 8\% = \text{Euro 16 million}$$

where 20% = BIS risk weight
      8% = regulatory capital charge

This assumes the originating bank gets an alternative favorable treatment on the equity risk of a 100 percent risk weighting and an 8 percent capital charge, due to taking advantage of ISP regulatory loopholes.

In rare cases, an aggressive interpretation gives a 0 percent charge for the equity for a total charge of Euro 15.76 million, but that treatment won't be supportable for long. If the bank is not in a favorable venue, the relevant regulatory capital charge is Euro 1.5 million for the equity. There is no advantage to an ISP, so the bank can retain the equity without structuring this feature, and the total regulatory capital charge is Euro 17.26 million (985 million × 20% × 8% + 1.5).

What is the position of the OECD bank arranger? The OECD bank arranger now has the synthetic tranches in its trading book. If it has counterparties for the synthetic risk, it can lay off the risk in back-to-back transactions. The OECD bank may enjoy model-based capital treatment in its trading book, and have a very much reduced regulatory capital charge versus a bank book. Several OECD banks have earned a fee simply for taking the risk off the balance sheet of a customer bank's bank book and putting the risk into their own trading books. The net value added to the banking system is only the exploitation of a regulatory capital arbitrage and a little paperwork. There is no net economic benefit.

I'm familiar with one bank that held the risk of every tranche of every synthetic deal they had ever arranged sitting in their credit default swap (CDS) trading books. They had no model to mark-to-market their deals. They didn't even have model-based capital treatment for regulatory capital purposes. Eventually, they set up repackaging special purpose vehicles (SPVs) to repackage the mezzanine risk so it could be sold to their cash bond investors.

The super senior tranches weren't funded, however, so the bank retained this risk in their trading books. They didn't have model-based capital treatment, so the return on regulatory capital was dismal. Over each quarter end, they did "bed and breakfast" trades to lay off the risk for one day with an OECD bank counterparty to reduce their overall regulatory capital charge. Even so, the small premiums earned on the super seniors left them with tepid returns on a regulatory capital basis, but at least it was a high single digit. Meanwhile, they continued to earn income on the large super senior positions. This was reported as accrual income (an anomaly in a trading book).

TRADING BOOKS AND CDOs: SHORT MEZZANINE AND LONG EQUITY

Traders that do not manage large flow books tell me they can't make money trading single name CDSs because they are too difficult to hedge. They wail that only firms with large flow books like J.P. Morgan Chase can make money by matching off transactions and capturing the bid/ask spread. They assert they can't exactly match off the trade in that way, and hedges are imperfect, so it is impossible to make money. They admit a one-sided bet could pay off and win big, but it is a lopsided risky strategy.

The same traders claim they have found a better way to make money. They claim they can make money structuring synthetic CDOs and retaining equity tranches, because they know how to hedge them. This is all the more remarkable, because they can't hedge single name CDSs. The game here is that they sell the mezzanine tranche and retain the equity tranche. They also often retain the super senior tranche.

Their claim is that by shorting the mezzanine tranche, they have created a natural hedge for the equity tranche. Furthermore, they selectively hedge some of the names in the portfolio as added protection for the equity tranche. The same traders who can't hedge their trading books when they are trading single names would have you believe they can now hedge single names in a portfolio of credit risk! It's magical.

A French bank exclusively relies on this strategy to report profits to its management, although they have very little distribution capability for this product. They provide funding for hedge funds that want to do TRORS against mezzanine positions. These banks have sold the idea to their management that this is a business model.

The manager at the London branch of the French bank mentioned above told me that his synthetic CDO strategy was virtually foolproof. I said I was puzzled that he should think this was foolproof. Was he aware that a large American investment bank lost so much money in the fourth quarter of 2001 on their "dynamically hedged" equity positions that they wiped out the substantial profits of the previous three quarters of their entire credit derivatives operation?

The synthetic CDO "arbitrage" is so juicy that the equity returns look good in a wide range of stress scenarios. The French manager mentioned above was thrilled with his strategy in the summer of 2002. He was not quite as thrilled in the fall of 2002 when the arbitrage got even juicier. Credit derivatives spreads widened so much that equity returns for synthetic CDOs more than doubled from around 25 percent to 60 percent for comparable collateral. (Returns are portfolio specific, so relative comparisons should be made for benchmark portfolios, if possible.) The slight widening of the BBB tranches the trader shorted could not compensate for the negative mark-to-market on his equity tranches, assuming he actually did mark them to market.

His exclusive reliance on this strategy became clearer to me when he explained that his group's compensation is a large percentage of the "profits" generated by this strategy. Needless to say, his employer has a few moral hazard challenges with this strategy.

Irrespective of the mark-to-market, is the default risk of the equity tranche actually hedged by shorting the BBB tranche and by selectively hedging single names? Based on what we already know, we can see it is not actually well hedged. How do I monetize the value of shorting the BBB tranche? If losses eat through the equity tranche, and if further losses threaten the BBB tranche, the value of the credit protection created by shorting the BBB position (now former BBB, since the credit has deteriorated due to the lack of subordination) increases.

One can envision a scenario, however, in which the equity tranche absorbs losses, but the deal matures with no losses ever touching the BBB tranche. Since the subordination has decreased, the mark-to-market of the short BBB tranche will increase. The BBB tranche is effectively downgraded, and the spread widens. The trading desk is short the widening spread, and therefore the position increases in mark-to-market value.

The BBB tranche does not have a claim to any residual cash flows in the deal. Furthermore, the value of the credit protection created by shorting the BBB tranche may not actually increase in value for individual names, making it difficult to monetize. In fact, if the remaining credits in the portfolio improve or remain stable, the value of the credit protection created by shorting the BBB tranche will not increase in value on a single name basis. If a hedge cannot be monetized, is it really a hedge? What protection does the short BBB position provide, in reality, that shorting single name credits— the strategy the trading desk admits it already failed at—provide? Is the total position marked-to-market or is it *marked-to-obfuscate*?

The short BBB position gives an illusion of a good hedge, but it is not.

The chief concern to investors in these deals is that the trading desk that retains the equity tranche will inevitably fight to create an equity tranche, which gives the trading desk the right to the residual cash flows of the deal. As we saw earlier, the moral hazard to investors in this type of structure is significant. Once losses eat through the original equity investment, the trading desk has a huge incentive to stuff the portfolio with high margin, risky assets to maximize the residual cash flows. If investors choose to participate in these deals, they need to carefully examine the structural handcuffs that will prevent trading to the disadvantage of the other tranche investors.

From the investor's point of view, even in the best-case scenario, they may not be getting the best deal available in the marketplace. Assume that the proper structural handcuffs prevent moral hazard–type trading. Even so, the trading desk is guessing which names will go sour. If surprise event risk such as the RBG metals fraud, American Tissue, or Enron is included in the portfolio—and who really knows?—selective hedging will only capture the risk by sheer luck. I agree it is better to be lucky than smart, but is that a business strategy? How would that conversation with your boss go? "I know I don't have a viable business strategy, but I feel lucky."

Selectively hedging single names and shorting the BBB tranche puts the trading book in the business of being the deal manager. Wall Street searches for experienced fund managers to do just that, and rating agencies consider the experience of the fund managers when rating the deals. The same trading desk that tells its boss that they can't hedge single name CDSs is telling investors they are the best managers for the CDO.

How is it that trading desks can make a case like this to their internal management and to investors? What is going on here?

If returns were marginal, traders would never be able to make this ridiculous case. But as we've discovered, the profitability of synthetic deals is boosted by about 45 bps per annum (or more) on about 90 percent of the entire deal. In addition, there have been periods where widening of CDS spreads has allowed base case returns on the equity tranche of investment grade synthetic portfolios to reach 60 percent and more (including the benefit of the super senior hived-off cash). As one manager at an investment bank said, "This is a no brainer."

The huge excess returns are what make this type of trading activity attractive. The large amounts of excess cash can cover multiple trading errors. But how profitable are these transactions in actual fact? Given the weakness in the strategy of these trading desks, should banks decline to participate?

I'm not in the business of regulating the legal behavior of consenting adults, but that never stopped me from suggesting that some types of conduct are more likely to promote a healthy outcome than others.

Several American investment banks opportunistically position these transactions, but they do not pretend this is their long-term business model. They view it as a calculated risk, and only participate when CDS spreads gap out as they did in the fall of 2002. This seems to be a sensible approach.

If a bank understands the implications of this strategy and wants to make this bet, there is no reason not to participate, particularly when CDS spreads gap out. When credit default spreads widen as they did in the fall of 2002, a well-chosen diversified portfolio can create very attractive returns. I agree that banks should put on these trades. These are extraordinary opportunities.

The challenge is not to delude anyone about the actual profitability of this strategy relative to other strategies, especially if a trading desk positions equity when CDS spreads are mediocre and they subsequently gap out. *My quibble with the way business is being done is the current obfuscation involved in an attempt to report greater profitability—or lower losses—than this strategy merits.*

If bank managers get a false picture of true value, no one in this business is well served. If banks express shock when losses occur or profits are lower than they anticipated, people with sound business models who run well-managed businesses come under suspicion because of the chicanery of others. The abuse doesn't occur because these products exist, it occurs because people are eager to overstate profitability to earn higher bonuses.

How does a bank protect its profitability from the game of "You take the risk, I'll state the profits"?

One reasonable way to approach this is to insist that risks are priced in a traditional fashion. For instance, suppose a trading book retains the equity portion of a synthetic CDO and also retains the super senior tranche of a deal. A bank might consider the spread of the original AAA tranche and calculate the amount of spread formerly earned for this risk that is foregone by creating super senior tranche. This amount can be subtracted from the "profitability" of retaining the equity tranche, because it was compensation that was formerly earned for taking AAA risk. This solves the problem of the arbitrariness of super seniors, and the fact that trading books inventory this risk indefinitely. This money, or part of this money, can be held in a reserve account to eliminate mark-to-market losses on the super senior tranche if defaults occur in the core portfolio.

The effectiveness of hedging equity positions by shorting a BBB tranche should be reexamined. Most trading desks that employ this strategy take inadequate reserves. Trading desks should accumulate large reserves that, over time, would cover potential losses to the equity tranche.

Traders that receive a percentage of "profitability" will vigorously resist this defense strategy, because it will reduce current reported profits. But if the strategy is viable in the long run, as more deals are booked and as reserves build, the trading book would have more stable profitability. As deals approach maturity, reserves earmarked to cover losses can be released into the profit and loss statement (P&L). If traders want high compensation, they will have to stick around and wait until their bets are covered by cash reserves, if necessary. The bank will then pay them based on true profitability.

The manager at the London branch of the French bank told me that his managers expected him to make as much profit as possible in the shortest time possible, and that is why he adopted the strategy of going long equity and shorting mezzanine tranches. This trading manager has no incentive to protect the bank's interest by properly stating AAA/super senior cash flows or by recognizing the inadequacy of his dynamic hedging strategy by increasing reserves.

Bank managers can change incentives by smoothing compensation. Rather than offer a percentage of profits for this type of business, it is more prudent to pay discretionary bonuses while building reserves.

HEDGE FUNDS AS INVESTORS

Hedge funds are important players in structured finance products, and are key investors in the leveraged tranches of CDOs. The potential for high returns, leverage, and funding attracts hedge funds. The key to doing business with hedge funds is to ask for full financial disclosure, and to require adequate collateral. Banks that don't insist on this are adding risk to their balance sheets. As we already know, many bank structuring groups are themselves hedge funds, whether or not their employers are aware of it.

Taking on credit risk allows hedge funds to diversify their leveraged strategies. Many hedge funds rely on prime brokers for financing, but the offered rates are variable and volatile. CDO managers can lever tranches of CDOs at cheaper rates, and usually constant rates, over the life of the CDO. The ultimate leverage is an unfunded investment in a synthetic CDO.

Hedge funds are private funds. Some make limited disclosure filings with the Commodity Futures Trading Commission (CFTC), but that only applies to hedge funds that invest in products regulated by the CFTC. Some venues outside the United States require principal guaranteed structures. The only other regulation is that they must either have less than 99 investors worth at least $1 million each, or they can sign up to 500 investors each worth at least $5 million. Some hedge funds have minimum net worth requirements greater than these guidelines, however.

Almost any fund that hedges risk can call itself a hedge fund, and anyone can start a hedge fund. Most financial professionals feel *the defining characteristic of a hedge fund is the heavy use of leverage*. Estimates about the number of hedge funds vary, but there are probably about 4,000 to 7,000 globally depending on who is counting, although the majority are in the United States. About 10 percent of them will fail this year.

Many hedge funds perform as expected for their investors. They are high risk and most years they offer high returns. Some quarters, or even some years, performance may be disappointing, but overall the return on investment can be high for long-term investors in well-managed funds. Several funds have long successful track records. Some well respected funds, such as Gotham and Long Term Capital Management (LTCM), go under after a few successful years. Others are new and untested. Hedge funds resist disclosing balance sheet information. A hedge fund can have less than $10 million under management or can have several billion dollars under management.

Why are individuals and financial institutions so keen to start hedge funds? It's because hedge fund managers usually charge high fees. For instance, a manager may charge a 1 percent (or more) per annum management fee plus an incentive fee of 20 percent of the upside of the investment strategy. Managers don't offer to refund 20 percent of the downside in a bad year, however. It's a great job. You use other people's money (OPM), you get paid a fee to risk that money, you get paid if you win money on your bets, and you don't refund money if your bets lose.

Managers of smaller hedge funds may not be able to live off the management fee, so they have to take leverage risk in an attempt to capture incentive fees. Leverage can make even a mediocre manager look good in the short run, if the manager is lucky.

In September 1996, I wrote about hedge funds for *Credit Derivatives: A Guide to Instruments and Applications,* published in 1997 by John Wiley & Sons:

> ...*the credit manager has no way to determine how much leverage the hedge fund employs.* ... *A hedge fund Counterparty seems to be a perversion of the concept of credit derivatives.* ...*If I want to lay off risk in the portfolio, to what degree am I hedged when the Counterparty is a hedge fund?*
>
> ...*The protection provided by the hedge fund is phantom protection. The only benefit is from the upfront collateral, which may reduce my exposure in the event of a default on the underlying asset.* ...*The question remains whether the enhanced spread income of LIBOR + 75 and more which hedge funds are willing to pay as a funding cost is enough to compensate banks for the credit risk.*

In August 1998, the Soros Quantum Fund lost $2 billion after Russia defaulted on short-term government debt obligations and the ruble was devalued. LTCM, founded in 1993, lost around $2 billion.

The managers at LTCM were meant to be among the best financial minds in the business, and they probably were. Myron Scholes and Robert Merton, cowinners of the 1998 Nobel prize in economics, pioneered equity option model pricing. John Meriwether, former head of Salomon's arbitrage group, and David Mullins, a former Federal Reserve Bank vice-chairman, were also partners.

Among other strategies, LTCM leveraged investments using total return swaps. LTCM managers refused to disclose positions or trades. They claimed they had to keep their transactions proprietary to protect their trading positions. In the end, others were probably grateful they couldn't copy LTCM's strategies. After several years of 40 percent-plus returns, and shortly after the Russia crisis, LTCM's net asset value (NAV) was down about 44 percent, meaning investors lost about 44 percent of their money if they were original investors.

UBS chairman Mathis Cabiallavetta and 3 other UBS executives lost their jobs after UBS disclosed it lost $700 million. Earlier, UBS had sold a seven-year call option on LTCM shares to LTCM's partners. They received a premium of $293 million, invested the majority of the call premium in LTCM, and hedged the call option by purchasing $800 million of LTCM fund shares. Unfortunately for UBS, the value of the shares plummeted.

Leverage is a very useful financial tool. Most of us use high degrees of leverage when we buy a home. But there is a difference between the way a bank treats you when you ask for a high degree of leverage, and the way many banks have treated hedge funds that ask for a high degree of leverage. Would you have been able to get a mortgage—even though you pledged your home as loan collateral—if you refused to disclose your financial details, including other debt, to the lending bank?

Why should a hedge fund that admittedly plans to employ high-risk strategies in a gambit to get high rewards be treated with unqualified faith?

Indexes try to track hedge fund performance. The Tremont index feels that the 380 funds they capture are representative of the hedge fund industry. Sandra Manzke, CEO of Tremont Advisers in New York, says you "don't need to own the S&P (the S&P 500 stock index) to get the S&P." True. But the various hedge funds are free to invest in anything they want. They aren't only investing in warrants and other leveraged stock plays. The Tremont index may have no utility at all when one is trying to figure out potential performance of an individual fund in which one wants to invest. Given that hedge funds can invest in any sector(s) of the capital markets, and can have any type of concentration risk they choose, indexes can't be relied on as indicators of value for a specific fund. As we know, many hedge funds invest in leveraged tranches of CDOs and further lever the investment through TRORS or other funding. This asset class is not even tracked by Tremont, at least in September 2002, when Ms. Manzke made her comments.

Jason Huemer, chief operating officer of York Capital Management in New York, calls this migration into new asset classes "style drift." The head of structuring at a U.S. investment bank calls this "competence drift." He said he's met some of the new hires that hedge funds have made for these investments, and he wasn't positively impressed. Nonetheless, hedge funds will increasingly migrate into this asset class, and will improve their expertise, since the lure of leverage and inexpensive funding is irresistible.

STRUCTURED FINANCE AND ACCOUNTING (KIDDER PEABODY)

Structured products are so difficult for many people to understand that they are ripe for accounting abuse. We've already discussed a few structures that could lend themselves to accounting abuse, but this isn't a new phenomenon, any more than the abuse of special purpose entities (SPEs) is a new phenomenon. The Securities and Exchange Commission's (SEC's) teeth have seemed more like gums in the recent past.

I recently asked a structurer if he'd ever heard of Kidder, Peabody & Co. (Kidder). He hadn't. Kidder existed about 4 structuring generations before his time, which in Wall Street terms, is less than 10 years ago.

Kidder was the turnaround success story of General Electric (GE), its parent company. GE's purchase of 80 percent of Kidder in April of 1986, for $602 million, earned it the name Generous Electric. Almost immediately after the purchase, the SEC required Kidder to implement a compliance system to detect fraudulent trading and pay a fine of $26 million after an insider trading scandal was exposed at the firm. Kidder's business declined, and it posted losses of $53 million in 1989 and $54 million in 1990. In 1990, GE earned further derision when they purchased the remaining 20 percent of Kidder for an additional $550 million in a bailout transaction.

At first, it seemed GE would have the last laugh. In its heyday, Kidder overwhelmed Wall Street with its dominant position as the top underwriter for MBSs. Its MBS underwriting volume surged to more than double that of its next largest competitor. Kidder started reporting profits in 1991 and 1992. In 1993, Kidder reported profits of $439 million. Unfortunately, the reports didn't reflect reality.

When Kidder failed in 1994, the major cause was false profits of $350 million reported by the government bond trading desk from 1991 through March 1994. In reality the desk was losing money, and actual losses exceeded $85 million over this period. The false profits were related to government bond reconstitution transactions and Kidder's control problems.

Orlando "Joseph" Jett traded treasury STRIPS (separate trading of registered interest and principal of securities). These are the strips of principal and interest portions of treasury bonds. The principal portion trades as a zero coupon bond as do the interest portions that represent strips of the coupon payments of the bond. Mr. Jett purchased the principal and interest portions of the same bond and reconstituted them for forward settlement. He reported record profits, supposedly because he was exploiting an arbitrage opportunity.

Melvin "Mel" R. Mullin, Jett's boss, was the managing director of the derivative products area for Kidder. Mullin held a Ph.D. in mathematics and was a former professor. He told a Kidder employee that part of his bonus was calculated based on Jett's revenues. He in turn reported to Ed Cerullo, the head of fixed income. Ed Cerullo's boss was the chief executive officer (CEO) of Kidder Peabody, Michael Carpenter.

When Jett began working for Mullin in 1992, Jett's profits were $32.5 million, double the Kidder historic record of $16 million for his trading area. Jett's reported trading profits for 1993 were $150.7 million. That's nine times the old $16 million historic record.

In December 1993, Kidder Peabody paid Joseph Jett a bonus of $9 million. Mel Mullin's reported bonus was $2.3 million, but that figure may not have included deferred compensation and other hidden pay perks. Ed Cerullo reportedly received $12 million.

In April of 1994, Kidder Peabody fired Joseph Jett. Kidder claimed Joseph Jett exploited an accounting glitch, and GE announced it would take a one-time $350 million charge to first quarter 1994 earnings to adjust for Jett's activity from 1991 through March of 1994.

There was no arbitrage. The reconstituted bonds and the strips used to create them were worth the same. In fact, other traders speculated that Jett even paid too much for the strip components at times. But Kidder's accounting system saw it differently. Kidder's trading system did not recognize that the present value of the reconstituted bond would be less than the settlement price of the bond, because the accrued interest, the coupon payments, belonged to the current owner of the strip. Coupon payments accrue between the transaction date and the settlement date and were included in the bond price, the *full price* of the bond. The coupon payment associated with this accrued interest was made after the settlement date of the reconstituted bond. While the owner of the coupon STRIPS is due the accrued interest, it didn't show up in the valuation of the STRIPS simply because the coupon payment was made after the settlement date. Even though it was impossible to make money, even though Jett was actually losing money, the Kidder system reported a profit for future settlement dates for reconstitution transactions.

Kidder claimed Jett was a rogue trader and that he acted alone. Jett claimed his supervisors, Mel Mullin and later Ed Cerullo, knew of his transactions and approved his activities. He claimed Mel and Ed encouraged his activities. Joe Jett pointed to his award as Kidder 1993 Employee of the Year as proof of their approval.

Mel Mullin and Ed Cerullo asked investigators to believe that Joseph Jett had an astronomical increase in profits, and they had no idea how Jett pulled it off. They claimed they never asked Jett how he did it.

GE employed attorney Gary Lynch to investigate problems at Kidder Peabody. Ed Cerullo and Mel Mullin told Gary Lynch's investigators that for a period of almost three years, they never once looked at one of Joseph Jett's trade tickets. They never once looked at a report that showed settlement dates of Jett's trades.

You or I might have asked a few questions along the lines of, "Hey Joe, just how are you making all that money?" Particularly if there were millions in it for us. Mullin and Cerullo claimed they never had enough curiosity to ask that question of Jett. Mullin and Cerullo would have you believe they were more than happy to collect their bonuses in this state of blissful ignorance. For his part, Michael Carpenter, the CEO, apparently relied on Mr. Cerullo's advice.

In December of 1994, GE sold most of Kidder's assets to PaineWebber Group Inc. for $670 million, representing a substantial loss from the total purchase cost of $1.152 billion.

In January of 1995, the SEC notified Kidder, Peabody & Co. that it planned to recommend filing civil administrative charges against Joseph Jett for securities fraud, Melvin Mullin for failure to supervise, and Ed Cerullo for failure to supervise.

Both Mullin and Cerullo suffered minimal repercussions. The SEC suspended Melvin Mullin for three months, and gave him three months of supervisory suspension from association with most financial institutions. He was also fined $25,000 for failure to supervise Jett. Contrast that with his $2.3 million bonus, which doesn't include the compensation his wife, another of his employees, also earned. Her compensation was believed to be $900,000 in 1992. Cerullo argued he couldn't be held responsible for the acts of only one of the 800 people he managed, not even the one that seemed to generate a huge chunk of the reported revenues. Cerullo was fined $50,000 and was suspended from the securities industry for 1 year. Contrast the fine with the $12 million bonus he received in 1993. It seems that for Mullin and Cerullo it was pretty good compensation for minimal accountability.

Joseph Jett runs a hedge fund in New York. No criminal charges were ever brought against him. Kidder and Jett's direct supervisors claimed he acted alone, and Jett was certainly vilified as the villain, but it seems unlikely that at least Mullin didn't have more knowledge of Jett's activities than he claimed. He spoke with Jett almost daily on the trading desk. Likewise, Jett's assertions that he actually did make money are ludicrous. When Jett appeared on *60 Minutes*, he claimed that Kidder held the profits in their coffers. He said this with a sincere straight face. Either he's a great liar, or he isn't as smart as he looks and was the pawn of his bosses. It's difficult to believe that Jett, a graduate of MIT and Harvard, didn't know the real score.

Michael Carpenter now works for Citigroup Inc.

THE SARBANES-OXLEY ACT OF 2002

The U.S. Congress seems to be fed up with the various excuses of corporate officers: "I'm responsible, but I'm not guilty. I'm guilty, but I'm not responsible. I'm not responsible, and I'm not guilty." Individual corporate managers grow wealthy, but somehow that elusive combination of guilt and responsibility belongs to someone else in corporate management. It seems those quickest to claim credit are also the most adept at denying liability.

The global marketplace tends to follow the lead of the United States, so I'm recapping the reaction of U.S. lawmakers to Enron, Global Crossing Ltd., WorldCom, and others. President Bush signed into law the Sarbanes-Oxley Act of 2002, which was passed by the U.S. Congress on July 30, 2002. The bill was named for Senator Paul Sarbanes (Democrat from Maryland) and Representative Michael Oxley (Republican from Ohio) who were instrumental in drafting the necessary compromises for passage. The act addresses issues of accounting oversight and corporate responsibility.

The act applies to companies that must file Form 10-K, 10-Q, and 8-K reports required by the Securities Exchange Act of 1934, but every U.S. company will consider its implications.

The part that seems to most affect structured finance is that the 10-K and 10-Q must disclose off-balance sheet transactions, contingent obligations, and relationships with unconsolidated entities. In other words, the financial reports should tell the entire story, and tell it accurately.

I'm astonished. Some of the provisions of the act merely seem to ask corporate officers to behave in a responsible manner. What I'm astonished about is that we have to ask people who are paid millions of dollars to do their jobs, ask them to do them honestly, spell out what would be considered dishonest, and threaten retribution if they don't.

The following are my broad-brush impressions of the parts of the Sarbanes-Oxley Act that I found most interesting, and its fallout. A detailed analysis would put a coffee addict to sleep. I only highlight what I feel is pertinent to how the act may affect structured finance, because the act doesn't specifically regulate structured finance, even though that is what sparked off most of Congress. Many of these products are difficult to understand and our congressmen and congresswomen weren't up to addressing them, since it is a specialized area of expertise. Nonetheless, the act is meant to discourage corporate officers from playing Enron-type games. It seems designed to put a scare into those who want to straddle the foul line.

My comments in italics follow my paraphrase of the provisions.

In each 10-Q and 10-K, CEOs and chief financial officers (CFOs) should certify the following:

- The signing officer has reviewed the report. *Officers were signing reports they hadn't reviewed?*
- To the officers' knowledge, the report doesn't contain any lies or misleading omissions. *We actually have to spell this out?*
- To the officers' knowledge, the financial statements actually represent the financial condition of the firm. *We mean to say that isn't what the signature represented in the first place?*

■ The officers who provide signatures are responsible for establishing and maintaining internal controls; *whereas before someone else signed, say the head of human resources?* The officers have designed such internal controls to ensure that the people reporting to them are actually doing it, are doing it on time, and are doing it honestly. *The officers are expected to manage their businesses.*

■ The signing officers have to report whether they have a grip on the situation to their company's auditors and the audit committee of the board of directors. They have to report any fraud involving management or other employees with a significant role. *As opposed to what— hushing it up?*

■ The signing officers have to come clean about whether there are any changes in internal controls or whether they had to correct weakness.

The Sarbanes-Oxley Act requires CEOs and CFOs to give up their bonuses for a year after the publication of a financial statement that needs to be redone because of misconduct. *But they get to keep their jobs?*

It's against the law for companies, directly or indirectly, to get a personal loan for any executive officer or director. Home improvement loans, consumer credit, charge cards, and limited broker/dealer loans other than for the purchase of company stock are OK, just as they are for any other employee. The prohibition does not apply to any loan made or maintained by a Federal Deposit Insurance Corporation (FDIC)-insured depository institution if the loan is subject to the insider lending restrictions of section 22(h) of the Federal Reserve Act. Personal loans made on or before July 30, 2002, are grandfathered. *Just when I thought they were going to get tough. . . .*

Financial statements must include correcting adjustments identified by a registered public accounting firm in accordance with generally accepted accounting principles (GAAP) and the rules and regulations of the SEC. *They were leaving this out?*

The 10-K and 10-Q must disclose off-balance sheet transactions, arrangements, obligations (including contingent obligations), and other relationships of the company with unconsolidated entities or other persons. *Report swaps and the activity of those offshore SPEs, so we can't be misled.*

The pro forma financial information must reconcile with the financial condition and results of operations of the company under GAAP. *You mean it didn't before?*

Executive officers and directors must report whether they bought or sold company stock within two business days following the day they did it. Within the year, they'll have to file this electronically.

The SEC will make companies say whether or not they have a code of ethics (and if not, why not) for their principal financial officers and comptrollers or principal accounting officers or persons performing similar functions. *Do we even want to hear the nonsense that would attempt to justify the absence of a code of ethics?*

There are newly created criminal penalties for tampering with records in federal investigations and bankruptcy. Destroying audit records or work papers within five years will get a criminal penalty, too. Certain securities fraud will also get criminal penalties. If CEOs and CFOs fail to perform the certifications the act told them to, they'll get a criminal penalty. If the company retaliates against a whistleblower, there will be a criminal penalty.

Why not mandatory minimums? How many people who violate this law will do even one day of hard time, as opposed to "soft" time in a minimum security, white collar crime, facility? The majority of prisoners in the United States serve hard time for nonviolent crimes. Mandatory minimum sentences are handed out to crack cocaine users and/or sellers, who are mainly African Americans. (White Americans tend to use powdered cocaine, and the punishment structure is different.) Justice is legally blind, but not color blind, or indifferent to class. Who has harmed the American economy more, the folks who inspired this act, or the folks who are currently long-term guests of the U.S. prison system? While I believe the U.S. system of government is the best in the world, there's room for improvement.

The corporation has to hire a public accounting firm registered with the Public Company Accounting Oversight Board (the "Oversight Board"). *The firm has got to find someone responsible to audit its books.*

Audit committees now have more responsibility by statute. Audit committees will be directly responsible for choosing, paying, and overseeing the auditor, and for resolving financial reporting disagreements. No member of the audit committee can have a conflict of interest, or take anything other than a director's fee. *No hidden payoffs.* They have to handle complaints about accounting, controls, or audits, even anonymous ones. *They were ignoring them before?*

The SEC will adopt rules for companies to disclose whether the audit committee of the company has at least one member who is a "financial expert," and if not, why not. This expert has to understand GAAP and audit committee functions. The expert must also have experience preparing or auditing financial statements and experience with internal accounting controls. *It's embarrassing that the SEC has to ask companies to make sure there is someone on the audit committee who is competent. It seems they left out something, however. They might have asked that at least one member of the committee have experience and understanding of structured products—if the company engages in them—since this expertise does not go hand-in-hand with accounting expertise. Some of the problems in recent history resulted partly because accountants were duped by structured products experts.*

In October 2002, the SEC published proposed rules implementing the Sarbanes-Oxley Act for comment. They are getting on with the job.

WILL SARBANES-OXLEY MAKE A DIFFERENCE?

How hard can it be to put together a credible audit committee? Apparently it can be pretty difficult. It seems even the former head of the SEC had difficulty putting together a new national board to oversee the accounting industry, as illustrated by the following events.

In late December, 2002, the SEC filed a lawsuit charging C. Gregory Earls, CEO of U.S. Technologies Inc. (UST), with one count of securities fraud, one count of mail fraud, and eight counts of wire fraud.

Allegedly, Earls used USV Partners LLC, an SPE that was a limited liability company, to misappropriate around $13.8 million that investors gave him to purchase UST's preferred stock and warrants. Although Earls said he'd get no management fees, he paid himself $4.7 million in management fees and $9.1 million he disguised as legal and accounting expenses. The SEC's complaint further says that Earls and UST covered up Earls' misdeeds. UST knew that Earls had previously been accused of misappropriating investors' funds in relation to other companies, but publicly praised his business acumen. UST failed to disclose its auditor's concerns about its controls. UST also forgot to mention that half of its board of directors resigned in the spring of 2002.

U.S. Technologies had an impressive sounding audit committee; after all, it was headed by William Webster, a former Federal Bureau of Investigation (FBI) director. Webster was chosen by the head of the SEC to head a new national board, the Public Company Accounting Oversight Board (PCAOB), created to police the accounting industry, until he resigned in November, 2002. He was to serve on the committee with Harvey L. Pitt, then chairman of the SEC, who also resigned. It turns out the SEC and Congress are investigating why Pitt chose Webster in the first place, given Webster's involvement with U.S. Technologies.

The incident reminded me of a World War I joke. A man stood on a corner in Berlin and yelled, "The Kaiser is an idiot!" Two policemen came to arrest him for treason. The man said, "You can't arrest me, I meant the Austrian Kaiser." The policemen retorted, "You can't fool us, we know who the idiot is."

The U.S. Senate is very likely to confirm Mr. Bush's nominee, William H. Donaldson, for the position of chairman of the SEC in 2003. If so, he'll help the SEC select a new head for the PCAOB.

This is great, but will it make a difference? If the following example is any indicator, it won't.

Frank Walsh, former head of Tyco International Ltd.'s (a Bermuda registered conglomerate) corporate governance committee, pled guilty to charges of securities fraud in December, 2002. When Tyco acquired The CIT Group in June 2001, for $9.5 billion, Mr. Walsh was paid a $20 million finders fee. He neglected to mention it to his board members. Mr. Walsh was trustee for a charity, and half of the fee went to the Community Foundation of New Jersey. (Those generous impulses sometimes come with some tax write-offs, but the contribution would have to be in Mr. Walsh's name, and the contribution may have merely been his recommendation.) The charges alleged he worked out the deal with Dennis Kozlowski, Tyco's former chairman.

So what happened to Mr. Walsh? The court directed him to pay $250,000 in fines to prosecutors, pay $2.5 million in fines to New York state and New York city, and to repay the $20 million to Tyco. In exchange, Mr. Walsh got a conditional discharge. No hard time for Mr. Walsh. No soft time for Mr. Walsh, either. In fact, no prison time at all. He immediately wrote the checks. I'm sure that left a dent in Mr. Walsh's financial portfolio, but it was nothing compared to the dent in Tyco's balance sheet and to the amount lost by Tyco shareholders.

When Tyco disclosed the news about Walsh, it appeared to cause a 1-day sell-off of Tyco shares, resulting in a decline of about $16 billion in market capitalization. At least that's what Tyco's civil law suit against Walsh alleges, so it may not be over for Mr. Walsh.

But what about all of that hard work on the June 2001 acquisition of The CIT Group for $9.5 billion? Surely some good had to come out of that?

In 2002, Tyco sold The CIT Group for about half that amount. Mr. Walsh's $22.75 million almost seems like a get-out-of-jail-free card. The payment can't make a dent in the real damages. As for Mr. Walsh, it is unlikely he'll suffer economic hardship.

It seems corporate malfeasance is a matter of risk and reward. Vast rewards come with limited downside. If economics is the only consideration, rational managers should do the crime. Recent history suggests they won't do the time.

The extraordinary payments that corporate executives earn for their services should also come with extraordinary consequences when things go badly wrong. The Sarbanes-Oxley Act may help regulatory bodies and the SEC cut some baby teeth, but it remains to be seen. So far it seems those responsible have much less downside than financial institutions that do business with them. This act will have little impact on executive behavior if the risk isn't commensurate with the rewards.

CHAPTER **9**

Super Senior Sophistry

Synthetics are a key driver of the collateralized debt obligation (CDO) market, and super senior tranches are a key driver of the synthetic CDO arbitrage. Super seniors were created to hide some unpleasant problems. Synthetics made super seniors possible, but the low margins on investment grade loans made them necessary. It was just too expensive to issue a AAA tranche, so the market created a cheaper tranche.

Super seniors first appeared in J.P. Morgan's BISTRO bank balance sheet deals. BISTRO stands for broad index secured trust offering, but in some circles it stands for "BIS total rip-off." Who is getting ripped off? Let's take a closer look at deals with super senior tranches to make sure it isn't you.

Originally, all venues considered the super senior tranche as 100 percent Bank for International Settlements (BIS) risk weighted. This meant that if the super senior were $1 billion in size, the capital charge would have been $80 million. If I'm earning 10 basis points (bps) on the super senior, my return on regulatory capital is only 1.25 percent. This is still the case for most non-U.S. venues, and that is why non-U.S. banks seek government guaranteed entities or Organization for Economic Cooperation and Development (OECD) banks as counterparties. With the 20 percent risk weighted OECD bank as counterparty, the capital required is only $16 million, and the return on regulatory capital for a 10 bps super senior is 6.25 percent. In the United States, the Federal Reserve already recognizes a 20 percent risk weight for super senior risk, and recently switched over to BIS II guidelines to allow AAAs to get 20 percent BIS risk weighted treatment. Even so, 6.25 percent is nothing to shout about. But that isn't the end of the story. For banks that can use model-based capital treatment, the return dramatically improves, because the regulatory capital requirement is usually very small, according to the models.

That's fine as far as regulatory capital goes, but that treatment merely allowed the deals to go forward. It wasn't the total driving force. We're aware the huge, low-cost super senior tranche dramatically lowers the all-in cost of a CDO. This is really convenient if you need to securitize low margin loans to alleviate balance sheet risk. Issuing a large AAA would drive up your all-in cost. It would be very unpleasant to have to explain that you booked loans at such tight levels that you will lose lots of cash if you securitize them. The super senior was the answer. Banks created a new, artificial, low-cost tranche. It erased some questions about the tight lending levels.

But even with the huge economic boost from the super senior tranche, several U.S. banks realized that economically they were often breakeven or worse on a balance sheet CDO. That suggests a review of bank loan activity is probably in order.

Super seniors spilled over into arbitrage deals driven from capital markets trading books. And why not? Everyone was saying this was free money. The market had magically created extra value in deals and created an enormous arbitrage where none had existed before!

How do you define super senior risk? Notice the exact definition hasn't come up until now. Were you even suspicious?

The reason is *there is no market standard definition of super senior risk. There is no standard means of pricing super senior risk.* The super senior is the most important driving force in synthetic deals and the super senior is the largest chunk of a synthetic deal. In fact, super senior tranches make up the major percentage of total CDO issuance, being 80 to 90 percent of most synthetic deals, which comprise the largest part of the CDO market. Yet the mark-to-market is open to wide interpretation. How can it be there is no standard pricing method and no standard definition?

It's incredible, but true. For instance, I can create two CDOs each using exactly the same underlying risks, rate them by the same rating agencies, and create different super senior tranches. The tranching in Table 9.1 shows two different ways of tranching an identical portfolio.

Which tranching is "correct"? *The disturbing answer is that they are both "correct."* The AAA attachment point is the same for both deals. By attachment point, I mean the amount of subordination that is required to achieve a rating of AAA by a rating agency. This super senior phenomenon is true no matter which rating agency or combination of rating agencies rates the CDO.

Once we have the AAA attachment point, the question is, how much subordination is required to deem the tranche above it a super senior?

I've seen several presentations in which the super senior tranche was labeled the AAAA tranche. Quadruple A. I wish it were true. Unfortunately, it is not.

I asked people at Moody's, Standard & Poor's (S&P), and Fitch how to determine the super senior attachment point. From the rating agency point

TABLE 9.1 Synthetic Static Arbitrage CDO Tranching
(Euro 500 million Baa2 Average Portfolio Rating)

Expected Rating	Principal (Millions)	Percent of Structure	Subordination
Super Senior	420.0	84.0%	16.0%
Aaa	25.0	5.0%	11.0%
Aa2	15.0	3.0%	8.0%
Baa2	20.0	4.0%	4.0%
NR	20.0	4.0%	NA

Expected Rating	Principal (Millions)	Percent of Structure	Subordination
Super Senior	432.5	86.5%	13.5%
Aaa	12.5	2.5%	11.0%
Aa2	15.0	3.0%	8.0%
Baa2	20.0	4.0%	4.0%
NR	20.0	4.0%	NA

of view, it is completely irrelevant. The rating agencies do not rate a super senior tranche. In fact, *the rating agencies do not acknowledge the existence of a super senior tranche.* The super senior tranche is a convention created by structurers. All the rating agencies care about is whether you have solved for the AAA attachment point in a manner consistent with their methodology. That methodology will be the same whether or not a structurer later creates a super senior tranche in the deal. As far as the rating agencies are concerned, the super senior is a retrofit that has nothing to do with them.

Except that it does.

THE AAA RIP-OFF

The rating agencies are overlooking the effect on the AAA rated tranches. When I asked a Moody's analyst about this, he said Moody's would think about this and get back to me. I'm still waiting. I got similar nonresponses from the rest of the rating agencies. Several analysts did not see how there could be any impact. The rating agencies might want to reconsider their position.

There is a compelling reason why the rating agencies might wish to take a point of view on super seniors in the context of their rating on Aaa (or AAA) tranches. I hear many arguments about rating agency models and how many angels can dance on the head of a pin. Oddly, I hear no arguments about AAA tranches. Getting distracted by models often makes us miss a

TABLE 9.2 Portfolio* Tranching with and without Super Senior Tranche

	Fully Funded CDO		Synthetic CDO	
Grade	Tranche Size	Percent of Portfolio	Tranche Size	Percent of Portfolio
Super Senior			414,500,000	82.9%
Aaa	439,500,000	87.9%	25,000,000	5.0%
Aa2	11,500,000	2.3%	11,500,000	2.3%
Baa2	14,000,000	2.8%	14,000,000	2.8%
Equity	35,000,000	7.0%	35,000,000	7.0%
	500,000,000	100.0%	500,000,000	100.0%

*Baa3 average portfolio rating. Up to 15% high yield and 10% asset backed.

huge problem that is right before our eyes. Let's take a look at how we can create a AAA on the cash Baa3 portfolio we tranched in Chapter 5. For the moment, let's assume this portfolio is on a bank's balance sheet. Let's assume we can either do a true sale structure and create an all cash deal, or we can do a synthetic structure and create a large super senior tranche along with some mezzanine tranches. Table 9.2 illustrates the tranching comparison.

The same portfolio can be tranched two different ways. The AAA attachment point is the same for both CDOs, as the rating agency models would predict. The amount of subordination required to get a AAA rating for a tranche of this portfolio is 12.1 percent. For the synthetic CDO, we add an extra step. After solving for the 12.1 percent AAA attachment point, we create a super senior tranche. The synthetic CDO has a super senior tranche that makes up 82.9 percent (17.1 percent subordination) of the portfolio. As we've already seen, we could just as easily have created a super senior tranche with a smaller or even a slightly larger size and still be "correct."

Both CDOs have a AAA tranche. Are you indifferent to owning the AAA from the fully funded deal versus the deal with the super senior?

The rating says you should be happy to buy either one. But you shouldn't be. Let's look only at the AAA level and up, and compare an investment of Euro 25 million in the AAA tranche of both of these CDOs. Figure 9.1 shows the two investments.

The second AAA is a first-loss tranche supporting the super senior tranche, or a *first-loss AAA tranche*. You may be asking yourself if it really makes all that much difference. Let's see. Suppose you were unlucky enough to have bought one of the deals that had WorldCom and Enron, each 1 percent of the deal, so that 2 percent of the total names in the portfolio defaulted. Chances are that other names in the portfolio were downgraded, so that the

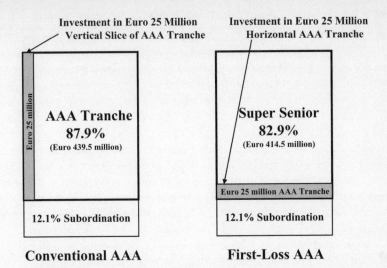

FIGURE 9.1　Two Different AAA Tranches of the Same Portfolio

amount of subordination to maintain a AAA rating would have to increase by more than 2 percent. But you know for sure that it would have to increase by at least 2 percent. Using this knowledge, let's take a look at the effect on our two AAA investments (see Figure 9.2).

The two AAA tranches are not equivalent in a nonstatic world. If everything else remained the same, but 2 percent of the portfolio defaulted, about

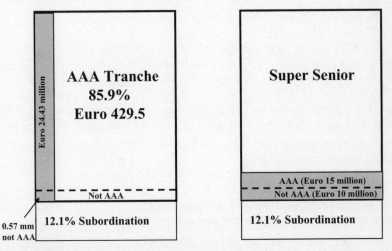

FIGURE 9.2　Effect of Default of 2% of the Portfolio on AAAs

0.57 million or about 2.27 percent of the Euro 25 million first AAA tranche would not be deemed AAA. If we restructured to add 2 percent more subordination to the total deal, about 24.43 million of this tranche would still be deemed AAA. The AAA of the synthetic CDO presents a different picture. Euro 10 million (40 percent) of this tranche would not be deemed AAA.

Almost all of the AAA tranches of static synthetic arbitrage deals initially brought to market traded close to levels of cash AAA tranches. None of them had added structural protections to benefit the senior noteholders. This is still the case with many of the deals brought to market today. The excess spread generated by the cheap super senior tranche was siphoned off for the benefit of the bank arranger. Most of the excess spread was not even passed through to the equity investor who accepted a maximum fixed coupon for the equity investment. The coupons looked good relative to a cash arbitrage CDO, but the clear benefit was to the bank arranger.

It seems that investors who bought AAA tranche structures like the one above didn't get the best deal possible, because they didn't know what to ask for at the time. As we saw in the discussion about equity tranches, there are several structural protections for senior tranche investors. Many structural features can be built into a CDO to protect senior noteholders. For instance, once losses exceed a certain threshold, excess spread can be trapped in a reserve account and used for the benefit of the AAA and super senior noteholders, if required. If the equity holder is promised a fixed coupon, excess spread can be trapped for the benefit of the senior noteholders, and revert to the bank arranger only if they are not needed to cover losses to the AAA and super senior investors. Other structural protections can be employed as well.

It isn't possible to determine the relative value of AAA tranches without knowing the entire deal structure. The way we price first-loss AAA tranches is due for a shake-up. It is darkly amusing just to combine the words *first-loss* and *AAA tranche* into a phrase that accurately describes a tranche of a CDO. For the most part, these risks and rewards have not been accurately represented to AAA tranche investors. As more of these investors become conversant with synthetic structures, they will become more demanding. It is logical they'll ask for some of the spread stripped off the super senior tranche, and will reject deals that do not trap sufficient excess spread in a reserve account.

RATING AGENCIES—MOODY'S TRANCHING

Even so, many firms will act as if all AAAs are the same. Bank of America's London office showed me the AAA tranche of a proposed restructuring of one of their Helix Investment Grade Hybrid Transaction Securities (HIGHTS) transactions. The original CDO had several dogs in the portfolio, and the small degree of subordination was aggressive to begin with. Due to defaults, Bank of America decided to restructure several deals to crystallize losses at the lower tranche levels and remarket the deals. The Bank of America marketer showed me the portfolio and told me the amount of subordination they were using to get to the AAA attachment point. The amount of subordination for the restructured tranche was insufficient to merit a AAA rating using a Moody's model. I explained this to the salesman. The salesman said that Bank of America was tranching the restructuring using the S&P model.

This highlights another CDO challenge. Different rating agency models produce different results. I pointed out to S&P that for every arbitrage deal I had time to look at, using both a Moody's and S&P tranching methodology, S&P was always insufficient relative to Moody's. They weren't aware of this, and hadn't done comparisons of their model versus Moody's.

Most market professionals and many investors feel that for corporate portfolios, Moody's dominates this field versus S&P. Although S&P seems to have more market acceptance than Fitch, the latter is rapidly gaining ground. When a deal is rated by more than one agency, the worst-case tranching is the one that dominates, and that is generally Moody's. Furthermore, Moody's tranching is used as the benchmark tranching in almost all of the unrated static arbitrage CDOs. It's true that some investors require an S&P rating. Nonetheless, investors would be remiss in not asking for Moody's benchmark tranching if it gives them more subordination.

I told the Bank of America marketer that he may find people to buy the tranche, but I wouldn't be one of them. Furthermore, a KMV analysis showed that the portfolio was worse than portfolios I was being shown from his competitors.

"Don't be afraid to make a bid at a much wider spread," he said. I couldn't imagine why he thought I'd be shy.

"OK," I said, "did you want me to give you a bid at a AA level? I would, except I'm not in the market for a AA tranche. I need AAA."

"Well, how much subordination does the Moody's model say you need?" he asked.

I told him. But that wasn't the entire point.

Bank of America was restructuring the deal to increase protection, presumably so investors could avoid getting burned the second time around. Their HIGHTs deals were suffering from a downgrade epidemic. Yet they were showing relatively lousy portfolios using S&P benchmark tranching and no structural protections at a time when many others were building these features into their deals.

The marketer called me a few weeks later to tell me Bank of America had sold the AAAs at much wider spreads than he offered me originally, but he didn't have the details of the exact spread. Neither of those facts surprised me.

A Goldman Sachs marketer sent me a portfolio in response to my request for AAA tranches. A few days later he began sending me e-mails asking me what I thought. I responded that after a KMV analysis, the portfolio looked promising, but I was awaiting details on the CDO structure.

After a few more days passed, I received more e-mails asking what I thought. I again asked for the deal structure. He responded by telling me the degree of subordination on the AAA tranche. I pointed out that the degree of tranching seemed insufficient relative to Moody's model. After a few days, he said they were hearing that from other customers, too, and had decided to tranche using Moody's as their benchmark.

He again asked what I thought. I responded that I needed to see the entire structure of the deal before I could comment. I said I needed to see each of the tranches and the structure of the cash flows for starters.

"How do you think they should be structured?" he asked. Goldman had an interesting approach. Were they actually asking me to structure their deals?

"With as many structural protections for the AAA tranche as possible," I responded.

AAA BASKET WITH 2 PERCENT FIRST-LOSS TRANCHE

Let's compare the pricing of 55 bps common throughout most of 2001 and 2002 for the first-loss AAA tranche shown in Figure 9.2 with pricing of a similar product. Baskets of AAA tranches of various CDOs are sometimes credit enhanced with a small first-loss tranche. The early deals securitized AAA tranches of CDOs backed by residential mortgages. At the time, the AAA tranches were trading around London InterBank Offered Rate (LIBOR) + 30 to LIBOR + 35 bps, or 30 to 35 basis points on a synthetic basis. The special purpose entity (SPE) bought protection on the first-loss risk of the basket through a "first-to-default basket swap." The first-loss piece was around 2 percent of the basket. Figure 9.3 shows this first-loss tranche.

The protection sellers received 100 bps for this risk. We know the residential mortgage collateral had a very high correlation across tranches, so one could view it as being similar to a large AAA tranche of one deal.

Returning to our previous discussion, some first-loss AAA tranches of synthetic arbitrage CDOs are only 2 percent in size. (I used an example of

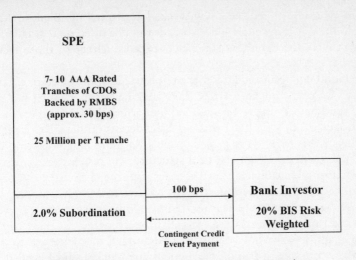

FIGURE 9.3   First-Loss on Basket of AAA Tranches

a AAA tranche that was 5 percent of the CDO.) The AAA tranches of those deals traded at only 50 to 55 bps at the same time the protection providers of the first-loss basket transactions received 100 bps. This suggests these investors were getting a bad deal.

These prices fluctuate. By the end of 2002, AAA tranches of synthetic investment grade arbitrage CDOs had widened to around 75 bps, but the AAAs of residential mortgage backed security (RMBS) backed CDOs had also widened, which suggests that investors in these first-loss AAAs are still getting underpaid.

SUPER SENIOR ATTACHMENT POINT

Structurers and rating agencies don't always agree on the AAA attachment point, but rating agency model results serve as benchmarks to frame the debate. There is no rating agency model for super seniors, however. How can we agree on a super senior attachment point, when there are no benchmark models?

One bank uses the Moody's model to solve for the attachment point at the 10^{-6} probability of default, and calls the amount above that super senior. The trouble is, no 2 analysts can agree on the 10^{-6} attachment point, even if they could agree it should be the criterion. If we examine historical data for corporates, different time series of data result in different values for volatility, recovery rates, and default rates. Correlation data is even more difficult to produce.

Another bank solves for the Moody's AAA attachment point and arbitrarily asks for at least a 5 percent AAA tranche underneath the super senior.

Other financial institutions have shown CDO structures with no AAA tranche whatsoever. They go from a AA tranche directly to a super senior tranche. In my view, they failed to meet the basic requirement for a super senior, which is to have AAA tranche subordination.

Ambac Financial Group, Inc. (Ambac) recently reviewed a 150-name corporate portfolio, and each of the names were of equal size. They liked the portfolio and were willing to bid on the "super senior" tranche. They asked for 10 percent subordination for the super senior, which would have been 90 percent of the CDO. In other words, they wanted the deal to be able to sustain the default of 15 names before the super senior tranche would be affected. The arranger found someone else to provide super senior protection. The alternate counterparty only required default protection for 12 names before the super senior would be affected. The definition of a super senior tranche is arbitrary.

SUPER SENIOR PRICING

Several factors influence super senior pricing. Bank arrangers who retain super senior risk in their trading books are often pressured by structurers to accept narrower spreads on the super senior tranche. The lower all-in CDO cost achieved by a lower spread on the super senior tranche can be the deciding factor in winning a mandate with an outside bank customer that wants to securitize balance sheet risk. The bank arranger's structurers earn fee income for structuring the deal. The super senior book is asked to "take one for the team." There's nothing logical about this pricing, other than a desire to win deal mandates. Since the mark-to-market on the super senior is rarely rigorously performed, this moral hazard is invisible to bank managers.

Trading books that retain the equity portion of CDOs use the cash they hived off the super senior tranche and incorporate it into equity returns. The extra cash is part of a slush fund that can hide a myriad of mistakes. Managers of banks have accepted this without much question. This ruse is about as sophisticated as the schoolyard prank of saying, "Look, your shoelace is untied!" And it works.

Some banks use model-based capital pricing. They have an internal benchmark for the super senior attachment point for a given set of data and volatility assumptions. They solve for the premium that gives them a target return on model-based capital. The results vary by financial institution.

Because this is merely a target, and because the data can be manipulated, there is a lot of latitude in super senior pricing.

Financial Security Assurance, Inc. (FSA), Ambac, and MBIA Inc. have internal capital models, which allow them to bid super seniors at tighter levels than most banks. In 2002, when many banks required super senior premiums of 8 to 12 bps for the super senior of corporate deals, the reinsurance companies were willing to take this risk at around 6 bps. For residential mortgage deals, they would be willing to go as low as 4 bps. Sometimes it was cheaper for a bank arranger to intermediate (or to find an OECD intermediary), between the originating bank and the reinsurance company, than for an OECD bank to take the super senior risk outright. Banks require much less capital for intermediations than for outright positions, and can usually intermediate for 1 to 2 bps.

By the end of 2002, FSA pulled back from being a super senior protection provider for corporate deals, due to corporate defaults in the portfolios in which they had already invested. MBIA stayed in the market and Ambac entered the market, but they asked for wider premiums of around 12 bps, and also asked for well-diversified portfolios with good levels of subordination. Due to the widening of corporate spreads, they were able to get what they asked for in many instances.

Many banks pulled back from the super senior market by the end of 2002. J.P. Morgan Chase had a large super senior portfolio and curtailed its super senior activities beginning in late 2001. Other banks instituted a policy wherein they would only retain super seniors on deals they were arranging, and would not invest in outside super seniors.

New banks entered the market. Banks doing arbitrage deals decided to keep the super senior and the equity tranches and go short the mezzanine tranche. We discussed that earlier, but there is a feature worth reiterating. Since the bank arranger owns the equity, which is itself subject to "investor acceptance" pricing, the arrangers can set the level of the super senior and the equity at will. The tranches are kept on the trading book, and there is moral hazard in the ultimate pricing as well as the structuring and ongoing deal management.

SUPER SENIORS OR SENILE SENIORS?

The rating agencies have downgraded the AAA tranches of many synthetic CDOs in 2001 and 2002. What does that mean for super senior tranches? We can use our earlier example to examine the effect of defaults of 2 percent of a synthetic corporate portfolio. For purposes of this example, we'll assume that the super senior and AAA are not written down by recovered

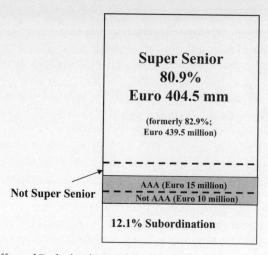

FIGURE 9.4   Effect of Default of 2% of the Portfolio on the Super Senior Tranche

amounts. We have to solve for the new super senior attachment point, just as we did for the AAA tranche. The new attachment point is shown in Figure 9.4.

Let's assume we mark the 2 percent strip of the former super senior to AAA levels of 55 bps versus 10 bps for the super senior tranche. The 45 bps difference is a loss of Euro 45,000 per annum. That doesn't seem too bad. Of course, we neglected the fact that many of the corporate names have been downgraded, and the overall subordination should probably increase more than 2 percent. The larger difference in the mark-to-market is from the portion that is still super senior. If Ambac is taking on board super senior risk at around 12 bps, banks will usually be about 4 bps wider. That suggests 16 bps might be a good benchmark level for the remainder of the tranche. That means there is a 6 bps loss in the mark-to-market of the remaining Euro 404.5 million. That's an additional Euro 242,700 per annum mark-to-market loss. The total mark-to-market loss on the super senior tranche is 287,700 per annum. Since volatility has increased, our internal model might suggest an even higher price, and even greater loss.

Notice our calculation above was for a small deal, only Euro 500 million in size. Most financial institutions have super senior portfolios of at least the equivalent of $10 billion, and for institutions like J.P. Morgan Chase, it is in the triple digits. A $10 billion corporate-backed portfolio might have experienced mark-to-market losses on the order of Euro 5.75 million per annum, and that is a generous estimate. But this mark-to-market loss won't show up on the profit and loss statement (P&L) of most trading books.

Since there is no visible market in super seniors, and since the definition is fluid, how can anyone say what the mark-to-market should be with complete conviction? Trading desks are counting on this ambiguity to obscure potential mark-to-market losses. One bank provided super senior protection for an early Deutsche Repon deal that had several defaults in the portfolio. Many of the remaining names had been downgraded. The AAA tranche was downgraded to AA. Nonetheless, the mark-to-market on the super senior didn't budge.

WHERE ARE THE REGULATORS?

Risk managers will have difficulty verifying mark-to-market losses they cannot observe. Super seniors aren't actually marked-to-market. They are marked to perception. There is a strong incentive for super senior providers to put low bids in the market, or reference the low bid of a reinsurance company, and declare victory. It is unlikely risk managers or senior bank managers will see those unpleasant mark-to-market losses show up on their desks in the magnitude I've described.

It's unlikely bank regulators will see it either, but then, they aren't asking the question in the first place. In the fourth quarter of 2002, I discussed this topic with a senior bank regulator. He was unaware of the issue, even though he is a "structured products expert." As we discussed the pricing of super seniors and the economics of synthetic deals, his brow furrowed in unaccustomed thought. If he thought about this hard enough, he might actually have to take a position. This was dangerous. New ideas and drive are not valued qualities in the regulatory network. "Team players" are highly valued. "Team player" is a code for toeing the party line. This means not rocking the boat and never introducing a new idea that may have political ramifications. Fortunately, the moment of thought morphed into a familiar lifetime of inertia. The regulator persuaded himself that it wasn't his problem. In fact, it isn't a problem at all.

"I've read that the market figures out all new products in around eighteen months, so this will soon be generally known." The official struck the precise tone of pompous complacency that resonates in bureaucracies the world over. Once again, he was relaxed and calm. All was right with his world.

As of the time of our conversation, BISTROs had been around for five years.

It is an interesting theory that the markets are efficient. It is one I subscribe to myself, in theory. The difficulty is that information distribution is not always efficient. Another difficulty is that humans only have so much time and life to analyze complex ideas.

In the long run markets are efficient, but in the short run, they are not. That is why "arbitrage" desks are often very successful. Many of the lucrative jobs in the capital markets exist because information distribution is not efficient in the short run. Sometimes it even seems inefficient in the long run.

Even if markets are efficient in the long run, bureaucracies are not. We can't take comfort in a notion that regulation makes our banking system safer. Countries that make bureaucracy an art form, such as Japan and Germany, are currently seeing the worst consequences of incompetent bank management, and the regulators are miles away from being part of the solution.

The responsibility for sound bank management lies with bank managers. A handful of banks have looked at the game of putting super seniors in the trading book for better capital treatment, and have declined to play the game. They rightly point out that they can't mark the super seniors to market, and the economics are a shell game. They expect that structures should add value other than providing a way to manipulate cash flows and siphon off fees for structurers. These managers didn't need to wait for "risk managers" or "regulators" to catch up; they studied the business and took their own decision. In the end, they will probably end up the winners in the shell game.

JUNIOR SUPER SENIORS

When banks and investment banks realized that monoline insurance companies would take super senior risk for much lower spreads than most banks, they were overjoyed. Occasionally, however, monolines didn't want the entire super senior tranche, only a portion of the super senior tranche. Furthermore, it was difficult to find additional buyers of the remaining vertical slice of the super senior tranche anywhere near the low levels to be had from the monolines.

Structurers could have created a smaller super senior tranche and a larger Aaa tranche, but this would have raised the cost of the securitization. Instead, many banks and investment banks offer a *junior super senior tranche*. They created another horizontal tranche in between the Aaa tranche and the super senior tranche.

The junior super senior is more likely to become a senile senior because a need for increased subordination to maintain a AAA rating will affect the mark-to-market of this tranche before the "super senior" (supersuper senior?) is affected.

Many of the original junior super senior tranches were priced from 8 to 12 bps, but recently super senior tranches traded at 12 bps. What does that say about the mark-to-market on those junior super seniors? We can see that the percentage mark-to-market loss will be greater than for an original super senior tranche, but there is no standard pricing for a junior super senior. The mark-to-market challenges for this tranche are the same challenges we faced for the super senior tranche.

Earlier we discovered that there is no standard definition of a super senior tranche. The junior super senior tranche adds more mud to the already muddy waters. There are no guidelines for the creation of this tranche. It is a distribution gimmick and an attempt to keep the costs of the liabilities to a minimum in the absence of buyers of the full super senior tranche.

The term "junior" super senior makes a mockery of the entire concept of the super senior tranche. Why stop at two "super senior" tranches? Why not have senior, junior, sophmore, and freshman super seniors?

SUPER SENIOR "INVESTORS"

If you think about super seniors in the context of AAAs, you could ask yourself the following question: "Would I rather own a AAA and earn a spread over LIBOR of 55 bps, or would I prefer to split the AAA into a small first-loss piece and earn 55 bps and a second large piece that pays me only 10 bps?"

No one needs a model to figure that out. This is exactly what banks have done with their balance sheet risk, but purely in response to regulatory capital pressure and cost pressures. Only the unfunded nature of the synthetic AAA allowed us to split it into two pieces and create one piece with such a low premium.

Many people remark that a repackaged super senior tranche (repackaged in note form that would require funding) should be ideal for "credit arbitrage" funds, structured investment vehicles (SIVs), that can lever the fund based on the quality of credit risk in the portfolio. Actually, super seniors would be a disaster for these funds.

These funds would get no benefit of additional leverage from a super senior tranche paying 10 bps than for a AAA tranche paying 55 bps, because the rating agencies consider the super senior and the AAA as having the same risk. The SIV would earn 45 bps per annum less, relative to their funding cost, and have no additional leverage. The SIV can buy a AAA tranche of a nonsynthetic deal and earn much more spread income than they would get if they purchased the AAA plus super senior of a synthetic deal, even if the underlying collateral was the same for both deals.

Who then are the "investors" in super seniors? Reinsurance companies and banks are the primary investors. Both are looking for off-balance sheet, unfunded, high-quality credit risk. Both can exploit model-based capital treatment or some variation to show a reasonable return even with the low premium.

The other "investor" is the bank originator that is eligible for a 20 percent BIS risk weight on super seniors, and retains the tranche. There is still a regulatory capital reduction for laying off mezzanine risk. If the bank originator retains the equity, it still captures excess spread, but for investment grade bank loans that spread is minimal due to the narrow spreads at which the loans were originated.

Another "investor" is the bank arranger that wants to earn fee income and has a trading book willing to take on the risk. Super seniors are nonliquid, never trade, and do not have a transparent mark-to-market. The capital market's trading book has become an investment portfolio for super senior tranches.

FINAL THOUGHTS ON SUPER SENIORS

It may seem as if I'm saying don't ever invest in super seniors, but I'm not advocating that. What I'm pointing out is that there are irrational dislocations in the current market. The way we tranche and accumulate super senior risk requires examination.

The lack of definition for super seniors and junior super seniors is a problem waiting to be solved. Earlier we discussed BIS II. It addresses super senior risk in an oblique way. Under BIS II, one of the ratings based approach classifications for AAA rated, thick tranches from highly granular portfolios might serve as the definition of a super senior tranche. The BIS II current proposed risk weight for tranches that meet the classification criteria is 7 percent, lower than the 20 percent risk weight already adopted in the United States for super senior risk that isn't accounted for using model-based treatment. To qualify, the Aaa rated risk must have 35 percent subordination and at least 100 obligors in the portfolio. Most super seniors today would only partially meet this test, and the rest might then be considered a lesser tranche. While this would at least be a consistent definition, it is arbitrary. It is no more arbitrary, however, than definitions currently in the market.

BIS II begs the question. Who got to BIS? If the rating agencies don't allow additional leverage—beyond that of a AAA tranche—for super senior risk in a credit arbitrage fund, why does BIS allow a reduction in regulatory capital beyond that of AAA risk?

If a bank has to create a new tranche that pays less than what they received earlier for taking the same slice of risk, just to make the economics look better, has any value been created?

I don't believe BIS came up with the idea of reduced regulatory capital for thick, highly granular tranches on their own. I believe they responded to the requests of banks that had already created super senior risk. If the most recent working paper is adopted, BIS II will create some new arbitrary rules ripe for arbitrage.

It's convenient to have super senior tranches in the trading book to take advantage of model-based capital treatment. It's convenient that super seniors are derivatives and are off-balance sheet. It's convenient to think of super seniors as having virtually no risk, yet the owner still gets paid to take it. One bank remarked it felt that super seniors were *free money*, but one must ask whether instruments that never trade belong in a trading book in the first place.

One head of structuring at a U.S. investment bank justified holding large stagnant positions of super senior positions in the trading book by asking, *"Has a super senior ever experienced a default?"*

No, of course not. But neither have most other publicly rated tranches, and none at the Aaa or Aa level. The risk of owning publicly rated CDO tranches (with nonmoral hazard with respect to the manager) is downgrade and mark-to-market risk. Why not apply this fuzzy logic to the other tranches of CDOs and earn a greater spread? Why not own large stagnant positions of AAAs in the trading book and earn more spread?

The answer is that holding stagnant positions isn't what the trading book was designed to do in the first place.

CHAPTER 10

Selected Structured Finance Products

FUTURE FLOWS: PAYMENT RIGHTS SECURITIZATIONS

How can a transaction get a rating higher than its sovereign rating? How can a structurer accomplish this without using a credit derivative or a financial guarantee?

A key concern for emerging market transactions is that a deal normally has a rating ceiling the same as the sovereign rating. Nonetheless, it is possible for a deal to get an investment grade rating even if the sovereign rating is below investment grade.

One structure that makes this possible is securitization of payment rights. For instance, if a bank generates payment rights sourced from export business and other foreign currency payments made offshore, there is a possibility of securitizing these receivables and getting a rating higher than that of the sponsor bank, or of the sovereign rating of the country in which the sponsor bank is located. Vakif Bank is rated only B by Fitch. It is located in Turkey, which is also rated only B by Fitch. Securitization of Vakif Bank's payment rights is rated BBB by Fitch, however. Other banks in Turkey and North Africa are keen to do these transactions, which can be done for any bank that has rating issues, if it securitizes foreign currency payments originated abroad.

The Society for Worldwide Interbank Financial Telecommunications (SWIFT) is the automated communication network that facilitates the transfer of currencies and financial information. Via SWIFT, the sponsor bank located in an emerging market country can divert offshore foreign currency payments to highly rated specified correspondent banks (SCBs) located in highly rated countries such as the United States, United Kingdom, and Switzerland. Asian banks located in Japan or other highly rated countries are also a possibility, but have not been used as frequently because most of the payments have not originated in Asia on deals done to date.

Foreign currency payments to banks in emerging market countries arise from various sources. One source is export business. Cash against goods transactions (CAGs), letter of credit transactions (LOCs), and cash against documents transactions (CADs) all result in foreign currency payments that normally transfer through the SWIFT system. SWIFT also handles check transactions. SCB accounts take in other foreign currency receivables from individuals and banks that are also transferred to banks in emerging market countries. These present and future foreign currency receivables are called *future flows* and the payment rights to these flows can be bought and sold.

The key to a successful future flow transaction is to capture the rights to the foreign currency deposits offshore, in highly rated SCBs in highly rated countries. The sponsor bank located in the emerging market country sells these rights to an offshore, bankruptcy remote, special purpose trust incorporated in a tax-friendly venue. Figure 10.1 shows a general schematic of a transaction for a Turkish bank. Note that the special purpose trust is located in Jersey, a tax friendly venue that is one of the United Kingdom's Channel Islands.

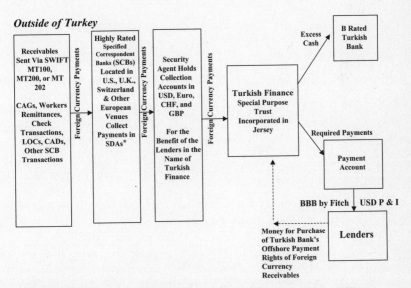

Outside of Turkey

*Turkish Finance purchases Turkish Bank Payment Rights & SCB transfers balance of SDAs to currency collection accounts.

FIGURE 10.1 Future Flow—Payment Rights Securitization

Although the payment rights originate in Turkey, the rights are sold and the SCBs are instructed to make payments to collection accounts offshore. The payments never pass through Turkey or through a foreign branch of the sponsor bank located in Turkey.

The tranches of the loan facility agreement receive an investment grade rating of BBB, and are denominated in a single hard currency. In our example, the tranche payments are denominated in U.S. dollars (USD).

The money paid for the tranches is used to buy the sponsor bank's payment rights. The sponsor bank notifies obligors of LOC, CAD, and check transactions that the payment rights have been sold to the special purpose trust, Turkish Finance, and are instructed to remit funds to an SCB. The special correspondent bank signs an acknowledgment that it will receive the funds in a specified deposit account (SDA). Since CAG transactions are completed between exporters and importers, the Turkish bank only promises to use best efforts to ask exporters to notify importers to remit payments through SCBs. This works in most of the transactions, but not all. CAG transactions may require special due diligence to ensure that payments are properly remitted. Fraud is always a potential issue, especially if there is no ongoing due diligence to check on importers, exporters, and instructions made to banks from the sponsor bank. It's not clear that the rating agencies take into account the full measure of this potential risk.

My personal view is that the rating agency assessment of the political risk of deals like this should be viewed with extreme skepticism. Since rating agencies rate deals, turnabout is fair play, and investors are free to rate the rating agencies' expertise. How qualified are they to assess this risk? How secure are cash flows when payment instructions to exporters can be changed to divert cash flows to accounts other than the ones previously specified at the SCBs?

Fitch relies on three major assessments to determine the rating of these transactions.

The first consideration is whether the sponsor bank located in the emerging market country will continue to operate. Depth and breadth of management expertise is a consideration.

A second assessment is the sovereign related risk. If there is a war, coup d'état, major law change, or other sovereign-related problem, will the structure insulate the foreign currency receivables from the reach of foreign intervention? Could a sovereign prohibit the foreign currency deposits from being transferred by the SCBs to the foreign currency collection accounts? Could the sovereign nullify the sale of the payment rights? Could the legality of the transaction be challenged in each of the foreign venues? These are questions for specialists in international law, and investors should invest some time and money to satisfy themselves on these issues. Investors should rightly demand a premium over more generic BBB tranches due to this extra documentation risk.

The third assessment is the debt service coverage ratio (DSCR). Fitch looks at the historical and potential generation of foreign currency receivables of the sponsor bank's payment rights processing business. The DSCR is calculated as follows:

$$DSCR = \frac{(\text{Diversified Payment Rights Cash Flows for Time Period } X)}{\begin{array}{c}(\text{Single Largest Loan Debt Service Payment} \\ \text{for Time Period } X \text{ over the Deal Life})\end{array}}$$

In other words, for the time period in which the largest debt service must be made over the life of the deal, Fitch looks at the receivables and calculates the DSCR. The DSCR may vary by deal, but a DSCR of around a minimum of 15 is expected for an investment grade rating of BBB, among other conditions.

Fitch looks for added structural protection with respect to the magnitude of the payment rights in the form of early amortization triggers. The following triggers are often included in a single securitization:

- Fall of monthly DSCR below a prespecified level.
- Fall of quarterly DSCR below a prespecified level (higher than the monthly DSCR trigger).
- Collection trigger based on a monthly rolling average.
- Annual collection trigger event.
- Audit test in which quarterly collections fall more than a prespecified percentage of the prior quarterly period or a lower preset percentage from the same quarter in the previous year.
- Specified correspondent bank events such as monthly collections from SCBs falling below a prespecified percentage of the total purchased payment rights.
- Fall of ratio of preexport loans to combined outstanding principal balance of the tranches to below a prespecified level.

Since future flows transactions are paper transactions, there should be some sensitivity to the possibility that documents can be falsified. If it were discovered that fraud was involved in the representation of receivables, for instance, that should be a trigger event in these deals. The type of fraud that should be of concern is where inventories are not where they are expected to be, or paperwork has been forged.

With the caveats that investors should satisfy themselves that the documentation is well-crafted, international law will support the transaction, and they are adequately compensated for the extra documentation risk. These deals may present opportunities for investors in the business of taking these risks. These deals tend to have short average lives. Investors with some experience in import/export businesses, and in analyzing bank foreign currency receivables, may find these transactions an attractive way to capture hard currency receivables and essentially offer a collateralized loan for high spreads to emerging market banks to which they otherwise could not lend.

EMERGING MARKET CAVEATS

All of the caveats mentioned above apply to emerging market collateralized debt obligations (CDOs). How much should an investor rely upon the rating agency rating? Can a rating agency rate an emerging markets deal as competently as a corporate deal or a mortgage backed security (MBS) deal? Does the BBB rating for an emerging markets CDO tranche reflect the same cash flow certainty as the BBB rating of an investment grade rated corporate deal?

A BBB rated tranche backed by corporate bonds will be downgraded if corporates in general are downgraded. Is ratings migration for a BBB rated tranche backed by corporate bonds comparable to the ratings migration risk of emerging market debt?

The answer to all of the questions above is no. Even if the initial BBB rating reflected exactly the same cash flow certainty, which it doesn't, the historical corporate ratings transition matrix shouldn't be used to attempt to predict ratings transitions for emerging market debt.

View these deals as separate types of risk, and let common sense and documentation be more of a guide than the rating assigned by the rating agencies.

The lack of experience and expertise with economic or political instability in a given country is a serious disadvantage to rating agencies. While Fitch feels they are taking this into account when assigning a rating for future flows deals such as the example in the previous section, the simple truth is they are guessing how severe sovereign reaction will be in times of economic or political crisis.

In the past few decades, we've seen governments turn sour fast. Some governments rise and fall based on whose gangs are more powerful. Educated people like bank managers are sometimes forced to flee for their lives. Documents are "lost." Deals made before the government collapse can be nullified.

I don't mean to pick on the Republic of Turkey, but—hold on—yes, I do, because it is a good example of how easy it is to lull ourselves into a belief that appearance is reality. Turkey has a lot going for it. Most people travel to Istanbul, and some even venture to Ankara. Bankers stay in the best hotels. The interior of a luxury hotel makes it difficult to tell what country one is staying in. Of course a country like Turkey looks well developed when viewed from the bottom of a crystal wine glass!

To its credit, parts of Turkey are better developed than many of its neighbors. Turkey is a political ally of the west. Turkish citizens elect their leaders. Turkey is progressive compared to many of its neighbors and near-neighbors. The bloody territorial disputes with Greece in the Aegean Sea and Cyprus seem to have calmed down.

It's true that the economy has been rocky in Turkey, but the International Monetary Fund (IMF) stepped in within the past year with financial support, and Turkey adopted a tighter fiscal policy and a major bank restructuring program. This was deemed necessary to maintain Turkey as a stabilizing force in this region of the world. Turkey is the global poster child for a liberal Islamic state that works.

Or is it?

Further east, some Turkish people feel they can be incarcerated without due process. The eastern road connecting Turkey to Iran is called "blood alley" because so many motorists were assaulted by roving bands of armed Turkish mountain men.

Let's not forget those friendly neighbors out east. Turkey squabbles with those even-tempered rationalists in Syria and Iraq over water development plans for the Tigris and Euphrates rivers. The skulls of 10,000 Christian-Armenian Turkish residents are decades old, but attest to lingering religious and ethnic intolerance. Armenians still claim this was attempted genocide, and that the actual death toll was much higher. Today the border with Armenia remains closed over the Nagorno-Karabakh dispute.

Religious tolerance is mere lip service, but there is little to be intolerant about. The Central Intelligence Agency (CIA) estimates 99.8 percent of Turks are Sunni Muslims, and only 0.2 percent of the population are Christians or Jews. There have been rumblings among fundamentalist Islamic groups that Turkish society and government is much too liberal for their taste, and there are attempts at political reorganization that could change the character of the government if they are successful. Sitting in a luxury hotel in Ankara, life is just as sweet as it was in Iran about six months before the Shah was overthrown. It's a very Western-friendly atmosphere, and the true stability is anybody's guess.

Not all governments are equal, just as some families are more functional than others. Governments that tend to concentrate power in favored factions, favored families, one favored family—or even worse—one man, are inherently unstable, even if they aren't currently challenged. The cliché, "Poor men want to be rich; rich men want to be kings; kings want to be gods," reflects a truism about human nature.

Good constitutions limit the power of monarchs. For instance, the United Kingdom is still the only European country in which its citizens are subjects of the crown as opposed to citizens of their country. Nonetheless, people in the United Kingdom have a high degree of confidence in their constitutional monarchy. The system of government has a strong system of checks and balances. Governments that administer according to rule of law are better governments for the people than governments that do not administer according to the rule of law.

But don't all governments administer by the rule of law, however unpalatable some of us may find the laws? No, of course they don't. Many governments administer by the rule of law when the law is convenient, but rule by executive fiat when the law is inconvenient.

When a government appears to administer by rule of law, one must ask how committed the government will be to rule of law in times of stress. A key factor in the stability of a government in times of stress is the system of internal checks and balances within the government, and that means power can't be concentrated in a single branch of government.

Inequity breeds hostility.

Even in a stable constitutional republic like the United States, there was recently nonviolent spirited disagreement about the legality of a presidential election. The stabilizing factor seems to be ultimate faith in rule of law, ultimate faith in checks and balances, ultimate faith in a well-crafted constitution, and ultimate faith that the government is for the people.

United States citizens can laugh out loud when Michael Moore lampoons stupid white men, they can laugh in public, and they can laugh without getting incarcerated or shot. Michael Moore doesn't grow old in prison; he grows rich in freedom.

Another feature of a stable government is the separation of church and state. A feature of unhealthy government is the claim of its leaders to know the will of God. (Not true! She only talks to me!) While the Securities and Exchange Commission (SEC) may not be able to arrest anyone for using this kind of inside information, the citizens of these countries don't seem to benefit. The separation of church and state is required not to protect religion from the grasp of government; it is required to protect government from the grasp of religious fanaticism.

Nothing can ruin your investment portfolio faster than a government takeover by religious zealots, except perhaps the zealots of Long Term Capital Management (LTCM). Armed with the claim that they have superior inspiration, zealots are universally crummy at managing risk.

If it sounds as if I'm encouraging you to be irreverent when evaluating ratings assigned by rating agencies, I am. Reverence has its place, and I encourage it, too. A show of reverence inspires people to explain themselves. Reverence is useful when one is attempting to gather information, attempting to understand the methodology, and attempting to better appreciate a point of view. The right time for *irreverence* is when you are evaluating the information you gathered, evaluating the methodology you understand, and evaluating the point of view you appreciate.

MULTISECTOR CDOs: CDOs²

Multisector CDOs are also known as *ABS CDOs, ABS of ABS, CDOs squared*, or *CDOs²*. This product emerged in 1999 in response to investors' desire to securitize their own positions of structured product. Both balance sheet and nonbalance sheet arbitrage deals have been done.

The spectrum of collateral for this product is more varied than for other CDOs. By that I mean that some multisector CDOs have been structured backed by AAA rated tranches of other CDOs, and some have been structured using BBB rated tranches of other CDOs. All types of CDO and nonCDO collateral have been added to the multisector collateral mix, including nonperforming loans.

Since it is possible to do a synthetic deal with highly rated collateral as we saw earlier, banks and insurance companies that need regulatory capital relief are happy to provide collateral for these CDOs, at least under the current regulatory capital regime.

Motives may change in the future. As more investors become aware of the structural risks of older deals on their balance sheets, they may seek to reduce the risk of poorly structured mezzanine tranches. For example, BBB tranches that are at risk of moral hazard trading of the underlying asset portfolio are likely securitization candidates. Two large U.K. banks recently completed synthetic securitizations of BBB tranches of various CDOs they had accumulated in their investment portfolios. The arbitrage was one motivation, but another may have been to reduce legacy structural risk.

Multisector CDOs include exclusively cash and exclusively synthetic collateral as well as a mix of both cash and synthetic collateral.

In one instance, a U.K. bank did an all synthetic deal referencing a multicurrency portfolio of BBB rated tranches of CDOs. The diversified portfolio consisted of positions of the Euro equivalent of approximately 10 million each.

These deals pose a currency problem unique to other synthetic deals. For instance, in many synthetic arbitrage deals, the deal may be brought in

Euros or USD and each name referenced will only offer protection on the prestated notional amount of the deal at the time the credit event occurs.

In a synthetic balance sheet multisector CDO, the bank is trying to hedge a physical or notional position in the exact amount of the relevant currency. The amount of deliverable is referenced from the start of the transaction, not at the time of the credit event. The currency mismatch risk must be borne either by the bank sponsor holding the assets or by the bank arranger, if any, helping the bank sponsor to bring the deal. Unwary investors may end up bearing this risk.

An American investment bank showed me the AAA tranche of a multi-sector balance sheet CDO and stated that the investor had no currency risk. I asked the investment bank how they were hedging the risk. Did they have a model to quanto the credit default protection that they (as bank arranger) were selling the bank originator? They said they didn't.

In many cases, bank arrangers will charge a currency mismatch fee, usually arbitrarily set at 2 to 5 basis points (bps) and take the currency risk in their trading books. This risk is very difficult for auditors and risk managers to find, and once found, it is difficult for them to quantify. This could probably be modeled using gross assumptions with a currency option model adjusted for the contingent credit event, but many firms do not take this extra step. This is probably an area where more general modeling will be done in the future.

STRUCTURED INVESTMENT VEHICLES (SIVs): CREDIT ARBITRAGE FUNDS

SIVs are offshore special purpose entities (SPEs) set up to invest in assets and issue notes at a funding cost low enough to enable the manager of the vehicle to earn an "arbitrage." These are also known as *credit arbitrage funds*, the first of which was Alpha Finance established in the 1980s by Citibank. Initially, many banks confused them with hedge funds and were reluctant to extend credit lines. Once the credit and investment constraints were better understood, these vehicles were able to issue AAA rated paper, and a downgrade would trigger a program unwind. These vehicles have produced triple digit spreads over London InterBank Offered Rate (LIBOR) for their equity investors, and equity investors have never experienced a loss. At least not yet, but SIVs have taken a variety of forms since the original structure.

The idea is that the diversity of the SIV's portfolio of assets makes this a very low-risk strategy for the equity investors, yet allows them to benefit from the leveraged investment. At least, this is the conventional understanding of SIV used in the marketplace, and that is what we will focus on in this section.

Other types of SIVs have been set up by various corporations and often with a variety of different objectives. For instance, it appears Enron sometimes used SIVs in order to engage in creative accounting. Hedge funds are limited liability partnerships, and they are occasionally referred to as SIVs.

The "credit arbitrage" SIVs are SPEs that are limited liability corporations. Many are incorporated in the Cayman Islands. The SPE engages in the activities of an investment company within proscribed parameters. A separately established "Investment Manager" conducts the investment activities of the SPE.

For SIVS in general, program credit enhancement is provided by capital raised in the market. The SPE's capital (commonly understood as equity) consists of pari passu "A" shares and "B" shares (preferred shares), and capital notes denominated in a variety of currencies. The ratio of issued and paid up capital to investments under management is on the order of 1 to 10 ($2 billion for $20 billion under management). Prime-1 rated bank liquidity facilities and liquid investment assets provide the necessary liquidity.

Optimization programs define the investment criteria. The SIV has constraints on credit quality, maturity, portfolio diversification, asset-to-liability maturity gap, and liquidity eligibility. The SIV purchases a portfolio of high-grade assets, generally with an average AA credit quality, and is allowed to lever AA rated investments up to around eight times. The gearing is adjusted for the rating of specific assets.

The attraction of credit derivatives is to allow the SIV to take advantage of the fact that credit default swap (CDS) spreads are often wider for the same credit risk than those in the capital markets. An added attraction is that there are often periods of high volatility and extraordinary widening such as in the fall of 2002. Capitalizing on spread widening is a matter of luck and timing. The volatility of returns will probably be greater for synthetic SIVs than for cash SIVs.

The first synthetic SIV was launched in 2002. Synthetic SIV managers have the added challenge of coping with CDS language. They will have to pay careful attention as the market becomes more sensitive to language issues.

HEDGE FUNDS AND COLLATERALIZED FUND OBLIGATIONS (CFOs)

How does one evaluate investments in hedge funds as collateral for a CDO? How does one tranche and rate the CDO?

Fund of funds managers are issuers of CFOs. A fund of funds is a pool of hedge fund interests chosen by the manager. The collateral is a diversified portfolio of hedge fund securities. CFOs are actively managed, market value CDOs. Obviously, the experience and track record of the manager is key to a successful launch of a CFO.

Moody's and Fitch rate these deals. Since the hedge fund strategies vary so much, the key to the ratings are the CFO's structural protections. That makes sense, but a key issue is the degree of structural protection required to make the ratings pari passu with more conventionally understood CDO structures. It's a guess, but the rating agencies are attempting to make it a more informed guess. CFOs incorporate many of the structural features of other CDOs, but the following are uniquely characteristic of CFOs.

The unrated equity tranches of these deals tend to be much greater in size than even the equity tranches of high yield backed collateralized bond obligations (CBOs). Equity subordination is often 30 percent and higher, and AAA tranches make up only about 40 to 45 percent of the deal.

CFOs must maintain a specified advance rate, which is expressed as the percentage of debt versus the market value of the underlying assets. The CFO will also have a volatility test. If the volatility on a rolling 12-month calculation exceeds a preset threshold, or if volatility exceeds a preset threshold for 3 consecutive months, the CFO must pass overcollateralization tests based on a second set of advance rates. CFO assets are marked-to-market monthly, and the advance rate is recalculated to see if the deal is in compliance. Just as one might expect, the cure is either to inject more cash collateral, redeem hedge funds, or reduce leverage by paying down tranches in order of seniority.

CFOs also have collateral quality tests (CQTs) with cures similar to that of the advance rate. Losses in excess of around 15 percent will usually start triggering CQTs. The overcollateralization test is a deleveraging trigger and requires the net asset value (NAV) times the advance rate to be greater than the remaining principal amount plus accrued and certain other senior liabilities (for instance, hedge costs, if applicable). If the overcollateralization test fails, the manager will have to switch some investments to cash (if possible at a profit to increase NAV), add capital, or delever until the deal passes the CQT.

The minimum net worth test is an unwind trigger in the extreme scenario. The CFO must exceed the prespecified minimum net worth requirement or else it must inject additional capital. If additional capital injection sufficient to pass the test isn't possible, the deal must be liquidated.

The manager is usually happy to retain the leveraged equity portion. Leverage and the cheaper funding available in the CDO market (versus prime brokers) make this a very interesting investment. Outright hedge funds might also be interested in the equity tranche, particularly if they could find a friendly bank arranger to finance the purchase. It would be the ideal hedge fund product, leverage upon leverage with financing to create further leverage.

FIRST (AND NTH)-TO-DEFAULT BASKET SWAPS

Some of the best financial institutions in the world disseminate pure nonsense about first-to-default protection and get the pricing wrong. *I have no confidence in any first-to-default pricing model I have ever seen.*

If you are an investor in this product, negotiate the best price possible, and be aware that you can challenge the output of any model using logical principles to make your case when negotiating.

If you manage first-to-default swap structurers and traders, take the model with enough salt to form an ocean from a fresh lake. It isn't possible to use single name CDSs to create a static hedge for the spread and default risk of a first-to-default basket. Traders must dynamically hedge this product. They will use the valuation model to calculate the hedge ratios. The same traders who say they cannot make money trading and hedging single name CDSs will claim they can dynamically hedge this product. What this really means is that they can make money if they are lucky. Many of the best firms have lost significant sums of money attempting to dynamically hedge this product, especially in our high credit default environment during the past two years. That also implies there are significant sums to be made.

If you can tolerate volatility in profit and loss statement (P&L), and if you want to make a few bets, go ahead. But don't try to claim there is more science or certainty to it than there really is. The fact of the matter is that when it comes to pricing and hedging first-to-default baskets, your informed guess is as good as mine, at least if your model is logically correct, but many are not.

In some cases, the models are simply wrong. The model price is outside the logical boundary conditions for pricing this product. One structurer asked me to look at his price, and our conversation went as follows:

"Risk management says this model is right. What do you think, is that price about right?" he nervously asked. He had worked for a couple of months on a simulation model, but still had no idea where he expected to end up.

"You may need to recalibrate your model. The answer you got is simply incorrect," I replied.

"Wait a minute," he said, trying to sound confident. "You can't possibly know that. You didn't do any calculations."

"I didn't use a model, but I know the answer your model calculated is incorrect. Have a cup of coffee while I explain," I replied again.

If you don't know where you are going, a model won't get you there.

Basket default swaps reference a small number of obligors, usually 10 to 20 or even fewer. A first-to-default swap pays a premium to the credit protection buyer to take the risk of the first default of any one of the reference obligors in the basket. The investor, or credit protection provider, in the first-to-default basket will only lose the loss amount of the first asset to default. The loss amount is simply par minus the recovery value of the first asset to default. Although the investor's risk is limited, the investor earns a higher spread than would otherwise be available.

The motive for the investor is *leverage. The maximum loss for the investor is defined, but so is the maximum upside, the leveraged premium on the basket.*

Figure 10.2 shows the mechanics of a typical first-to-default basket swap.

Most first-to-default basket swaps are cash settled. The basket is usually a well-diversified basket of investment grade names. Figure 10.2 shows a basket of reference obligations from diversified and relatively uncorrelated industries: electronics, finance, retail stores, and automotive. The basket has only one prespecified name from each industry and each has an investment grade rating of either A2 or A3.

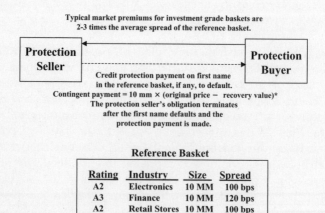

Typical market premiums for investment grade baskets are 2-3 times the average spread of the reference basket.

Protection Seller ← **Protection Buyer**

Credit protection payment on first name in the reference basket, if any, to default.
Contingent payment = 10 mm × (original price − recovery value)*
The protection seller's obligation terminates after the first name defaults and the protection payment is made.

Reference Basket

Rating	Industry	Size	Spread
A2	Electronics	10 MM	100 bps
A3	Finance	10 MM	120 bps
A2	Retail Stores	10 MM	100 bps
A3	Automobile	10 MM	120 bps

* Most transactions are cash settled, and recovery value is market price of an allowable reference obligation for the reference obligor that is the first to default.

FIGURE 10.2 First-to-Default Basket Swap

A single name CDS for each of these assets pays a premium of 100 to 120 bps. Notice that I chose relatively uncorrelated assets. I chose notional amounts that are the same for each asset in the basket. I chose assets with an investment grade rating. Each of the reference obligors/assets has a low absolute value of probability of default. Each asset is a senior unsecured obligation, meaning each asset is in the same seniority category for the respective reference obligor. The street will price first-to-default basket swap premiums on this type of basket at around two to three times the average spread of the basket. The average spread on this basket is 100 bps, and it is common to see market prices of around 220 to 330 bps.

Theoretically, the price of a first-to-default basket depends on the default correlation of the names in the basket. In other words, we want to know how likely it is that the names in the basket will default at the same time. In the above basket, I chose investment grade names in industries that are diverse, which means the names in this basket will have a low default correlation.

Several factors affect pricing: the default correlations of the names in the basket and the volatility of the assumed correlations; the absolute value of the probability of default (the potential for coincident default); the volatility of the probability of default; the ranking of potential reference assets in the reference obligor's capital structure, for example, senior unsecured debt; the dispersion of the premiums of the individual names in the basket; the notional amount of each of the assets in the basket; and the dispersion of potential recovery values.

It is possible to define the upper and lower bounds for pricing a first-to-default basket swap. I once saw an example using four credits: A, B, C, and D. The assets have the following single-name CDS spreads: 30, 35, 40, and 50 bps, respectively. Note that the sum of the spreads is 155 bps, the widest spread for any asset in the basket is 50 bps, and the narrowest spread for any asset in the basket is 30 bps. The example went on to say that if the credits are highly correlated, one would apply a lower percentage to the total to come up with the pricing for the first-to-default basket. The example calculated the highly correlated case as follows:

$$155 \times 0.15 = 23 \text{ bps}$$

What is wrong with this example?

The lower bound will never be as low as 23 bps. The example giver knows this product well, but this was a simple case of not paying attention. *The lower bound for the basket must be higher than 30 bps, the spread of the narrowest asset in the basket.*

This was exactly the same error made by the coffee-sipping structurer. *In fact, the first-to-default basket swap premium will be higher than 50 bps, the highest individual spread in the basket, which is asset D, for any correlation of the names in the basket less than 100 percent.* The probability of exercise of the option is greater than just the probability of D's default, so the protection seller must earn the premium for D plus something more. We need to assess the probability of default of *either A or B or C or D.*

Let's further assume this is a 2-year transaction. The individual 2-year cumulative probabilities of default for assets A, B, C, and D are respectively as follows: 0.7 percent, 0.5 percent, 0.6 percent, and 0.7 percent. The probability of default for either one of those assets is not the product of the individual probabilities of default. First one must calculate the probability of no default for the basket. This is simply the product of each of the probabilities of no default. The probability of no default for each of the individual assets is simply:

Probability of No Individual Default = (1 − Probability of Individual Default)

The probability of no default in the basket is: $(0.993 \times 0.995 \times 0.994 \times 0.993) \times 100 = 97.52$ percent. The 2-year probability of at least one default in the 2-year period is simply $(1 - .9752) = 0.024768$ or 2.48 percent for the 2-year period. Notice this is higher than the default probability of any of the individual names: 0.7 percent, 0.5 percent, 0.6 percent, 0.7 percent, and is slightly below the sum of the individual correlations. Since these are investment grade credits, the absolute level is still very low. Remember, we assumed no correlation between the assets in this basket when we calculated the probability of at least 1 default in the 2-year period of 2.48 percent.

The probability of no default increases with increasing correlation, meaning the probability of no default is lower for higher correlation between the names in the basket. Uncorrelated credits will have a higher spread than correlated credits because any of four different types of causes could be responsible for a default of uncorrelated assets, whereas the causes of default for correlated assets are more limited.

What then is the upper boundary limit of the first-to-default basket premium? Is it the sum of the individual CDS spreads, or in our case 155 bps? Some of the finest minds in the business will talk about investment grade baskets and tell you this is the answer. They are incorrect, but they are on the right track.

The argument for the sum of the individual CDS premiums is that the credit default probability of the basket is almost the same as the sum of the probability of default of the individual credits. That's an error. *The protection seller will make a credit event payment on only one of the credits, not on all four.* The protection seller is compensated only for the worst-case default probability—in reality the highest single premium in the basket—plus the increased likelihood of a default occurring because there is more than one obligor in the basket. If that incremental likelihood is low, the probability of payout is low, so the incremental premium is low.

Consider a basket made up of synthetic AAA tranches of four CDOs. The underlying collateral for each of the CDOs is different. Assume, for the moment, that the underlying asset classes for each of the tranches are entirely uncorrelated. Each of the AAA tranches pays a spread of 55 bps. Each of the AAA tranches is 10 million in size. Would the protection seller expect to get paid a first-to-default basket swap premium close to 220 bps to take the risk of the first of the 10 million size tranches to default? Of course not. The reason is that the absolute probability of default is still very low.

Default correlation is correlated to credit rating. Higher grade assets—investment grade assets—exhibit less default correlation than noninvestment grade assets. Noninvestment grade assets tend to be highly leveraged and economic affects may tend to affect all leveraged companies, even those in uncorrelated industries. Furthermore, noninvestment grade assets have a higher probability of default. Even in the absence of an economic downturn, two uncorrelated assets may experience a coincident or nearby timeframe default. Even if default isn't coincident, it is likely that other credits in the basket will have deteriorated so that a second-to-default or even a third-to-default is imminent.

With noninvestment grade assets, we are dealing with much higher individual probabilities of default. The individual 2-year cumulative probabilities of default for high-yield assets A, B, C, and D are respectively as follows: 11.71 percent, 14.20 percent, 13.50 percent, and 14.20 percent. The 2-year probability of no default in the basket is: $(0.8829 \times 0.8580 \times 0.8650 \times 0.8580) \times 100 = 56.22$ percent. The 2-year probability of at least one default in the 2-year period is simply $(1 - .5622) = 0.4378$ or 43.78 percent for the 2-year period. Note that this is for uncorrelated assets. The magnitude of the difference between this basket of noninvestment grade assets A, B, C, D and our earlier example using investment grade assets A, B, C, D is summarized in Table 10.1.

Of course, structurers can't get enough of a good thing, and assume investors can't either. Investors who want less risk and less income can provide second-to-default credit protection. Pricing second-to-default basket risk is as much an art form as pricing first-to-default basket risk. Some firms will create nth-to-default structures, and investors can earn a premium to provide protection for the first-, or second-, or third-, or nth-to-default risk.

TABLE 10.1 Comparison of Individual and Basket Default Rates for Assets of Different Credit Quality

| | Investment Grade Assets | | High Yield | |
| | Individual Cumulative P_d | Basket Cumulative P_d | Individual Cumulative P_d | Basket Cumulative P_d |
Asset	Two-Year	Two-Year	Two-Year	Two-Year
A	0.70%	2.48%	11.71%	43.78%
B	0.50%	2.48%	14.20%	43.78%
C	0.60%	2.48%	13.50%	43.78%
D	0.70%	2.48%	14.20%	43.78%

Moody's will provide ratings on the mezzanine risk of default baskets. These ratings should be viewed as a convenience for investors who require ratings. I don't believe these ratings should be taken seriously. As we've already seen, the rating agencies haven't been doing too well with ratings over the past five years. In a basket we have a very small sample, and the sampling error is likely to be huge when one tries to draw conclusions from statistical analysis, even in the best-case data scenario. But we already know that we aren't in the best-case data scenario. Historical rating agency data has let us down in the past two years in terms of its predictive power of credit risk. Couple that with the biases introduced by using a small sample that is not necessarily representative of the credit spectrum it is meant to represent, and you are begging to be misled.

Nonetheless, if your mandate is to make market bets, if you want to diversify your market bets, and if you require pricing models and ratings in order to get permission to make those bets, the models and ratings come in handy. Consider them as guidelines. Just don't expect them to precisely or even accurately predict your outcomes.

PORTFOLIO SWAPS

As we saw earlier, any synthetic balance sheet CDO or trading book arbitrage CDO could be classified as a portfolio swap. Bank for International Settlements (BIS) II distinguishes portfolios by granularity, so first-to-default baskets and any portfolio with 32 reference obligors or fewer would be considered nongranular pools. Portfolios with 100 or more obligors would be considered highly granular. As the size of the pool becomes larger, a synthetic swap is often referred to as a *portfolio swap*. The terminology is very ambiguous, so it is best to get clarification from the speaker.

Evaluation of the loss distribution, or of the probability of default, and the recovery rate become key. Some portfolio swaps simply have only two tranches: a senior tranche and a subordinated tranche. SCOR Reassurance, the French insurer, likes to issue guarantees on a 30 percent first-loss tranche for a diversified pool of around 30 to 50 investment grade corporate names. SCOR Reassurance is rated A+ by Standard & Poor's (S&P), so the first-loss tranche is eligible for this rating. Since the first-loss tranche is so large, the senior tranche would be considered super senior risk by today's standards. Under the proposed BIS II treatment, it would not make the seniormost tier, however.

For most portfolio swaps a 90 percent senior tranche to a 10 percent subordinated tranche is more common. The structure for the subordinated tranche is usually the least advantageous to the investor. As losses occur, the notional amortizes down. The spread paid remains a constant percentage of the remaining notional. The portfolios are usually static, and the notional on the senior tranche steps down by the amount recovered.

Investors weren't sensitive to the disadvantage of this structure versus alternatives in the cash market, and seemed to willingly accept these structures. Nonetheless, most of these early structures were a clear disadvantage to the investor. If a structuring group were to retain the first-loss, they wouldn't accept this type of structure. Instead, they would insist on receiving the residual cash flows of the deal. Investors should compare the offered spread on this type of structure with the internal rate of return (IRR) had the investor received the residual cash flows instead. Except in cases where they are being offered an extraordinary spread relative to the residuals, stress test analysis will show that receiving the residual cash flows is the better deal.

MULTILINE INSURANCE PRODUCTS: DISAPPOINTMENT AND PROMISE

The market is accustomed to the timely payment of credit-enhanced cash flows by the AAA rated monoline insurers such as Ambac Financial Group, Inc. (Ambac), Financial Security Assurance, Inc. (FSA), and MBIA Inc. As we discussed earlier, J.P. Morgan's disappointment with the performance of surety bonds is an indication that contracts with multiline insurance companies are often not equivalent to the financial guarantees with monoline insurers, upon which structurers and investors traditionally rely. The recent disputes over claims for payment will inspire structurers to avoid using multiline insurance companies. We'll discuss one of the most famous, Hollywood Funding, in this chapter.

When we discussed credit derivatives, we contrasted them with insurance contracts, which are contracts of indemnity. Under a credit derivatives contract—in contrast to an insurance contract—the protection buyer does not have to sustain an actual loss in order to receive the credit protection payment once a predefined credit event has occurred. Guarantees, such as financial guarantees provided by monolines, are just that. Monoline credit enhancement has satisfied both investors and structurers with timely payment of credit enhanced cash flows.

An insurance policy issued by a multiline insurance company, on the other hand, may not assure timely or even ultimate payment of cash flows. Insurance contracts require a loss on the part of the insured, and also have several defenses against payment. Even when it appears defenses against payment are waived, disputes occur. The assurances of rating agencies and investment bankers carry no weight when investors cannot get their claims honored by the insurance providers.

Future flow deals will probably not successfully close if multiline insurance contracts are used to "credit enhance" the cash flows. Recent disputes may have soured the market's appetite for this type of multiline insurance product.

Insurance companies have a variety of other structured finance products. Catastrophe linked issuance in the property market has not lived up to its initial promise. There has been virtually no volume growth in the past 5 years; the annual issuance is flat at around $1 billion.

Other products such as mergers and acquisitions (M&A) enhancement and contingent capital show some potential, but have yet to indicate they can become significant factors in the marketplace.

M&A enhancement is a form of transaction insurance. Insurance companies mitigate a wide variety of risks such as tax liability, successor liability, reps and warranties, and other risks that may occur. Given recent payment disputes by insurance companies, investment bankers may question whether insurance companies will challenge their obligation to pay in the event a deal doesn't go as planned. For instance, if reps and warranties were misrepresented, would the insurance company be able to defend against payment due to fraud?

Contingent capital transactions enable investors to earn interest—enhanced by premiums—and principal for prefunding an SPE, which provides contingent event protection to an insurer. If the event occurs, the insurance company gains liquidity in the form of the SPE's cash, and investors agree to accept a debt instrument that will pay them back over time. The structure may or may not be reinsured with respect to interest, principal, or both.

LEXINGTON (AIG) AND HOLLYWOOD FUNDING

Lexington Insurance Co., a AAA rated insurer and wholly owned subsidiary of American International Group Inc. (AIG), issued an insurance policy to provide credit enhancement to a deal issued by an SPE named Flashpoint Inc. Flashpoint securitized future receivables from Hollywood film productions. The CDO proceeds would provide financing for the movies to be made. The SPE issued series of notes called Hollywood 1, 2, 3, 4, 5, 6, and 7. Each series was linked to specific movie projects. The receivables were supposed to be the future revenues from future movies made by Hollywood film productions. Lexington credit enhanced Hollywood Funding 4, 5, 6 with insurance contracts. The Hollywood 4, 5, and 6 transactions were rated AAA by S&P due to Lexington's credit enhancement. Figure 10.3 is a schematic of Hollywood Funding No. 5 Ltd.

But it looks as if these films won't be made, and Lexington Capital and AIG take the view that the credit enhancement was an insurance contract, not a guarantee of timely payment of principal and interest. Since the films were never made, no payment of claims is due under their interpretation of the contract.

HIH Casualty and General Insurance Ltd. provided credit enhancement for Hollywood Funding 1, 2, and 3, and they reinsured their risk—or so they thought—with AXA Re, New Hampshire Insurance, and others. These

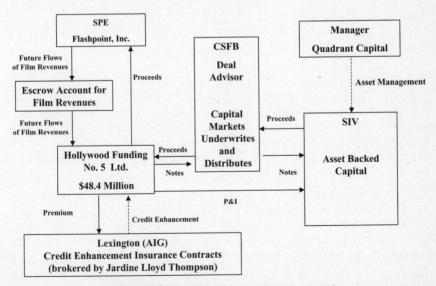

FIGURE 10.3   Hollywood Funding No. 5 Ltd.

deals are the center of U.K. litigation. The case is *HIH Casualty and General Insurance Ltd. v. New Hampshire Insurance Company and others*. The reinsurance companies disputed HIH Casualty's and General Insurance's claims. The court ruled that breach of warranty issues, coverage issues, and fraud can properly be raised as defenses to payment. The decision is being appealed.

Lexington's case seems virtually identical. Therefore, Lexington feels confident that they have defenses to payment in their Hollywood Funding 4, 5, and 6 deals. Disputes concerning Hollywood Funding 4, 5, and 6 are being litigated in the United Kingdom.

Asset Backed Capital, managed by Quadrant Capital, is suing CSFB, Jardine Lloyd Thompson, and Weil, Gotshal & Manges (the legal advisor). Asset Backed Capital bought all of Hollywood Funding 4 and 5, and most of 6. The bond trustee is suing AIG and Lexington.

Standard & Poor's said it believes the policies are absolute and unconditional, that there are no conditions or warranties that need to be satisfied in order to draw on the policies (other than the money in the escrow account being insufficient). They believe Lexington has waived all of its defenses to payment on the policies. They further believe the policies meet the standards of the capital market for credit enhancement of financial market instruments. Nonetheless, they downgraded these deals from AAA to BB.

We've already seen several instances where a deal's rating may be a convenience, but it isn't necessarily an accurate representation of the quality of the cash flows. If there is a dispute, the rating agency will never step in to make an investor whole, no matter what rating they have placed on a security. Ratings are a convenient way to evidence that steps were taken to evaluate the cash flows, but they are entirely irrelevant when an investor is attempting to interpret whether the documentation assures he will get paid. An investor should never rely on a rating agency rating as assurance that documentation is in order. Rating agencies don't take losses, investors do.

One can't rely on the structurer or marketer to assure you that your cash flows are properly protected, either. We'll revisit this point in the next section when we look at a "Transformer."

The reasons I focused on AIG's involvement with Hollywood Funding are twofold. The key reason is that the investor is suing Lexington, and the investor is suffering the consequences of nonpayment. In the HIH case, HIH protected the investors, but reinsurance failed HIH. Since a high profile investor has been burned in the later Hollywood deals, insurance protection will come under closer scrutiny by other investors.

A secondary reason is that it appears Lexington/AIG's defense is having repercussions for AIG's ability to bring other structured finance deals with insurance contract protection to market. In the summer of 2002, AIG postponed AIG Credit Premium Finance Master Trust Series 2002-1. The deal was backed by premium finance loans to AIG's customers—so they could spread their insurance premiums over a year—from AIG's subsidiaries. AIG tried and failed to bring the same deal to market in April of 2001.

There is tremendous confidence in the creditworthiness of AIG, but investor confidence in the specific business of credit enhancement in the form of insurance contracts is at an all-time low.

TRANSFORMERS

While monoline insurance companies such as Ambac, FSA, and MBIA seem to have mastered the art of credit wrapping to make structured finance investors feel as comfortable as if they bought credit default protection, the same statement isn't true for multiline insurance companies.

Many multiline insurance companies and reinsurance companies also want to participate in the CDS market. Several have created special purposes corporations called *transformers* to act as counterparties in CDS contracts. The claim is that the SPEs should pay off under the terms of the CDS contract in a similar fashion to CDSs. This product has not taken off for multiline insurance companies, however.

One well-known, well-respected, American investment bank asked me to consider protection from one of their "transformer" vehicles. They asked if the bank I worked for would intermediate a CDS transaction. Requests for intermediation are common. Many banks need an Organization for Economic Cooperation and Development (OECD) bank counterparty for regulatory capital purposes. If the structure is right, the intermediation fee can allow the intermediary bank to earn a reasonable return on the minimal capital required, and all parties are satisfied.

The investment bank sent over their documentation. It was a paltry two-page document, whereas monolines will send a small booklet and make their lawyers available to discuss language details. When I looked at the document, I realized that the transaction was unsuitable. Figure 10.4 shows the gist of the proposal, without embarrassing those who should be.

The investment bank assured me they would give me proper CDS documentation incorporating whatever language I wanted. If a credit event occurred, the bank would look to the SPE to make payment under the terms of the CDS, and I could design the terms.

I declined.

The investment bank invited me to a meeting at their offices. Four tailored Armani suits or better appeared at the meeting. If life were a fashion

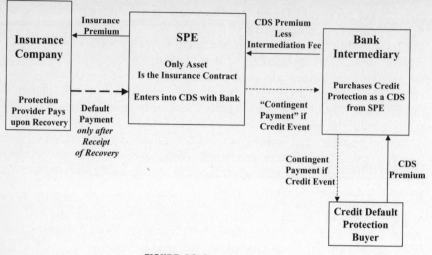

FIGURE 10.4   Transformer

war, the investment bankers would be winning. They were confident and took victory postures. They attempted to persuade me to do the transaction. I continued to decline. I could sense their building frustration. They couldn't understand why they weren't getting my agreement. After all, they were taller, they were louder, and they were in the majority.

So what was the problem?

I picked up a cookie—the meeting didn't have to be a total loss—and explained. I didn't want to play their shell game. The problem was that my counterparty for the CDS protection would have been the SPE, a shell corporation. The only asset of the SPE was an insurance contract. The SPE would only receive a credit default payment after the insurance company determined its actual recovery, after taking the matter through bankruptcy proceedings. The SPE had no way of assuring timely payment under the terms of the credit default swap confirmation.

The transformer wasn't even worth the price of the child's toy of the same name for the purpose they were suggesting. Sure, the SPE would have ultimately gotten paid and the bank would ultimately have received payment, but that wasn't the point. The point was that the SPE did not have the resources to perform under the terms of its transaction with the bank. It could not pay on a timely basis, no matter how cleverly crafted the CDS confirmation. If a credit event occurred, the bank would have to fund the credit default payment to the ultimate protection buyer until the SPE finally received its payment from the insurance company. The investment bank only offered the usual CDS intermediation fee, but the bank had additional risk beyond the CDS agreement.

It's possible that the well-dressed guys weren't aware of this until I pointed it out. The implications of that are ugly enough. But if they were aware, the implications are even uglier. I couldn't help wondering how many other counterparties they had already approached or were planning to approach. Would their counterparties look through the SPE to the ultimate obligor, the insurance company?

It is possible that other multiline insurance companies have put together sound transformer structures allowing them to provide credit default protection that stands up to the acid test of default, but the lack of growth in this product suggests otherwise.

Future Developments in Structured Finance

Bank for International Settlements (BIS) II will affect the way regulatory capital is assessed for securitized products. It's only fair to attempt to forecast what this will all mean for structured finance going forward.

PLAYING THE GAME WITH BIS II

Any arbitrary system begs to be arbitraged, and the new regulatory capital treatment will be no different from the old on that score. One of the key differences is that the regulatory capital for retaining senior tranches of collateralized debt obligations (CDOs) will be greatly reduced. This means that instead of trying to get "super senior" tranches and Aaa tranches off the balance sheet, it will now make sense for banks to retain these tranches. Many of the outstanding synthetic balance sheet transactions will be called when BIS II is implemented.

The tranches that banks will want to securitize are the BBB and below rated tranches. On a relative basis, these tranches will look much less attractive.

All banks can default to the standardized approach, but many banks, both originating and investing banks, will strive to become eligible for the internal ratings based (IRB) approach. Table 11.1 shows the risk weights for tranches rated BBB− and greater. For the IRB approach, I'm assuming that the originating bank's calculations show it can use the ratings based approach (RBA).

Assume I'm not eligible for model-based capital treatment, and I want to look at the implication of retaining the tranches of a synthetic securitization under BIS II versus the return on capital of retaining the tranches under BIS I. I have more than 100 obligors in the diversified highly granular

TABLE 11.1 Risk Weights for Tranches Rated BBB− and Greater

Long-Term Rating	Standardized Approach	Thick Tranches Highly Granular Pools	Base Case	Nongranular Pools
Aaa	20% All	7%	12%	20%
Aa	20% All	10%	15%	25%
A	50% All	20%	20%	35%
Baa1	100% All	50%	50%	50%
Baa2	100% All	75%	75%	75%
Baa3	100% All	100%	100%	100%

pool. I'll further assume that the equity tranche will get a 1:1 deduction. See Table 11.2. Suppose the structure is a synthetic CDO tranched today as follows (see Table 11.2):

- Super senior tranche priced at 10 basis points (bps) comprises 88 percent of the deal.
- Aaa tranche priced at 60 bps is 6 percent of the deal.
- A rated tranche is 3.6 percent of the deal priced at 180 bps.
- Baa2 rated tranche is 0.9 percent of the deal.
- Equity tranche is 1.5 percent of the deal and returns 800 bps.

Notice that under BIS II, the extra credit risk of the BBB and lower tranches makes them poor choices on a return on regulatory capital basis versus Aaa risk. Of course this depends on how one defines Aaa risk. Note that only a portion of today's super senior tranches of highly granular portfolios will be eligible for the minimum RBA capital. Even so, the return

TABLE 11.2 Tranched Synthetic CDO

Tranche	Return on Regulatory Capital		
	BIS I	BIS II—Standardized	BIS II—RBA
Super Senior	1.25%	6.25%	13.37%*
Aaa	7.5%	37.5%	62.5%
A	22.5%	45%	112.5%
Baa2	50%	50%	66.6%
Equity	8%	8%	8%

*$(35/88) \times (10/56) + (53/88) \times (10/96) = 13.37\%$.

on the super senior tranche as it stands is still double-digit for a very high credit quality asset.

Note that the top 35 percent of most cash asset-backed CDOs with 100 or more obligors would be eligible for the lowest BIS II risk weighting, too. Let's compare the return on this 35 percent slice with an eligible super senior 35 percent slice. The AAA of a CDO backed by cash assets is a funded investment, and a super senior is unfunded. The cash collateralized CDO slice pays 55 bps, whereas the super senior pays 10 bps. The regulatory capital for each is 8 percent × 7 percent = 0.0056 or 56 bps. The return on regulatory capital for the cash CDO slice is 98.2 percent. The return on the super senior slice is only 17.8 percent.

Super seniors and Aaa tranches are due for an overhaul. The regulatory capital returns under BIS II should encourage that process beyond the incentives we have today.

The sales pattern of risk will change. Banks will have more incentive to retain highly rated assets. Instead of retaining equity tranches, banks will seek to find buyers of equity risk. Variations on the original secured loan trust (SLT) structure may become more popular.

Banks and investment banks will cultivate alternative investors who can take equity and BBB risk, even on a financed basis. This suggests that banks will have to find ways to become comfortable with alternative investors such as private equity investors and hedge funds, because this customer base is a key consumer of leveraged risk. They do not have the same regulatory capital constraints as banks.

TREND TO RISK DISTRIBUTION

Banks have learned a hard lesson in the wake of defaults of highly rated, high concentration risks on their balance sheets. Banks will seek more ways to distribute risks. Loan syndication and loan repackaging will become a major focus for large exposures.

Banks will question principal finance groups and structuring groups that park huge positions on the balance sheet. At a minimum, reserves must increase. Due diligence needs to increase, too.

United States bank managers may question mark-to-market values more carefully in the wake of the Sarbanes-Oxley Act. The Securities Exchange Commission (SEC) regulates all U.S. banks that have publicly traded equity. Managers may become nervous about signing off on the financial statements of their capital market's groups when they can't understand how trading instruments are being marked-to-market. They may also get nervous about trading books being used as investment portfolios. They'll also be nervous about recognizing income on an accrual basis in trading portfolios.

Finally, management might take more time to investigate the structuring activity that occurs under their noses. Ignorance will no longer be accepted as an excuse.

You'll recall these changes aren't happening because business managers woke up one day and decided they needed to change the way they were doing business. As in the case of Citicorp and J.P. Morgan Chase, the changes are occurring because the U.S. general public's tolerance for suspect practices—as reflected by Congress—is at an all-time low.

Structures that do the traditional job will become a key focus. Structures that reduce balance sheet risk will get more attention. Structures that create value for investors will get more attention. Structures that are transparent will get more attention. It seems the market is efficient, after all.

Acronym Key

ABCP	Asset Backed Commercial Paper
ABS	Asset Backed Security
AIG	American International Group
Ambac	Ambac Financial Group, Inc.
BaCa	Bank Austria Credit Anstalt
BAFin	Bundesanstaltfür Finanzdienst-leistungsaufsicht (Bundesbank Regulations and Guidance)
BBVA	Banco Bilbal Vizcaya Argentaria S.A.
BBA	British Banker's Association
BEY	Bond Equivalent Yield
BIS	Bank for International Settlements
BISTRO	Broad Index Secured Trust Offering
BOJ	Bank of Japan
BP	Basis Point
C&I	Commercial and Industrial
CAD	Cash Against Documents
CADR	Constant Annual Default Rate
CAG	Cash Against Goods
CBO	Collateralized Bond Obligation
CBOE	Chicago Board Options Exchange
CBT	Chicago Board of Trade
CDO	Collateralized Debt Obligation
CDS	Credit Default Swap
CEO	Chief Executive Officer
CFO	Collateralized Fund Obligation and Chief Financial Officer
CFTC	Commodities Futures Trading Commission
CLN	Credit Linked Note
CLO	Collateralized Loan Obligation
CMO	Collateralized Mortgage Obligation
CN	Combination Note
COO	Chief Operating Officer
CP	Commercial Paper
CPR	Constant Prepayment Rate

CQT	Collateral Quality Test
CSFB	Credit Suisse First Boston
CSFP	Credit Suisse Financial Products
CSLT	Chase Secured Loan Trust
CSO	Credit Spread Option
CUSIP	Committee on Uniform Securities Identification Procedures
DAX	Deutsche Aktienindex or German stock index
DBA	Doing Business As
DSCR	Debt Service Coverage Ratio
DTC	Depository Trust Company
DWOE	Duration Weighted Optimal Exercise
EC	European Community
ECB	European Central Bank
EU	European Union
EMTN	Euro Medium Term Note
FASB	Financial Accounting Standards Board
FASIT	Financial Asset Securitization Investment Trust
FED	Federal Reserve Board and the Federal Reserve System
FDIC	Federal Deposit Insurance Corporation
FHLB	Federal Home Loan Bank
FNMA	Federal National Mortgage Association and Fannie Mae
FHLMC	Federal Home Loan Mortgage Corporation and Freddie Mac
FRN	Floating Rate Note
FSA	Financial Services Authority (UK) and Financial Security Assurance, Inc.
GAAP	Generally Accepted Accounting Principles
GARP	Global Association of Risk Professionals
GBP	Great Britain Pound (Sterling currency)
GDP	Gross Domestic Product
GLPC	Guaranteed Loan Pools Certificate
GmbH	Gesellschaft mit beschränkter Haftung (limited liability company)
GNMA	Government National Mortgage Association and Ginnie Mae
HIGHTS	Helix Investment Grade Hybrid Transaction Securities
HLT	Highly Leveraged Transactions
IA	Investment Advisor
IBCA	International Bank Classification Agency
I/C	Interest Coverage Ratio
ICO	Instituto de Credito Official
IO	Interest Only (tranche)
IOR	Istituto per le Opere di Religione (The Institute of Religious Work also known as the Vatican Bank)

IMF	International Monetary Fund
IMM	International Money Market
IRB	Internal Ratings Based Approach
IRR	Internal Rate of Return
IRS	Internal Revenue Service (U.S. Tax Department)
ISDA	International Swap and Derivatives Association, Inc.
ISP	Interest Subparticipation Piece
KfW	Kreditanstalt für Wiederaufbau
KMV	KMV Corporation now owned by Moody's
LIBOR	London InterBank Offered Rate
LOC	Letter of Credit (also LC)
LSTA	Loan Syndications and Trading Association
LTCM	Long Term Capital Management
M&A	Mergers and Acquisitions
MBIA	MBIA Inc. (formerly Municipal Bond Insurance Association)
MBS	Mortgage Backed Security
MIE	Multi-Issuance Entity
MTN	Medium Term Note
N/A	Not Applicable and Not Available
NAIC	National Association of Insurance Commissioners
NAV	Net Asset Value
NER	Non-Economic Residual
NPV	Net Present Value
O/C	Overcollateralization Ratio
OCC	Office of the Comptroller of the Currency
OECD	Organization for Economic Cooperation and Development
OPM	Other People's Money
OSFI	Office of the Superintendent of Financial Institutions
OTC	Over the Counter
P&I	Principal and Interest
P&L	Profit and Loss Statement
PAC	Planned Amortization Class
PCAOB	Public Company Accounting Oversight Board
PIK	Pay-in-Kind and Payment-in-Kind
PN	Participation Note
PO	Principal Only
PROMISE	Program for Mittelstand-loan Securitization
PPN	Principal Protected Note
PPS	Principal Protected Schuldschein
QIB	Qualified Institutional Buyer
QMM	Quarterly Money Market
QSPE	Qualifying Special Purpose Entity

RBA	Ratings Based Approach
RP	Repurchase Agreement or REPO
REIT	Real Estate Investment Trust
REMIC	Real Estate Mortgage Investment Conduit
RMBS	Residential Mortgage Backed Security
RTC	Resolution Trust Corporation
R.O.S.E.	Repeat Offering Securitization Entity
S&L	Savings and Loan
S&P	Standard & Poor's, also common usage for the S&P 500 stock index
SBC	Swiss Bank Corporation
SCB	Specified Correspondent Bank
SCOR	SCOR Reassurance
SDA	Specified Deposit Account
SEC	Securities and Exchange Commission
SFA	Supervisory Formula Approach
SIV	Structured Investment Vehicle
SLMA	Student Loan Marketing Association and Sallie Mae
SLT	Secured Loan Trust
SME	Small to Medium-Size Enterprise
SPC	Special Purpose Corporation
SPE	Special Purpose Entity
SPV	Special Purpose Vehicle
STRIPS	Separate Trading of Registered Interest and Principal of Securities
SWIFT	Society for Worldwide Interbank Financial Telecommunications
T-Bill	Treasury Bill
T-Bond	Treasury Bond
TRORS	Total Rate of Return Swap also TRS or Total Return Swap
UBS	Union Bank of Switzerland
USD	U.S. Dollar
UST	U.S. Technologies, Inc., and U.S. Treasury and U.S. Treasuries (bonds)
VAR	Value-at-Risk
VAT	Value Added Tax
WAC	Weighted Average Coupon
WAM	Weighted Average Maturity
WARF	Weighted Average Risk Factor
YTM	Yield to Maturity

Selected Bibliography

Basel Committee on Banking Supervision, "Second Working Paper on Securitization Issued for comment by December 20, 2002," October 2002.

Brealey, Richard, and Stewart Meyers. *Principles of Corporate Finance.* New York: McGraw-Hill, 1981.

Brooks, Brady, Roger J. Vos, and Diane Vazza. "Corporate Defaults Peak in 2002 Amid Record Amounts of Defaults and Declining Credit Quality—Hazards Remain," Standard & Poor's Ratings Direct, January 23, 2003.

Carty, Lea, Dana Lieberman, and Jerome S. Fons. "Corporate Bond Defaults and Default Rates 1970–1994." Moody's Investors Service Global Credit Research. New York: January 1995.

Caouette, John B., Edward I. Altman, and Paul Narayanan. *Managing Credit Risk: The Next Great Financial Challenge.* Hoboken, New Jersey: John Wiley & Sons, 1998.

Cialdini, Robert B., Ph.D. *Influence—How and Why People Agree to Things.* New York: William Morrow and Company, 1984.

Dowd, Kevin. *Beyond Value at Risk:The New Science of Risk Management.* Hoboken, New Jersey: John Wiley & Sons, 1998.

Efrat, Isaac, Ph.D., Jeremy Gluck, Ph.D., and David Powar. "Moody's Refines Its Approach to Rating Structured Notes." Moody's Investors Service, July 3, 1997.

Fabozzi, Frank J. *Handbook of Structured Financial Products.* Pa., Frank J. Fabozzi Associates, New Hope, Pennsylvania 1998.

"Global Market for Derivatives," *Wall Street Journal,* December 19, 1995, p. 1.

Gordy, Michael. "A Risk-Factor Model Foundation for Ratings-Based Bank Capital Rules." 2002.

Gordy, Michael, and David Jones. "Capital Allocation for Securitization with Uncertainty in Loss Prioritization," December 6, 2002.

Hessol, Gail I., Francis Parisi, Mark Puccia, and Joanne W. Rose. "Credit Comments," Standard & Poor's Structured Finance, November 1995.

Hull, John C. *Options, Futures, and Other Derivatives.* 4th ed. New York: Prentice-Hall, 2000.

International Swap Dealers Association, "Confirmation of OTC Credit Swap Transaction Single Reference Entity Non-Sovereign," ISDA, 1999.

Lee, Peter. "Masters of Credit or Hype?" *Euromoney*, July 1997, 44–49.

Natenberg, Sheldon. *Option Volatility & Pricing*. New York: Richard D. Irwin, 1994.

Nelken, Israel, ed. *Option Embedded Bonds*. Los Angeles: Times Mirror, 1997.

Poundstone, William. *The Prisoner's Dilemma*. New York: Doubleday, 1992.

Rosen, Dan. "Effectively Measuring and Integrating Market Risk & Credit Risk." *Algorithmics Inc.*, New York, January 29, 1997.

Southern District of N.Y. *J.P. Morgan Chase Bank v. Liberty Mutual Insurance Company*, no. 01-CV-11523. March 5, 2002.

Tavakoli, Janet. *Credit Derivatives and Synthetic Structures: A Guide to Instruments and Applications*. 2d ed. Hoboken, New Jersey: John Wiley & Sons, 2001.

Westlake, Melvyn. "The Credit Crucible." *Emerging Market Investor*, 2, February 1997, 10–14.

Winkler, Robert L. and William L. Hays. *Statistics Probability, Inference, and Decision*. New York: Holt, Rinehart & Winston, 1975.

Interesting Web Sites

These are prefixed by http://www.

bafin.de—Bundesanstaltfür Finanzdienst-leistungsaufsicht (BAFin), Bundesbank Regulations and Guidance (formerly backred.de)

bba.org.uk—British Banker's Association web site

bloomberg.com—online version of the system we know and love

bis.org—Bank for International Settlements web site

bis.org/publ/bcbs_wp11.htm—download site for Working Paper 2

boj.or.jp/en—Bank of Japan web site

derivatives.com—financial derivatives and risk mangement news

fdic.gov/bank—Federal Deposit Insurance Corporation web site

fitchratings.com—Fitch rating agency home page

frbservices.org—U.S. Federal Reserve Regulations and Guidance

gloriamundi.org—web site for VaR resources and risk professionals

isda.org—International Swap and Derivatives Association, Inc.

loanpricing.com—Loan Pricing Corp.'s web site

mof.go.jp/english—Japanese Ministry of Finance web site

moodys.com—Moody's Investors Service homepage

occ.treas.gov—web site for Office of the Comptroller of the Currency (U.S.)

risk.ifci.ch—introduction to risk management

riskmetrics.com—risk management tools

savvysoft.com—cutting edge financial engineering software developers

sec.gov/news/press/2002-150.htm—SEC supplements to the Sarbanes-Oxley Act

sec.gov/new/digest.shtml—SEC updates on investigations

standardandpoors.com—Standard & Poor's home page

tavakolistructuredfinance.com—consulting services, education, and expert witness testimony in structured finance.

Index